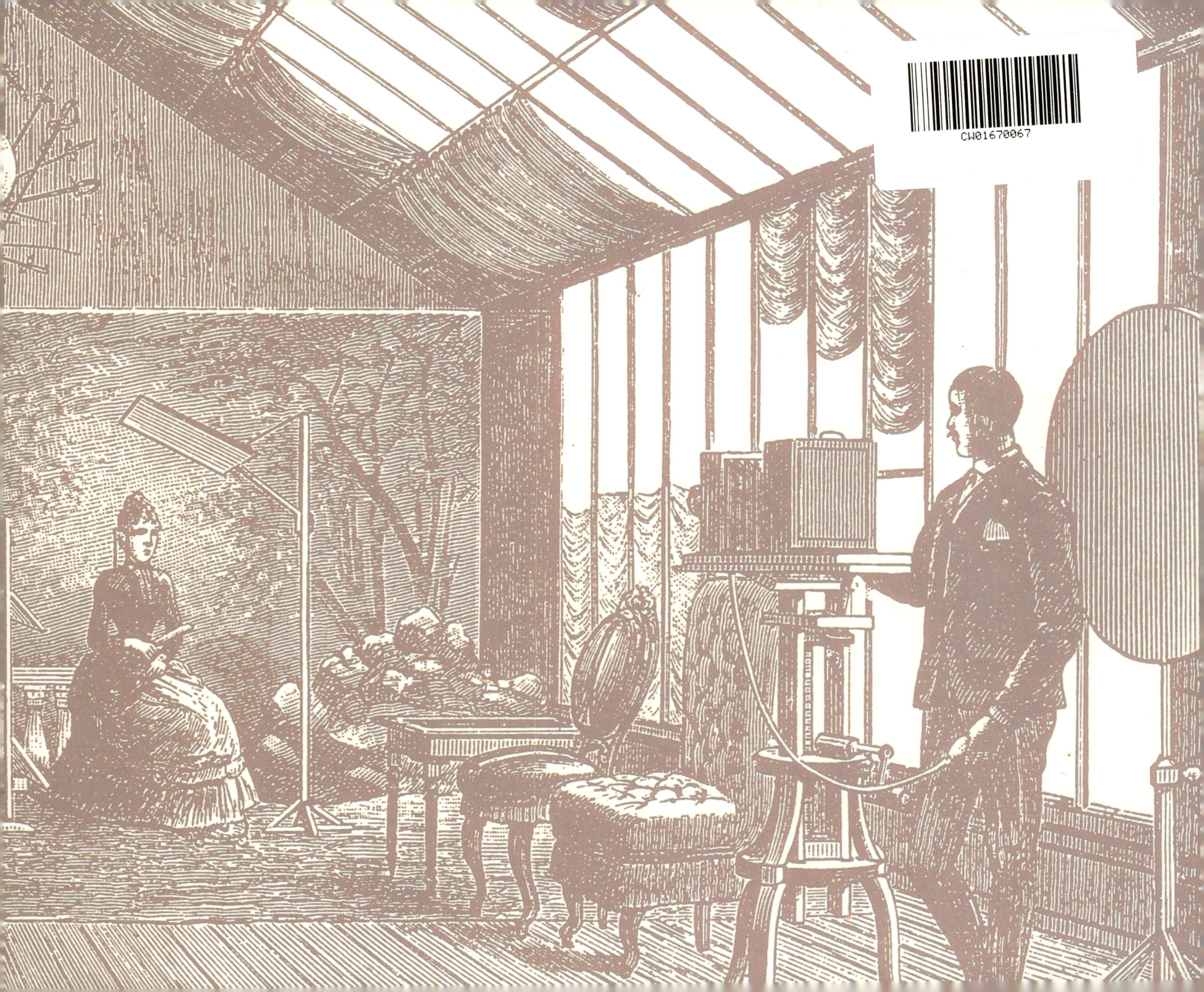

Case Histories

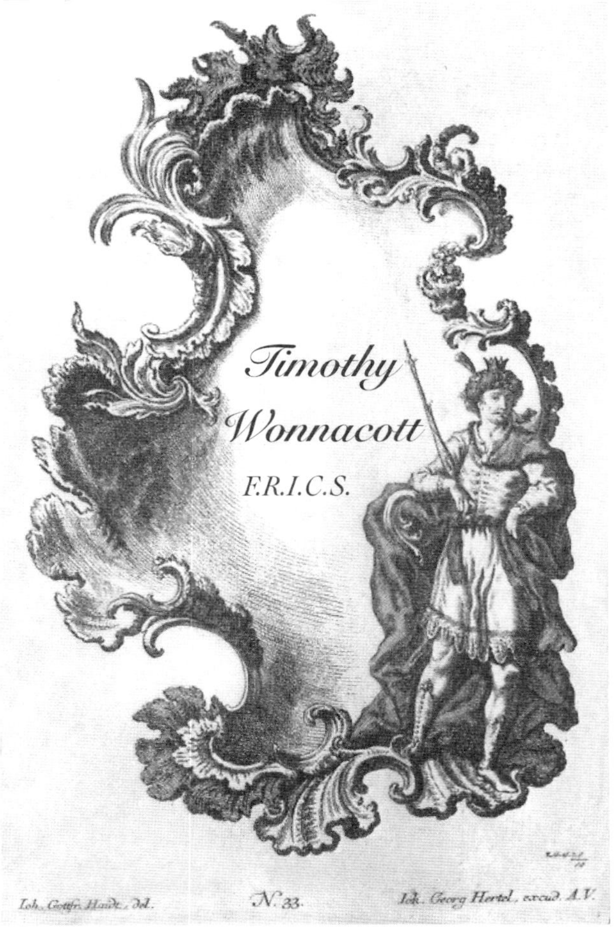

Case Histories

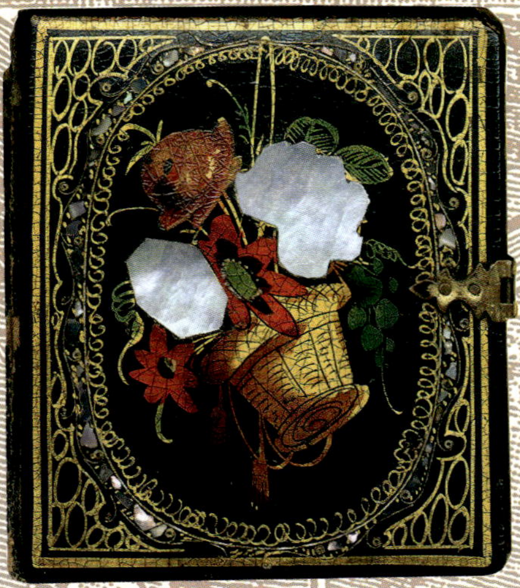

The Packaging and Presentation of the Photographic Portrait In Victorian Britain 1840-1875

John Hannavy

About the Author

John Hannavy is a well known writer and broadcaster on the history of photography. Author of over twenty books on photographic history, and photography as a means of accessing history, he has also been reponsible for several major photographic exhibitions in the UK, and two acclaimed series of television films on the history of photography.

He lives in Lancashire, and is Research Professor in Art & Design at the University of Bolton.

He was awarded a Ph.D. in 1985 for his research into the Waxed Paper process of photography.

Professor Hannavy has been an active collector of cased photographic portraits for more than thirty years, and all the illustrations in this book are drawn from his personal collection.

By the same Author:
Roger Fenton of Crimble Hall.
Thomas Keith's Scotland.
Masters of Victorian Photography.
Fox Talbot.
The Victorian Professional Photographer.
A Moment in Time – Scottish Contributions to Photography.
Victorian Photographers at Work.
Images of a Century – the Centenary of the British Institute of Professional Photography.

ISBN 1 85149 481 2

British Library Cataloguing-in-Publication Data
A catalogue record for this book is available from the British Library

Printed in China
by the Antique Collectors' Club Ltd., Woodbridge, Suffolk

Contents

Acknowledgements

This book is somewhat unusual in that all the illustrations come from my own collection of nineteenth century photography. A general word of thanks, therefore, is due to all the friends and dealers who, over the past thirty years, have drawn my attention to specific images and cases which they knew would appeal to me. My obsession with this aspect of photographic history knows few bounds but, thanks to friends and associates, this collection has been built up without mortgaging the family silver – if we ever had any to mortgage!

Over the years during which I have been collecting, an ever-growing list of fellow collectors, and of experts in museums and galleries throughout Britain and America have all shared their time and expertise with me, and broadened my understanding of this period of photography's history. To them all, my continuing thanks are due. I must also record my appreciation of the advice and help offered by collectors and experts in the areas of early plastics who have helped me unravel the mysteries of Victorian plastic moulding methods.

While is would be impossible to list them all, some individuals and institutions have always been especially helpful. A personal note of thanks must go to Dennis Firkins, Alvin Moss and the late June Stevens. To many members of both the Photographic Collectors' Club of Great Britain, and the Daguerreian Society of America, thanks are also due for their willingness to share snippets of information.

The advice of Colin Harding and other members of the staff at the National Museum of Photography, Film and Television in Bradford, and at the London Science Museum before that, have, over the years, been invaluable.

My many dealer friends have also played their part and without their detective work, many of the cases illustrated here might never have come my way.

The detective work done by Floyd & Marion Rinhart for their pioneering 1969 book *American Miniature Case Art* set me on more than thirty years of obsession, and has been invaluable to me as a collector. Like many others, I stand in awe of the amount of research carried out by Clifford & Michele Krainik, with Dr. Carl Walvoord for their 1989 study of the thermoplastic *Union Cases*. Both these earlier works remain essential reading.

Paul Berg's 2003 book *Nineteenth Century Photographic Cases and Wall Frames* – the expanded second edition of his 1995 work – offers an important perspective on case designs, manufacture and collecting, and is a further milestone in our understanding of the subject.

I must not leave out the dealers who were affronted when I suggested that their highly priced 'jet' cases were in fact plastic, nor those who sold me treasures for a song!

This is a totally absorbing subject for all of us touched by the obsession, and I hope that the information contained in this work adds a little to the story.

John Hannavy, Standish, 2005

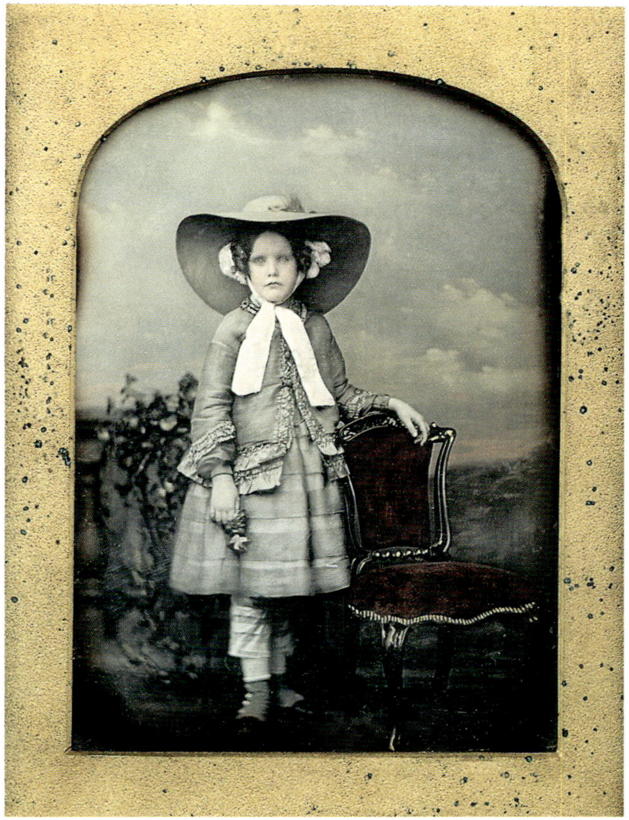

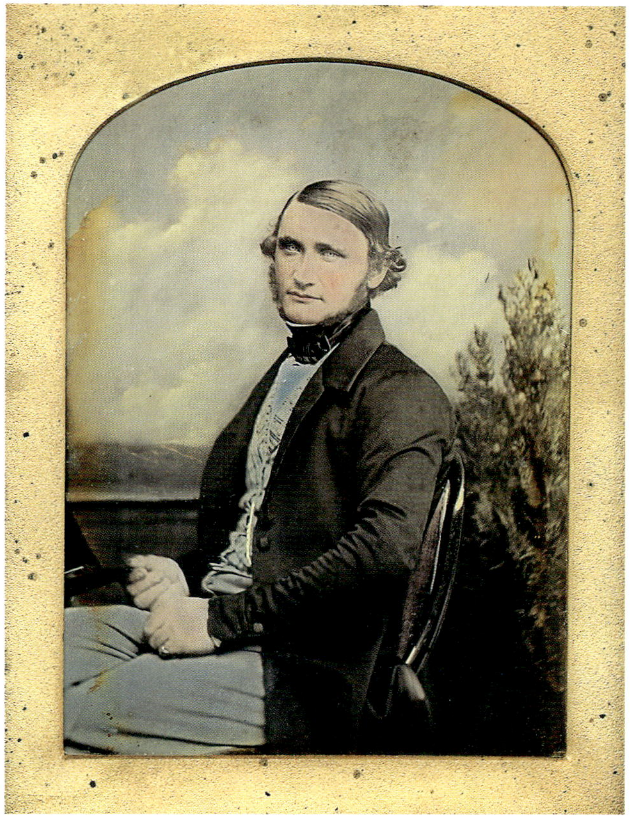

Two hand-coloured quarter plate daguerreotypes by William Kilburn, whose studio at 234 Regent Street, was open only from 1852 until 1855, so dating these images is simple. Both are housed in quality leather cases with brass hinges. Kilburn offered a high qualty service at a high price, and used excellent materials in the process. It would seem that slight movement by the child during the long exposure was not considered to detract from the charm of the image and did not render the result unacceptable, despite the high cost of the portrait sitting. In his advertisement in The Athenæum, *April 10th 1847, Kilburn, aware that his potential customers were already familiar with the established traditions of the cased miniature painting, assured them that 'the likeness taken by the photographic process serves merely as a sketch for the miniature, which is painted by M. Mansion'.*

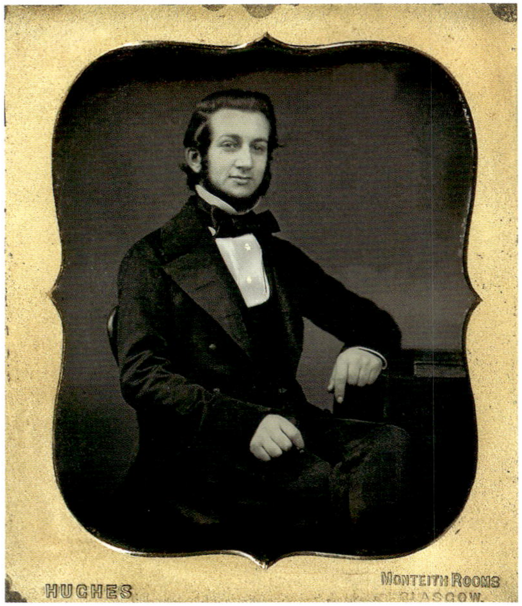

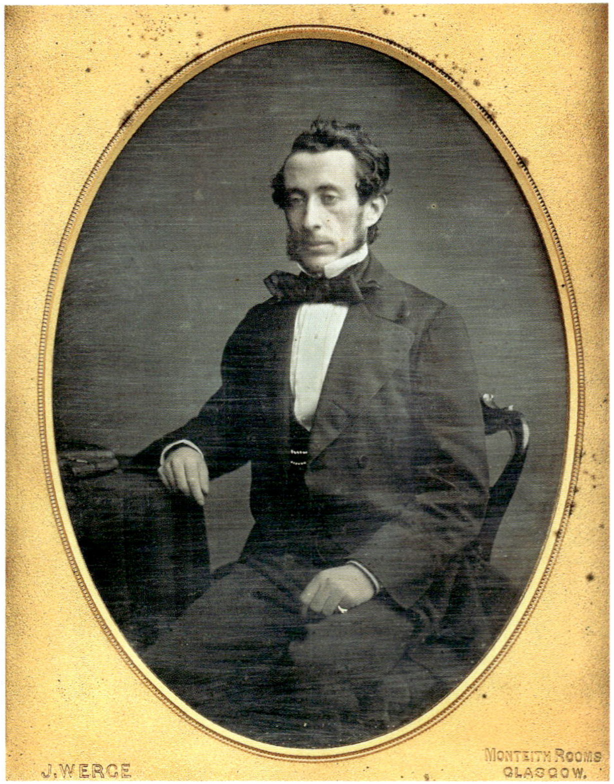

The length of time during which individual photographers stayed in business in the early years was sometimes short, giving early studios an often quite rapid turnover of owners. The Menteith Rooms at 67 Buchanan Street, Glasgow, was originally opened as a studio in 1846 by John Bernard. By 1848 Bernard had been joined by Cornelius J. Hughes, who was in sole ownership of the studio by 1850. In 1856 Hughes sold out to John Werge who spent three years at the premises before leaving in 1859. He later became a respected author of photographic texts as well as an accomplished portraitist.

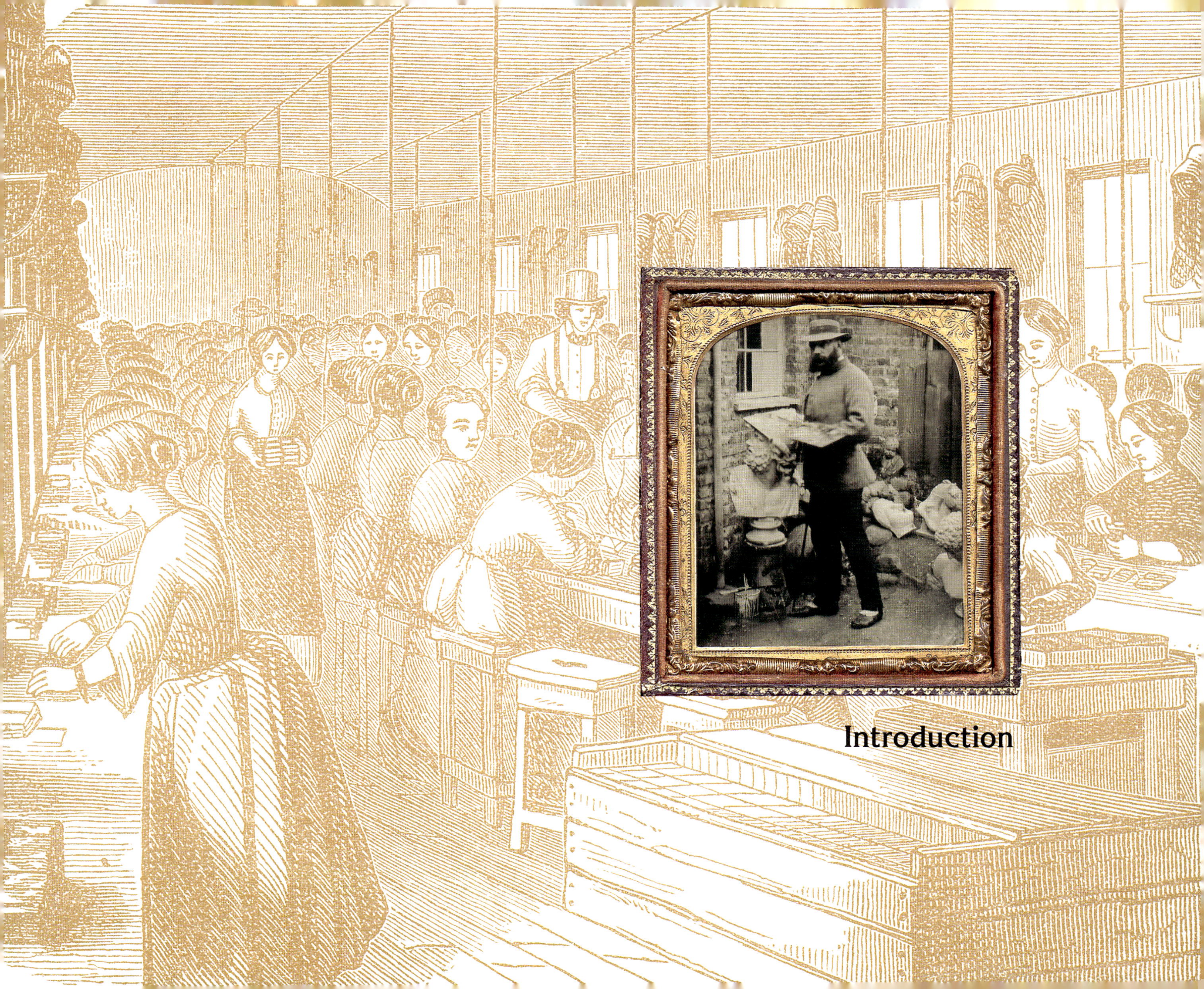

Introduction

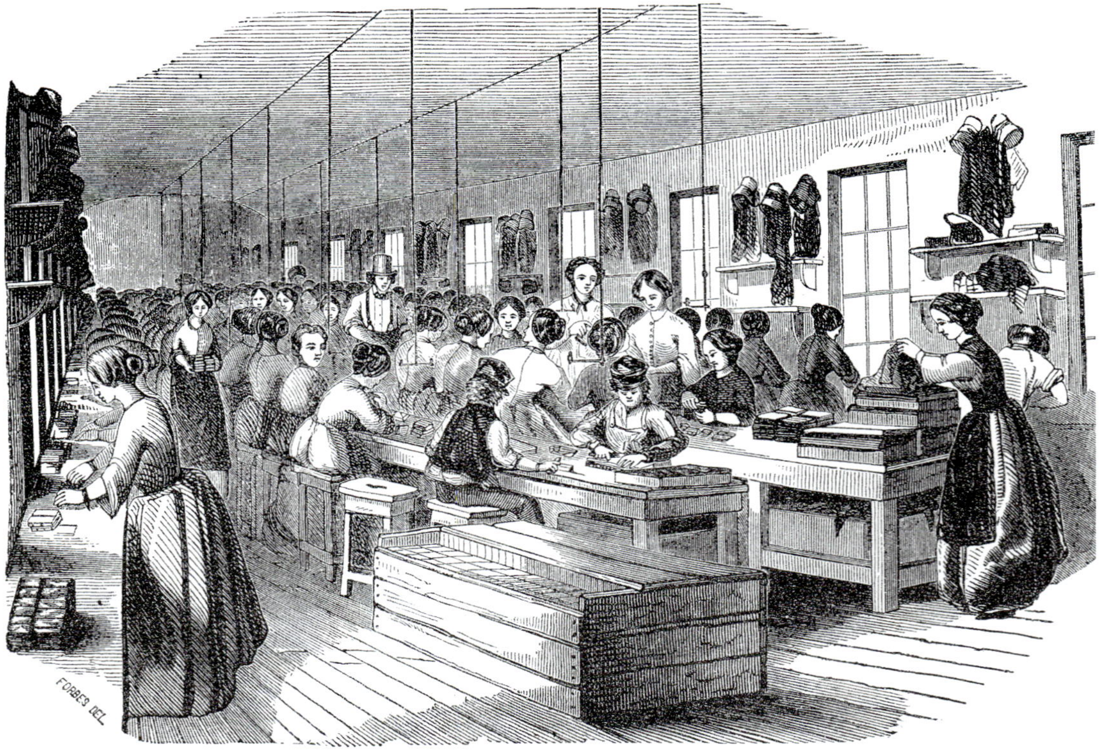

In this contemporary woodcut of the 'Covering and Finishing Room' at Edward Anthony's New York factory, a considerable number of young women are engaged in the covering and polishing of leather daguerreotype cases.

Introduction

The cased photographic portrait enjoyed almost three decades of unrivalled popularity between the early 1840s and the later 1860s. During that period the art of presenting the unique character of the daguerreotype, the ambrotype, and the tintype to a public willing to part with not inconsiderable sums of money, reached heights of both manufacturing technique and aesthetic sophistication. Today we are left with examples of early packaging considered by many to be every bit as much *objets d'art* as the pictures themselves – and often more so.

The evolution of photography, and the public perception of the value of the photographic image itself, were both reflected in and paralleled by the decoration of the cases in which the pictures were sold. From little more than a simple unadorned box in which to house and protect the delicate image, the miniature case evolved into a celebration of nineteenth century craftsmanship and mass manufacturing technique.

Within a few years, case manufacture had been developed on to a grand scale, with hundreds of designs, many and varied methods of manufacture, and closely guarded – and often bitterly fought over – patents in both Britain and America.

The cased photograph was predominantly a British and American phenomenon – although not exclusively so. There are many examples of cased portrait photography throughout Europe, but seldom on the scale found in America and Britain. Mainland Europe seems to have displayed a marked preference for framing rather than casing photographs – with many of the manufacturing techniques and materials evident in American cases evolving in slightly different ways to meet European presentation needs.

Indeed, manufacture of plastic cases at least was predominantly an American prerogative, with the majority of such cases used in Britain certainly having been imported from America. While there was a thriving industry and substantial market for the output of British makers of leather and papier mâché cases, so far only one British manufacturer of thermoplastic cases has been discovered – but where there was one there may be others! Most of the design variants found in UK collections and used by British photographers are clearly of American origin. There are, of course, exceptions, with a number of specifically British designs having been identified in the course of the research for this book.

Bearing in mind that the bulk of the printed cards and albums (both leather and plastic) required by the enormous carte-de-visite market in the 1860s and '70s were produced by French manufacturers – Marion & Co of Paris in particular – the British professional photographic industry seems to have been fairly heavily dependent upon imports from the very earliest days. Little has changed!

The importation of packaging materials from America was not entirely a one-sided affair. There is strong evidence of at least some two-way traffic. There were a number of high quality case manufacturers in Britain, at least in the early days when quality leathers were used for the outer skins of the cases. One or two of those British case makers did clearly export to America. The existence of Wharton patent daguerreotype cases in America is considerably greater than might be expected to have been achieved either by the movement of people or of complete and cased photographs across the Atlantic during the years in which cases were popular. That there was an export market from the Midlands manufacturer to the United States is certain – but the scale of that export is unrecorded.

A note of caution should be noted here as the widespread export of British and European antiques by the container load to America must necessarily have distorted the figures and increased the likelihood of such cases being found in collections and locations where they were unknown in contemporary times. The frequency with which some of John Smith's Birmingham-made thermoplastic cases are found in American collections is an example. Research undertaken for this book suggests that the majority of British

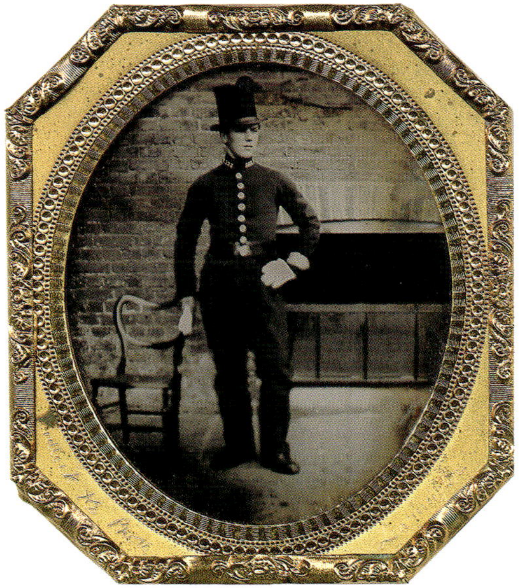

Portrait of a Policeman c.*1856, sixth plate ambrotype by Bullock & Co., Photographic Portrait Gallery, Royal Assembly Rooms, Bedford Street, Leamington, Warwickshire. The image is housed in an octagonal thermoplastic Union Case by Littlefield, Parsons, & Co. Bullock & Co. were at this address from 1855 until 1861.*

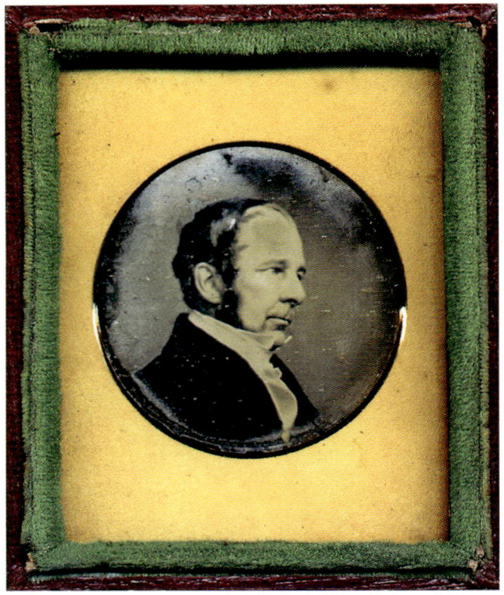

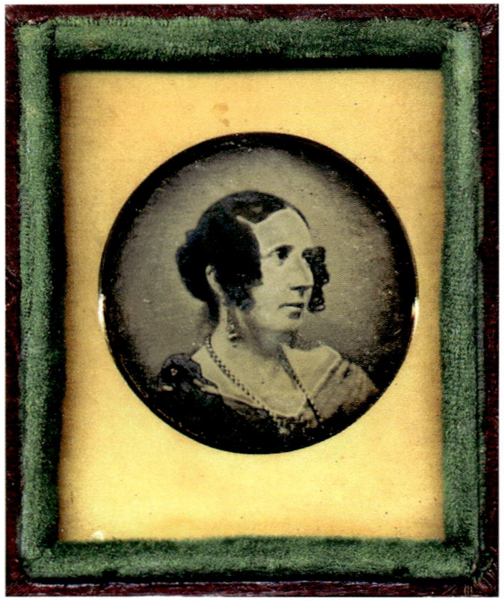

Ninth plate daguerreotype portraits of a lady and gentleman, by the Photographic Institution, Salop. Fine leather cases with studio gilt stamp on base. Case size 72mm x 69mm, plain matte, with circular aperture size 38mm diameter. The studio was active in the second half of the 1840s.

plastic cases currently found in collections in the United States may be recent imports rather than contemporary with their commercial life.

It is not, however, the purpose of this book to assume a totally local standpoint when discussing and chronicling the history and evolution of the cased photograph. It is probable that unless identified otherwise on the pictures themselves, the majority of the illustrations for this book were taken in Britain. Certainly they were nearly all purchased in Britain, as this book is unusual in being illustrated from a single privately assembled collection rather than the usual method of assembling a collage of illustrative material from a selection of national and private sources. Only a very few illustrations are of cases acquired in the United States.

Several potentially dangerous assumptions might be made by virtue of the fact that almost all the material has been collected in the UK. As many of the cases have been identified as being from American manufacturers, and there is minimal (although increasing through facilities such as eBay) movement of photographic antiques from America to the UK today, it might be assumed with reasonable safety that these cases were imported in the heyday of the cased portrait.

The fact of single images identified as being from American studios being found in out-of-the-way places in Britain has been interpreted as evidence that there was a degree of traffic across the Atlantic in the 1840s, '50s and '60s by way of gifts and so on. As collecting becomes increasingly transatlantic, however, the frequency with which the (usually unmistakable) work of American studios is offered for sale in Britain is increasing sharply

A great deal of care, and special technique, has gone into the preparation of the illustrations of many of the cases, to enhance the relief effect of the patterns found on case covers, and by that means, to make them easier to identify. This has, in some cases, made the motifs seems stronger and more distinctive than they actually are. The relief effect has been electronically heightened using computer technology. Seeing many of the cases in reality, designs are much more subtle. That subtlety would be lost in the printing process were these enhancing techniques not used. This is an instance where the latest electronic and digital technology has been brought to the aid of these early images and cases.

There has been a tendency in the recent past to write about daguerreotypes, ambrotypes and so on without reference to their cases – to treat photographs and cases separately. Yet they were designed to be seen together. In many instances the hand-colouring of the image was echoed by subtle choices of colour available in the soft velvet pad on the left hand side of the case. Indeed it is often a good if arbitrary method of checking whether or not a picture has been paired up with a case for which it was intended. If tinting on the photograph, and colouring on the velvet pad do not harmonise, there must be a strong possibility that the photograph has been separated from its original case and married up with another!

Certainly from contemporary catalogues it is clear that velvet pads in a range of qualities and with a variety of embossed designs were available in a wide range of colours to fit all case sizes. There exists therefore the likelihood that photographers stocked either a variety of completed cases with different coloured pad inserts, or as they were available separately, stocked empty cases and a stock of pads to be married together to meet specific customer needs. Three examples of the union case design known either as 'The Deer and the Pine Tree' or 'The Proud Elk' inspected in the course of research for this book have pads of quite different colours, embossed with different motifs. The edging strip around the image bearing side of each case is also colour-coordinated to match the respective pad colour, and the tinting on the images. The packaging of the nineteenth century photograph spawned a vast manufacturing and marketing network which readily took on the most advanced production methods available. The sheer scale of the operation is hinted at by the fact that one of the first successful uses for mass-produced plastic was the manufacture of photographic cases in the mid 1850s. For at least one known British casemaker, this was a profitable spin-off from the manufacture of plastic imitation horn buttons!

It started with the daguerreotype, reached a peak in the mid to late 1850s and, by the time the carte-de-visite reached the peak of its popularity, photographic case manufacture had returned almost to the level of cottage industry. This book is the story of those decades.

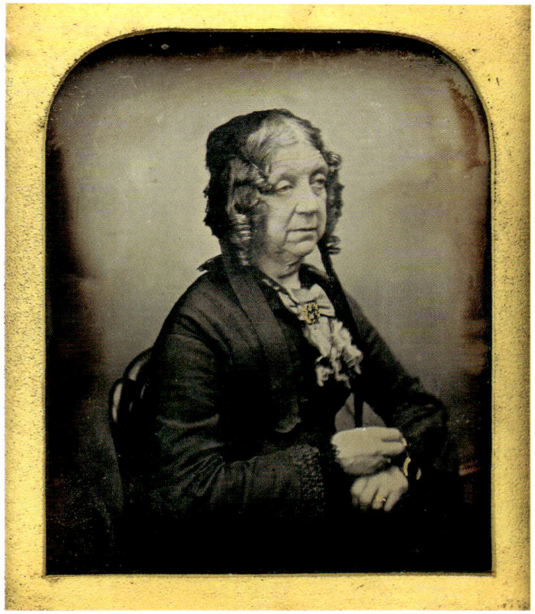

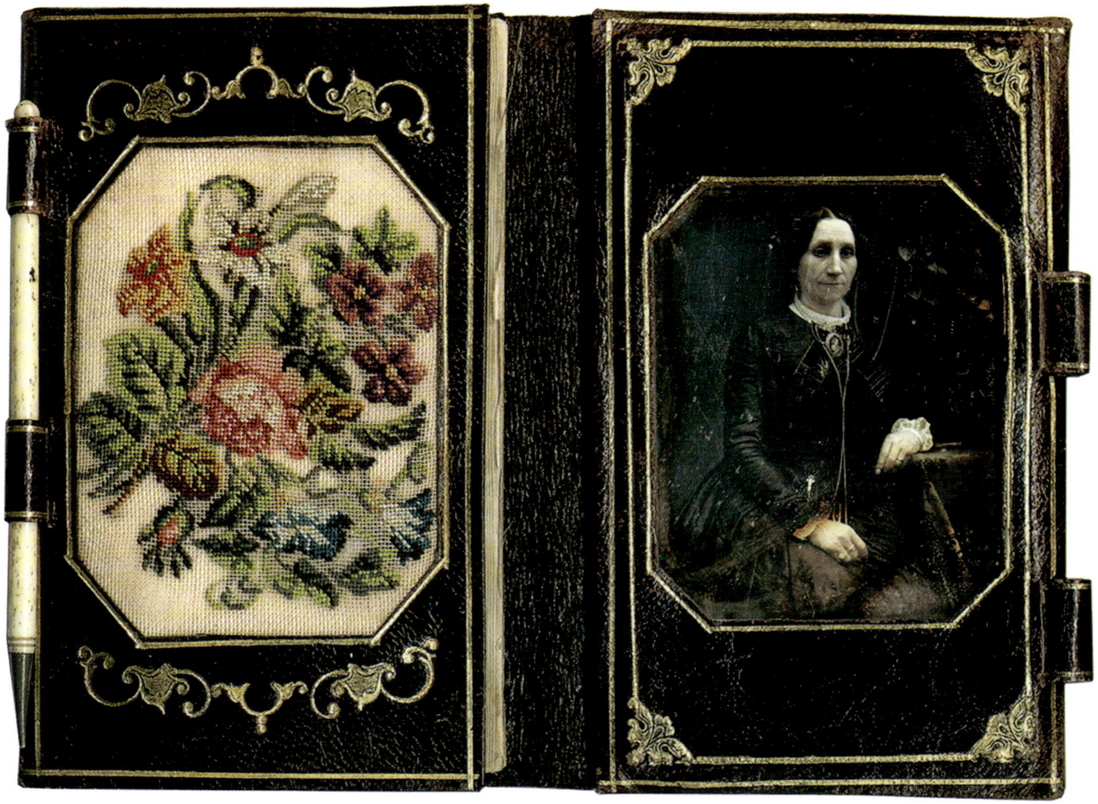

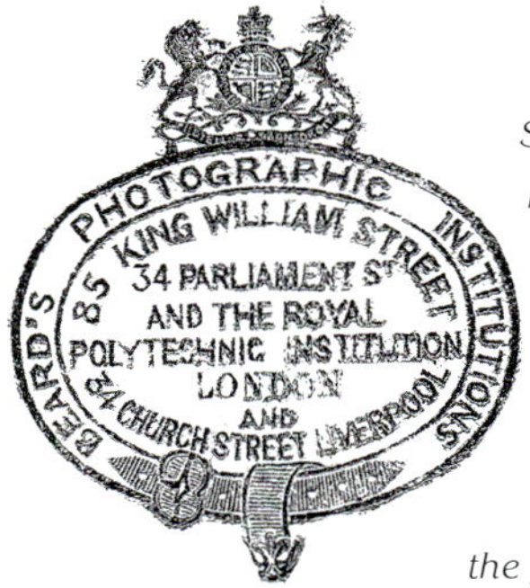

Above: Sixth plate daguerreotype portrait by one of Beard's London Photographic Institutions, early 1850s. Originally tinted and gilded. Beard's high quality leather cases usually bore a version of the gilt embossed stamp, left.

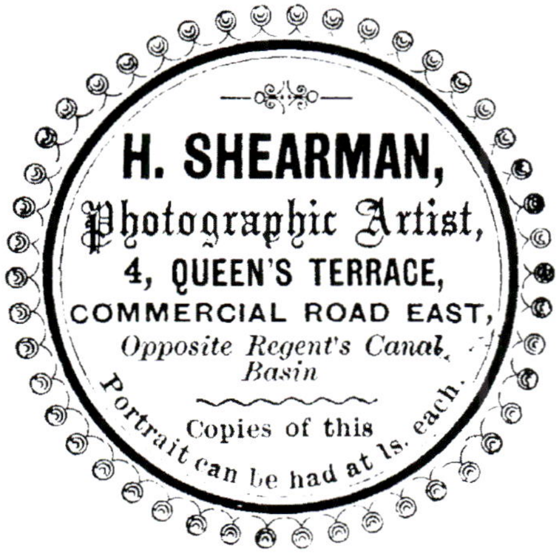

Above: Leather bound notecase & pocket book 1851. Hand embroidered pad, set in gilded and tooled leather. Ivory shafted lead pencil, with vellum notepad. Sixth plate Daguerreotype. Photographer unknown. Image size 72mm x 62mm. Aperture size 66mm x 53mm. The silk-covered notebook is inscribed 'to Alexander Douglas from his Mother, May 10th 1851.'

Left: Label affixed to images by H. Shearman, Photographic Artist, 1860s. Shearman occupied these premises from 1861 until 1867, turning out high quality ambrotypes. The example of his work from which this label comes is housed in a thermoplastic union case.

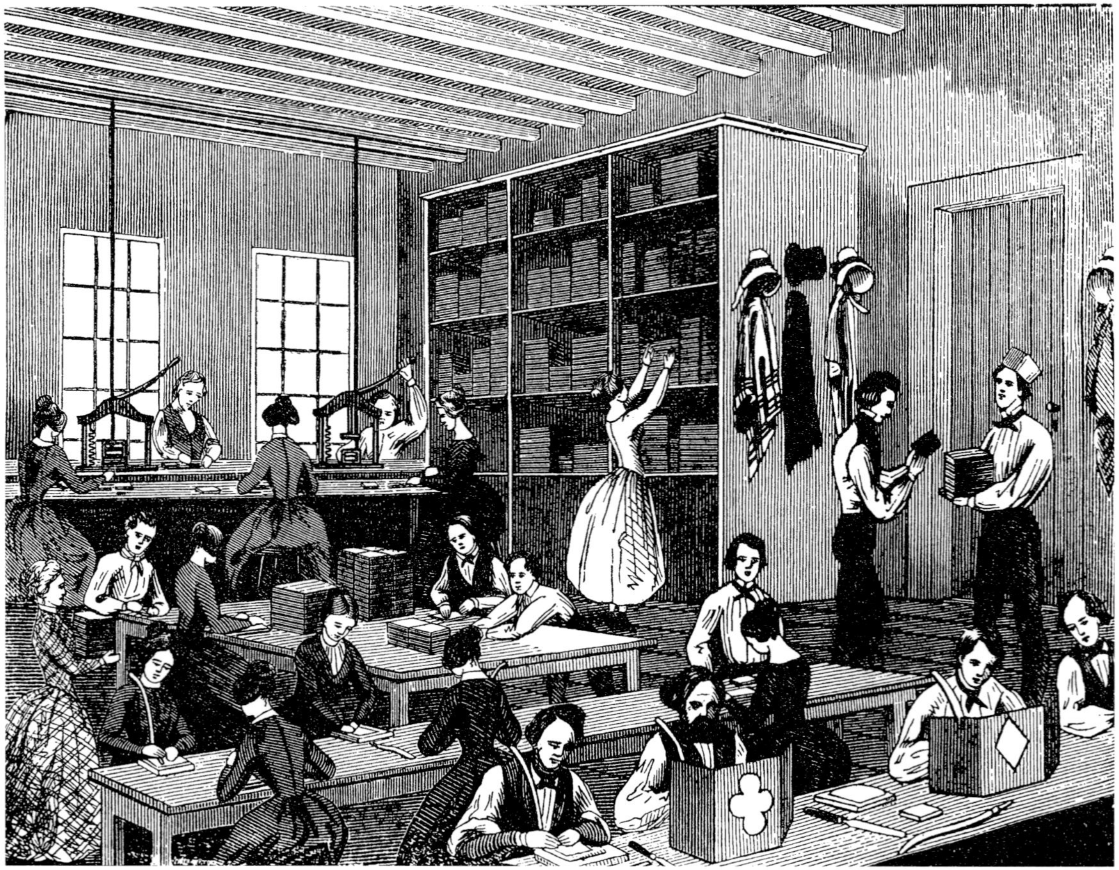

In the 'Gilding Room' of Anthony's factory, 1854, gold leaf decoration is being applied to case fronts. On most case designs this would have been simple gold leaf borders, but other more elaborate patterns were also produced. The Gilding Department was one of four in Anthony's factory, described in his catalogue as 'one for making the wooden boxes which form the substratum or body of the cases; one where these boxes are covering with leather and trimmed, one where the leather covering and the cushions are embossed and stamped, and one where the cases are gilded.'

Chapter One

Marketing the Photographic Portrait

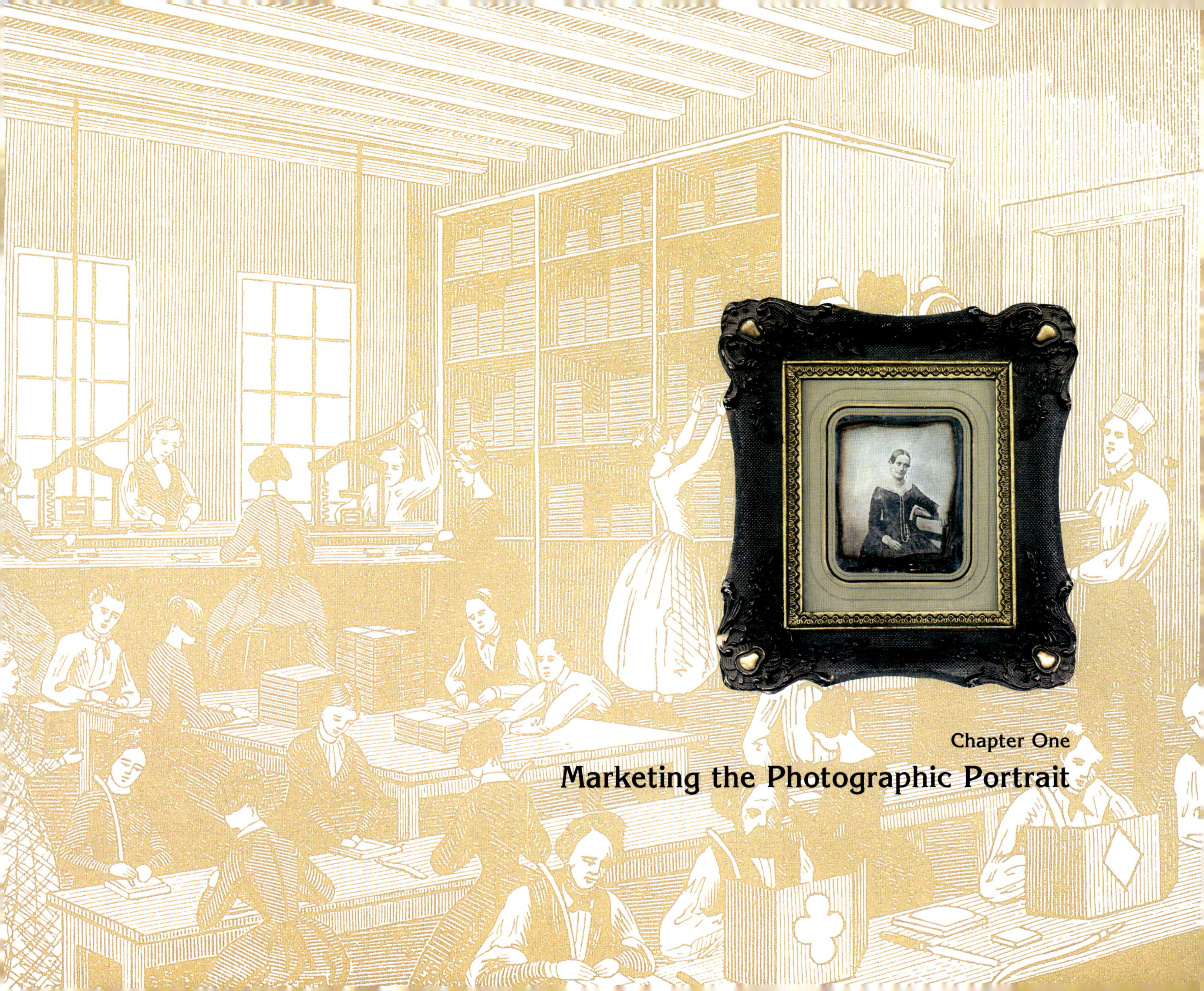

Chapter One:

Marketing the Photographic Portrait

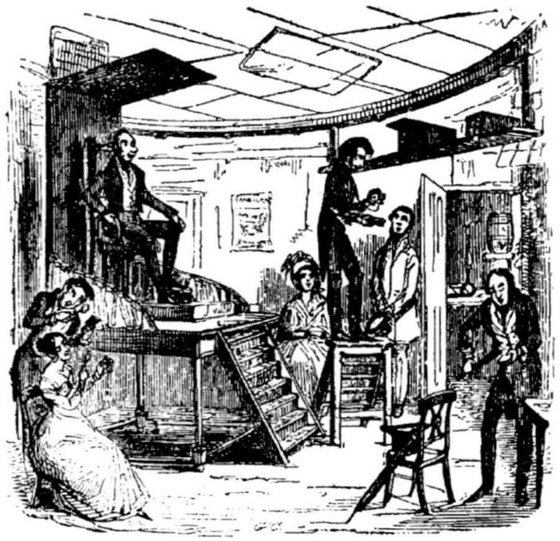

Above: Cruikshank's famous cartoon of the first daguerreotype studio in London, opened in 1841 by Richard Beard. The camera is mounted on rails around the top of the studio, while the subject is seated on a movable platform. Thus the subject could always be facing the sun, and the camera facing the subject. The muslin diffusers above the sitter's head cut down the top light coming in through the glass roof.

While photography did not introduce the idea of the cased portrait – miniature paintings had been available in leather cases at least since the end of the eighteenth century both in America and in Britain – it did take the manufacture of cases out of the small hand-crafted industry and into the realms of low unit cost mass production. As the daguerreotype was seen as a new method of portrait painting when it was first introduced, it was both logical, and commercially sound, to present it and market it in a manner which echoed the tradition of which it claimed to be the logical successor. Indeed many newspaper accounts of the introduction of photography – or more specifically the opening of the first photographic studios in each newspaper's locality – headed their articles with variations on the theme of 'painting by the new process'.

Initial fascination with photography surrounded the ability of the camera to capture finer detail and more accurate detail than had been possible with the painter's brush on such a small scale, and to do so at a cost which brought the miniature portrait within the financial reach of a wider sector of the population. The report published in the *Dumfries & Galloway Courier* is typical of that carried in many other newspapers. While one could dispute some of the generalisations it contains, the fascination that photography held – and the writer's inability to find appropriate words with which to describe the miracle process – are clearly evident. The photograph – and if the newspaper account is to be believed, the photographer as well – had a scarcity value, and the opportunity to acquire such a treasure should not be ignored.[1]

'Mr. Edwards, a cadet of the Adelaide Gallery which has turned out some of the finest specimens of the art, has established his painting rooms, to speak in the old phrase, in a handsome saloon, 43 Buchanan Street Glasgow, erected for the purpose, so that the light of day, which acts to him the part of a pencil, may have free and uninterrupted access. There he has produced some very beautiful living portraits in the short space of a few seconds, and has even transferred prints and celebrated oil paintings. Not a few of his works contain all the severity of truth and, in addition to the countenance and aspect of the individual, the form of a breastpin, the crease of a ruffle, or the petals of a flower which may be worn in the breast, are most faithfully portrayed. In fact the artist can neither flatter nor detract from the appearance of an object which is presented to him; he is merely a secondary agent and the work is painted with a pencil of light.

'None who desire to possess likenesses of themselves or of their friends, such as the pencil can never possibly equal, should miss the opportunity they now enjoy for the first time.'

The account went on to say that, with his Glasgow studio now firmly established, Mr. Edwards was making a short visit to Dumfries, where he had established another studio, at Mrs Williamson's in Irish Street, where likenesses could be made for one guinea, which included a handsome case or frame.

Mr. Edwards was not a man to settle for long – indeed his Dumfries advertisement mentioned that he would be in the town for only a very short time as he had pressing engagement in *'Russia, Prussia etc and may not return to Dumfries again, if ever, for a lengthened period of time'.*[2]

Those engagements cannot have been anything more than a device to ensure a queue of customers outside Mrs. Williamson's boarding house. Nor can they have been all that long or all that pressing, for a few weeks later Mr. Edwards was advertising in the Stirling newspapers that he had established his *'painting rooms'* at Mrs. Stirling's in Melville Terrace, Stirling, where he would, once again, remain for only a very short time!

Edwards was one of a number of photographers who travelled from town to town setting up temporary studios and introducing the daguerreotype to hundreds of willing customers. He had originally been trained in the art of photography by Antoine Claudet of the Adelaide Gallery in London.

The daguerreotype was the subject of a somewhat confused patent situation in England – a situation which required all potential users of the process initially to acquire a licence to use it.

Shortly after the announcement of the process in France, Louis Daguerre took out patents in England and Wales through his agent Miles Berry. Within a few months of his original announcement of the process, he had embarked upon negotiations with the French government designed to transfer all his French interests to the government in return for national recognition and a substantial pension.

After agreeing terms, the French Government in a typically expansive gesture, promptly gave the process free to the people of France. In Britain, matters were not resolved with such ease or simplicity. Antoine Claudet in London proposed that the British Government might do the same for British photographers and, on hearing that Daguerre, through Berry, wished to dispose of the British rights, even offered his services as intermediary to arrange this. His proposals came to nothing.

Subsequently, to protect Daguerre's interests, and generate income, Berry patented the process in England and Wales 'and the town of Berwick upon Tweed' on Daguerre's behalf – as the patent states *'being a communication from a foreigner residing abroad'*. The patent specification included a brief background note which referred to the French negotiations:–

'Before proceeding to the description of this invention, I think it proper to make the following remarks.– This Invention or discovery relates to photogenic drawing, or the spontaneous reproduction of images, pictures or representations of nature by the action of light that is, by the process or method now well known under the name of "daguerreotype". I believe it to be the Invention of Messrs. Louis Jacques Maude (sic!) *Daguerre and Joseph Isdodore* (sic!) *Niepce, junior, both of the Kingdom of France, from whom the French government have purchased the Invention, for the benefit of that country.'*[3]

Almost as soon as Berry completed the patent application, Antoine Claudet acquired a licence and paid considerably for the privilege. The complicated licensing system in England was both unusual and highly restrictive. It is interesting that Daguerre's instructions to Berry seem to have been to 'petition her Majesty to grant Her Royal Letters Patent for the exclusive use of the same within these kingdoms' suggesting that the original idea was to include Scotland and Ireland within the area covered.[4]

The first professional photographer to open for business in England was Richard Beard, a former partner in a coal merchant's business, who established England's first photographic studio at the Royal Polytechnic Institution in Regent Street.

Beard himself had little or no initial knowledge of photography and employed two chemists to carry out a considerable amount of research work at the Institution designed to increase the sensitivity of the plates and considerably reduce exposure times. Those two chemists may even have taken photographs for him as well in the first months.

When Daguerre, through Berry, chose to dispose of his patent rights in England and Wales, it was to Beard that they were sold. The transfer of Berry's interests in the patent to Richard Beard, however, left both Beard and Claudet in curious positions.

By 1841, Beard, now sole patent holder for the daguerreotype in *England, Wales and Berwick Upon Tweed*, not to mention the *Colonies and Plantations*, had sole jurisdiction over the process with the exception of Claudet's Adelaide Gallery – and Claudet was in direct competition with him! Claudet's licence acquired from Berry had legal standing over and above any arrangement reached between Berry and Beard!

One thing did separate the two men, however, and that stemmed from the fact that Beard's initial interest in the daguerreotype had come from America rather than France. Beard had been impressed by the innovative work on the process and particularly on camera design carried out by

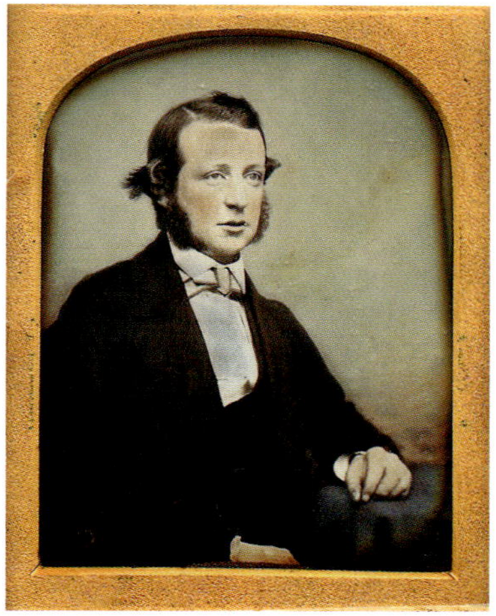

Inside the top-hinged leather-covered case housing a ninth plate daguerreotype by Thomas Chapman Browne of Leicester, his business card lists all the other activities he undertook to support his photographic studio. It seems even in a town the size of Leicester in the 1850s, there was not sufficient demand for a full-time photographer. Browne was in partnership with J.J.Hewitt from 1844 until 1848, at the Bible and Crown Printing Works, and this image dates from around 1850.

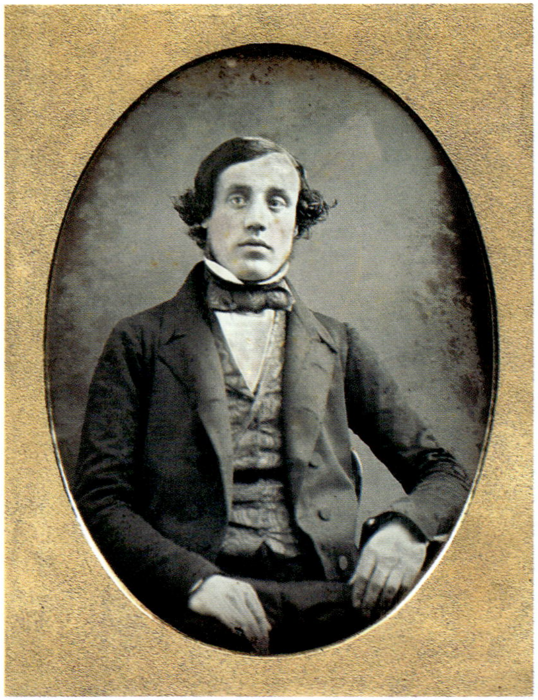

Quarter plate daguerreotype by Thomas Jones, 1854-56. Photographer's gilt stamp on plain leather case. Case size 113mm x 87mm. Oval matte, aperture size 88mm x 64mm. Trim and pad in burgundy velvet. Jones opened his first studio at 498 Oxford Street, London, in 1850, before moving to the Royal Arcade, 537 New Oxford Street in 1854 – where he took this portrait – an address he occupied for only two years.

the American, Alexander S Wolcott, and patented in America on May 8th 1840.[5] Beard patented the camera design in England within his British Patent *Apparatus for Obtaining Likenesses &c.*[6]

The 'official' camera which carried Daguerre's seal of approval – built by Alphonse Giroux in Paris – was of what might be considered a conventional design with a lens at the front and a plate holder at the back. It created a laterally reversed image. The early meniscus lens fitted to the camera – between f/11 and f/16 – gave long exposures and was quickly replaced by an f/6.7 design by Charles Chevalier, and an f/3.5 design by the German Professor Petzval.[7]

Wolcott's camera design used a concave mirror at the back instead of a lens, reflecting the image back to a plate fixed on to a focusable slide near the front panel, rather in the method used in reflecting telescopes even today. The effect of this was to correct the lateral reversal of the image, and produce a small positive image which read the right way round. The large mirror focusing light on to a relatively small plate gave relatively short exposures from the outset. The image was small, and rather soft, but thanks to the light-collecting qualities of the large mirror, exposure times were very short.

Later Claudet and others corrected the reading of their daguerreotypes by using a reversing prism in front of the camera lens.

Beard had originally opened Britain's first photographic studio without seeking licence authority from Miles Berry, asserting that the differences between the American and French methods were so fundamental that he was outwith Berry's patent control. However after persistent demands from Berry, he appears to have agreed to the payment of a fee in return for a percentage interest in the patent. It was only several months after his entry into photography that Beard assumed total control of the patent, after paying a substantial amount to buy out Miles Berry's interests completely.

Once totally in control of the process, Beard was able effectively to control the growth of photography itself, and – with the exception of Claudet – control those photographers who engaged in commercial portraiture. In real terms, this meant that studios were only opened where Richard Beard wanted them to be opened. By this time he was in partnership with John Johnson, and between them they set about establishing a chain of Photographic Institutions throughout the country.

Prospective photographers found themselves in a difficult position if they wished to set up studios themselves. There were three options open to them – the same three options which would have faced Mr. Edwards when he made his decision to leave Claudet's employment and set up on his own.

Firstly, they could elect to pay the asking price for a licence to open a studio – assuming of course that Beard was prepared to sanction a studio in the photographer's chosen town, and that he had not already sold exclusive rights to use the process in that area. Beard's excuse for the high fees was, after all, that he guaranteed a degree of exclusivity – with no competition. No other photographers would be allowed to move into an area covered by a Beard Licensed Photographer, or one of Beard's own operations.

Secondly, if the patent fee was too high, the photographer could elect either to become one of Beard's managers, or to go into partnership with Beard himself. In the former case the photographer drew a salary, while in the latter Beard would take a percentage of the studio earnings.

The third option – and the one chosen by Mr. Edwards – was to move outside Beard's patent control. This usually meant a move to Scotland where he could use Daguerre's process freely.

The drawback to that, of course, was the relatively small number of heavily populated centres in Scotland from which a photographer could derive a guaranteed living – thus the frequency with which *itinerant* photographers were found north of the border. The market potential of each town could, therefore, effectively be exhausted – temporarily at least – within a matter

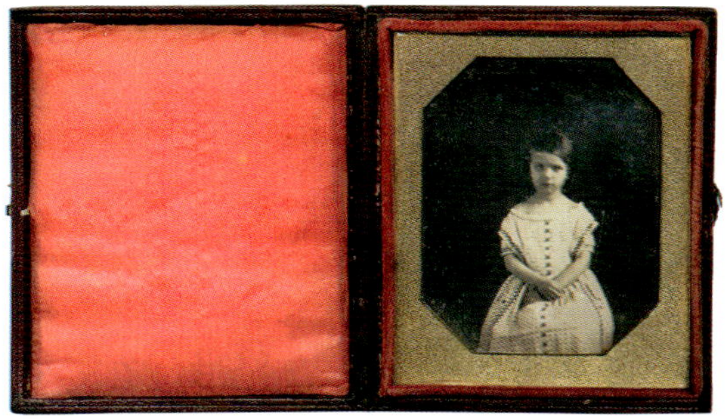

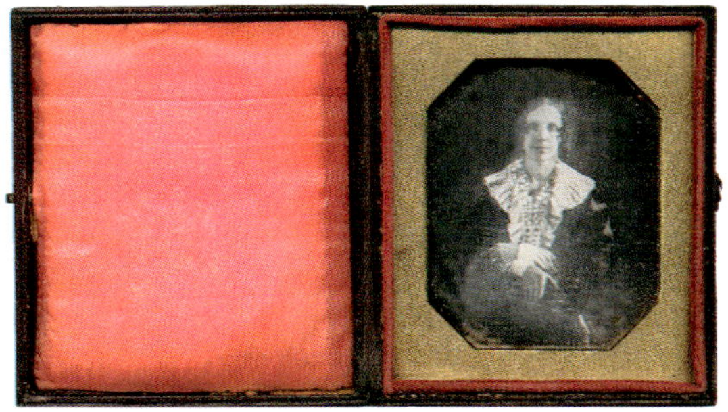

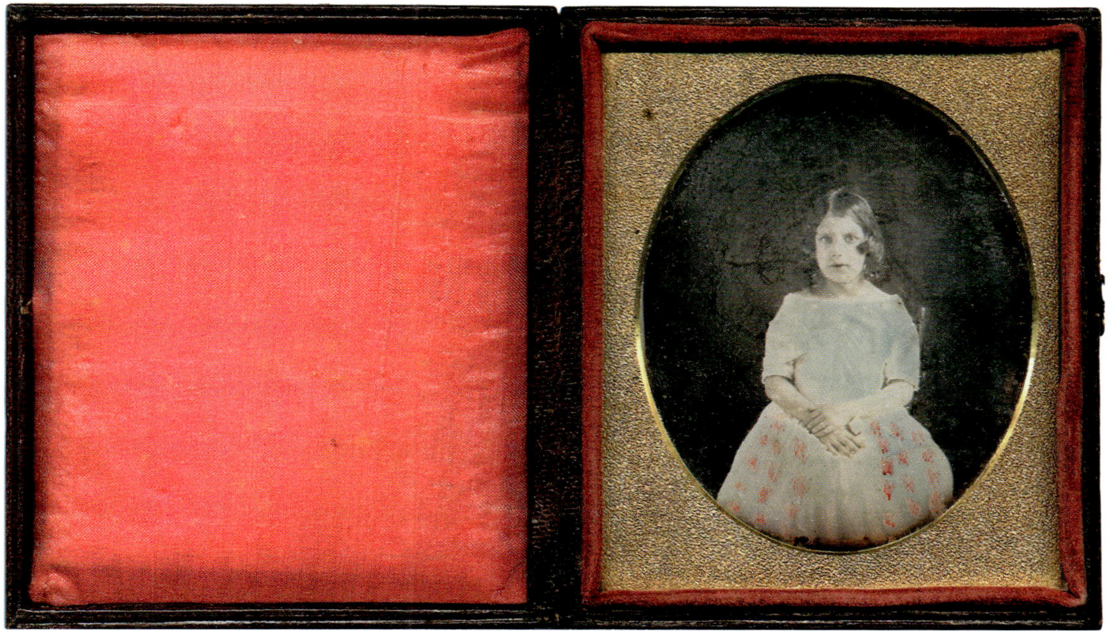

of months. The photographer would then have to move on in search of pastures new – which had not already been exploited by someone else!

Initially Beard & Johnson set up a relatively small number of studios – and Johnson himself managed Manchester's first studio in Ducie Place for the first few months after it opened in 1841. Their managers worked studios in Liverpool, Bath, Brighton and elsewhere and, having established them and operated them for a few months, often transferred the licences to local photographers they had themselves trained, and set off to open new operations in other towns and cities.

Thus it was that James T. Foard arrived in Liverpool. He had started out as a Beard manager – probably first in the Birmingham studio in 1842 before moving to Sheffield and then to Liverpool in 1843 or 1844. At first he ran Beard's Liverpool studio for him, before apparently setting up on his own for a few years. By the late 1840s, with Richard Beard facing bankruptcy, Foard teamed up with Richard Beard Jnr. and opened Beard &

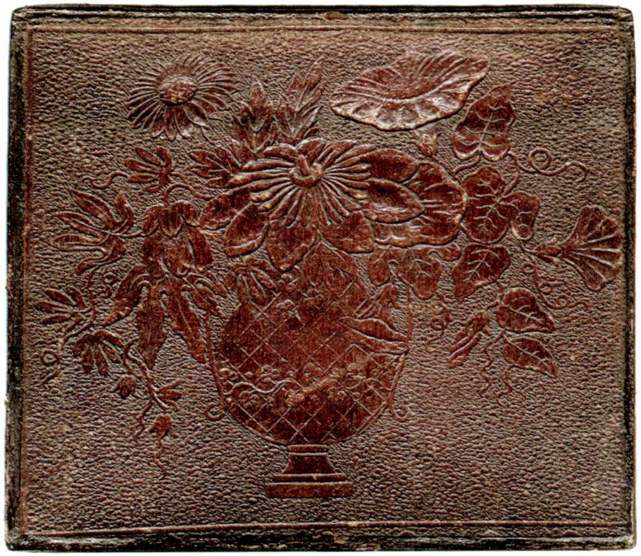

Sixth plate daguerreotype case reputed to be by John Plumbe Jnr, 1843-5. Plumbe is credited with introducing the embossed leather case, and this 'Grecian Urn' design is believed to be his earliest. A trio of these cases was used to hold the three daguerreotype portraits of a mother and her daughters above. All are believed to be American, and by the simplicity of the mats and the pink silk pads, they date from c.1843-4.

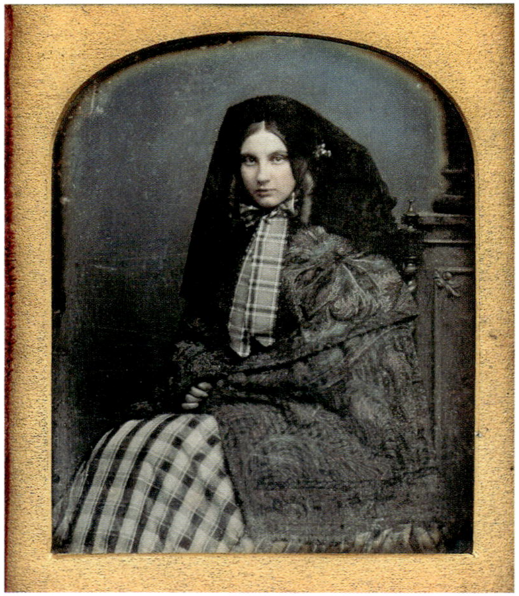

Tinted sixth plate daguerreotype Portrait of a young girl, by Richard Lowe of Cheltenham, 1850s. Embossed paper-covered case, with photographer's gilded stamp. Case size 94mm x 80mm. Aperture size 55mm x 43mm. Lowe's studio on Cheltenham's Promenade operated as one of Beard's Photographic Institutions from 1841 until 1856. It was sold to Richard Marklove in 1844 or 1845, and then bought back by Richard Beard Jnr in 1849. By 1850 Lowe, the former manager, was trading under his own name. He eventually disappeared leaving considerable debts, and is believed to have travelled in Europe before returning to America. The studio was subsequently re-opened by Charles Pottinger.

Foard's first joint studio at 34 Church Street Liverpool in 1849 and, five years later, a second studio under the joint name in Manchester's St Ann's Square. The Manchester studio, however, survived for only three years before being taken over by Alfred Brothers in 1857.

Interestingly, while these two northern studios were trading under the 'Beard & Foard' title, their names and addresses were listed on the back of some cases from Beard's London studios simply as 'Beard's Photographic Institutions'. Equally interesting is the reverse of that story – for on some cases dating from the 1850s the London studios are listed under the umbrella title of 'Beard & Foard's Photographic Institutions'.

Returning to the 1840s, however, the real effect of Beard's patents – whatever his initial intentions – was to retard quite significantly, the development of photography in England and Wales. By 1850 Liverpool had only three studios, while similarly sized towns in Europe could boast many times that number. Considering that he and his staff had been instrumental in bringing about considerable improvements in the process, it is of course quite reasonable that they should wish to protect their investment until such time as a reasonable return had been achieved on their initial outlay.

Those patent rights were rigorously defended and, like Fox Talbot over his calotype process patents, Beard became involved in several celebrated court cases, usually trying to bring to heel photographers who had been using the daguerreotype without permission – often for several years before Beard's lawyers caught up with them!

While Talbot was sufficiently wealthy to meet the often huge costs of patent protection, Beard apparently was not, and by the end of the decade he had filed for bankruptcy – but not before his rights had been upheld in a variety of courts. When the patents were ultimately allowed to lapse, daguerreotype portraiture was finally given the chance to develop and establish itself as it already had done throughout the rest of Europe and America.

While Beard himself was originally seen, in the eyes of many of his contemporaries at least, as nothing more than an opportunist, his involvement with the process produced considerable improvements in both the technical and aesthetic qualities of the images. He also became a formidable portraitist in his own right – a fact borne out by the many fine surviving examples of his work. In addition to establishing a string of studios, he established standards of operation and of operator training which helped lay down a foundation of quality in the early years. He also pioneered hand colouring of the images – taking out a patent in 1842 for Daguerre's own colouring process 'communicated to me by a certain Foreigner living abroad' – and pioneered a variety of ornate presentation styles.[8]

While the majority of portraits found in Beard cases are the work of his managers and assistants, some images do survive which bear his own ink signature.

The output of Beard studios falls into three categories. First there is the body of work found in cases embossed with the 'Beard Photographic Institution' logotype. As already mentioned, these cases bear several of the addresses from which Beard photographers worked. In London alone he operated seven studios with addresses – in addition to the Polytechnic Institution – at King William Street, Regent Street, Parliament Street and elsewhere.

Secondly a group of images bear the 'Beard Patentee' blind stamp on the matte or on a label inside the case. Such studios were clearly licensed by Beard, although some 'Beard Patentee' cases do appear with Beard's own signature in ink across the label.

Thirdly, there are the studios which were run in partnership with Richard Beard Jnr. – such as the Manchester, Liverpool and Birmingham operations at various times.

Many of the photographers who entered the business after the demise of the patent restrictions were not as confident as Beard of the earning potential of photography. Initially few of them were willing to abandon their previous occupations and devote themselves exclusively to photography. Even fewer were willing or able to meet the cost of custom-built premises such as those boasted by Mr. Edwards on the roof of 43 Buchanan Street in Glasgow. Indeed many of the early studios were temporary affairs attached to the backs or roofs of an assortment of buildings – public houses being a particular favourite.

This practice of setting up studios in inns or pubs was both widespread and long-lived. In the late 1860s, for example, well after the demise of the daguerreotype, research into those photographers working in Wigan, near Manchester, has shown several of them still classified as 'photographer and innkeepers' or 'photographer and beer retailer', with seven of the town's studios being established in local inns!

Although there were few studios in England in 1841, there were many more in America. In America too the idea of casing the miniature painting was already more firmly accepted, with many casemakers already well established and well known. By 1842 or 1843 at the latest, Britain's photographic studios were offering the leather case as a natural alternative to the wood or plaster frame, and it seems likely that many of these cases were imported from the American east coast.

Although there remains an element of conjecture in such suppositions, it can be fairly conclusively assumed that daguerreotype portraits found in American cases in Britain are, generally speaking, of British subjects. Subtle distinctions between American and British fashions are easy to recognise.

Early cased daguerreotypes fall into two categories – those in plain leather cases with no decoration and either with or without the photographer's gilt embossed stamp, and embossed cases almost always without any identification of the photographer.

The cost of having cases especially made and embossed with the photographer's name and address may well have been an unwarranted expense for a newly established studio, especially bearing in mind the burden imposed by the huge licence fee payable to Beard. For photographers operating outwith Beard's licence control, the itinerant nature of their lifestyle would have made such decoration commercially pointless, as they seem to have stayed only a few weeks in any one location, certainly for the first few years of their professional careers.

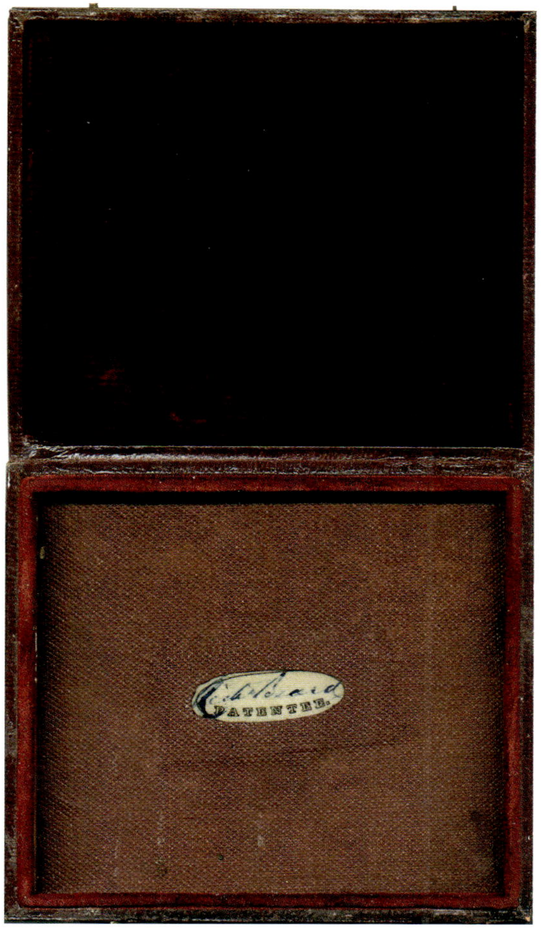

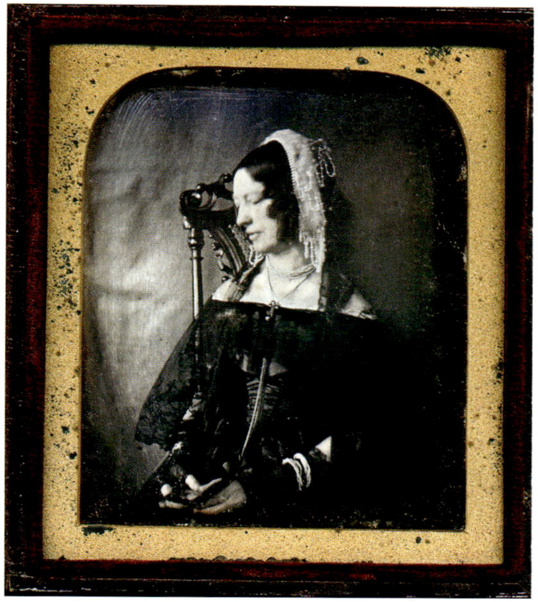

Sixth plate daguerreotype of a lady holding a cased daguerreotype. The 'Beard Patentee' label inside the burgundy leather case is signed in blue ink 'Rich'd Beard' suggesting that this image may have been taken by Beard himself. The case is of very simple design, and the daguerreotype plate itself is of a very thick gauge, typical of the earlier years of the process. c.*1847.*

The practice of case identification seems only to have come into common use by the end of photography's first decade, by which time studios were better established and photographers more certain of their market potential. A few of the early workers did insert paper cards or labels either inside the case, or fixed to the backs of the plates themselves. Others scribed their names and addresses into the brass mattes used to protect the delicate images.[9] Framed portraits with labels on the backs of the frames seem to have been fairly common since the mid 1840s.

There were a few exceptions. Mattes stamped 'Beard Patentee' can be found in some very early cases, while the Wharton matte and preserver for daguerreotypes – which also usually carried the royal coat of arms in an embossed stamp – was introduced as early as 1841.

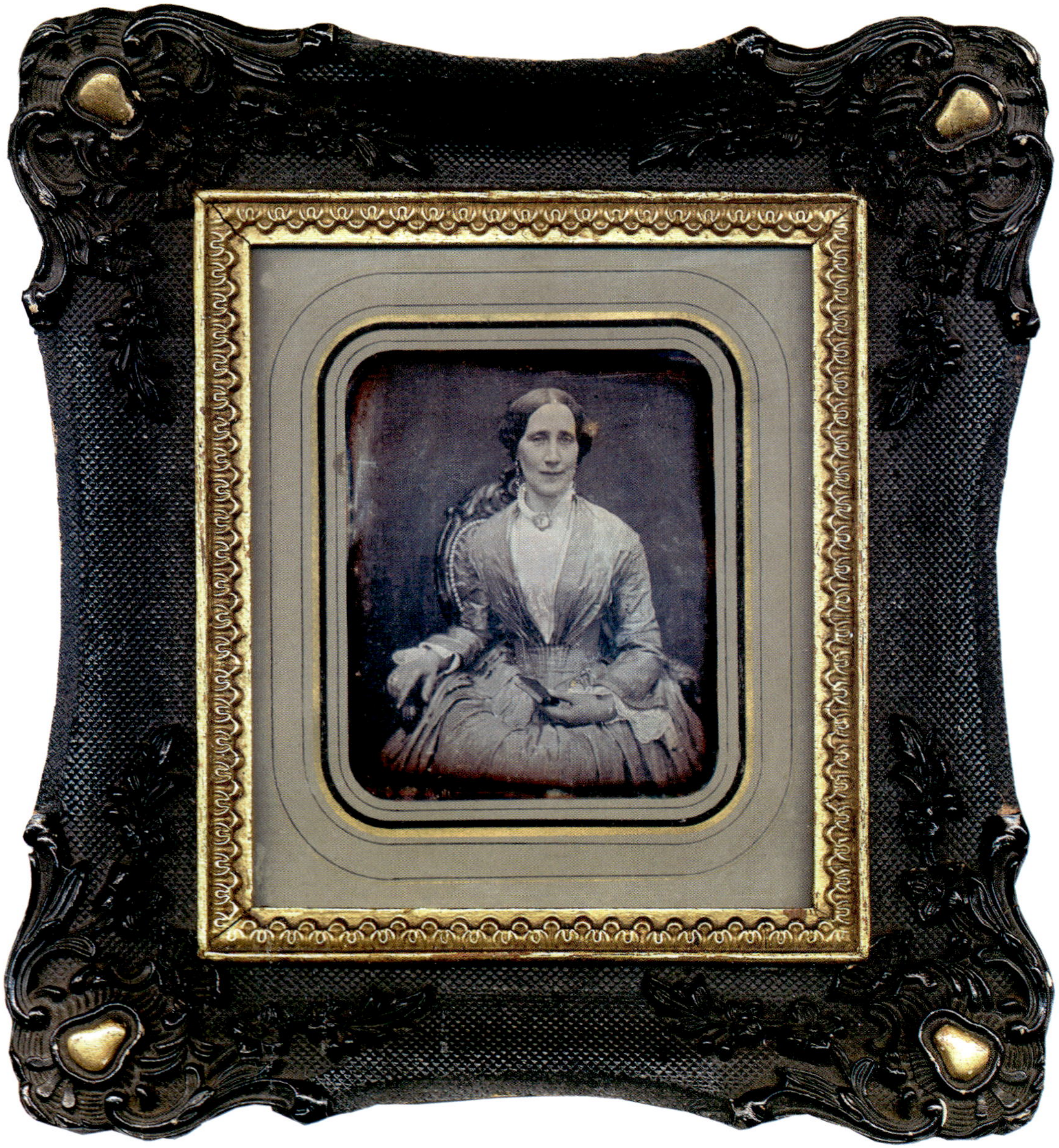

Sixth plate daguerreotype by Gustav Oehme of 20 Jagerstasse, Berlin, one of Germany's first professional photographers. Oehme was a former pupil of Louis Daguerre himself, and opened his Berlin studio in the early 1840s. This portrait, identified in pencil on the reverse as 'Aunt Louise Brause, née Bencke', is one of a pair sent to Britain as presents c.1845. Both are housed in gilded wood and plaster frames, 180mm x 165mm.

By the early 1850s, the American companies supplying the brass mattes were offering to stamp them with the photographer's name and address on to one or two corners, and at no extra cost. It is therefore a little surprising that so few photographers availed themselves of this opportunity to personalise their presentation methods. Later still, by the mid 1850s, American case makers were offering a service whereby the name and address of the studio could be stamped into the velvet pad which protected the face of the picture inside the case itself.

It can only be assumed that even the minimum order requirement from the manufacturers before they were willing to undertake these services was still too large for some small-town operators.

During its commercial life, the daguerreotype progressed from a fairly unsophisticated portraiture medium to a level of high art. The artistry and skill of the photographer was augmented by the skill of the miniature painter, thanks to a patented process for adding colour and gold leaf to the portrait.

While the daguerreotype is often presented as a medium which enjoyed its heyday in the 1840s, this is a misrepresentation. Clear evidence exists to support the view that daguerreotypes and ambrotypes enjoyed periods of predominantly contemporary success – with the early years of the 1850s largely being the peak of daguerreotype production in Britain. Beard's patents and his system of controlling and restricting the issue of licences were largely responsible for this. In his first round of licences in 1841-2 he sanctioned the establishment of less than a dozen studios. London, Manchester, Liverpool, Birmingham, Nottingham, Bristol, Bath, Cheltenham, Brighton, Southampton and Plymouth were first in line, with Derby, York and Newcastle following very shortly afterwards. It was only after the patents lapsed that the process really became popular.

In London, the restriction was such that even by the end of the 1840s, only five photographers had set up businesses – or at least only five were advertising themselves in trade directories. By the end of the following decade, with all patent restrictions lifted, over one hundred and fifty were operating in the London area alone.

Licence fees were high – and considering that Beard had probably paid only £800 for the exclusive patent rights in England Wales & Berwick on Tweed – profits must have been exceptional. Records show that Beard took over £3,000 in the first few months of operating his own studio, and that licence fees per year ranged from £300 to £1,200 per studio. Some licences were to operate a single studio, while others were to have exclusive rights to a designated area. The asking price for the Manchester area was reputed to be £1,000, but was not taken up, resulting in the profit sharing partnership of Beard and Foard.

It is interesting to note that several of the best known names today from the history of the daguerreotype did not enter the market place until the early 1850s – Thomas Jones in 1850, William Kilburn in 1852, and J.E. Mayall not until 1853.

Also of interest are the apparent differences in the dates for the first photographic businesses in towns throughout Britain. As might be expected, the towns of the south of England were amongst the first – London, Brighton, Bath, Cheltenham, Southampton and Plymouth all had working studios in 1841. So did Liverpool, Manchester and Nottingham, while Birmingham joined the ranks the following year, along with Oxford and Leeds. While the people of Edinburgh, Glasgow, Stirling and Dumfries had been introduced to the new portraiture medium in 1843, the good citizens of a city the size of Cardiff did not apparently support a professional photographic studio until well into the 1850s. Further research may prove such dates to be much too late!

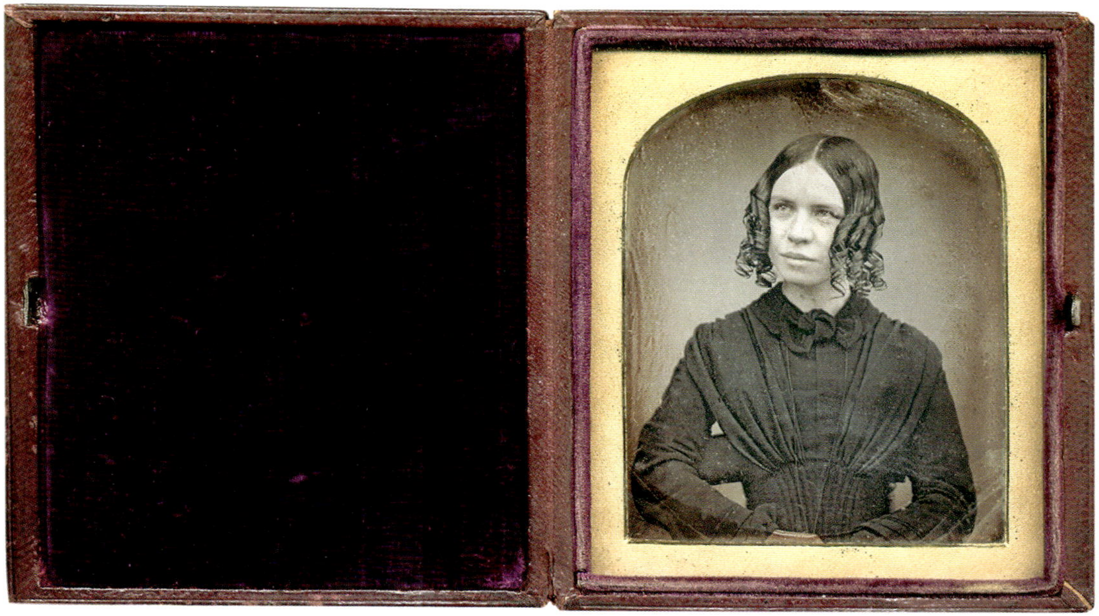

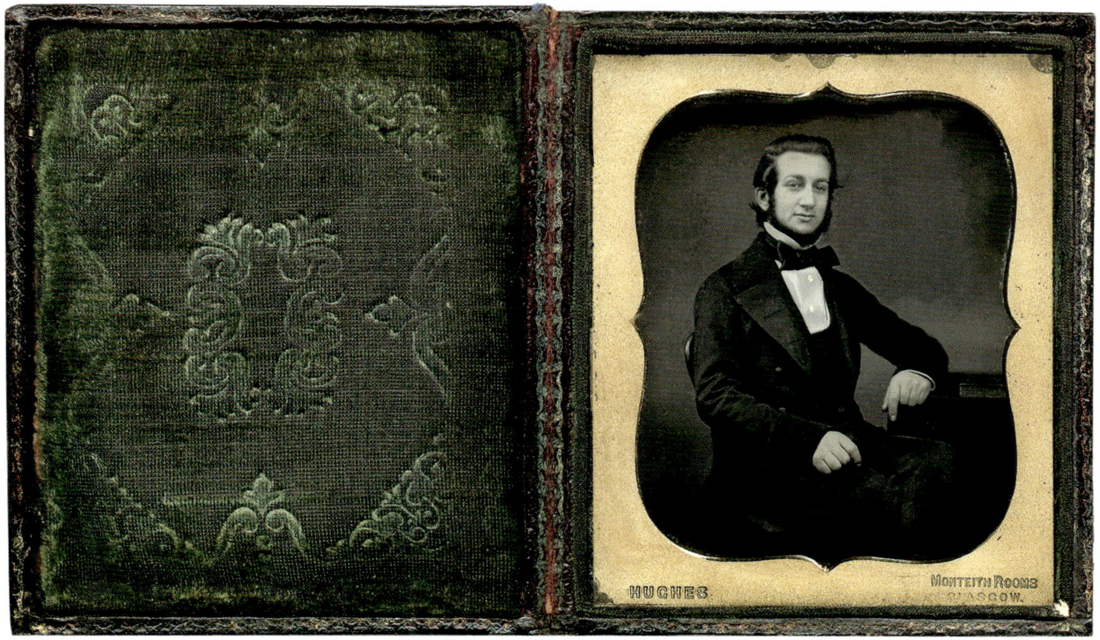

Above right: a sixth plate daguerreotype, c.1855, photographer unknown, with light tinting to the face, housed in an embossed leather case with deep purple pad and trim. Purple is found only rarely in case fittings. Below right: Sixth plate daguerreotype by Jabez Cornelius Hughes, 1850-56, housed in a plain burgundy case with rich green trim and an embossed green velvet pad.

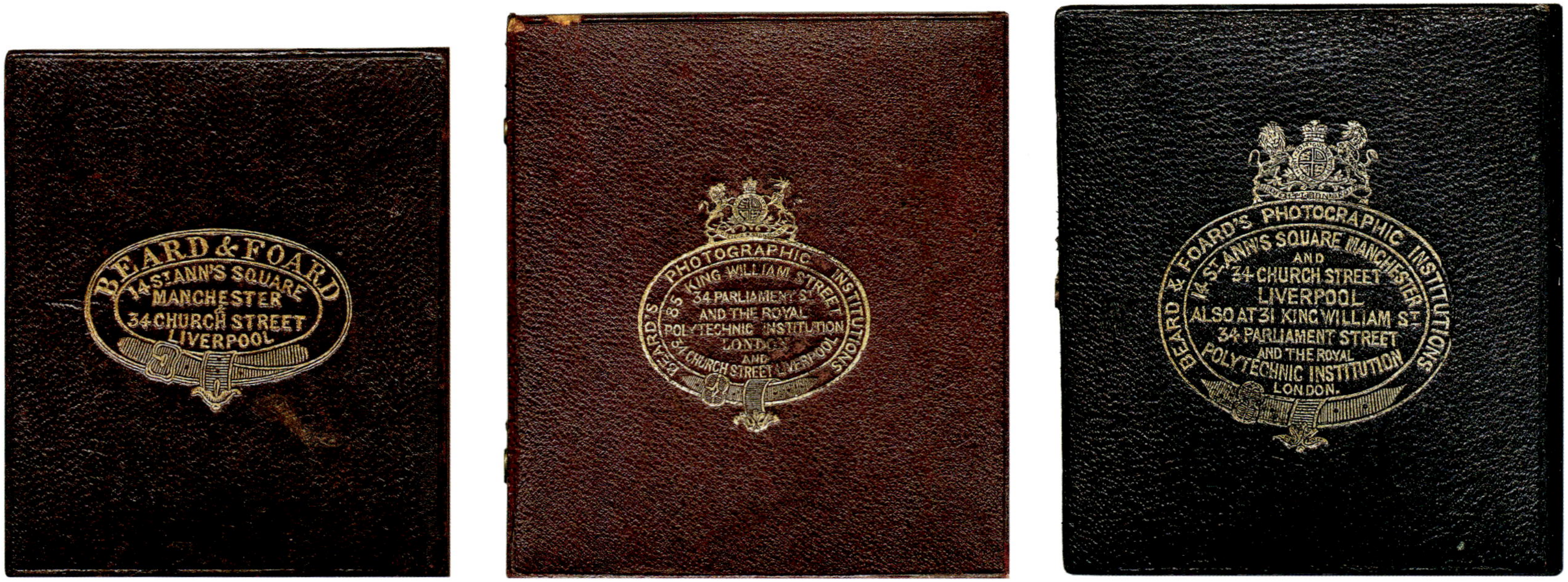

These three cases offer a progressive view on the fortunes of Richard Beard. The centre case dates from 1852-54 and houses the 1/6th plate dagerreotype illustrated on page 13. Beard's original studio at the Royal Polytechnic Institution is listed along with his two other sites in Parliament Street and King William Street, from which he worked between 1843-54 and 1843-56 respectively. At the end of 1854, or early 1855, the King William Street studio was moved to No.31. Beard also had studios at 17 and 18 Wharf Road, City Road (1843-44 and 1844-48), 309 Regent Street (1842-49), and at New Millman Street (1849-53). The sixth plate Beard & Foard case, above right, dating from 1854-56, advertises the two James T. Foard studios in Liverpool and Manchester in which Beard had a share, and also promotes the three London studios. Interestingly, very few other examples of cases exist where Beard's advertising inadvertently implies that his provincial partner also has an interest in the London studios. Most Beard & Foad cases only advertise the Liverpool and Manchester studios, as in the ninth plate case, above left. The daguerreotype housed in this case is illustrated on page 29.

Footnotes

1. *Dumfries & Galloway Courier* (based on articles previously published in the *Glasgow Herald* and the *Scotsman*) March 27th 1843, less than three years after photography first became publicly available.
2. ibid.
3. British Patent Number 8194, AD1839 Miles Berry: *Obtaining Daguerreotype Portraits &c.* It is often suggested that the French government gave the process free to the 'civilised world', and much entertainment has been drawn from the exclusion of England and Wales from that definition of 'civilisation'! The wording of the patent makes the French government's intention quite clear. Daguerre himself wrote that the government's gesture was for 'the benefit of all my countrymen' clearly restricting the patent freedom to France alone!
4. Beard's Scottish Patents No.114 (December 1840) and No.148 (November 1841) and his Irish Patent No.229 (April 1841) covered his improvements to the process, and the Wolcott camera. Thus Daguerre's original process remained free for all to use in those countries. There appears little evidence that the Scottish or Irish Patents were enforced with the same vigour as those in England and Wales.
5. US Patent No.1582, granted on 8th May 1840 is believed to have been the first US Patent relating to photography.
6. British Patent Number 8546, AD1840, *Apparatus for Obtaining Likenesses &c.*, includes the designs for the camera itself, as well as for the circular studio immortalised in Cruikshank's well known contemporary cartoon, illustrated on page 16.
7. The Petzval lens first appeared in May 1840, having been manufactured by Peter Voigtlander in Vienna to Petzval's design. For further detailed information on the Wolcott mirror design, and the early fast lenses by both Petzval and Chevalier see Sidney Ray: *The Era of the Astigmatic lens* in 'Technology & Art', proceedings of Royal Photographic Society Historical Group Symposium 1989, Royal Photographic Society, London, Ed. Michael Pritchard
8. British Patent Number 9292, AD1842.
9. The inscription 'Bullock & Co. Photo, Leamington' can be seen hand-scribed into the lower quadrants of the matte surrounding the portrait of a policeman which accompanies the introduction on page 11.

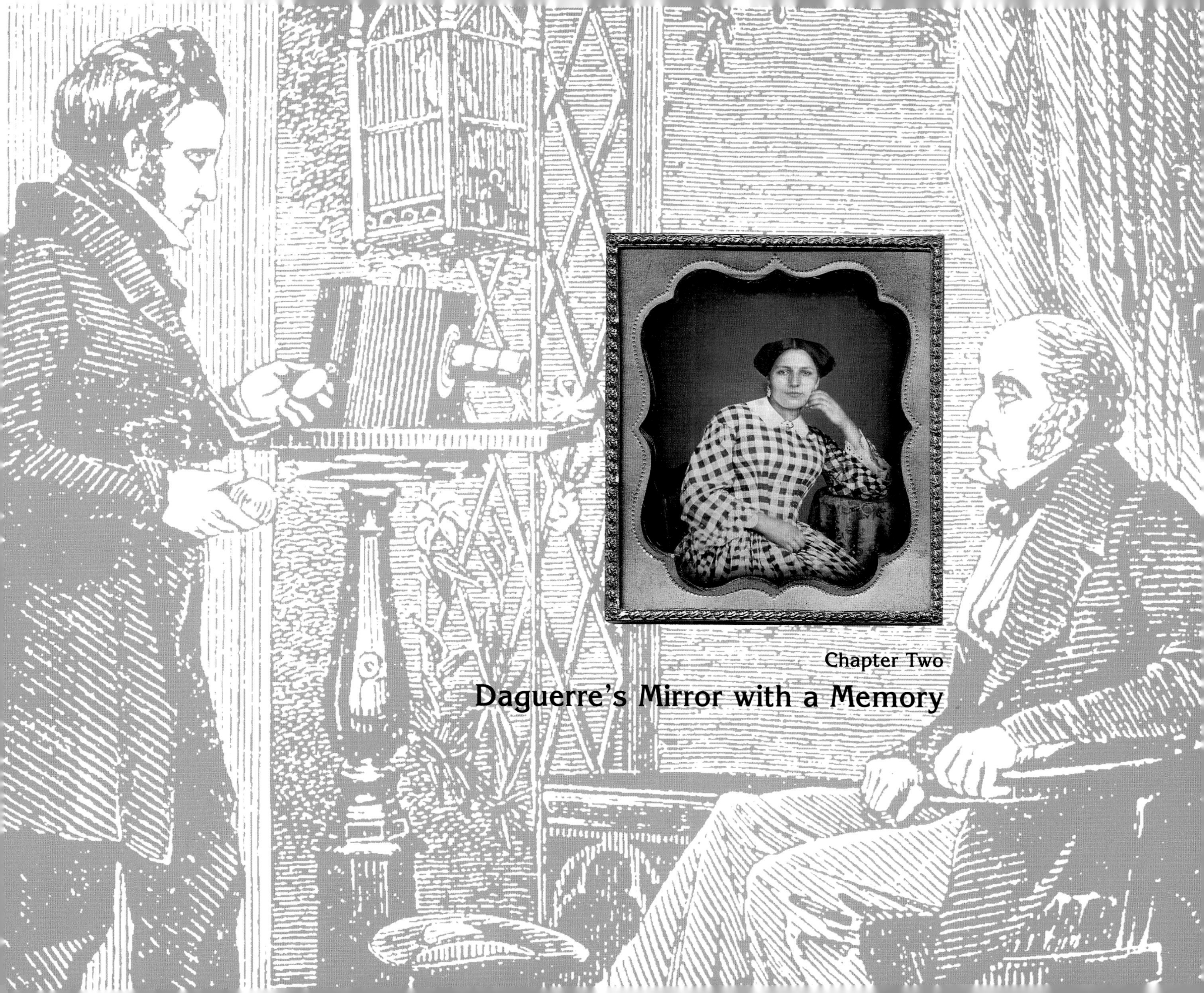

Chapter Two

Daguerre's Mirror with a Memory

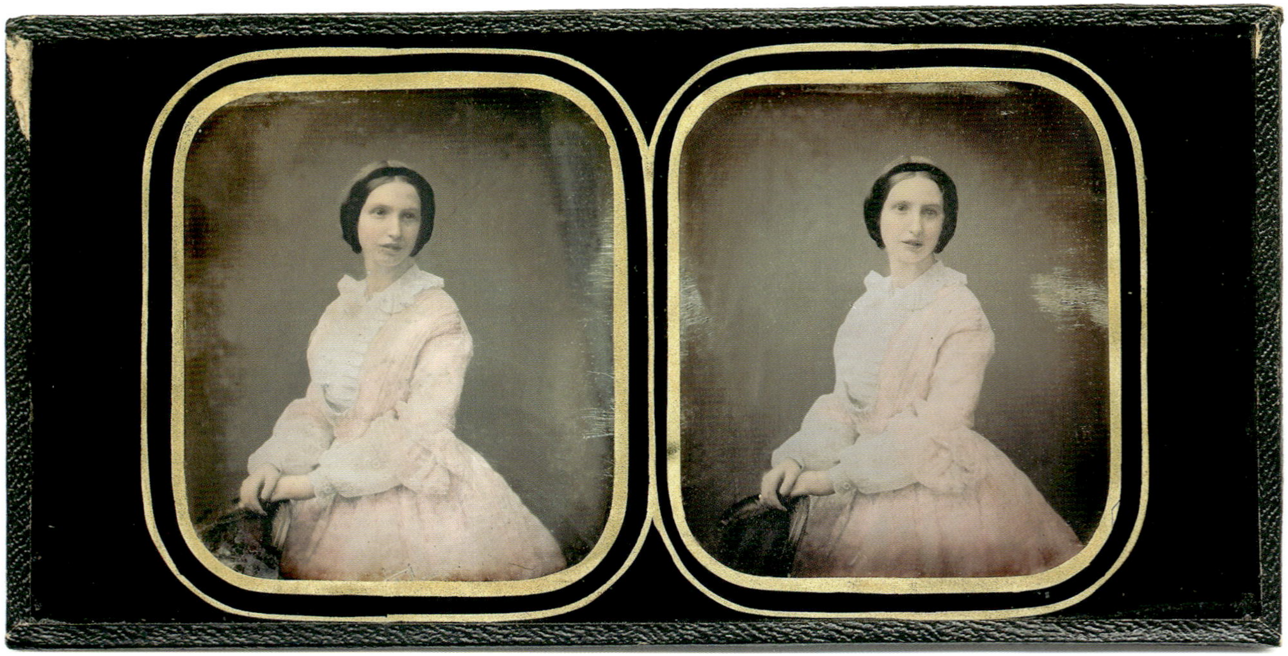

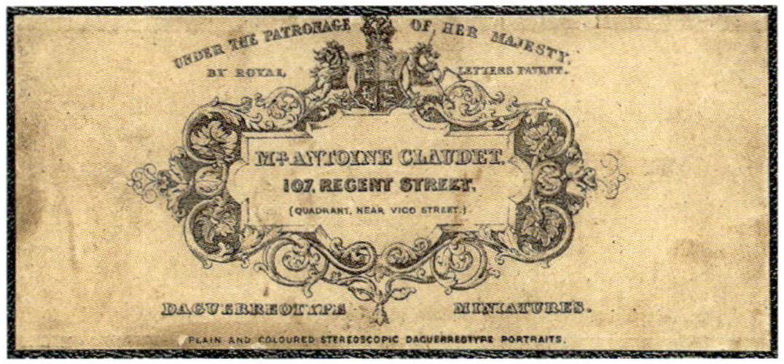
UNDER THE PATRONAGE OF HER MAJESTY.
BY ROYAL LETTERS PATENT.
MR. ANTOINE CLAUDET.
107, REGENT STREET,
(QUADRANT, NEAR VICO STREET.)
DAGUERREOTYPE MINIATURES.
PLAIN AND COLOURED STEREOSCOPIC DAGUERREOTYPE PORTRAITS.

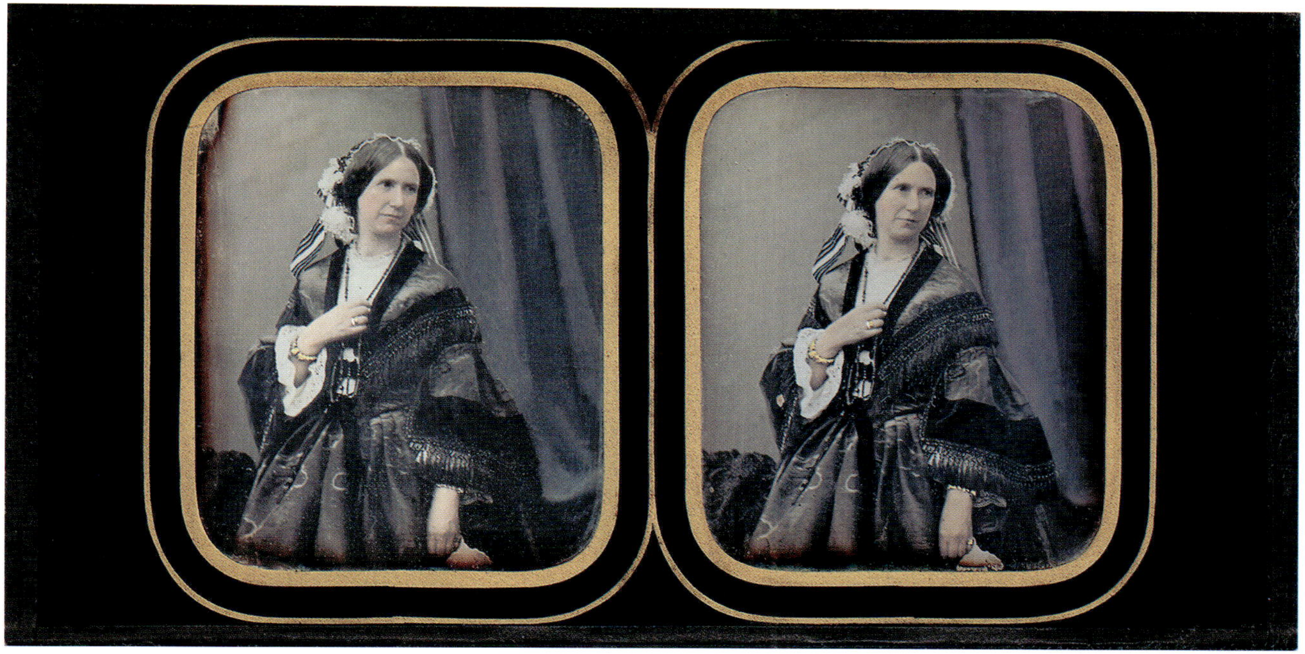

With the rise in the popularity of the drawing-room stereoscope in the 1850s, many customers eschewed the intimacy of the cased portrait for the amusement and enhanced reality afforded by the stereoscope. The 3-D portrait achieved the height of its popularity through the vehicle of the card-mounted paper print, but also enjoyed some success through a limited number of studios producing the highly exclusive stereoscopic daguerreotype. Amongst the high artists of this medium were Antoine Claudet and T.R.Williams. These two stereoscopic portraits of unknown sitters come from Claudet's Quadrant studio at 107 Regent Street, an address he occupied from 1852 until 1858. The fashions of these two subjects date their portraits as early 1850s. Claudet opened his first London studio, on the roof of the Adelaide Gallery near the Strand, in June 1841, having acquired his licence to use the daguerreotype direct from the inventor himself. Thus, he remained outside the controls afforded by Richard Beard's rights in Daguerre's patent. He continued to practise as a portrait photographer long after the daguerreotype was superseded, first by the colodion positive and later by the paper carte-de-visite.

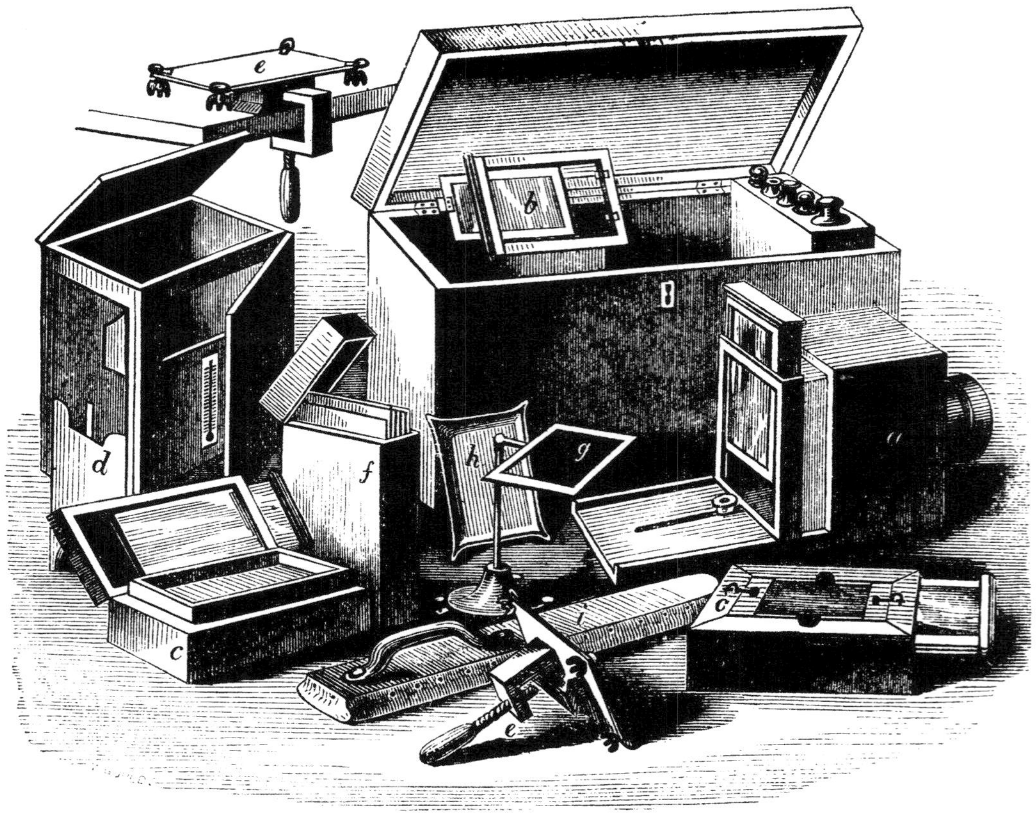

A typical daguerreotype photographer's outfit, as illustrated in Robert Hunt's Manual of Photography, *1857 edition. Everything was included in the kit to prepare and sensitise the silvered copper plates, and expose and process them.*

Chapter Two:

Daguerre's 'Mirror with a Memory'

The daguerreotype was the process which established photographic portraiture as a commercial proposition. It was the medium which first caught the imagination of the Victorian public, and it was the daguerreotype image, with its infinite detail, which appealed to artisan and aesthete alike. While only the wealthy could initially afford the image produced by the camera, others aspired to the social class which could afford such an acquisition.

The daguerreotype used chemistry which damaged the health of all who used it, produced an image which was destroyed by being touched, and in terms of its chemistry was a cul-de-sac.

Yet the daguerreotype portrait more than any other photographic medium established the idea of the family portrait as an icon of its time. To be able to afford a daguerreotype was to occupy a clearly recognised rung on the social ladder.

Producing the daguerreotype involved a skilled and complex series of operations, some undertaken just moments before, and the others immediately after the exposure of the portrait.

The American photographer and author Henry Snelling wrote a succinct account in 1854 of the processes and equipment involved[1] —

'1st Cleaning and Polishing the Plate, For this it is necessary to have plate blocks, plate, vice, spirit lamps, buffs, (round or machine), nitric acid, or ammonia and alcohol, rottenstone, rouge, or prepared powder, and prepared cotton, or common flannel; it would also be of service to have a galvanic battery for silvering the plate.

2nd Applying the sensitive coating, requiring an iodine box, bromine box, resublimed iodine, and bromide of lime or other accelerating substance.

3rd Exposure of the Plate to light, requiring the photographic camera.

4th Bringing out the picture, or mercurialising requiring the mercury bath and perfectly pure mercury.

5th Fixing the Image requiring hypo-sulphite of soda, a porcelain dish and bowl, a pair of pliers and a spirit lamp.

6th Gilding the Image requiring chloride of gold, or hyposulphite of gold, a pair of pliers, or gilding stand, and a spirit lamp.'

In his book Snelling attributes the invention of the daguerreotype to both Louis Daguerre and Joseph Nicéphore Niépce – a generosity no longer entertained. While Niépce's early experiments certainly inspired Daguerre, the commercial process he gave his name to was uniquely his own[2]. What is interesting from Snelling's account, is the range and complexity of the equipment required to 'impress' an image on the 'silver tablet' as the silvered copper plate was often described.

The plates themselves could be bought from suppliers in a range of sizes and qualities. Two weights were usually available, giving plates of approximately 1mm and 1.6mm thickness respectively. When exposed, processed, and packaged in a robust wood or plastic case, with a cover glass and a fine quality brass matte and frame, the thicker plates produced a very heavy portrait indeed.

Typically, a 1/6th plate daguerreotype

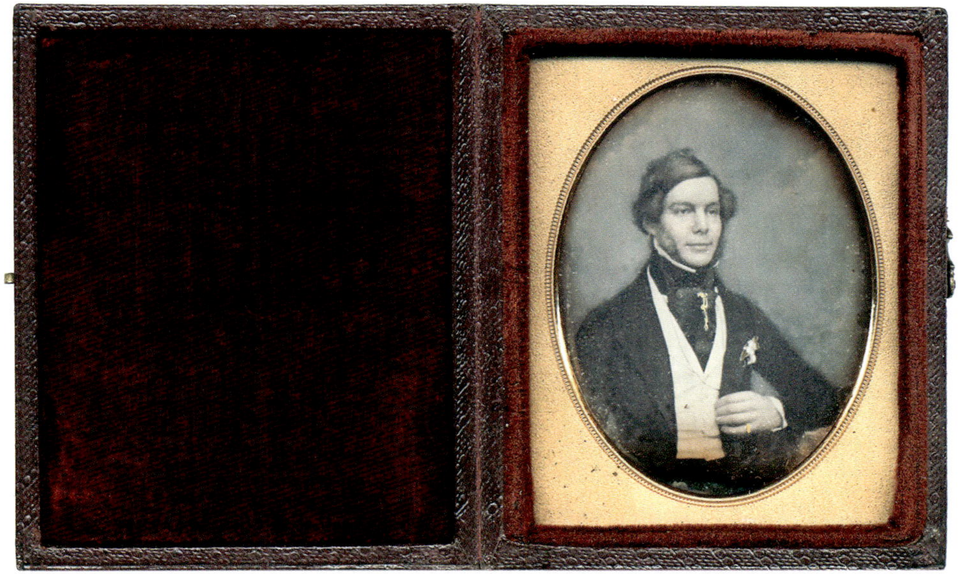

Ninth plate tinted and gilded daguerreotype by Beard & Foard's Manchester studio. James T. Foard, who had entered into a partnership with Beard in a Liverpool studio in 1849 after managing premises for Beard in Birmingham and elsewhere, opened the Manchester studio in 1854. While the Liverpool business enjoyed considerable success, the Manchester studio in St Ann's Square apparently did not, and Foard sold it after only three years. It was taken over in 1857 by Alfred Brothers. The case is in plain burgundy leather, with the studio's gilt stamp on the base - see opposite top left. Case size 73mm x 61mm, oval aperture size 55mm x 43mm.

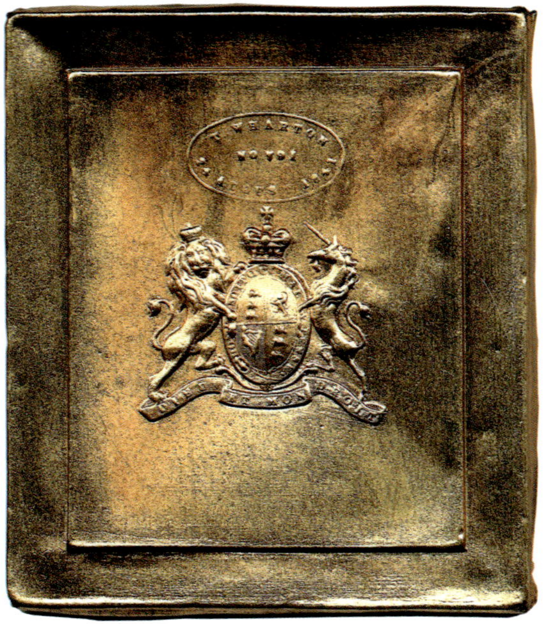

The design for a daguerreotype pan and preserver was registered by Thomas Wharton of Birmingham on August 24th 1841, only a few weeks after the commercial introduction of the daguerreotype. It was one of the first designs for a photographic product to be thus registered. Design registration was itself a relatively new protection for designers – this design is No.791. Small daguerreotypes taken with a camera fitted with a large lens helped keep exposures down, and sixth plate cases were already in widespread use for miniature paintings. This ingenious design of plate holder brought the two together, and enabled a ninth plate daguerreotype to be presented in the larger case. The base of the metal pan shows the royal coat of arms and the date and number of the registered design.

produced on the heavier plate, once matted and cased, would weigh over five ounces – 160gms. Later productions, using light case materials, thinner mattes and glasses and, of course, thinner Daguerreotype plates, reduced that weight by a factor of up to 50%.

The plates were sized according to the traditional size of a sheet of glass. The full plate of 6½in. x 8½in., described as '4-4th size' in many American catalogues, was more usually known as 'whole plate' in Britain. The other common fractions were 1/2 plate, 1/4 plate, 1/6th, 1/9th and 1/16th plate, 1/4, 1/6th and 1/9th being those most commonly produced and sold. In the American style, the fractions were described as 4-4th size, 1-2 size,1-4th size, 1-6th size, 1-9th size, and 1-16th size.

The process itself involved a series of complex steps, an accident with any one of which could render the portrait unsaleable.

First of all, if the photographer was silvering his own plates, then the copper plate had to be carefully clean and coated with silver, usually by electroplating – although many operators preferred to buy their plates ready silvered as this was perhaps the most 'uncertain' of the operations. However, an increasing number of photographers grew dissatisfied with commercially prepared plates and re-silvered their own. Once silvered the plate had to be cleaned and then polished to a high gloss. Only with a completely clean plate could the high quality and fine detail for which the daguerreotype was renowned be achieved with any consistency.

To achieve this state of perfection, the plate was first shaped with special pliers – bevelling the edges down and away from the silvered surface. It was then firmly secured to a plate block and cleaned with a paste made of dilute nitric acid and either very fine pumice or rottenstone (a finely-particled silicaceous limestone ideal for cleaning) applied with cotton wool. Once cleaned, it was buffed with a mixture of rouge and lampblack (soot/pure carbon) until a high polish was achieved. The direction of the final polishing was critical – care being taken to ensure that the direction of polishing was left to right when the final picture was viewed. For landscape pictures, therefore, buffing along the longer dimension was advised, while it was across the shorter dimension for portraits.

Next, fitted into a frame to hold it securely, the plate was introduced silver side down into the iodine box, where iodine vapour chemically reacted with the silver to produce a layer of silver nitrate. Next it was 'accelerated' or 'excited' in the bromide box, where it was exposed variously to the vapours of bromine, iodine bromide and iodine chloride, creating silver bromide and silver chloride in the image-bearing layer. In later versions of the process, the more sensitive chloro-bromo-fluoride salts were sometimes introduced at this stage.

While all these chemical preparations were taking place in the darkroom, the subject was being prepared for photography.

The daguerreotype was always relatively low sensitivity. In its early days it was very slow, requiring long exposures, and even in its heyday, sitting for one's portrait was not a comfortable experience. Given this fact, the spontaneity and apparent relaxation of many of the sitters is all the more remarkable.

In order to minimise the discomfort for the sitter, it was necessary to maximise the access of light into the studio. Studios were frequently built on the tops of relatively high buildings – the studio opened in Glasgow by Edwards referred to in the opening chapter was on the roof of a five storey building in that city's premier shopping street.

In a well known cartoon by Cruikshank[3] *(see page 16)*, a layout for a daguerreotype studio designed to employ the best of the light irrespective of the time of day is illustrated.

In this layout, the subject sat on a raised dais which was equipped with castors so it could easily be rotated always to face the light. A black panel was suspended above the seat to ensure that not too much light came down directly on top of the subject's head from the glass roof above, while ample direct light, lightly diffused by sheets of muslin, illuminated the subject's face and body in a natural manner. The daguerreotype camera, on a platform suspended from a rail running round the circular room was pre-focused, pre-positioned vis-à-vis the subject, and could yet be moved round to follow the light. The darkroom was accessed through a door beneath the camera platform.

What Cruikshank's drawing does not show, are the devices used to keep the subject fixed in place for the duration of the exposure. On dull days, that could be several minutes, while even on a bright day, it was long enough to require these firm clamps.

The clamp held the subject's head in a U-shaped device which fitted behind the ears, its ends usually covered with hair. Where that was not practical, a lower clamp rested round the back of the neck, with a single ball-ended spike at the rear of the head to assist in the retention of the precise position required by the photographer. It is any wonder that the expressions of so many of our forefathers lack humour or enjoyment? They were experiencing neither. A portrait photograph represented such a significant investment, and the actual process of acquiring it was so uncomfortable, that movement was not only expensive but painful. As a result, an entire generation has been misrepresented in the portraits they left us! Despite the sombre image their photographs portray, the Victorians were frequently amused!

The clamp continued to be used throughout the daguerreotype era. Photographers using the later ambrotype and carte-de-visite processes also employed it, and indeed on many carte-de-visite portraits the feet of the clamp can be seen beneath chair legs, an oversight frequently included in the portrait when children were photographed standing on chairs.

Posing in their best clothes – the affluent upper class in the early 1840s, the middle class as the 1850s progressed and prices were reduced – our Victorian ancestors suffered for their small cased daguerreotype of vanity. Trying desperately hard not to blink too often – the occasional blink would not matter but too frequent a lapse softened the

Below: An assortment of headclamps typical of the types used in Victorian photographic studios.

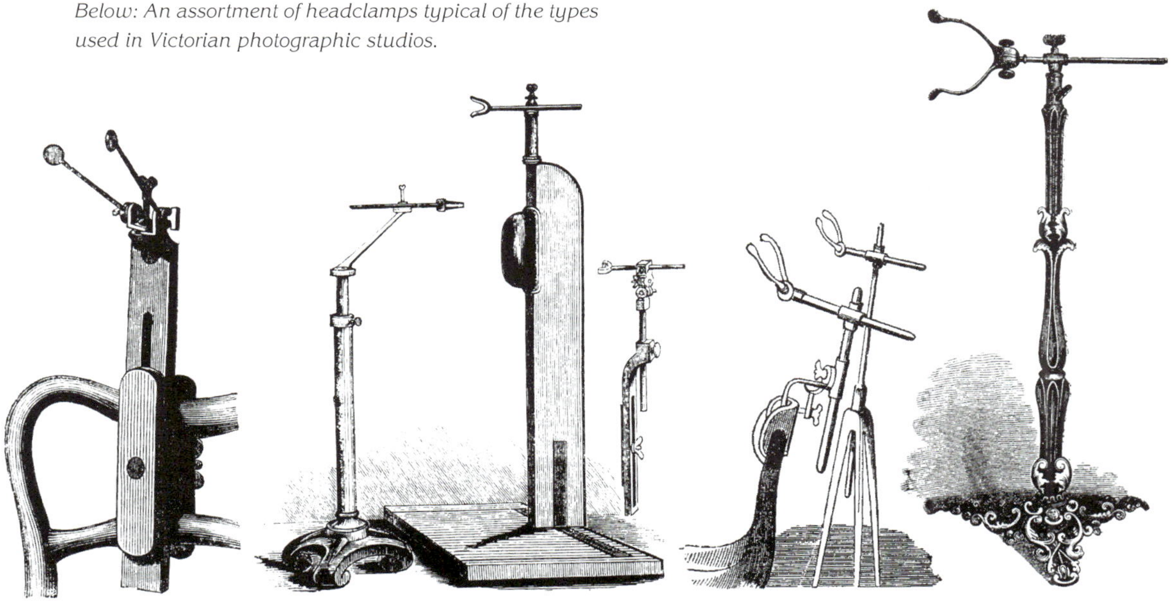

Ninth plate daguerreotype, photographer unknown, in sixth plate top-hinged case, Wharton pan and preserver.

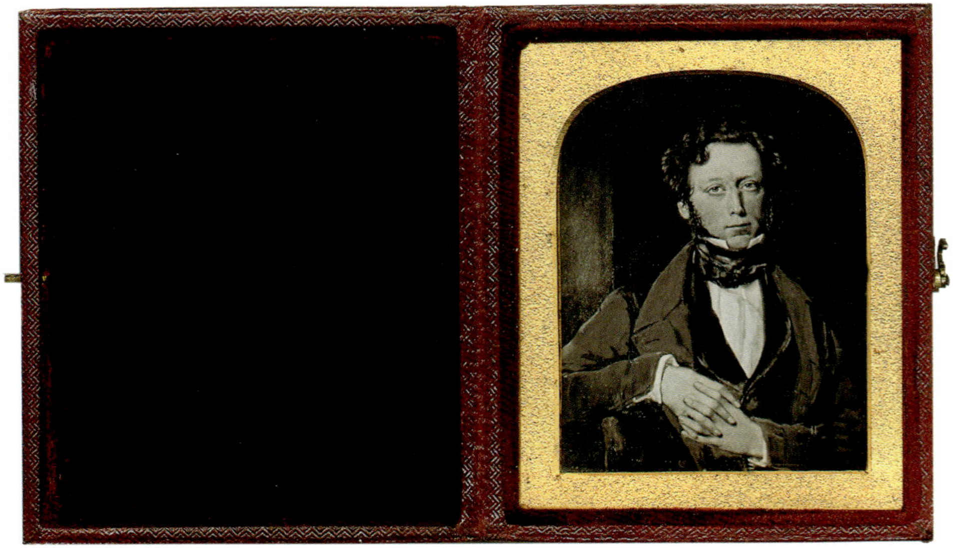

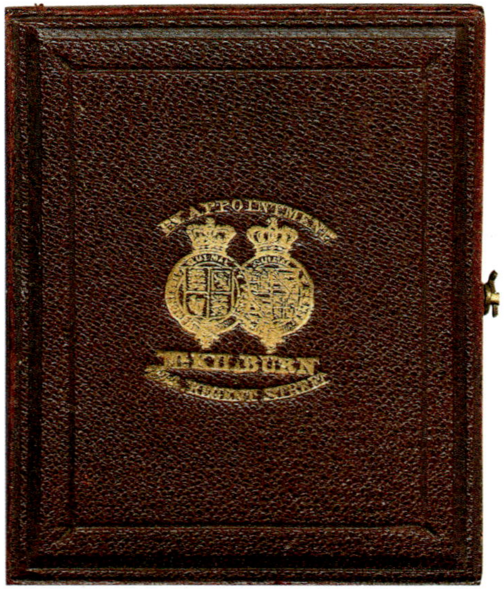

Ninth plate daguerreotype copy of a painting by William Kilburn, in embossed leather case, studio gilt stamp on front face, 1850s. Case 72mm x 58mm, simple oval-topped matte.

eyes – they adopted the relaxed and sombre facial expressions we see in their images. Smiling is achieved by tensing muscles – and tensed muscles cannot be held for a minute or two.

Very early poses can often be recognised by profile or semi-profile positioning of the subject, with eyes turned down *(see page 21)* – not for any reasons of modesty as has sometimes been suggested, but simply to reduce the blurring effects of eye movement on the final portrait image.

It would, however, be an over-simplification of the story to suggest that it was primitive science and technology which forced these long exposures. While the science may have been primitive, it had improved considerably within the first few years of the daguerreotype's life.

Even when exposures became markedly shorter, the Victorians declined to smile, as to do so was incompatible with the status of the portrait.[4]

The technology evolved rapidly in the early years. The most common camera lens of the late 1840s and the 1850s was that designed by Professor Joseph Petzval[5] – indeed it became the standard tool of both portrait and landscape photographers for over forty years. That lens offered portrait photographers a maximum aperture of f/3.6 by the mid 1840s, admitting fifteen times more light to the camera than Daguerre had been able to use at the start of the decade.

By 1860 and the heyday of the carte-de-visite portrait, photographers had at their disposal a Dallmeyer modification of Petzval's lens with a maximum aperture equivalent to f/2.2. Smaller apertures were achieved by inserting slides with different sized holes into a slot in the lens barrel.[6]

It would be many years later before the terminology of f/stops was adopted, and for the daguerreotype photographer the lens might be described as being fitted with a 1/4 inch stop, the measurement referring to the diameter of the aperture itself.

With the subject firmly clamped into position, the lighting adjusted by using blinds to reduce or eliminate light where it was not needed and thus create three-dimensional modelling, the coated and sensitised plate was loaded into a darkslide and inserted into the camera.

Exposure was delivered by removing and then replacing the lens cap after an appropriate exposure, the darkslide was then reinserted, and the plate holder removed to the darkroom so that the photographer could deal with that part of the process described in the manual as bringing out the picture and rendering it visible.

Development was effected by carefully removing the plate from the darkslide and suspending it at an angle over a small bath of mercury heated to a temperature of 170° Fahrenheit, and leaving it there until, viewed by candlelight through a small door in the side of the developing box, the image became visible as a strong white salt on the plate's surface.

Fixing was achieved with sodium thiosulphate – as still widely used today – known in error then, as now, as 'hypo' as nineteenth century chemists originally thought it was sodium hyposulphite.[7] Washing in pure distilled water followed fixation, before the plate was gently dried over the flame of a spirit lamp.

The mercury vapour was extremely toxic, and many users of the daguerreotype suffered from the long term effects of its use. This did not, however, restrict its almost unbridled popularity.

While most daguerreotype portraits were produced in sizes smaller than 1/4 plate – 1/6th plate and 1/9th plate undoubtedly being the most popular, it is interesting to note that several American suppliers offered plates up to 11in. x 14in. in size, and a mammoth 25in. x 30in. is still in existence.[8]

Not surprisingly, few large images survive – perhaps reflecting their scarcity even in their heyday. Whatever the complexities of coating exposing and processing a quarter plate might have been, manipulating a giant plate must have posed unique problems.

In any event it was the miniaturisation of reality which caught the public imagination, gave the process its unique quality, and which pioneered the idea of the portable likeness – the townscape reduced to half plate or quarter plate, the portrait reduced to the size of a miniature painting or even smaller, yet as perfect in every detail as nature herself.

As the columnist in the *Scottish Guardian* commented in March 1843, *'the artist is equally au fait at copies of paintings; and is producing miniatures within the diameter of a ring or a sleeve button, yet as distinct in their detail as the camera can make them.'*

For the soldier at war in India, the Crimea, or the American Civil War, or for the pioneer opening up the Empire, the African continent or the American West, it was the durability of the daguerreotype which appealed. The weight may have had its drawbacks, but the images survived where others – paper or glass – might not have been so fortunate.

In the earliest days of the commercial exploitation of the process, it commanded a significant price premium, restricting its market to only the wealthiest members of society.[9] With a relatively small cased daguerreotype portrait costing a small fortune even from a relatively ordinary studio – 'terms one guinea for a portrait including a handsome miniature case or frame' – few could avail themselves of the service of the professional photographer. One guinea (£1.05) represented two weeks' earnings for a relatively skilled man in the mid 1840s.

With prices initially restricting access only to the wealthy, there is no doubt that those who could afford it advertised their wealth by the abundance of photography they could acquire! Daguerreotype brooches and rings, as expensive as the larger portrait sitting themselves, were worn while their owners were photographed! Choker brooches containing a daguerreotype portrait of mother – often re-photographed from larger examples – were a frequent if ostentatious part of public mourning, and the double-faced brooch containing a portrait on one side and a lock of hair in the other were a common part of the rites of both courtship and death.

However, true commercial exploitation of the process only became possible as prices were reduced, and price reductions were not really

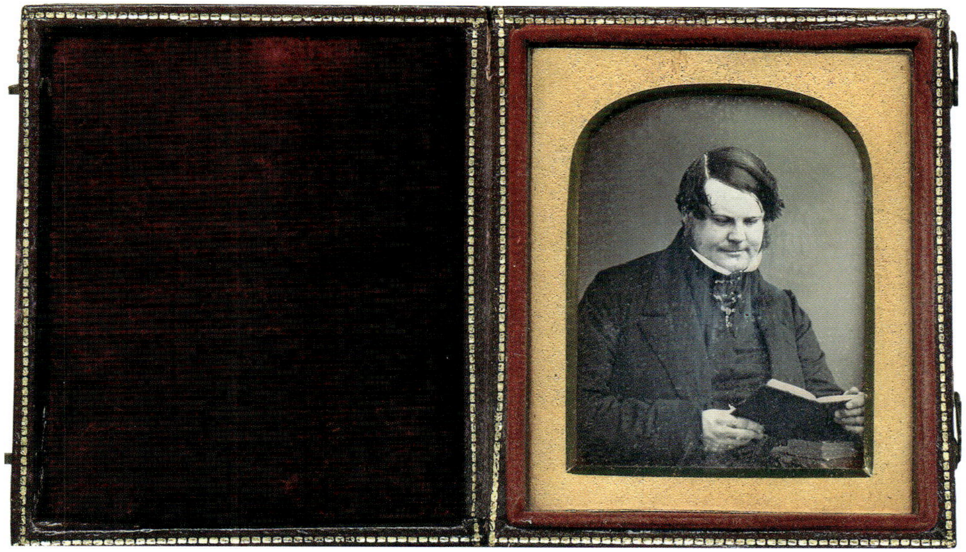

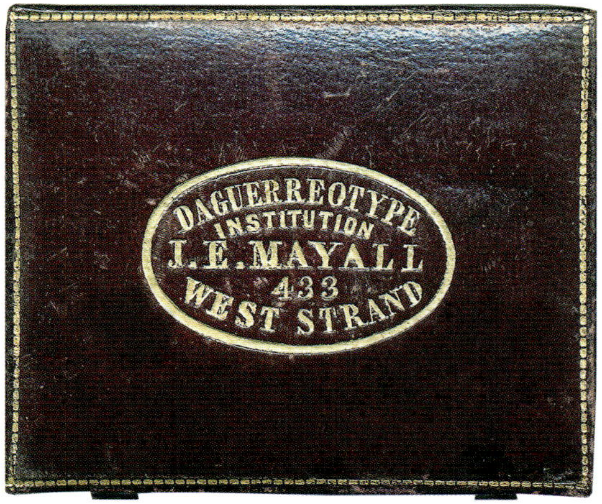

Ninth plate daguerreotype by J.E. Mayall, 433 West Strand, London. Leather case with gilt stamp on upper face. Deep burgundy velvet pad and trim. Mayall advertised from this address in 1847, and again from 1853-55. He originally styled his studio as the 'American Daguerreotype Institution'.

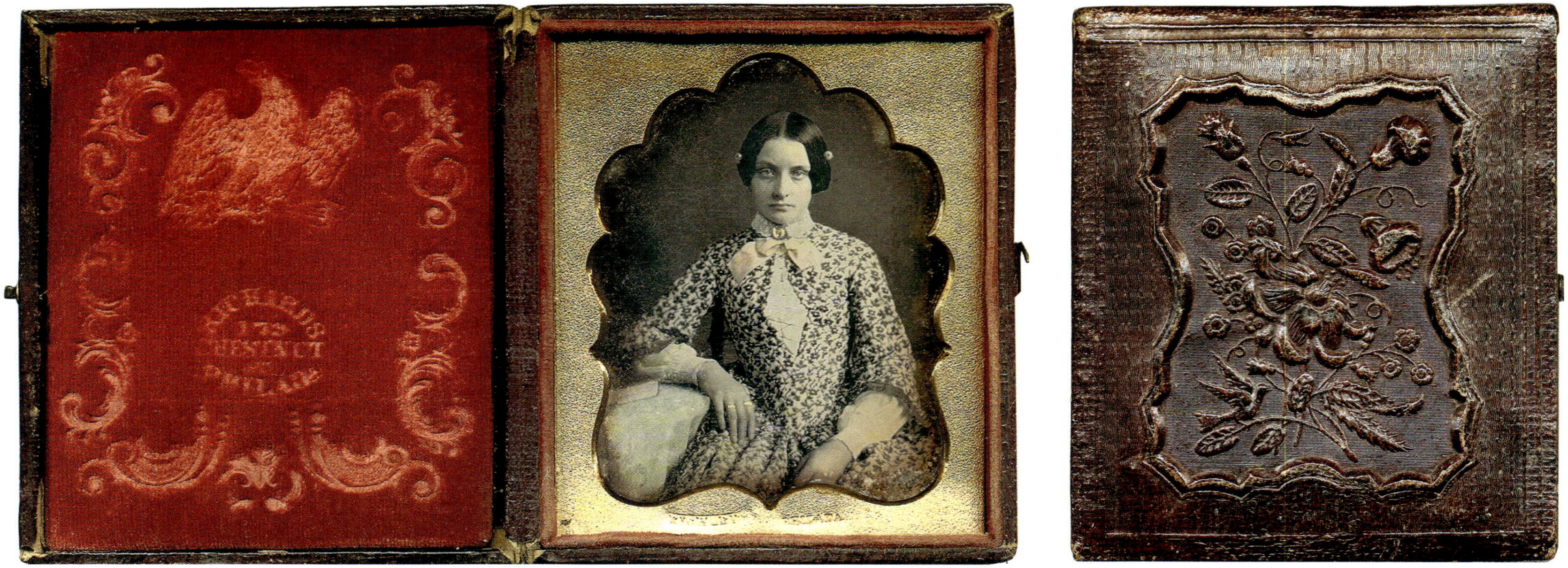

Sixth plate daguerreotype portrait of a young lady by Frederick de Bourg Richards of 179 Chesnut Street, Philadelphia, 1850s. An eminent photographer in his day, celebrities were frequent sitters in his studio – and his portraits of Jenny Lind and Lola Montez still survive. His original studio at 144 Chestnut Street opened in the 1840s, but he moved to No.179 in 1851. Photographer's name stamped into brass matte and embossed on to rose-coloured velvet pad, which also carried the popular emblem of the American eagle. Portrait tinted and gilded. The matte style is identical to one marketed by E. A. Anthony of New York in the late 1840s. The image is housed in an embossed leather case with flower motifs, 78mm x 91mm.

entertained until there was a degree of competition not only from other daguerreotype photographers after the patents lapsed, but also from the cheaper glass plate 'ambrotypes' or 'collodion positives'.

With those two factors bringing prices down to a level affordable by all but the poorest, the era of the shilling portrait in Britain and the 25 cent portrait in the United States helped elevate the portrait to the status of universal icon, accepted and understood by almost everyone, and all but endowed with the characteristics and personality of the sitter it depicted.

By that time, the fears of some eminent people when first confronted by photography seemed so far in the past. Yet the time taken from the introduction of the medium on a commercial basis, to almost universal acceptance, was less than two decades.

The idea, proposed by Balzac,[10] that each time one was photographed, a layer of one's being was whisked away to be fixed to the daguerreotype plate – and that therefore being photographed too often proposed a risk – had been consigned to history, as had ideas that photography was the work of the devil!

The medium however, did retain the popular name of the 'black art' and well into the era of mass production of photographs. The photographer with his chemistry and his mysterious skills was still seen as something of an alchemist.

The daguerreotype enjoyed a significant period of popularity, despite the introduction of cheaper methods of portraiture. The brilliance of the image and the social caché which went with it, gave is a status which placed it above the cheaper alternatives.

Despite the widespread popularity of the cheaper ambrotype throughout the 1850s, many of the major studios stayed loyal to the silvered plate well through that decade. As noted earlier, many of the finest and best known exponents of the daguerreotype did not take it up commercially until the years following the introduction of the ambrotype. Only when prices were dramatically forced down by cheaper alternatives, did they abandon the more complex process.

That did not happen either suddenly or early. The daguerreotype enjoyed continuing, albeit limited, success through into the 1860s, especially in places and under conditions where the fragility of the glass plate ambrotype made it unsuitable.

In 1853, well into the collodion era, J.H. Croucher, writing in his *Practical Hints on the Daguerreotype*[11] opened his treatise with the comment that *'Notwithstanding the many valuable discoveries with which the researches of Sir John Herschell, Mr. Fox Talbot, Mr. Robert Hunt, and other distinguished philosophers, native and foreign, have enriched the science of Photography, or, as it is now termed, actino-chemistry, the Daguerreotype process, first divulged in 1839, still retains the highest place in public estimation. The extreme beauty and delicacy of the pictures produced by this method, and the comparative simplicity and certainty of the operation, fully justify the preference, and account for the large number of amateurs who are pursuing it in the present day with more or less success.'*

It is interesting that Croucher refers to the simplicity of use, as many photographers found the process prone to solarisation if over-exposed, and introduced quite complex chemistry to try and increase the certainty of a saleable result.

Four years later in 1857, Robert Hunt, in his *Manual of Photography*[12] still felt the process had sufficient popularity to be worth a chapter devoted to its manipulation, and an illustration of the paraphernalia required to employ it.

The daguerreotype was almost completely out of use in Great Britain by 1860, but continued to be used in the United States for a little longer. Some were sad to see it finally go out of fashion.

In his book *Sunlight Sketches,*[13] the American writer and photographer Henry H. Snelling summed up the impact of the daguerreotype's eventual demise with a poignant eulogy –

'O sad fate of the beautiful daguerreotype! I would to heaven I could forget it. But it lingers in my soul like the fond rememberence of a dear departed friend.'

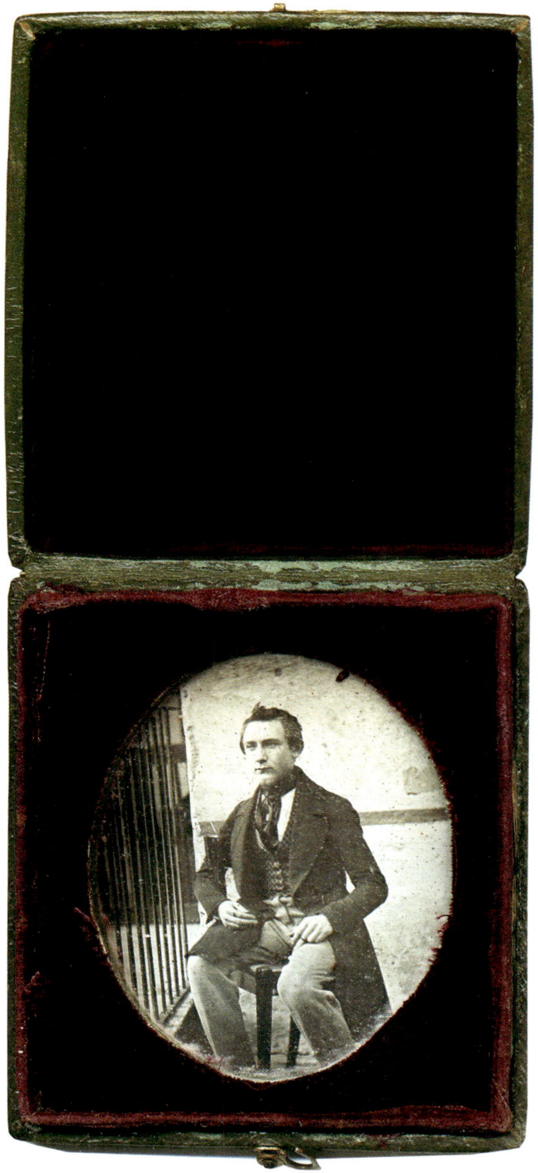

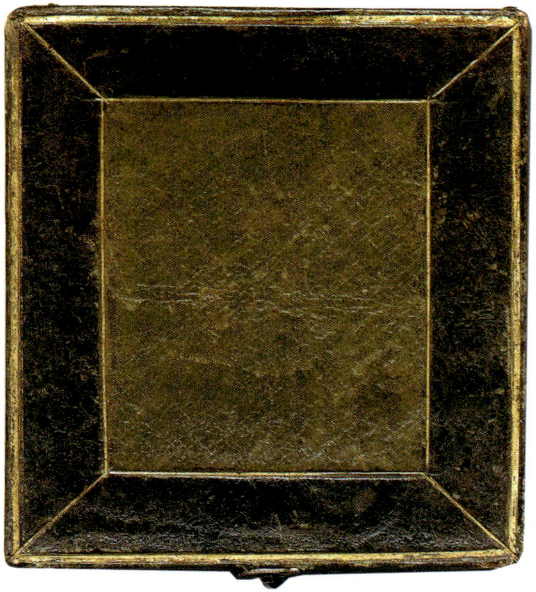

Sixth plate daguerreotype of a gentleman, late 1840s or early 1850s, taken outdoors, photographer unknown. Inlaid green leather case with gilt decoration. The base of the case is embosed bright green paper. Deep purple velvet pad and trim. In place of the traditional brass matte, the image is housed behind a purple velvet matte. The image is believed to be British, and the location may be outside the traditional glass house studio on the roof of a building. Case size 82mm x 91mm.

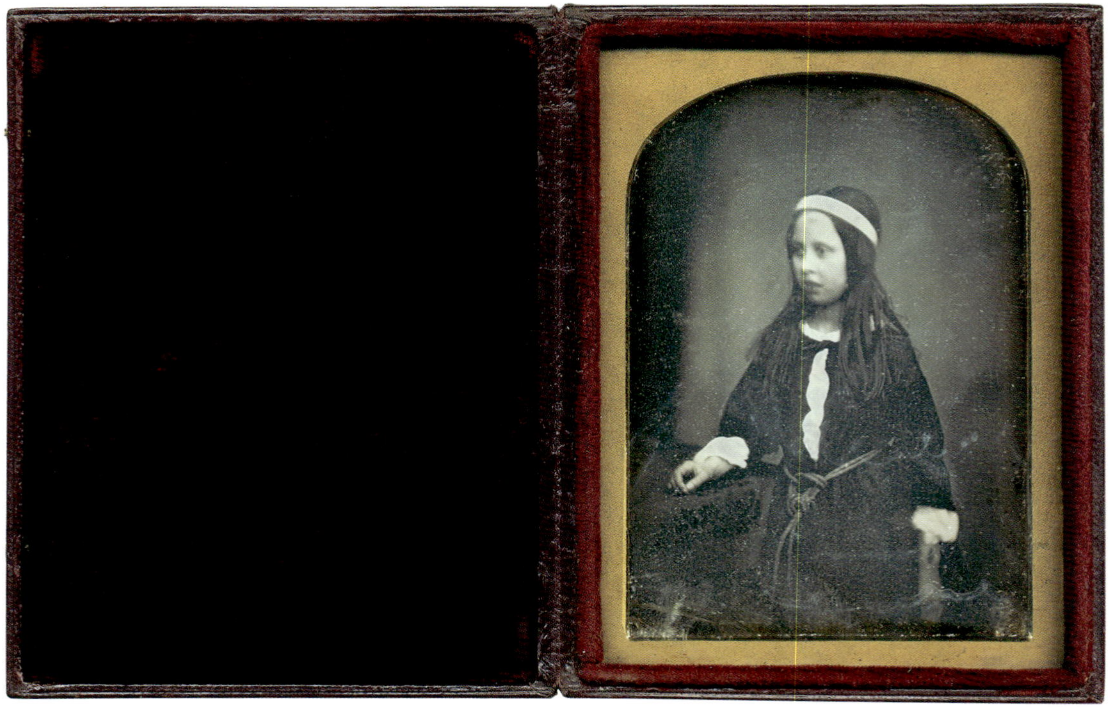

Quarter plate daguerreotype portrait of an unidentified young lady, by Ross & Thomson, 90 Princes Street, Edinburgh, 1850s. The image is housed in a plain burgundy leather case, 85mm x 100mm.

Footnotes

1. *The History & Practice of the Art of Photography* by Henry H. Snelling, published by G. P. Putnam, 155 Broadway, New York, 1849, and re-published in facsimile in collaboration with George Eastman House, Rochester, New York, by Morgan & Morgan Inc, Hastings-on-Hudson, NY, and the Fountain Press, London, 1970 with a foreword by Beaumont Newhall.
2. Niepce's relationship with Daguerre, and his involvement with what became the daguerreotype process is a complex one. While Niepce took the earliest surviving photograph in the 1820s, and Fox Talbot's salted paper process was used to make the first negative in the mid 1830s, it was Daguerre's process which marked the real start of photography as a commercial proposition. Niepce and Daguerre formed a partnership in 1829 ostensibly to develop Niepce's ideas but Niepce died in 1832 before any of their ideas reached fruition. Many of the ideas embodied in the original daguerreotype process probably emanated from that partnership, and while Daguerre gave full credit to Niepce at the time, it was Louis Jacques Mandé Daguerre whose name entered the history books as the inventor of photography's first commercially successful process.
3. Captioned 'Photographic Phenomena, or the New School of Portrait-Painting', George Cruickshank's cartoon was created to illustrate a poem entitled *The New School of Portrait Painting* by L.S. Blanchard, and first appeared in 1842.
4. Photography, in its endeavour to be accepted as art, adopted many of the conventions of the portrait painting, where a timeless, and some said passionless expression was considered desirable. The fact that the limitations of the process made such lack of animated expression a necessity worked in photography's favour. A useful perspective on Victorian expression, posing, and the etiquette which was expected to be demonstrated in photographic portraits can be found in Audrey Linkman *The Victorians: Photographic Portraits* Tauris Parke Books, London, 1993.
5. In his *Manual of Photographic Manipulation*, Houlston & Stoneman, London, 1868, William Sparling described Petzval's portrait lens design as *'a front crown of unequal convex curves, to which are cemented a doublet flint lens of unequal concave curves; the back combination is a crown lens of unequal convex curves, and a concavo-convex flint lens a little distance from it.'* He also commented that *'for more than a quarter of a century, this lens, without further changes in its construction than modification of its curves, has been used not only for the class of pictures its name denotes, but for a variety of others.* In the short history of photography before Sparling wrote his manual, such longevity had been unknown.
6. The practice of altering aperture by inserting slides into the lens barrel with different size holes was popularised by John Waterhouse in 1858, and his Waterhouse Stops were widely used until the iris diaphragm became the preferred method for controlling light into the lens.
7. The abbreviation 'Hypo' in all probability predates photography. It was understood to be a synonym for Sodium Thiosulphate fairly early on in its application as a fixer, but the misnomer has survived, perhaps because of its simplicity and ease of recognition.
8. An example of the very largest daguerreotype is in the collection of the National Museum of Photography, Film & Television, Bradford, UK.
9. Audrey Linkman *The Victorians: Photographic Portraits* Tauris Parke Books, London, 1993.
10. According to the photographer Nadar (reported in 1900) Balzac believed that *'each daguerreian operation was therefore going to lay hold of, detach, and use up one of the layers of the body on which it focussed'.* However, as Balzac was a portly gentleman, he had no fear of being photographed too often!
11. *Practical Hints on the Daguerreotype*, J. H. Croucher, A. Hart, Philadelphia, 1853.
12. *Manual of Photography*, Robert Hunt, Richard Griffin and Company, London, 1857.
13. *Sunlight Sketches, or the Photographic Text Book*, H.H. Snelling, New York 1858.

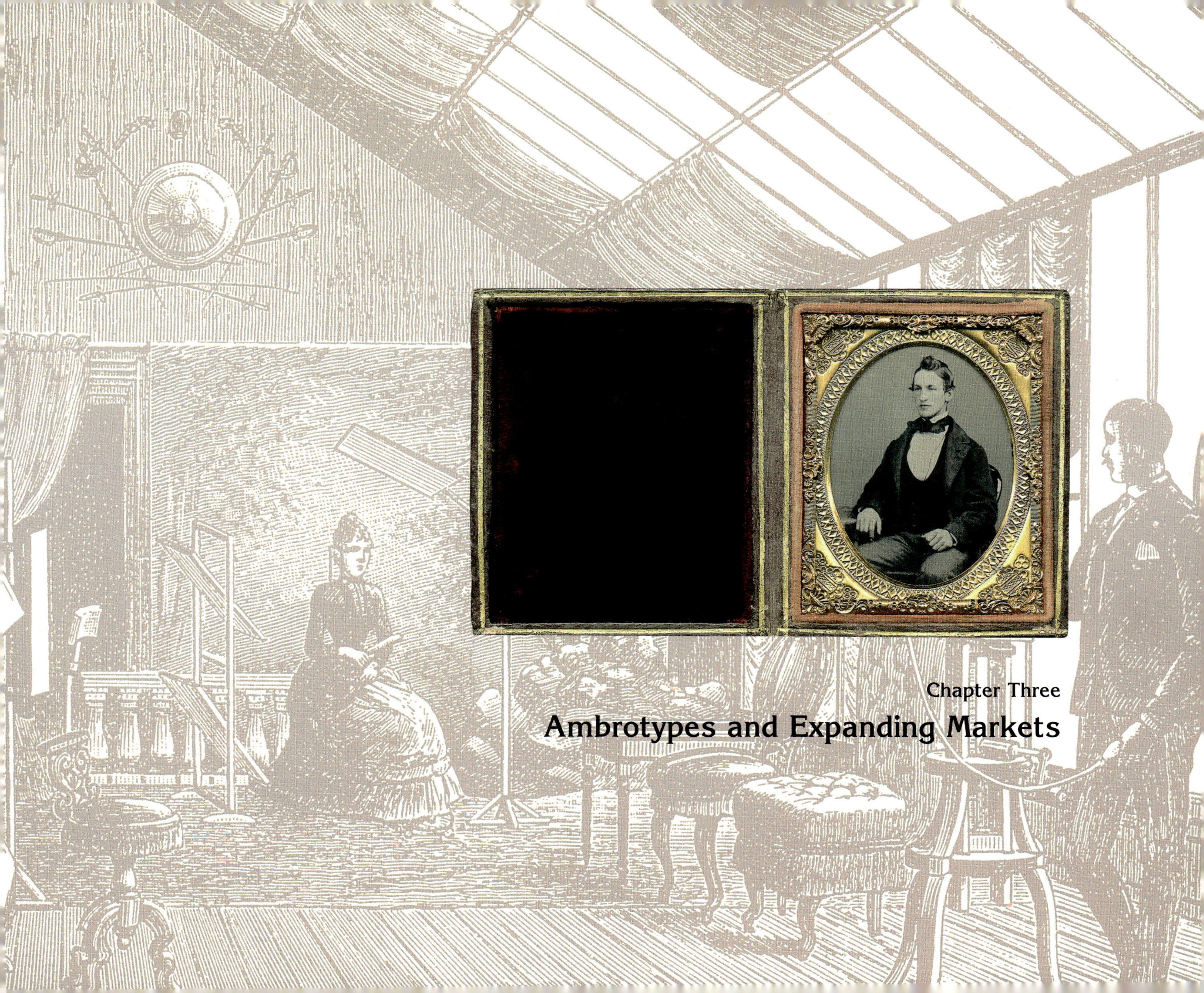

Chapter Three

Ambrotypes and Expanding Markets

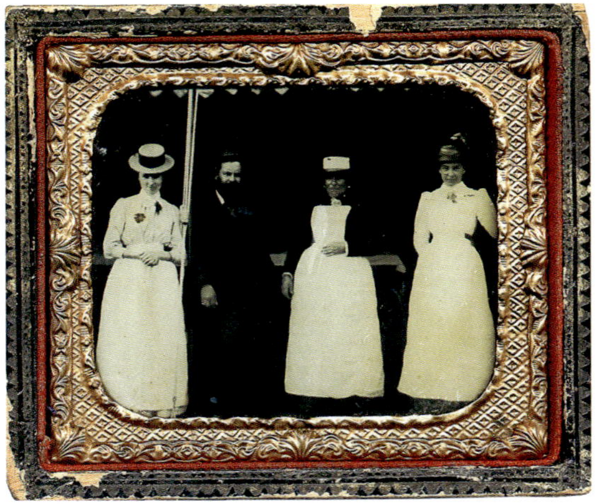

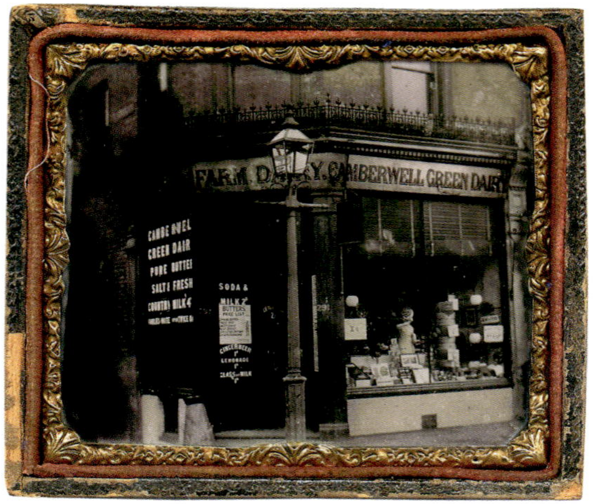

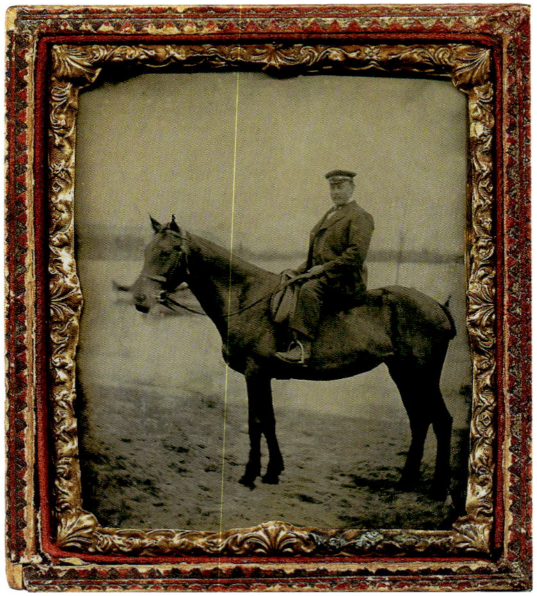

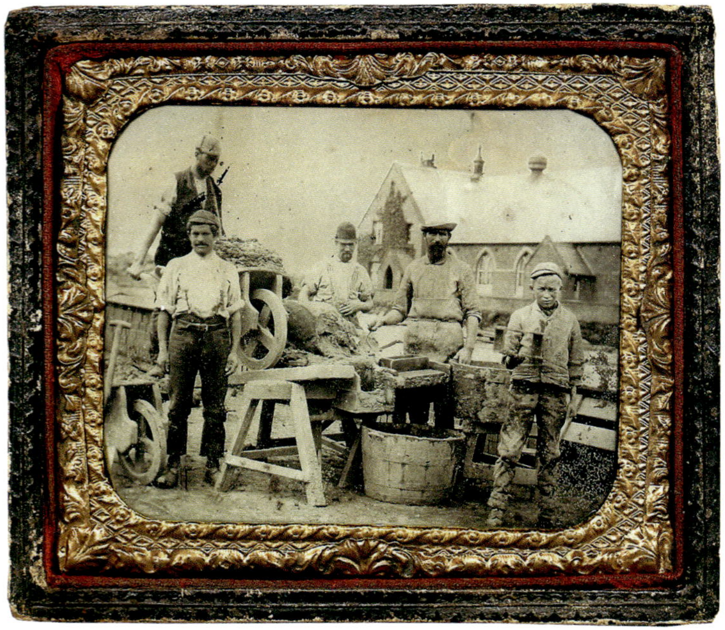

Framed ambrotypes were produced at the cheaper end of the market, and were very popular with itinerant photographers whose output was usually limited to only two sizes – sixth plate and quarter plate.
From top left, Group of servants in a marquee, 1860s, photographer and location unknown, 97mm x 83mm; Camberwell Dairy, 1860s, sixth plate ambrotype, photographer unknown, 94mm x 80mm; Gentleman on Horseback, sixth plate ambrotype by Thomas Harrison, South Beach, Scarborough, c.1870, 83mm x 94mm;
Left: Sixth plate ambrotype of tilemakers or brickmakers with their rough moulds and tools, location and photographer unknown, late 1850s, 95mm x 83mm.

Chapter Three:

Ambrotypes and Expanding Markets

The relationship between the daguerreotype and the collodion positive, or ambrotype, in photographic history has always been confused by early attempts to write the history of the photographic process as a strict chronological sequence, rather than viewing the introduction of new processes as being a means of broadening photography's market appeal and potential.

While it is undoubtedly true that the introduction of the daguerreotype predated the collodion positive, it is equally true, as has already been noted, that the two achieved their peak of popularity at about the same time – thanks to the relaxing of the daguerreotype patents, and the absence of any serious attempts at patent control on the use of wet collodion – Fox Talbot excepted.

The daguerreotype has often been referred to as photography's 'false start' – presumably because none of the manipulative stages involved in its production bear any relationship to successive processes or those with which we are familiar today. If indeed it was a false start – and whether or not one believes that depends on whether chemical compatibility or commercial viability is used as a yardstick for measurement – then the ambrotype or collodion positive was also a false start. It too produced a single positive image which was unique and incapable of easy duplication.

What both the daguerreotype and the ambrotype did for photography – and for portraiture in particular – was to give respectability by allying the new photographic portrait to the established form and style of the miniature painting. In that respect, rather than both processes being false starts, they gave photography a strong and commercially viable foundation upon which to build. Indeed it was perhaps the only possible foundation from which the new profession could have been developed and expanded.

It was the ability of the photographic portrait, by whatever process, to mimic the established portraiture medium which generated public interest – and in particular it was the ability of photography to mimic the miniature painting in moments rather than days, and with a truthfulness hitherto undreamed of, which the Victorians found both magical and exciting. Once the idea of the photographic portrait had been established – painted as the reviews put it 'with a pencil of light' – then photography as a medium was able to stand on its own feet and develop a photographic tradition rather than merely extend an established painting tradition.

The ambrotype, therefore, served a dual purpose in the evolution of a public appreciation of photography. Firstly, by reducing the unit cost of a photographic portrait, it broadened photography's market base and introduced the medium to a larger market. Secondly, it introduced a measure of standardisation in the techniques of photography – for the same equipment, materials and chemicals used by the wet collodion photographer producing glass negatives from which prints could be made were also used by the production of collodion positives.

The influence of the process's introduction also had a significant effect on both earlier photographic processes – the daguerreotype and the calotype. While both were covered by fiercely protected patents, there were no patents – in Britain at least – restricting the use and spread of either wet collodion negative photography or the use of the collodion positive variant.

Although it was initially free from all patents – and therefore available to any photographer who wished to use it – the ambrotype was later the subject of several celebrated court cases resulting from dubious patent claims on both sides of the Atlantic.

Those court actions fell into two groups. First of all there were a number of photographers who tried to patent spurious 'improvements' to the process in order to make money from the sale of licences. Secondly there were legal actions brought by both Henry Fox Talbot and Richard Beard against photographers using the wet collodion and collodion positive processes for claimed infringements of their patents.

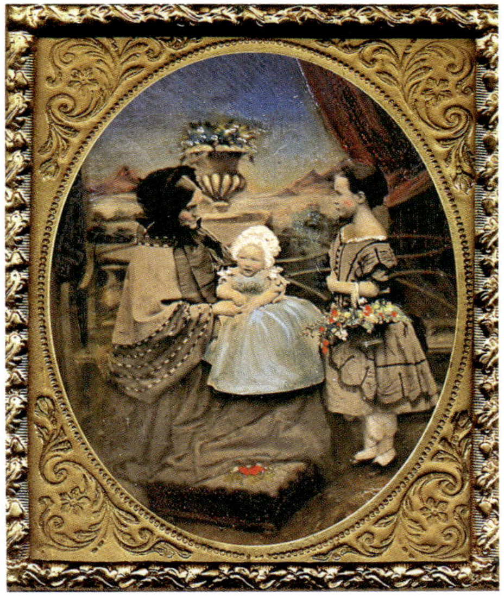

Ninth plate ambrotype, richly tinted and gilded. Photographed by W.H. Franklin, 173 Lower Street, Deal, Kent, c.1860.

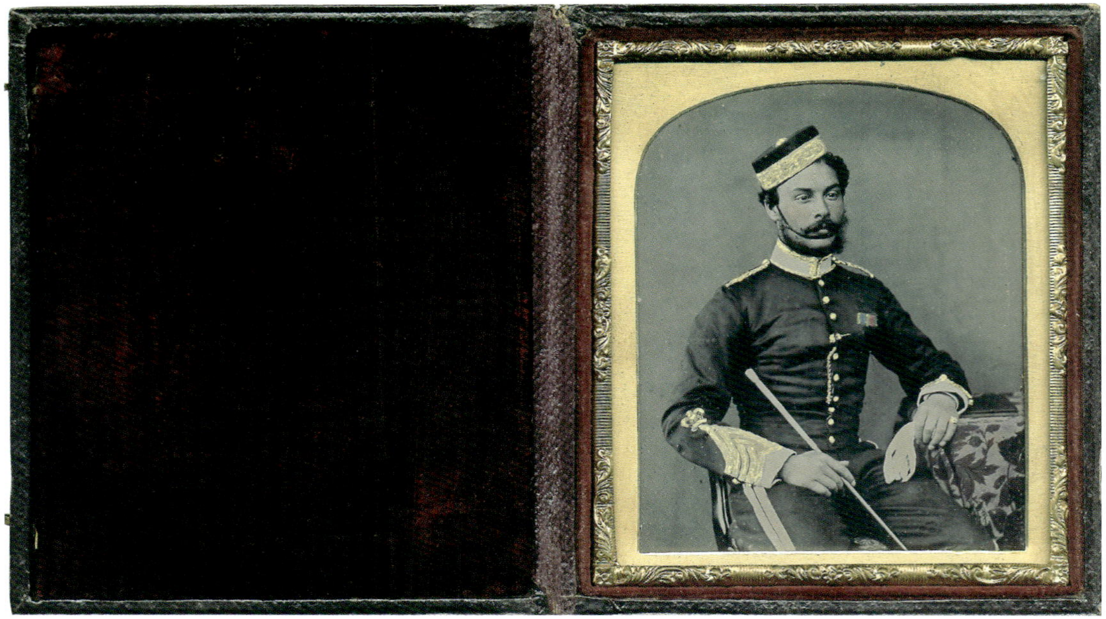

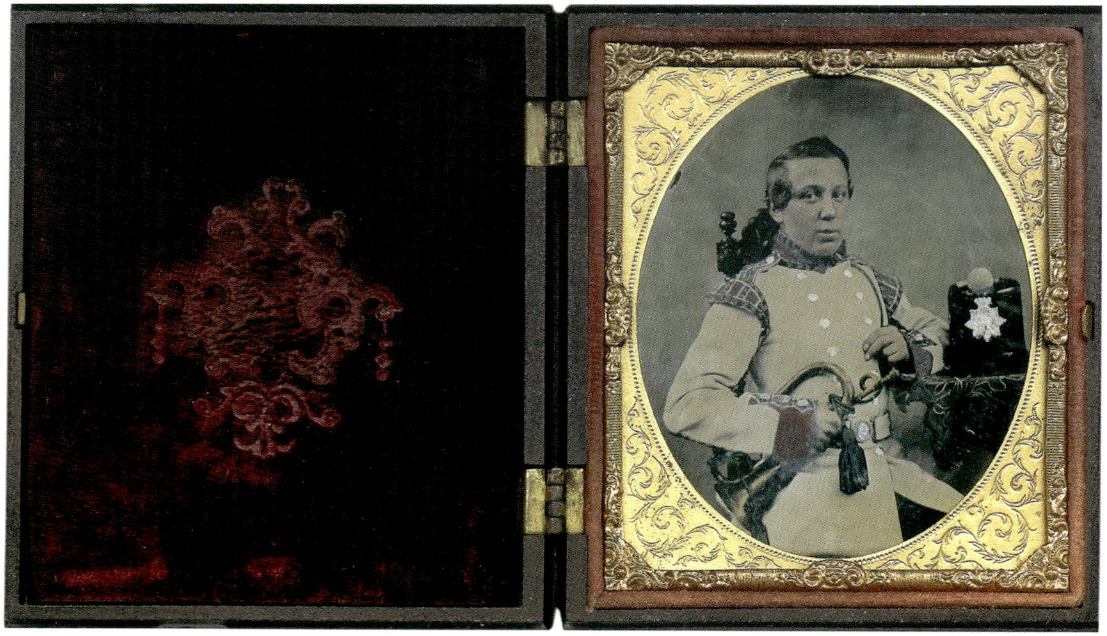

It is not however within the sphere of this study to become concerned with the many celebrated court cases of the 1850s, but it is worthwhile noting that the outcome of the patent disputes was complex and not a little cruel. While Talbot had his calotype rights upheld in court – not that they were ever in doubt anyway – and Richard Beard's right to control and license the use of the daguerreotype was also upheld – again never really in dispute anyway – Frederick Scott Archer, the inventor of the practical wet collodion process was treated as if he did not exist. It was a number of other photographers who were taken to court over their use of Archer's process. It was the courtroom testimony of those other photographers which helped establish Archer's process as being outside Beard's and Talbot's patents and which helped define the limits of those patents.

Archer stayed almost entirely in the background, and ultimately died in poverty – although it was his process which had set photography off on the road to real commercial success.

While it is Frederick Scott Archer who is celebrated in all the history books as the inventor of the wet collodion process and, with Peter Fry, of the ambrotype or collodion positive, he was merely one of a number of workers experimenting with collodion as a carrier for the light sensitive photographic chemistry. Gustave le Gray, credited with the *waxed paper process*, claimed to have a working collodion process the year before Archer announced his version in the March 1851 edition of the journal *The Chemist*.[1]

The concept of the collodion positive was contained within Archer's original published account of the process. He – and indeed British photographers in general at the time – much preferred the term 'collodion positive' to the American term 'ambrotype'. It is perhaps a testament to the power of American influence that 'ambrotype' is an almost universally accepted term amongst photographic historians today.

The ambrotype went through two distinct developmental phases as far as its chemical

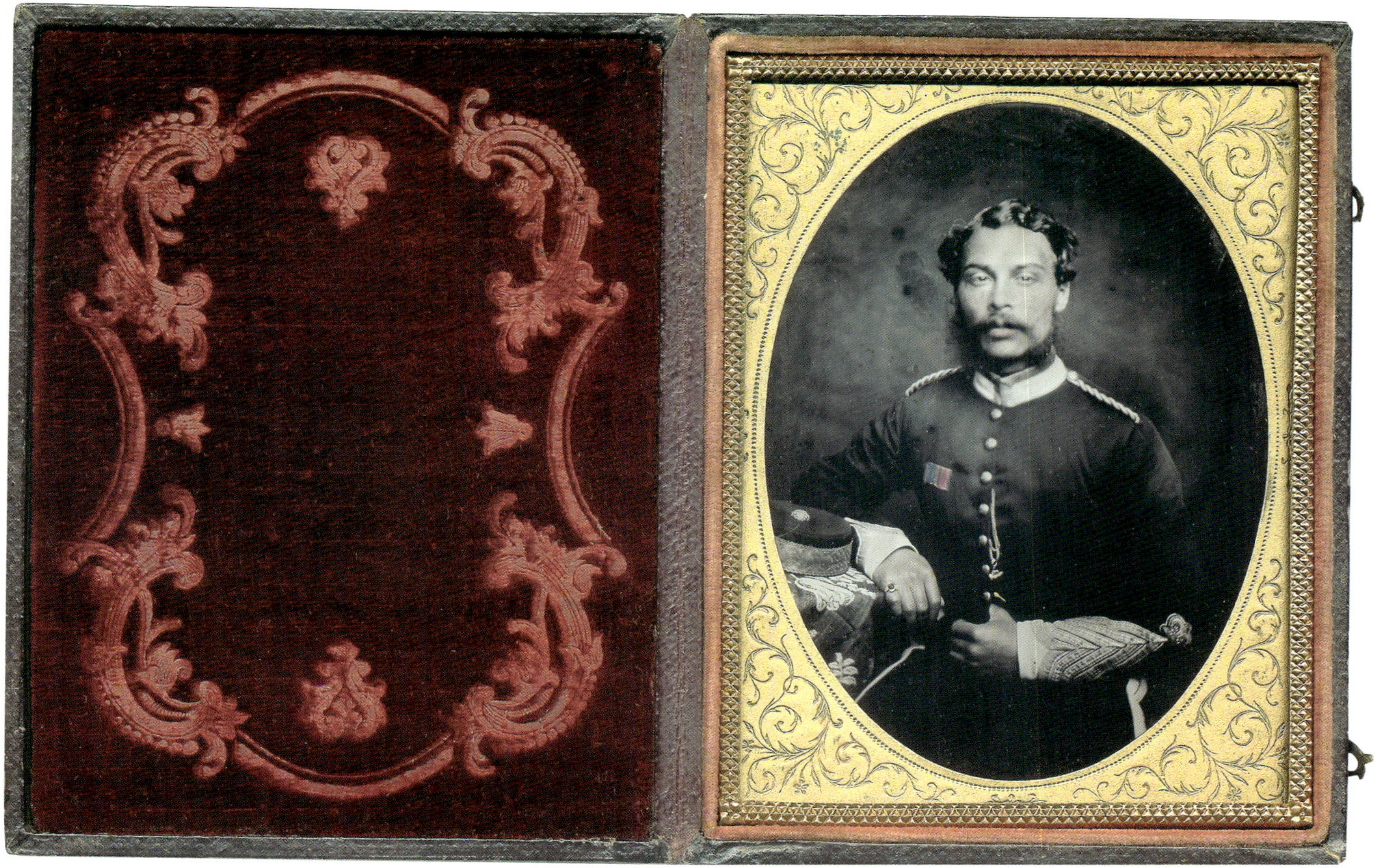

The images on this page (quarter plate, actual size) and top opposite (sixth plate) show two portraits of the same Regimental Sergeant Major in the undress uniform of the 17th Light Dragoon Lancers, 1850s. The quarter plate image, above, is presented emulsion side up in an embossed leather covered case. The image is therefore presented laterally reversed, with tunic buttons and decorations on the wrong side. The sixth plate image, opposite, is presented emulsion side down, thus giving the image its correct orientation.

Below left: Sixth plate tinted and gilded ambrotype portrait of a young bugler in an unidentified regimental uniform, photographer unknown, late 1850s. The image is housed in a thermoplastic union case. The cased ambrotype was a popular vehicle for military portraits in the 1850s. The image was bright, easy to view under all lighting conditions, unlike the daguerreotype, and yielded a high quality unique portrait at a fraction of the cost.

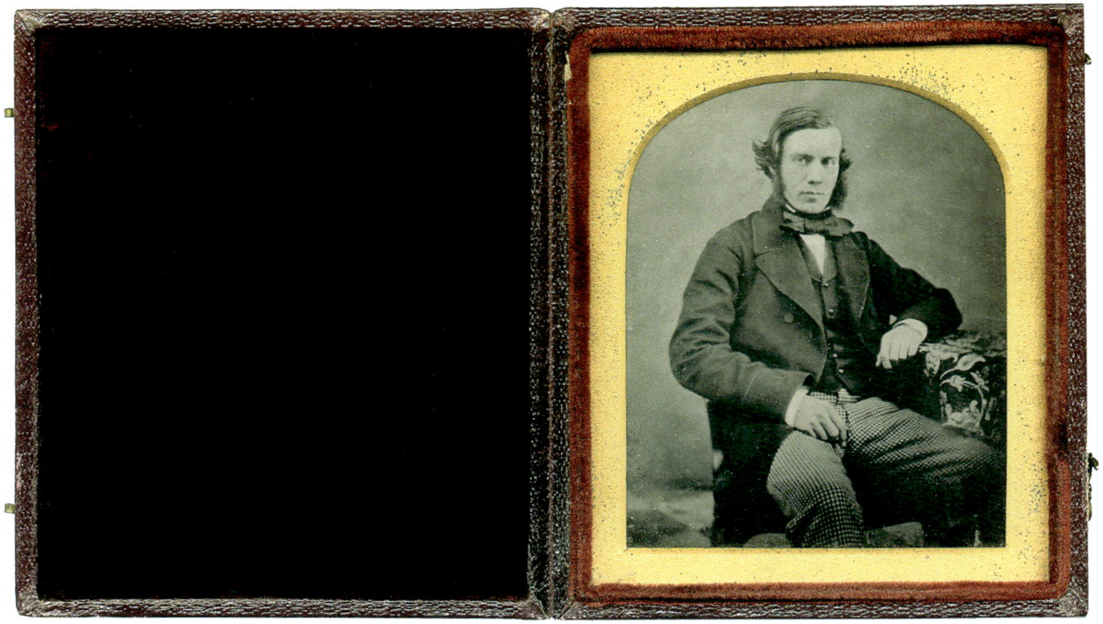

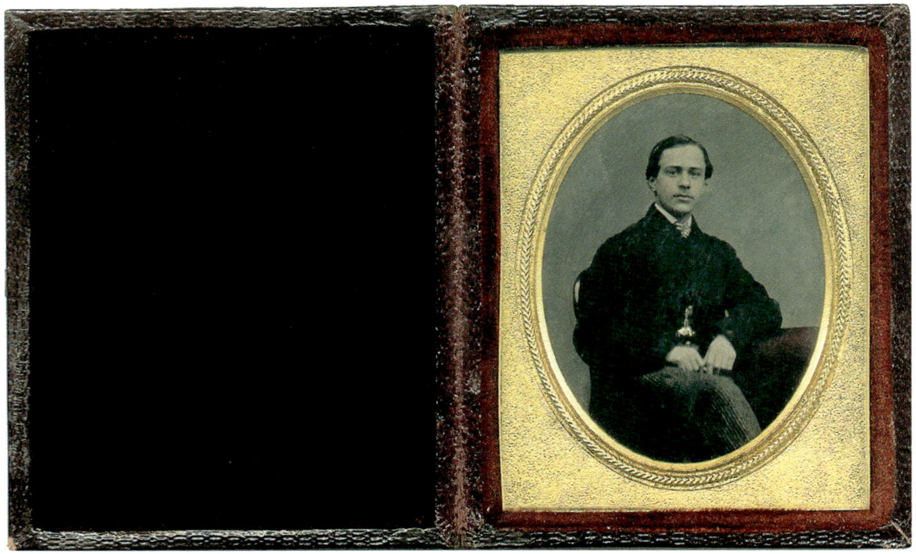

Top: Sixth plate ambrotype by Beard & Foard, housed in a plain leather case (opposite, top left) embossed with the same gilt stamp used for their earlier daguerreotypes.

production process was concerned. Initially Archer & Fry demonstrated that a thin (underdeveloped but not underexposed) wet collodion negative could be treated with nitric acid, or with mercury bichloride, changing the black metallic silver of the thin negative image into an opaque white salt. That image, now white on clear glass appeared as a strong positive image when laid on black velvet. Alternatively, the black velvet could be replaced with a coating of black shellac applied directly on to the emulsion, creating a permanent positive – that latter device also serving as a protection against abrasion for the image itself. The result was a unique positive image without the distracting reflectance so characteristic of the polished metal base of the Daguerreotype.

However, this method appears to have been short-lived – or at least few examples of it have survived – and the commercial exploitation of the process proceeded without the bleaching stage. Excluding that step in the production stage, but with development carefully controlled, good positive images could still be produced, albeit without quite the same brilliance as Archer and Fry's original examples. They could, of course, be produced more quickly and, therefore, more cheaply.

Indeed, by the time of the publication of Philip Delamotte's book *The Practice of Photography* [2] in its second edition in 1855, no mention of the bleaching stage whatsoever was made in the directions for producing collodion positives. The year before in *A Dictionary of the Photographic Arts* [3] that step had been considered essential.

Used in either variant, the collodion positive assumed considerable popularity – although in the minds of some more select photographers, a slightly downmarket stigma was always attached to it!

Indeed, relatively few of the major daguerreotype photographers are believed to have used the process. Some recent accounts have claimed that leading photographers such as Antoine Claudet never used it at all – and that would be a strange irrationality in the man if true, as he later exploited the even cheaper mass-market carte-de-visite format of paper print with considerable success, producing some very fine portraits indeed.

Whilst there are no examples of Richard Beard using the ambrotype, James T. Foard, onetime partner of Richard Beard Jnr. in both Manchester and Liverpool certainly did. Equally Edinburgh's Ross & Thomson offered both processes to their clients throughout the 1850s.

Certainly the majority of the surviving examples of the process bear no photographer's name whatsoever, but no conclusions as to quality ought to be drawn from that fact. For instance, the bulk of surviving examples of the daguerreotype are equally anonymous, reflecting, perhaps, more the size of the studios involved than the social standing of the photographs they produced.

It is also worth remembering that the thermoplastic union case – examined in depth later in this book – was considered an expensive and rather up-market method of packaging the photographic – usually ambrotype – portrait, and very few examples of these identify the photographer or studio concerned.

For small studios, the additional cost of having their names applied to the cases may well have proved prohibitive, given that large quantities would have had to be ordered in order to make the addition of name and address economically viable. Mention has already been made of the fact that American casemakers would stamp and gild the name and address of the photographer on to the leather or paper cases free of charge – but it can be fairly certainly assumed that this would only have been for bulk orders.

A studio ordering only a few dozen cases in each size would hardly have been considered an economic investment for the manufacturers. However, wider use of the relatively inexpensive practice of pasting a paper label inside the case beneath the image used sadly only by a few photographers might have considerably improved the lot of the image historian!

Just as with the daguerreotype, however, the larger studios with bigger turnovers produced often lavish and personalised packaging for their

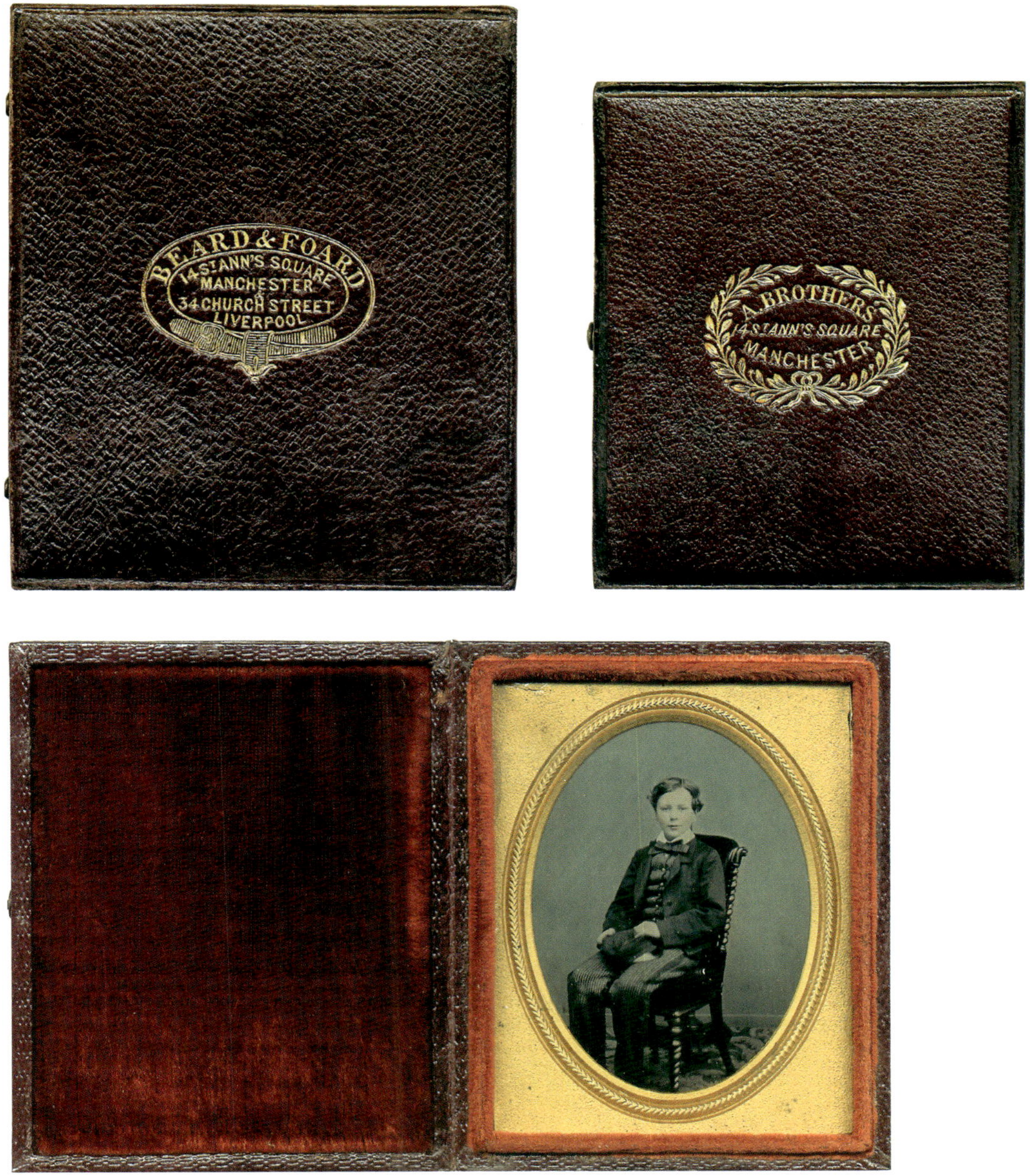

Above and opposite: Pair of ninth plate tinted ambrotypes of boys by Alfred Brothers who took over the studio from James T. Foard in the late 1850s.

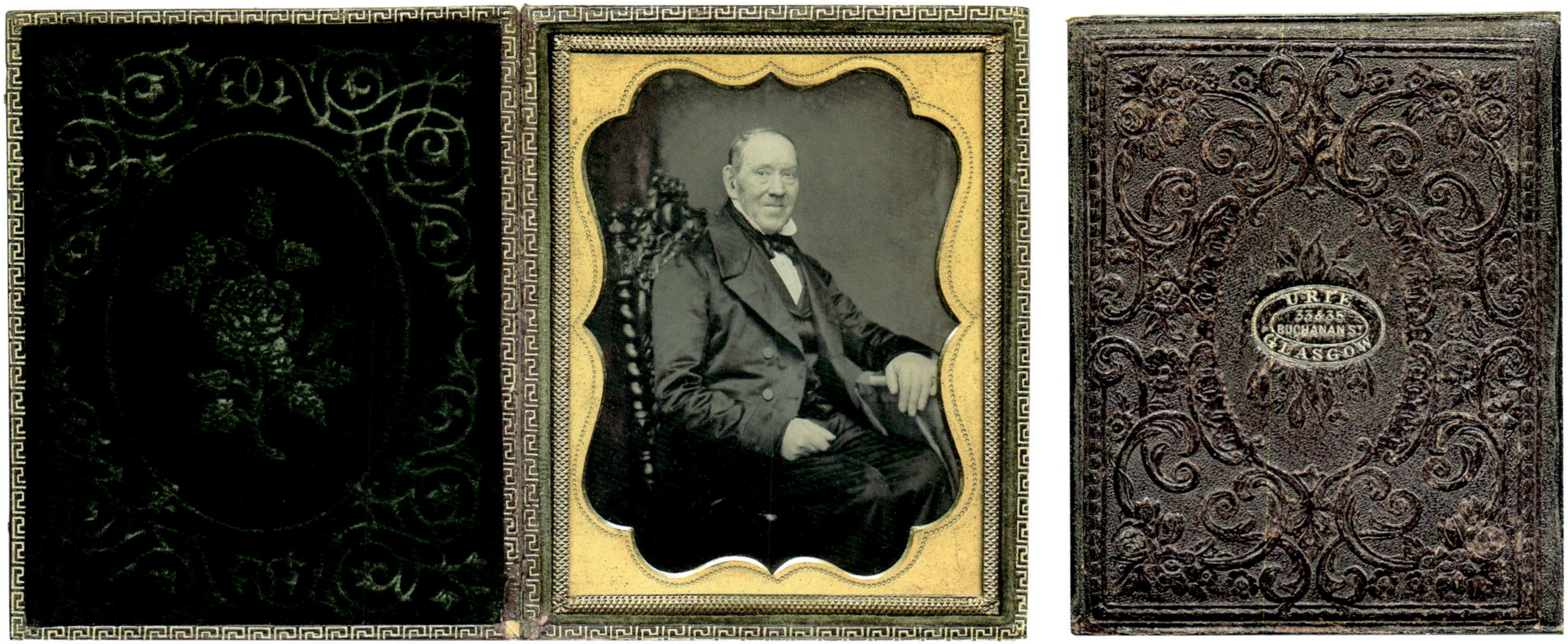

Quarter plate tinted and gilded ambrotype portrait of a gentleman, by John Urie, 33 & 35 Buchanan Street, Glasgow. Urie moved into these premises in 1854 and occupied them until at least 1897. This portrait comes from c.*1860. It is housed in an embossed paper-covered imitation leather case. The pattern is the same on both faces. The central motif, obscured by the studio gilt stamp, is an embossed bouquet of roses.*

portraiture output. Indeed many of them evolved particular presentation variations which they marketed initially as exclusive.

One such variation introduced by Glasgow photographer John Urie was recounted in issue 74 of the *Mechanics Journal* in 1854.

'The "relief pictures" of Mr Urie of Glasgow are amongst the latest of the important additions to our modern course of practice, giving a depth and roundness hitherto quite unattainable in photographic delineations and, indeed, combining the two very distinct effects of sculpture and painting. This clever artist whose perseverance has brought to light many minor improvements in the collodion process, now produces pictures possessing all the illusory appearance of a bold relief, the image having the effect of standing well forward from its background. After the picture is developed and finished in the usual manner, the back of the glass, or the surface opposite that on which the image is taken, is coated with a black varnish or dark pigment, care being taken to confine this reverse coating to the exact area opposite to or covered by the picture. After this treatment the picture is mounted in the usual way; the result is that the reverse coating cheats the observer into the idea that he is really looking upon a prominent formation. The opaque film, indeed, forms a species of background, from which the image, distant from such ground glass to the extent of the thickness of the glass or picture plate, appears to project well forward.

'Instead of this pigment coating, paper or other dark material may be laid on the reverse side of the glass. Indeed, any matter which will give an opaque or partially opaque background may be thus employed – as for example, one dark one for the reverse of the actual figure, and a light one for the general background of the picture. The extent and roundness of the relief is also capable of great improvement by graduating the reverse coating to suit the actual rounds of the picture.'

Much has been written in other histories of photography about Urie's 'relievotype' process. As can be seen from the preceding account - and as a justification for quoting such a large proportion of it – the actual manner of producing these unusual images is very different from several recently published accounts of it.

The important characteristic of the relievotype is that the image was placed in its case emulsion side up rather than the usual form of emulsion side down whereby the plate of glass itself was used as a cover glass. With the relievotype, the shellac or other backing was on the reverse side of the glass to the image – giving the separation needed to create the three-dimensional effect – so a separate cover glass was required for the portrait.

Urie also suggested the use of chemically induced tints into the backgrounds for further unusual effects in his ambrotypes. From several other photographers came equally innovating suggestions, and ambrotypes survive today with backings of a wide variety of soft tints and colours. Grey, green, pale and dark blue, and even soft browns – which may indeed once have been reds – are also known to have been produced.

There were a number of patented modifications to the ambrotype. Although the original process as outlined by Archer and Fry was not and could not be patented, minor modifications to the process were. Indeed in some cases patent specifications included exact duplications of the original formulations – implying, whatever the patentee might claim – that the process itself was patented.

One patent taken out both in Britain and in America by James A. Cutting – who also coined the name 'ambrotype' for collodion positives from the Greek for 'eternal' and not because his middle name was Ambrose as some sources claim – patented a specific and supposedly advantageous method of protecting the image from the ravages of exposure to air. Ironically, the examples of the Cutting Patent Ambrotype which have survived the last hundred and thirty years or so have generally fared worse than those produced without the benefit of Mr Cutting's 'improvement'.

His method, originally patented in the USA – and in Britain under British Patent No. 1638 – in July 1854 involved sealing the image between its own glass and a top cover glass using a solution of Canada balsam. In addition his patent claimed the introduction of the use of alcohol to expel moisture from the collodion, and the use of camphor to 'increase the vigour and delineation of the positive pictures'.

There was a disclaimer at the end of the patent specification in which Cutting did make it clear that only these three elements were the subject of his patent, and recognising that the process itself was in the public domain. However the three variations were in themselves both minor and also – in two cases at least – also already within the public domain.

Cutting later conceded that many photographers did already use alcohol's astringent properties to help dry their plates, and that balsam was already widely used to seal microscope slides.

Like the daguerreotype, ambrotypes were initially available in fractions of the established 'plate' sizes.

Commonest were the two smaller sizes – 1/6th plate and 1/9th plate, with 1/4 plate next in prominence. These fractions were nominal divisions of the standard plate of 6½in. x 8½in. However the rapid advance of photography in the wet collodion period – and the desire of photographers for lightweight cameras which could be easily transported – brought about the introduction of a glass negative size which did not conform to the established scale of multiples or divisions of the plate. 10in. x 8in. very quickly became the most popular size for glass negatives – with 10in. x 10in. achieving considerable popularity due to the ease with which both vertical and horizontal images could be cropped out of it.

Many small portraits, therefore, became based on the logical quartering of the 10in. x 8in. sheet of glass – thus introducing the 5in. x 4in. format into photography, a format which along with 10in. x 8in., remains the principal professional negative size to this day.

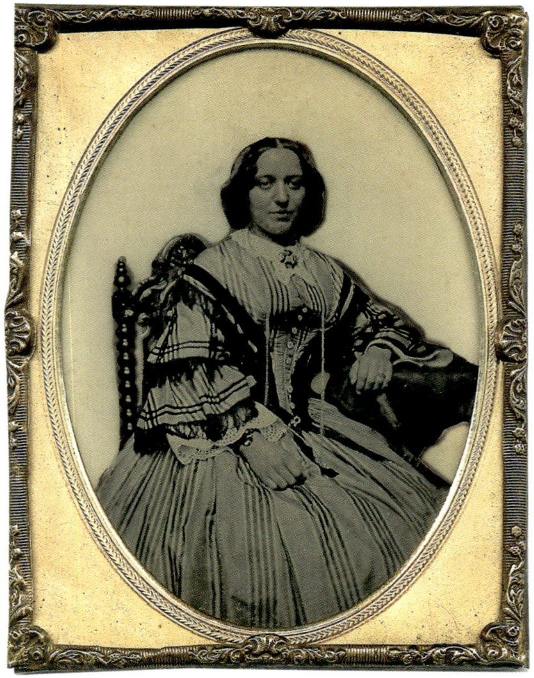

Quarter plate relievotype portrait, taken according to Urie's published description, by Alfred Booker, Photographic Artist of Redditch, late 1850s. As Urie stated, the 'pigment coating, paper or other dark material may be laid on the reverse side of the glass. Indeed any matter which will give an opaque or partially opaque background may be thus employed – as for example, one dark one for the reverse of the actual figure, and a light one for the general background of the picture'.

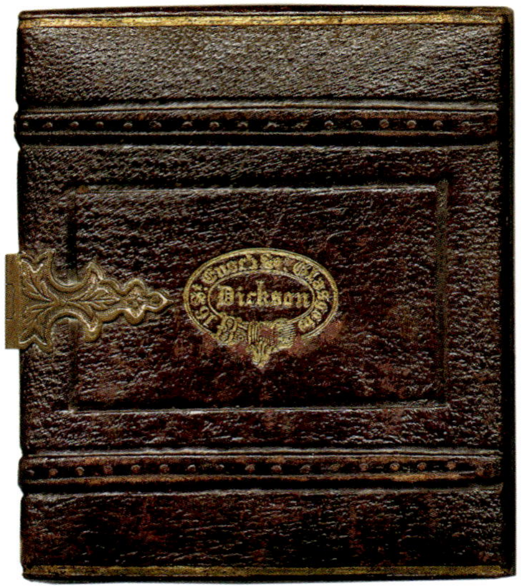

Tinted and gilded sixth plate ambrotype by William Dickson of two young men. Dickson opened his studio at 16 St. Enoch Square, Glasgow, in 1859, and produced this ambrotype of two young men in the early 1860s. The subject is perhaps surprising given the repressive nature of Victorian society, yet there was an already well established posing code for male friends, understood throughout both Britain and America. The embossed leather case with its raised decorative bands is based on a mid-1850s patented design by Harold Eichmeyer of Philadelphia. With its rounded edges and the ornate clasp, it was perceived as a luxurious and up-market pattern. The clasp is embossed with lily leaves on either side, and a single lily flower across the edge of the case.

Opposite page: Sixth plate ambrotype by Edinburgh photographers Ross & Thomson, late 1850s. Those studios which had established a strong reputation for introducing interesting poses and striking lighting into their daguerreotypes, adapted the ambrotype to produce work of similar artistic merit. The image is housed in a blue leather case, with embossed motif on the face, and photographer's gilt stamp on the base.

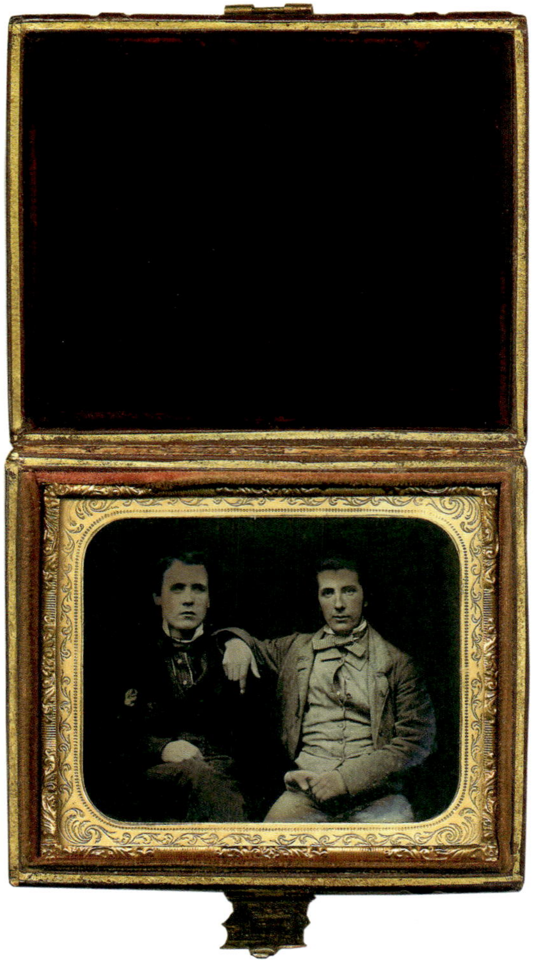

The advantage of working with fractions of the whole plate were, of course, considerable. The same cases could be used for packaging both ambrotypes and daguerreotypes. This may have had the effect of limiting the use of those formats which did not conform to plate sizes to ambrotype photographers alone, with daguerreotypes forever remaining restricted to the established range of dimensions. Certainly this writer, while familiar with 5in. x 4in. ambrotypes, has not found any daguerreotypes of that size.

There are no figures of the numbers of photographers producing ambrotypes in the 1850s and '60s, although increasingly valuable lists of professional photographers working within those decades are being compiled by local and national historians. No accurate assessment, therefore, can be made as to the likely output of British photography within the period. The figures are likely to have been considerable, and the range and availability of cases within which to present the portraits was clearly very broad indeed.

Edward Anthony's 1854 catalogue of photographic materials and equipment[4] gives some idea of the scale of the market. In all some six hundred and seventeen case variants are offered for sale. Variations in quality of finish, quality of glass, variety of clasps, snap closures and so on, different types of hinges, leather, paper or papiér mâché coverings and, of course the usual range and variety of sizes, not to mention the variety of colour options in trim and pad available for each size, offered photographers almost limitless variety in the packaging combinations they could offer to their customers.

Bearing in mind that Anthony's were almost exclusively offering other than plastic cases – so several hundred plastic designs in a variety of sizes should be added to that already considerable total – the ultimate range of choices available to photographers in Britain and America may have been twice that size.

As the market was based on supply and demand, the number of ambrotype images and daguerreotype images being produced during the period must have been enormous to support such a well established and broad based case and frame manufacturing enterprise.

While the daguerreotype case market in the 1840s was generally catered for by relatively simple designs – with a few more lavish exceptions such as the Plumbe 'Urn' cases and other embossed leather designs – it was the ambrotype market which saw the real multiplication of designs and broadening of the range of manufacturing techniques.

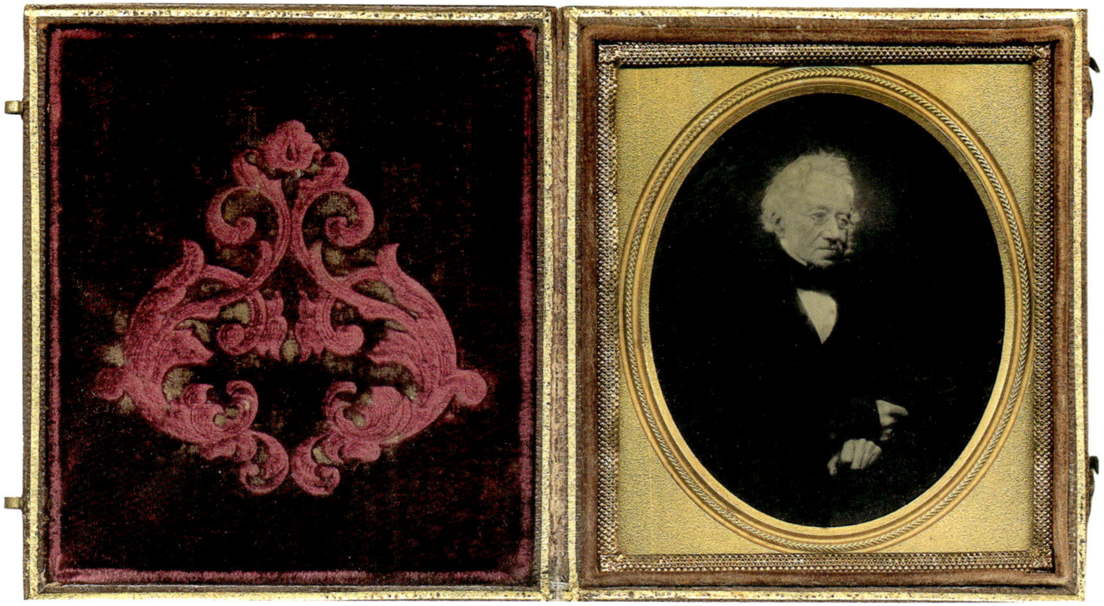

To keep the unit cost of a cased ambrotype portrait low – or in order to be able to offer a cheap version at the bottom end of each studio's range – simpler and at the same time more elaborate case designs were evolved.

While the earlier case makers varied their prices within a range determined by the cost parameters of different qualities of Morocco leathers, the considerable expansion of both the range of case designs and of the gap between the top and bottom ends of the market was only made possible by advanced manufacturing techniques which linked low production costs with apparently sophisticated design.

Thus top grade leather was replaced first by poorer leather skins, and then by a variety of other materials as a means of covering the traditional case, and the wooden frame itself was abandoned in favour of less labour intensive manufacturing techniques. Using lower quality skins was less obvious if an embossed pattern obscured flaws in the leather.

Paper covered and papiér mâché cases were by far the most common – and are so today amongst survivors of the medium. Early paper cases may have been very simple, but very quickly techniques for embossing and moulding papiér mâché evolved to take the initial cheap variant into a whole new era of design.

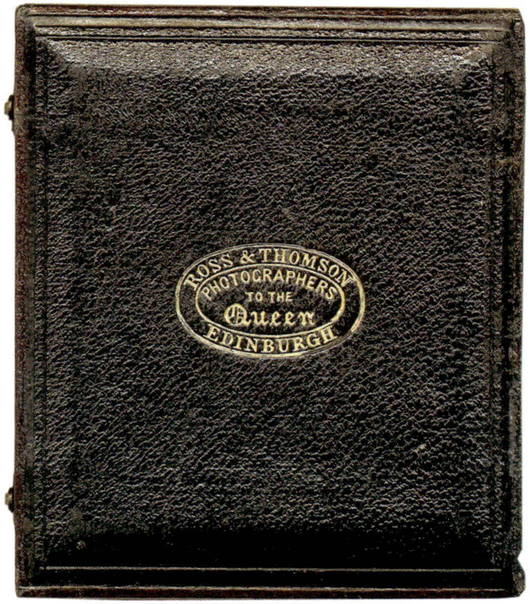

It was that response to market demands which characterised the development of the photographic case. This was in no way a matter of manufacturers imposing their will on their clients. Client demands were clear – sophisticated packaging, and well-designed packaging, at an affordable price. The paper case which had started out as a utilitarian product soon became a well-designed and well-manufactured commodity. The paper case was originally a cheap imitation – nothing more. It was the imitation leather suitcase of its day – a cheap copy of something which the owner would like to be able to afford. The market was, however, big enough to be worth developing – so design conscious case-makers did devote considerable energies to improving the

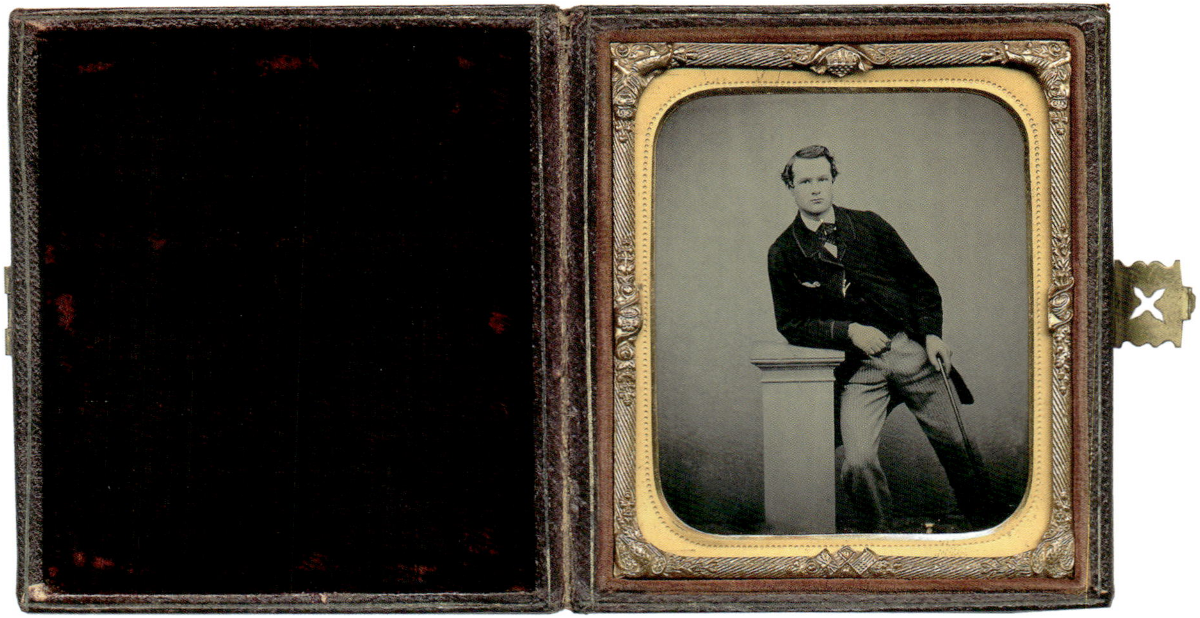

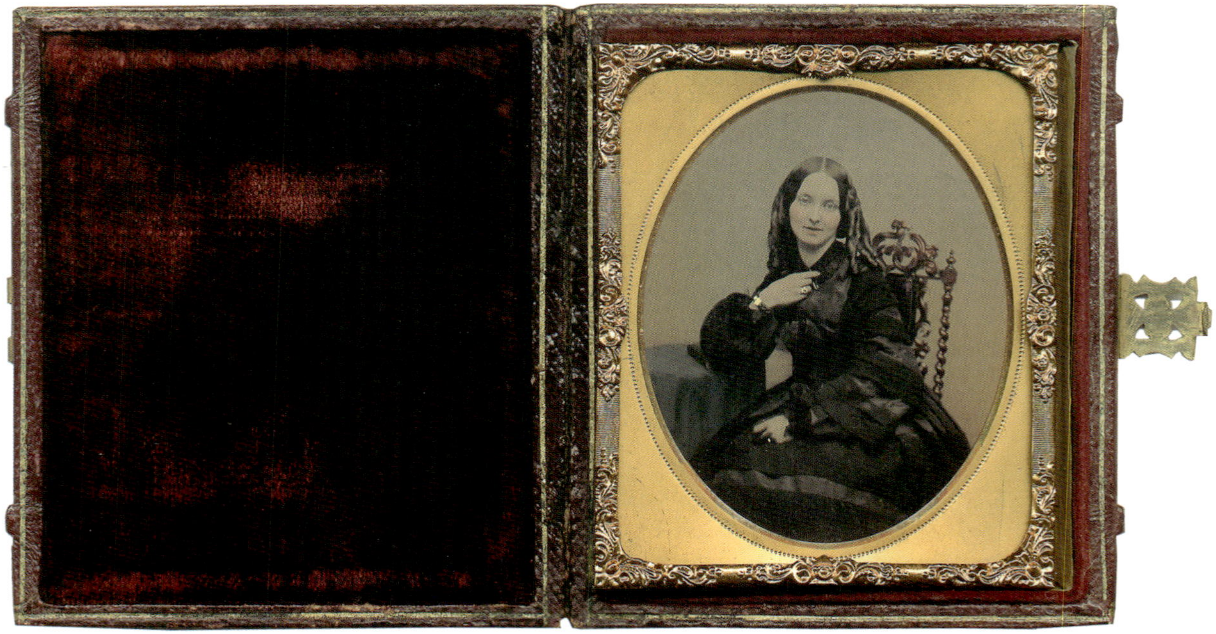

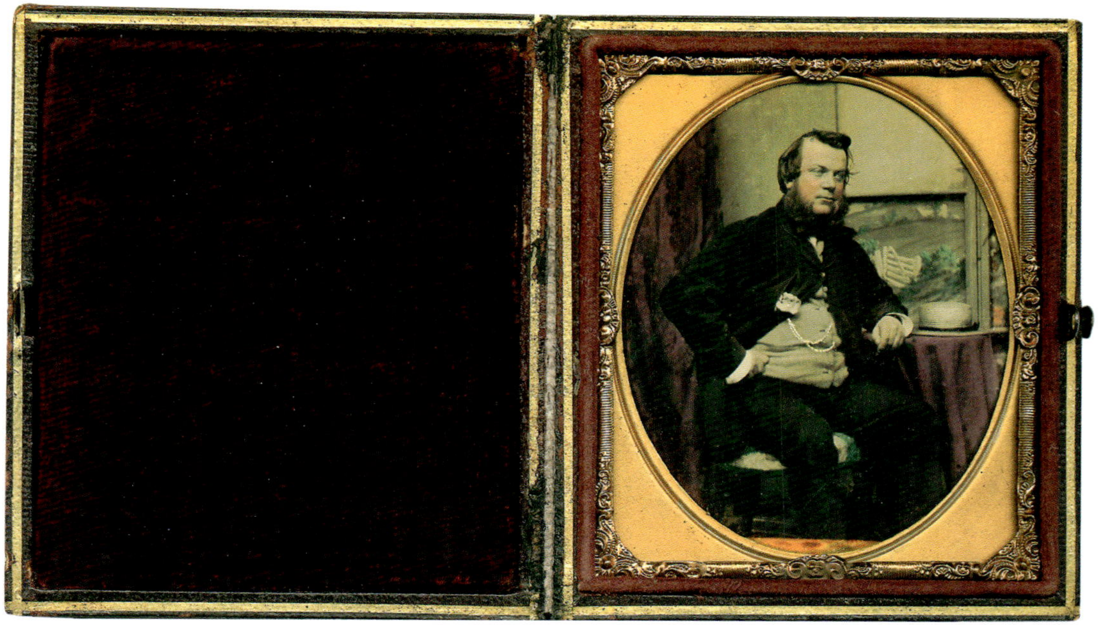

Wayne & Rothwell's studio in Douglas, Isle of Man, was responsible for the production of some very sophisticated ambrotype portraits from the mid 1850s into the 1860s. They produced a high quality product, using sophisticated natural lighting, striking poses, delicate tinting and gilding and high quality Eichmeyer and other cases. The example opposite is presented in a leather-covered case with push-button closure, while the two portraits on this page are both contained in Eichmeyer cases. Inside each case, the photographers' label can be found beneath the image.

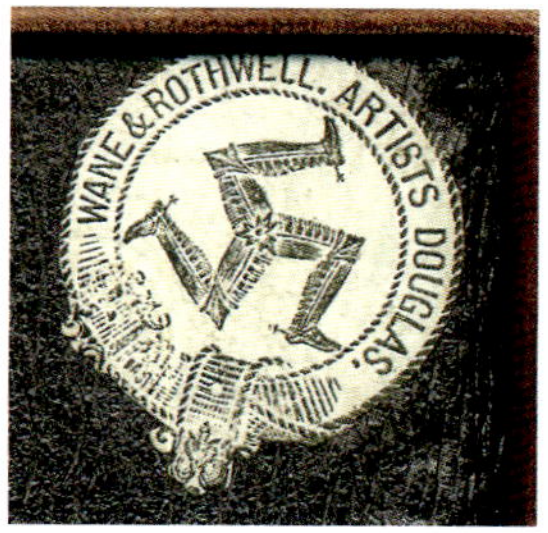

appearance of the product while at the same time reducing costs. The qualities of the materials themselves were exploited to bring to the paper and papiér mâché case characteristics which were uniquely theirs. From about 1852/3, paper cases were common and in many cases very attractive and desirable objects.

In support of all these casmakers, allied industries produced mattes and preservers in a range of qualities. While many were imported from America, many others were British made, largely in Birmingham and London.

At the same time as the cheaper end was being catered for by mass production on a hitherto unprecedented scale, the upper end of the market was also being introduced to a moulded material – and a material which was to revolutionise the developed world. Moulded thermoplastic offered qualities which were impossible with paper, leather or any other previously used material.

Footnotes

1. Writing in the introduction to *Plain Directions for Obtaining Photographic Pictures upon Glass and Albumenised Paper*, Richard Willats, London 1853, Charles Heisch commented:
Much Discussion has recently taken place as to who first proposed the use of collodion as a substance upon which photographs might be obtained. The question who first suggested its use? is more easily asked than answered. I myself first heard its use proposed by a friend in 1847, almost immediately after Professor Schoenbein had announced that rather bad guncotton would dissolve in ether. It is, however, easier to say who first published an account of using it. This was undoubtedly le Gray in the appendix to his work Traité Pratique de Photographie sur Papier et sur Verre *published in June 1850... the appendix seems to have been most curiously overlooked...*
Heisch went on to describe le Gray's process and to attest to the fact that it was – or at least appeared to be – a practical working process. Needless to say Archer had his own views – and dismissed le Gray's claims in a few lines. Heisch himself quoted Archer's view that le Gray *'did not give the public the advantage of following him and that in his work in 1850 the subject [collodion] is dismissed in three or four lines.'*
Certainly a great deal more information would have been necessary to convert le Gray's few sketchy details into a working process – although he did actually state that he had used the process, and quoted specimen exposure times. It was Scott Archer, however, who published the first full working account of the process in 1851.
2. Philip Delamotte, *The Practice of Photography – a Manual for Students and Amateurs*, second edition, London, The Photographic Institution, and Low & Son, 1855. Delamotte, claiming that collodion positives 'resemble in many respects Daguerreotypes, but are free from the objectionable glare peculiar to the polished silver plates' offers a very simple process for preparing ambrotypes, warning of the risks of over-development which, he noted, resulted in negatives!
3. Henry H. Snelling, *A Dictionary of the Photographic Arts* written and published by H.H. Snelling, New York, 1854. Snelling, at this stage still using the term 'collodion positive' notes that Archer's bleaching process with bichloride of mercury – which could be reversed returning the image to a rich black negative – produced a 'most perfect white positive'.
4. *A Comprehensive and Systematic Catalogue of Photographic Apparatus and Materials Manufactured Imported and Sold* by E. Anthony, published by H.H. Snelling, New York, 1854. The introduction contains detailed descriptions of the processes involved in manufacturing daguerreotype plates, cameras, ancillary equipment, and the range of leather, wood and papiér mâché cases listed in the catalogue.

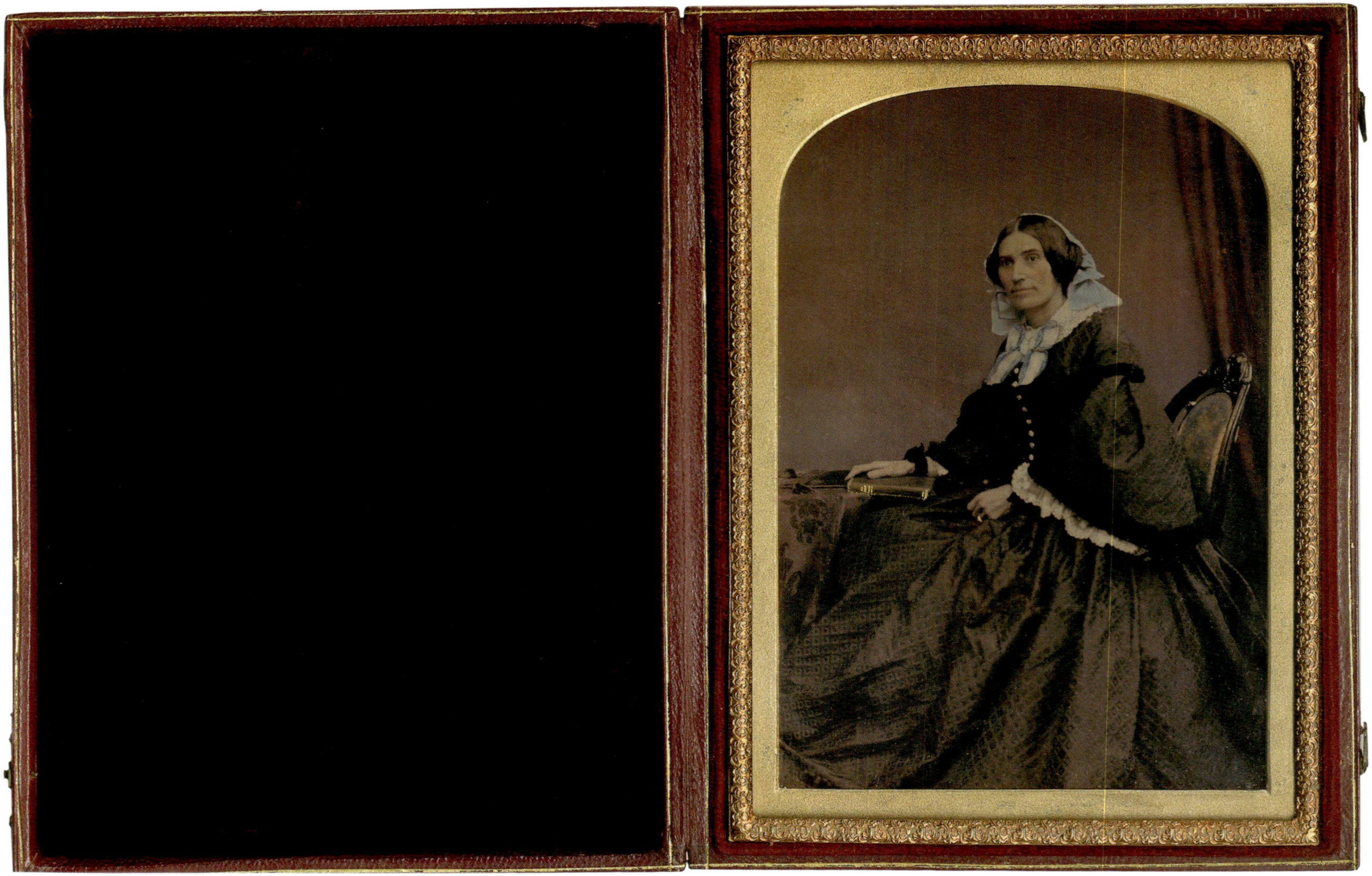

Half plate tinted and gilded ambrotype by G. & D. Hay, Photographists, 68 Princes Street, Edinburgh, c.1860. Ambrotypes of half and full plate are relatively uncommon because of their cost, but also perhaps because of their weight, and because of the fragility of the glass plate itself. While images up to quarter plate in size are regularly found both coloured and uncoloured, large images were usually tinted and gilded, as the cost of this additional decoration was presumably well within the financial reach of customers at this level. Many cased images of this size have been damaged as a result of the inherent instability of the cases themselves. Large cases made of soft wood had a tendency to warp, causing the plate itself to crack. The example in which this image is housed is showing signs of splitting across the seams which held the three wooden sections of each face together. The construction of a leather-covered, wood-framed case is discussed in detail in Chapter Four.

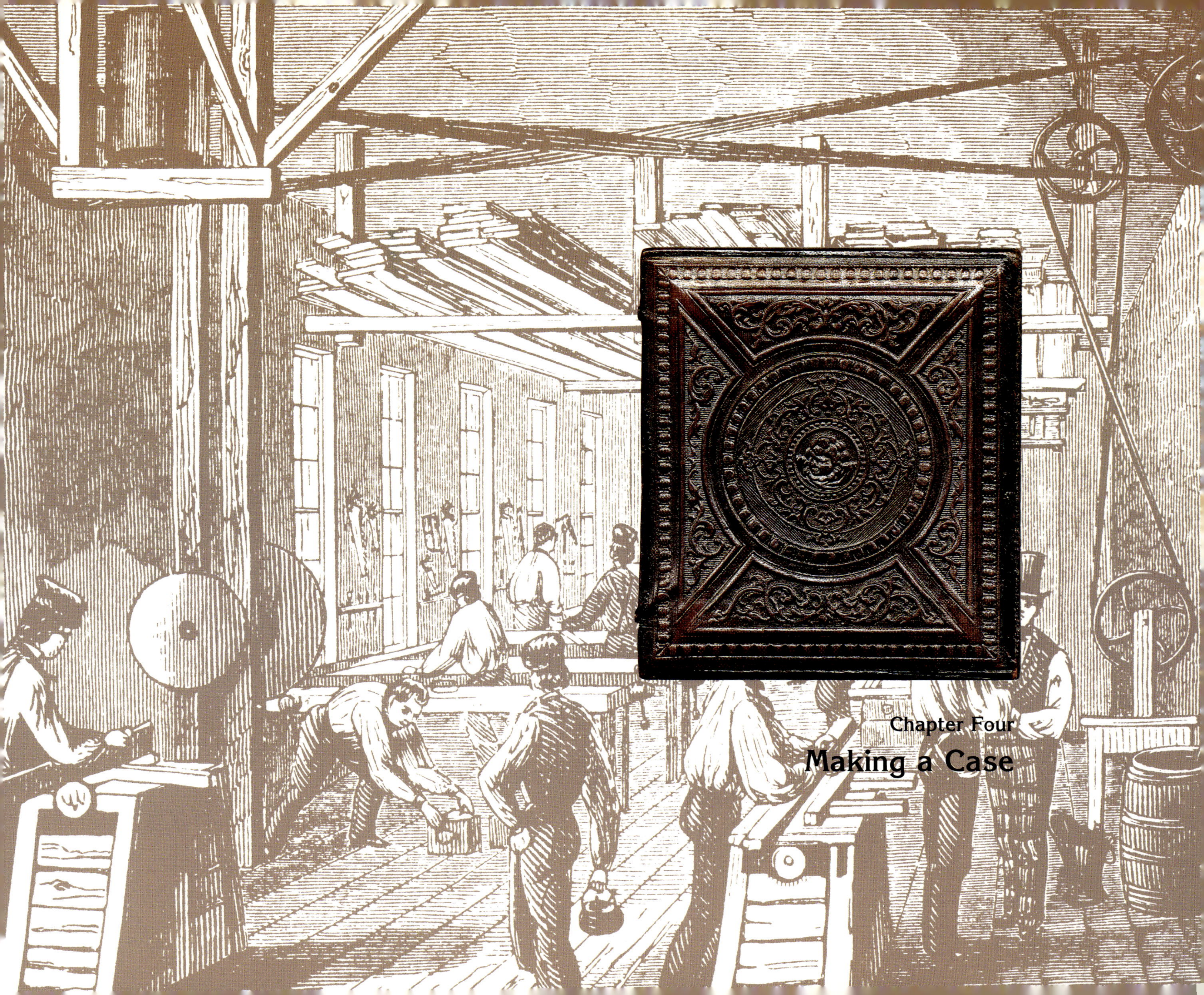

Chapter Four

Making a Case

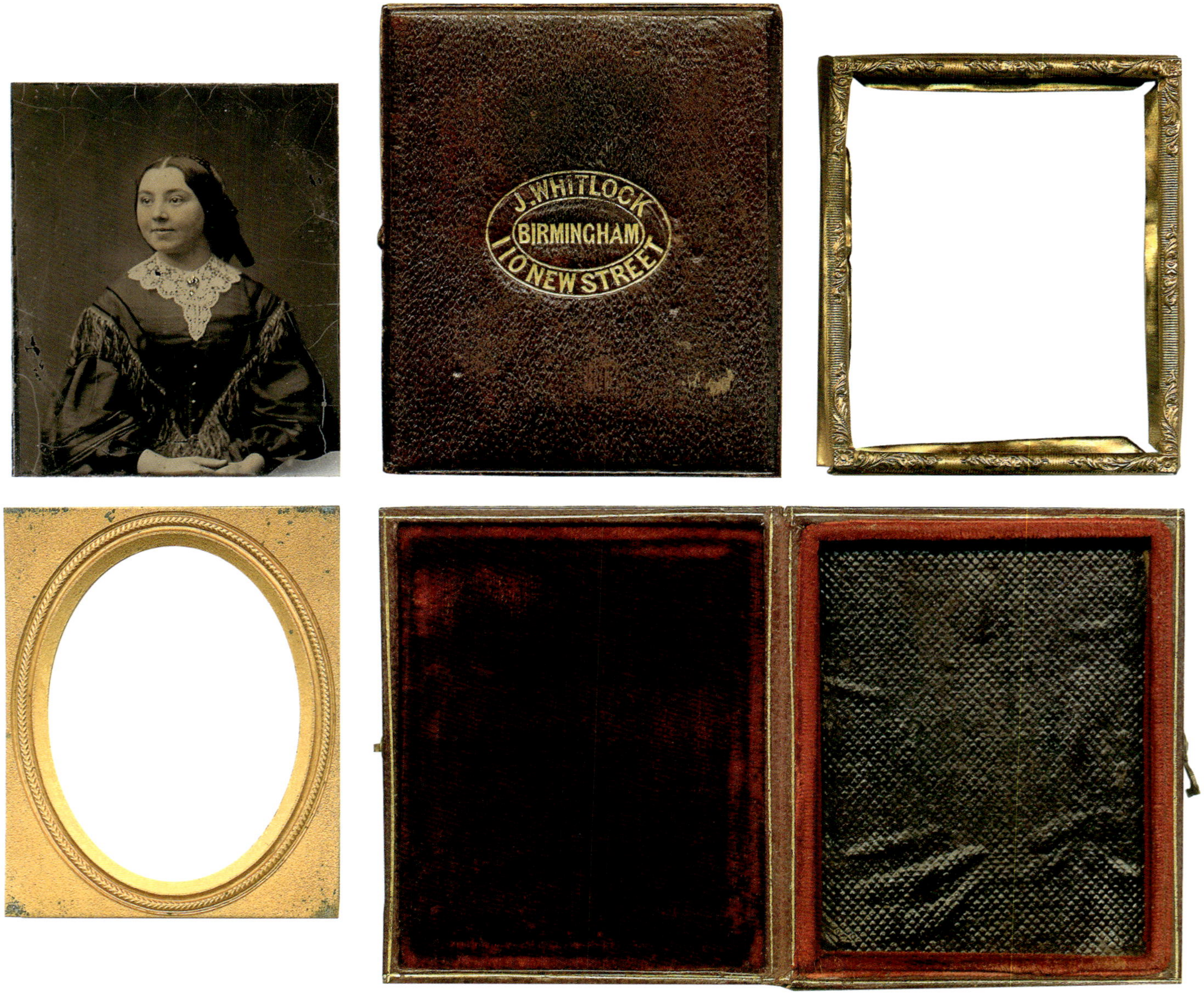

The cased ambrotype portrait was the result of an elaborate and time consuming process. The case itself, was made of fourteen pieces of wood, between two and ten pieces of leather, assorted pieces of paper and a velvet pad, and was held shut by a small metal clasp. The collodion plate was set behind a matte and a cover glass, and held in place by an embossed brass frame which fitted snugly into the velvet case trim. The emulsion on collodion negatives was notoriously liable to crack after it had been backed with black shellac varnish – clearly visible in this example – but once placed in the case with dark paper behind, the cracks became invisible. The cased image, opposite, shows no trace of the cracking.

Chapter Four:
Making a Case

Just as the miniature painting had been offered to sitters in a variety of mounts and presentation styles, so it was from the outset with the daguerreotype. Both framed and cased photographic portraits were available from Beard licensees in England and Wales, and from the range of itinerant photographers elsewhere. This fact, evident from contemporary advertising, draws attention to a particular problem when applying late twentieth century perceptions to a mid nineteenth century invention.

It is true that the framed daguerreotype was a difficult image to view – even in its heyday in the mid 1850s writers were drawing attention to the infinite superiority of the ambrotype (or collodion positive) in that respect. In 1855, the writer and photographer Philip H. Delamotte in his work *The Practice of Photography* described collodion positives as pictures which *'resemble in many respects daguerreotypes, but are free from the objectionable glare peculiar to the polished silver plates.'*[1]

However, daguerreotypes were by no means impossible to view – and their popularity in frames of all shapes and sizes and degrees of decoration attests to that popularity. The significant difference between our perception of their ease of viewing and that of their original purchasers and owners is one of lighting conditions. The daguerreotype is an image which is much more easily viewed by directional light. Victorian drawing-rooms were often darker in their decoration – heavy wall hangings and curtains by day, and lit by relatively local directional candle, gas or lamplight by night. In contrast, our houses today are lit by bright diffuse lighting, and decorated with much lighter furnishings. The daguerreotype was therefore a portraiture medium much better suited to its contemporary surroundings than to today's.

The case, therefore, must be viewed as a presentation medium which had other attractions and values. Ease of viewing, while better with a cased portrait, was by no means an overriding influence. Framed portraits made specific statements to all who visited a Victorian household – not least of which would have been the simple fact that the owner was able to afford a large framed daguerreotype.

The case did serve several useful purposes – ease of carriage, and ease of storage whilst also imparting considerable protection from fading and damage which was not afforded by the displayed framed portrait.

It may well have been the established tradition of treating personal treasures more intimately in Britain which gave the case its special attraction. In America, the protection offered by the case perhaps played a greater role in its success. With a considerably more mobile population, the safety of the image within its case was substantially greater than in a frame.

Whatever the reason, the predominance of frames in Europe and cases in Britain and America seems to have been established relatively early on in photography's history.

The extent to which those differences had already been established by the mid-1840s is, however, worthy of comment. At the same time as

Ninth plate portrait of a young lady, tinted, taken by Joseph Whitlock, 110 New Street, Birmingham, in the late 1850s. The Whitlock studio first opened at No.120 in 1848, and the business remained active in Birmingham for well over a century.

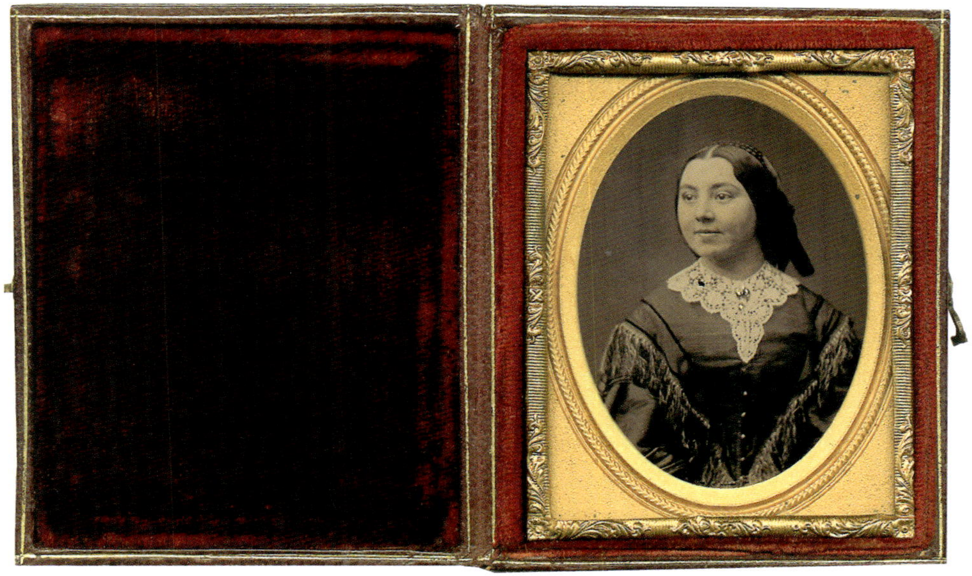

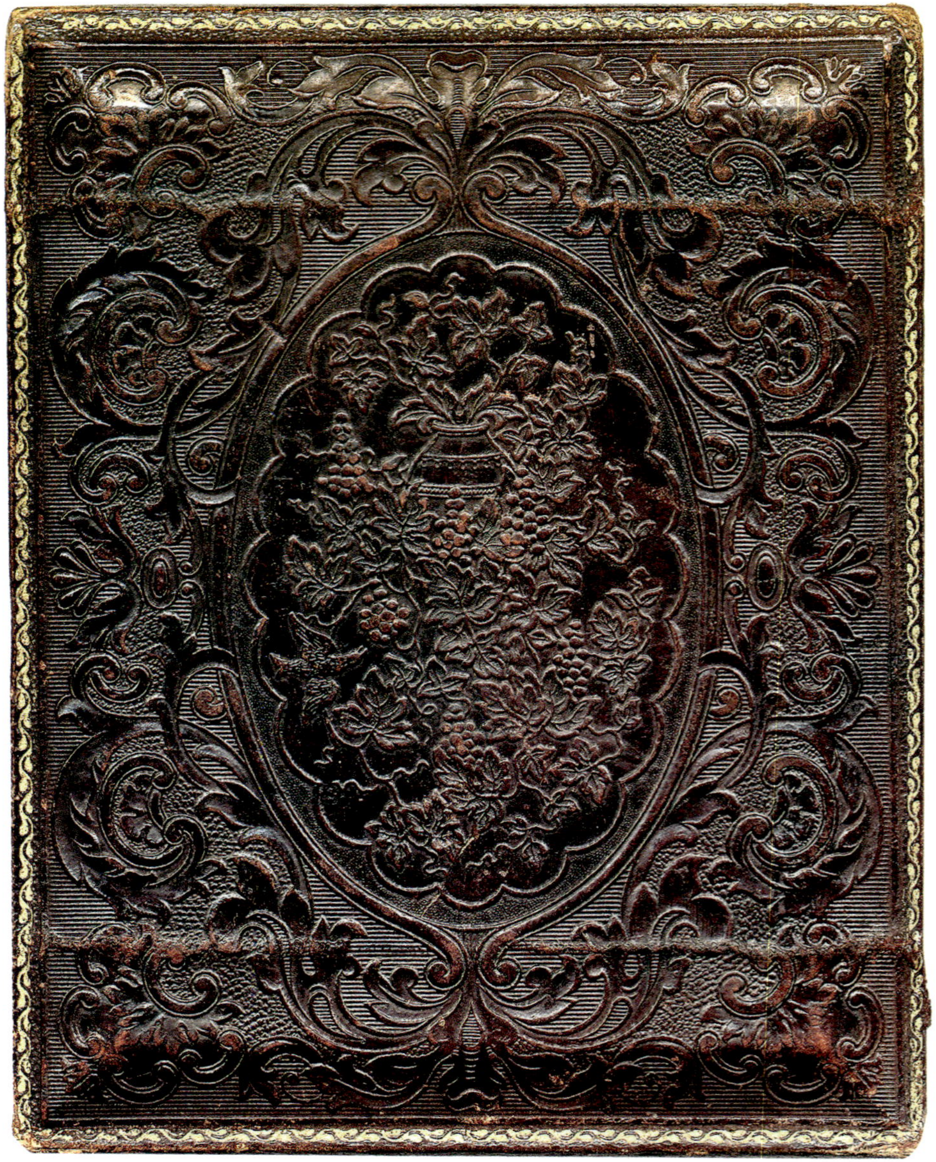

Half plate leather-covered and gilded case c.*1852, embossed with floral motif. This case contains an ambrotype set in a brass matte embossed with the legend 'Cutting's Patent'. James Ambrose Cutting took out a patent covering a number of matters relating to the production of collodion positives. While many of them were ideas already in the public domain – and therefore should not have been included in a patent – he did include a means of sealing the ambrotype image to its cover glass, thus allegedly protecting it from deterioration due to damp and atmospheric pollution.*

Mr. Edwards was opening his first photographic studio in Glasgow – at a time when even London could boast only two (those operated by Beard and Claudet) – cities such as Berlin could list nearly as many studios as were to be found in the whole of England. That greater development of photography supported a more sophisticated presentation industry.

German photographers such as Gustav Oehme,[2] a former pupil of Daguerre who had opened his studio early in 1843 at 20 Jagerstrasse in Berlin could offer his clientele a wide range of stylish and ornate frames, while his (few) British contemporaries were only able to offer a much smaller range of plainer cases and frames.

Britain's native case-making industry was already established in the pre-photographic days supplying cases for miniature paintings. One such maker, Thomas Wharton of Birmingham,[3] adapted the deep top-hinged cases he had been making for years to meet the demands of the new market.

Wharton, a manufacturer of bronze ware and brassware in addition to his interest in japanned wood frames and morocco cases for miniature paintings, already had all the expertise necessary to produce fine quality packaging for the daguerreotype. That his range of photographic packaging styles was limited would, one supposes, be a reflection on the size of the market rather than the plainness of British tastes.

He registered his design for a matte and preserving pan for the daguerreotype in August 1841, only a month after Beard had acquired exclusive patent rights for the process itself. Given the small market in the early years, one can assume with a degree of confidence that Wharton anticipated a greater market for the photographic process and therefore for his cases than was to follow as a result of Beard's manipulation of the market.

The Wharton pan and preserver had two useful characteristics – firstly it held the image firmly in place protecting it from damage, and secondly it allowed Wharton to sell larger (1/6th plate) cases for the small 1/9th plate photographic portraits which were the standard in the early days.

There were also aesthetic considerations – the larger case set the image in a larger space, accentuating its visual qualities as well as giving it an increased perceived value and, with the ornament afforded by the chased matte itself, creating an altogether more luxurious product.

Most Wharton cases are top-hinged, rather than the usual side-hinged variety which opened like a book. Top-hinged cases are frequently found housing miniature paintings, and are rarely found outside the UK. As far as can be ascertained, they were exclusively British made.

Wharton cases are also about 50% deeper than most other designs. It can also be argued that the smaller recessed pan of the Wharton preserver permitted a larger proportion of the daguerreotype plate to be used for photography – or a larger proportion of the portrait to be viewed. If photographic plate and matte are the same size, quite a lot of the image is hidden from view behind the metal frame.

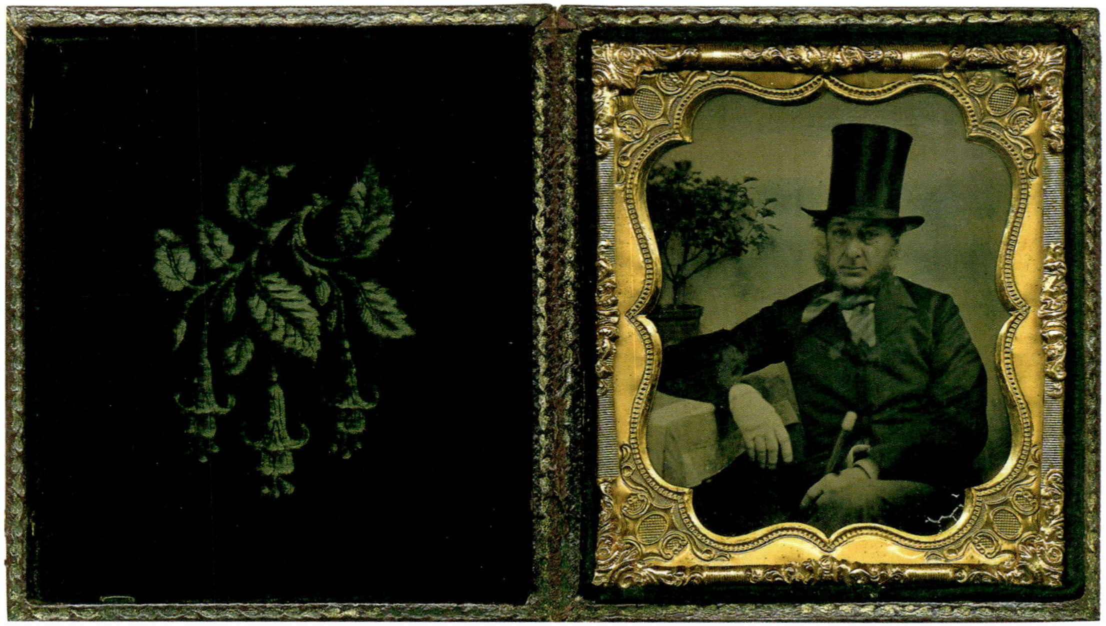

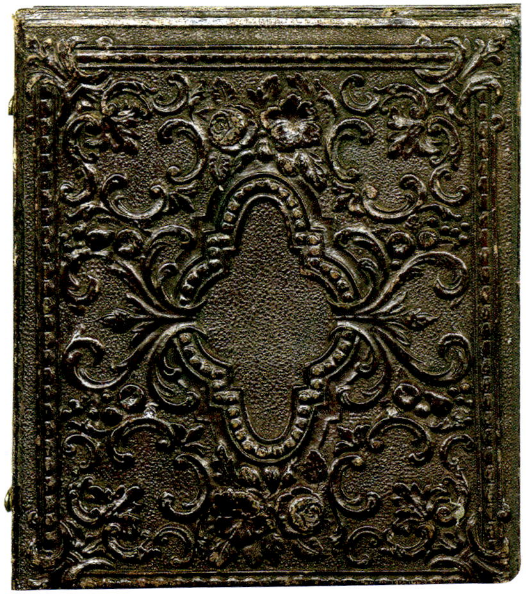

Ambrotype by F. Reynolds Photographic Gallery, Leamington, in embossed paper case, late 1850s.

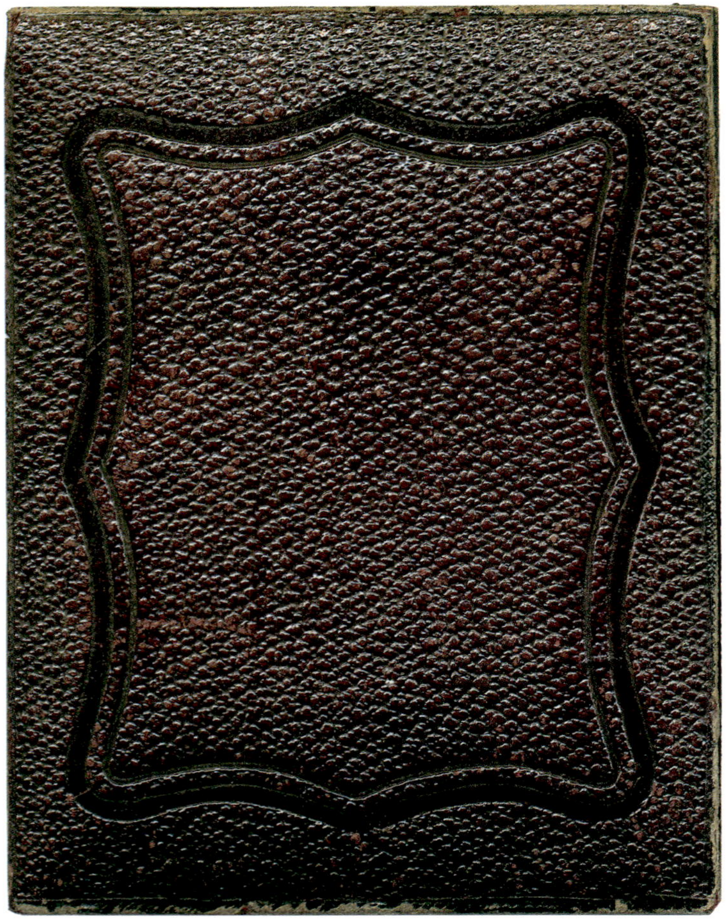
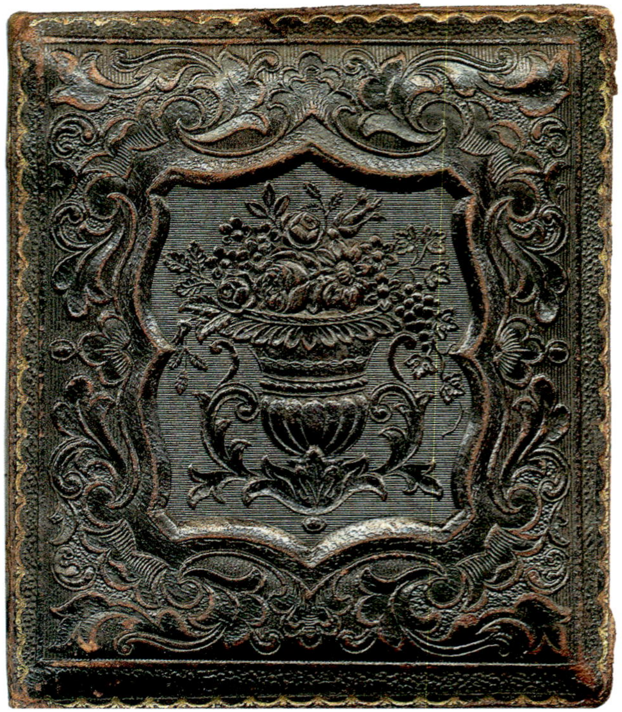

Above left: A typical quarter plate case from the late 1840s, made of high quality leathers, embossed with a simple pattern. The case is of simple construction, each half being made up of five sections, four framing bars and a single sheet of wood for each face.
Above right: A sixth plate case from the mid 1850s, also made of leather, this time embossed with an elaborate motif of an urn of flowers. The construction of this case is of the more typical seven-piece construction, with cross-grained strengthening pieces in the face to prevent warping. Both cases are illustrated here at actual size, 94mm x 120mm for the quarter plate, 80mm x 93mm for the sixth plate.

The deeper case design is, perhaps, a by-product of its construction method, and as will be seen, much slimmer cases later became the norm.

Wharton mattes and preservers are usually embossed – the preserver with an oval containing Wharton's name and the number and date of his English registration date (No. 791 24th August 1854). He never patented the idea, merely registered the design. The mattes are frequently also embossed with the legend 'Beard Patentee'.

That latter fact does not imply that Wharton himself was a Beard Patentee – the patentee in Birmingham was Beard himself – but probably suggests that Beard insisted on his patent interests in the daguerreotype itself being recognised by all his licensees. As, with the exception of Claudet, all Wharton's initial customers were Beard Patentees – or ought to have been – Beard would thus be ensuring that his name assumed prominence at all times.

Indeed even Beard himself used cases with 'Beard Patentee' labels affixed to the inside of the base, suggesting that he had effective control over the photographic cases produced by casemakers at the time.

The actual construction method employed for the cases themselves went through several phases before the common case of the late 1850s and the 1860s evolved.

Considering that the portrait case was not a novelty when photography arrived, the fact that many of the early cases were of a fundamentally unsound design is difficult to understand or explain. Once an early example and a late example of daguerreotype cases are stripped of their outer coverings, the differences in construction can easily be seen.

The problem was the case material itself. The softwoods used for miniature cases are dimensionally unstable materials, and if they are to be constructed into robust products, the nature of the construction itself has to take into account the natural characteristics of the wood. Where hardwoods were used, the case construction was flawless, and robust.

The earliest cases consisted of five pieces of wood for each half of the case – the four outer framing bars, and a sheet of thin wood for the face of the case itself. This is an inherently flawed design, as dampness – such as that likely to be encountered during a case's life in a Victorian house – could tend to induce a degree of warping, with the case curving outwards from the edges at right angles to the running grain of the facing timber. Viewed in antique shops and many private collections, a high proportion – but not all – of early cases exhibit this problem, which manifests itself most clearly in the cases failing to close properly.

A notable exception to this is the design of the Wharton deep case. In the course of the research for this book, not a single instance of a warped Wharton case has been encountered. It is perhaps the additional strength and rigidity afforded by the taller – and therefore stronger – side members which keeps the case perfectly shaped.

The John Plumbe cases illustrated in this book are also of relatively sound construction. By their age, they too should be of five-piece construction, but so far none has yet been found in poor enough condition to be suitable for dismantling, so the actual construction method cannot be ascertained. Their slim profile should have left them prone to warping.

However, the seriously warped cases which have been dismantled – and there have been many during the course of the research for this project – have without exception been found to be of five-piece construction. On the other hand, cases of seven-piece construction, and later origin, are dimensionally more sound.

As can be seen from the accompanying illustrations, the faces of later cases are constructed to resist movement of any sort due to the instability of the wood itself. Each half of the case is constructed from seven pieces of wood rather than five. The central panel has vertically running grain, while the upper and lower panels have their grain running at ninety degrees to the central one. Once glued and assembled, this

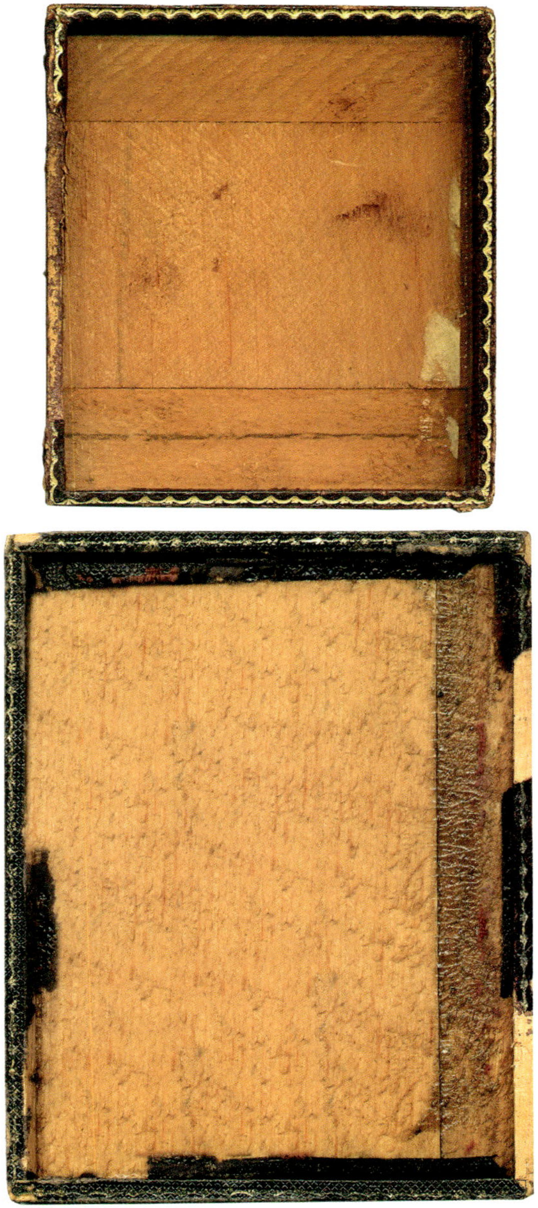

Above: The interiors of the two cases illustrated above, with the interior paper covering removed to show the construction differences between the two designs.

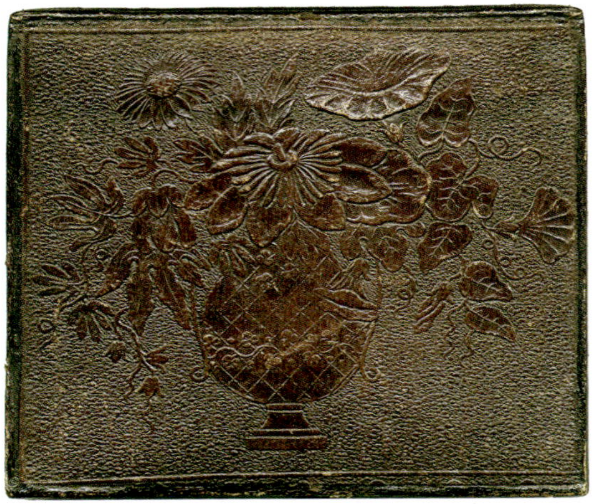

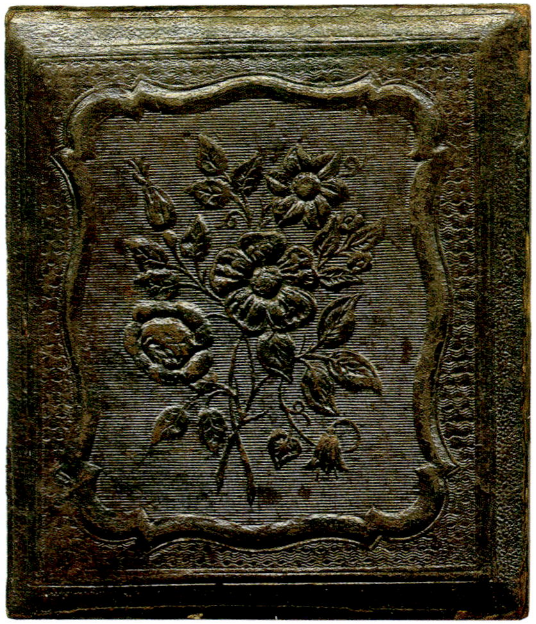

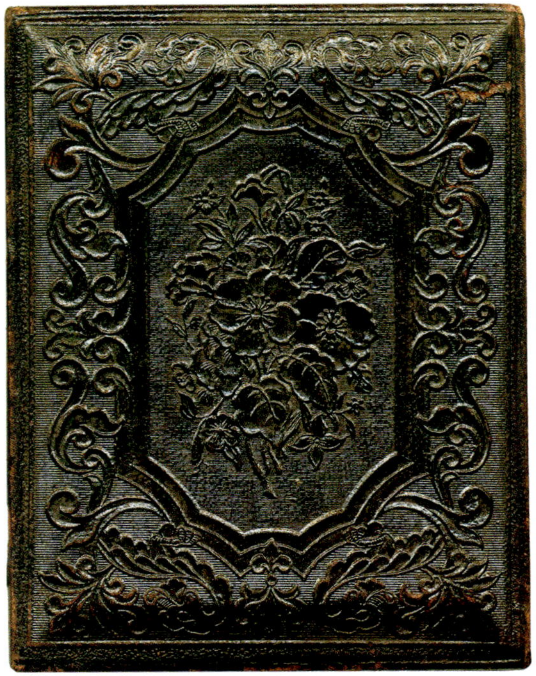

seven-piece construction is both stable and very strong indeed. Where even that construction has proved to be weak is when the jointing has failed, and the upper and lower face woods have curved away from the central panel – on occasions tearing the leather or paper outer coverings.

The insides of the cases vary considerably. Early cases were available with either silk covered pads on the left face, or velvet ones. Both the silk and velvet options were available in a variety of colours – with cream or pink by far the most common amongst surviving silk examples, and red, green and purple apparently the most common in velvet – if it can be assumed that the survivors are representative of the styles and colours which were originally available.

On the outside, leather was the common covering material in the early days – with individual casemakers having their own preferred way of applying it, from the ambitious who prided themselves in using one single piece of leather, to the more realistic who realised that anything up to ten pieces could complete the job much more quickly!

Many early leather covered cases are completely unadorned – as might be expected at the beginning of a mass industry when only high quality materials are being used.

The notable exception to this was John Plumbe, whose early case designs ranged from simple plain leathers to elaborately embossed ones in the first half of the 1840s. Researches carried out by the Rinharts for their 1969 book *American Miniature Case Art* [4] led them to believe that the fine and delicate *Urn and Flowers* case was designed by Plumbe and produced by or for him as early as 1841. This is remarkably early, and adds strength to the argument that case makers in Britain and America had, in many instances, years of experience in manufacture and decoration before the photographic era dawned. Thirty-five years later, the Rinharts' claim has not been seriously disputed.

What is unusual about the date for the 'Urn' design is that other similarly ornamented cases did not become common until *c*.1850.

The plain case was the work of a craftsman – reference has already been made to casemakers priding themselves in being able to cover a case with a single piece of leather. Embossing, gilding and other forms of decoration achieved several things apart from ornament – the relief effect concealed imperfections in poorer quality leathers, and gilding helped camouflage joins in the covers. To ornament a good quality hide was certainly unusual, and yet the condition of the Plumbe case illustrated here certainly suggests that they were made of the highest quality materials.

Mechanisms for opening and closing the cases also varied considerably from maker to maker. While many cases have a simple strip of leather (and later paper or linen) as a hinge, others used a variety of metal hinges. Full length piano hinges were quite frequently used – especially for larger high quality cases – as were small brass hinges pinned and glued into the edges of the case's wooden framing bars.[5] Piano hinges are more common on larger cases from high quality studios, and on cases designed for two daguerreotypes. The greater weight the hinge had to bear – and its tendency to be pulled out of its softwood spine – influenced such decisions, rather than simple considerations of cost!

Closures came in a variety of styles and forms as well. From a single clasp to hold the smaller cases shut – with two on larger varieties – held in place by small metal pins, to recessed snap closures in a variety of styles and sizes, manufacturers were able to offer a considerable range of options to their customers.

Eichmeyer[6] and imitation Eichmeyer cases used a single, often ornate, metal clasp which was pinned in place on both faces of the case, and which folded across the profile of the closed case.

Other cases used a leather-covered flap which folded across the front face and was held in place in a raised brass slot.

The leather used on cases was traditionally red morocco, but by the early 1850s this had been extended to include a range of shades of reds and browns. Deep green, black, blue and even beige leathers were making significant inroads into the market by the mid 1850s, and in both Britain and America even velvet covered cases were popular. Their poorer resistance to wear gave them a shorter life, however, and few good examples survive today. Some highly attractive oval cases, covered in blue, purple and red velvets survive, often containing paper carte-de-visite prints.

Gilt ornamentation on the upper face of leather cases also became widely available in the 1850s, again presumably at a premium price.

As the demand grew, and the range of styles expanded, there was also a market developing for cheaper products. Price considerations were controlled to an extent by the unit cost of the photograph itself.

While the high unit cost of the daguerreotype prevailed, there was little resistance by the small consumer market to the high cost of quality cases. However as the collodion positive or ambrotype,

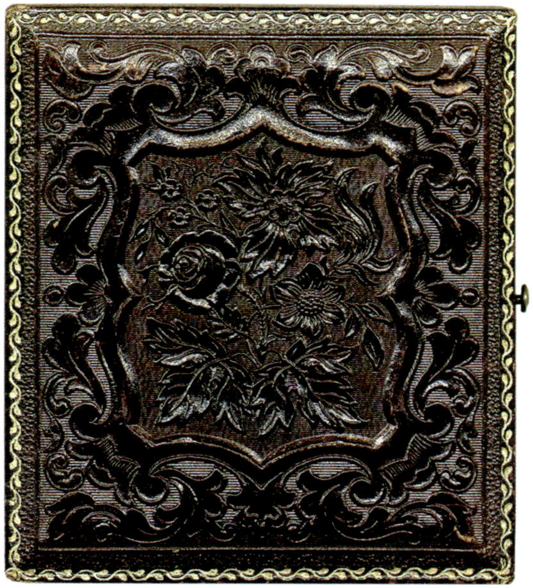

The interpretation of motifs was influenced by the case design itself and by available technology. The 'Urn' case by John Plumbe Jnr (opposite page, top) dates from the early 1840s, the sixth plate case (opposite left, from c.1847, and the quarter plate (opposite right) from c.1855. Each face of the sixth plate case is of five-piece construction, and covered in high quality leather. The quarter plate case is of seven-piece design, lower quality leather and much heavier embossing.

The highest relief decoration on this sixth plate case (left) dates from the late 1850s. It uses a very heavily embossed leather, a push button closure, and applied gilding to the edges. It contains the fine ambrotype of two small girls, below, and is probably American.

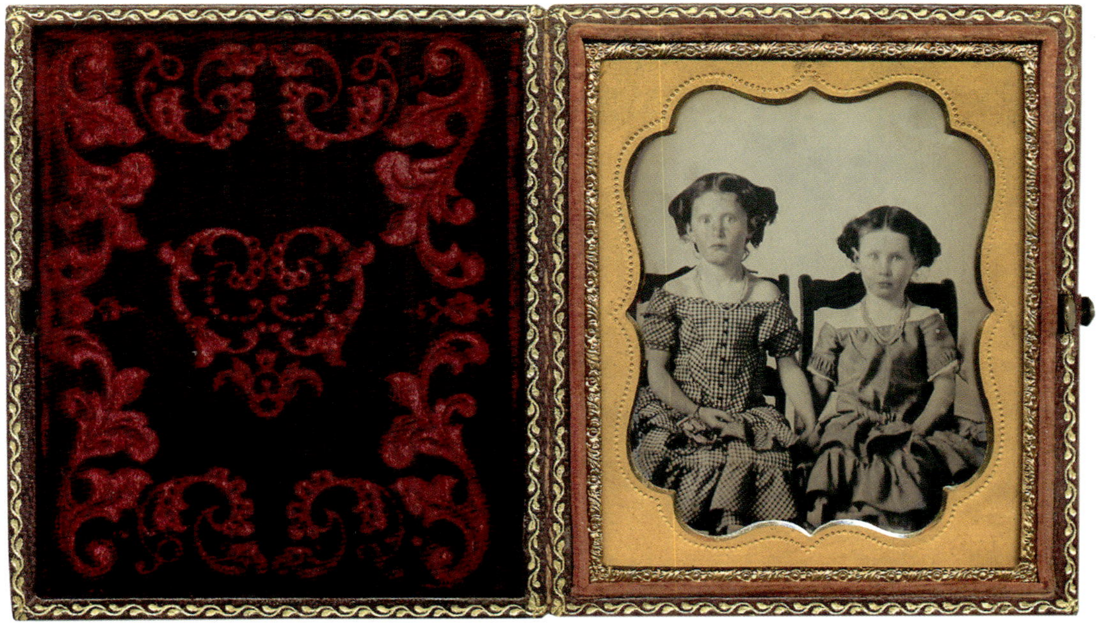

Sixth plate case covered with thin embossed leather. The case has narrow reinforcing panels top and bottom, according to the construction method advocated by Anthony. Due to the partial failure of the glued tongue and groove joints, the case is warping at one side, causing damage to the covering.

and later the tintype, expanded the market and reduced unit costs, a less affluent stratum of society began to buy photography.

Some savings in case costs were achieved by offering 1st and 2nd grade leathers – only really close inspection would have revealed the difference.

Cases with flexible leather hinges were cheaper to manufacture than metal-hinged one, and these soon became the norm. Metal hinges required better woods for the frames – denser woods being required to retain the locating pins for the hinges. With leather hinges, lighter and softer wood could be used without the risk of pins splitting the framing bars. These were more easily and more quickly worked, further reducing the production costs.

In their 1854 catalogue, E. Anthony of New York gave a detailed description of the casemaking process, and also offered a rationale for their operation.

'I propose to describe somewhat in detail the different processes of their manufacture; promising that it is only by the sub-division of labor and the manufacture in large quantities and by labor saving machinery that they can be produced at a price which enables the public to procure pictures of a certain class at the present low prices.[7]'

In other words, the first application of mass production methods in photography was in case production. That the market could demand such an approach by the early 1850s clearly defines the scale of the photographic portraiture business in America and the United Kingdom. Britain was an essential part of Anthony's market place, with their products imported direct to British photographic studios by mail order!

The move to softer woods for the framing bars may coincide with a change in the structure of the three-piece construction of the case face. The earliest three-piece faces use a large central panel with smaller upper and lower panels, sometimes mounted on a harder wood frame. Stable cases with softer woods required a smaller central panel with proportionately larger top and bottom sections if rigidity was going to be achieved.

It can perhaps be safely assumed that in the earlier cases utilising a three-piece face, the stability of the case itself owes more to a combination of face strength and strength of the framing bars than just to the three-piece face construction itself. As casemakers moved to softwood with lighter and slimmer framing bars, the face had to be completely stable, as the bars could not be relied on to offer much assistance in that matter.

Most surviving cases are of pitch-pine construction – a wood hardly renowned for its strength or stability, certainly in such light section. In order to achieve any great strength in the finished case considerable attention had to be paid to the gluing of the case itself.

Early cases had mitred joints for the four framing bars with the glue joints at the mitres and between bars and face adding considerably to the strength. However as the wood moved and curled, such simple joints just pulled apart, destroying the shape of the case completely. To overcome this some manufacturers used mortise and tenon joints, and some even tried a simple dovetail – no mean feat with such slender strips of wood.

The combination of the three-piece face and a mortised joint proved to be the best in strength terms, while also being relatively inexpensive in manufacture.

By the mid 1850s it had been almost universally adopted. Additional strength was achieved by overlapping the three pieces of the case faces – creating a greater gluing area.

Making the cases up from ten pieces of wood and a great deal of glue required both accuracy and speed – no easy combination when the strength of the finished product depended on how carefully the assembly was carried out. And why ten pieces of wood when each face apparently has seven components? The clue is contained within a lively and enlightening text describing Anthony's manufacturing processes.

'The revolution of the pullies, the rapid motion of the belting which every four feet extends from

the ceiling to the floor, the brisk motions of the boys, the flying of the nascent 'woods' from the saw or lathes to the box in which it is conveyed to the next operation in its course of 'development' the flashes of sawdust evolved in the process of 'grinding', the 'crirr' of the saws, and the hissing of the sand paper which present to the beholder a busy sound. The operations going on are at first sight inexplicable. He is shown at the same time a finished 'wood', smooth even, top and bottom fitting each other to the smallest fraction of a hair, and a pile of rough 'frames' and 'tops', and fails to perceive the remotest connection between the two; and the mystery is still further enhanced by showing him a wood which has passed through every operation but the last. He sees nothing but what appears to him a solid block of pine wood...[8]

'Anthony then goes on to explain that amongst the many things which need to be explained to his visitor is *...finally why you take the trouble to make an article that looks like a solid block of wood, and then deliberately saw it into two pieces. You assure him that the box with the nicely fitting top and bottom were at one time just such another solid block... an inspection of these two pieces however, shows him that what he took to be solid was in fact hollow...*'

In other words, the perfect fit was only achievable because the framing bars which held each face of the case together were in fact made as one frame and sawn into two unequal halves – the slightly higher half making the base of the case, the slimmer one the lid.

Anthony's description of the manufacture of the 'woods' concluded with the comment that '*...between the cutting of the lumber into strips of proper widths and the finishing of the woods, it passes through at least twenty different manipulations.*'

The ambitious casemakers in the 1850s introduced oval and circular cases, with framing bars curved and shaped under steam and pressure, and covered them with leather or velvet.

The complexity of the task of covering the case was, from a practical standpoint, dependent upon the covering being used. If a plain leather was being used – in sections – covering was a relatively straightforward if somewhat delicate task.

For an embossed leather, the embossed faces were made separately – using the very highest grades of leather – and fixed into place with very thin strips of colour-matched hides.

While the early John Plumbe cases stand out as being markedly different from the other designs then currently available, by the mid 1850s, a wide range of embossed designs was available. Many of these were made in the United States and imported into Britain by a small number of entrepreneurs, but locally-made products were also available.

The range of designs available in America was always greater than in Britain – reflecting both the relative sizes of the markets, and the American preference for patriotic designs for their cases. The number of American cases depicting designs based on the Stars and Stripes, or the American Eagle is considerable.

Angels, fairies, dancers, lyres, cupid, castles, Jenny Lind 'the Swedish nightingale', Daguerre himself, beehives, and a wide range of birds and animals have all been embossed on to cases, establishing a set of themes which would later be extended and refined in moulded materials.

Few casemakers made their own tops, with most subcontracting out this aspect of the work to specialist die-makers and stampers. Edward Anthony, however, completed the entire manufacturing process in-house. He underlined his view that this was not skilled work by announcing that *...the work here, which is very simple, is done mostly by boys and girls.* The tops were made slightly larger than the case to be covered and were fixed into place using glue and a controlled amount of pressure. Once in place, they were trimmed to size and then bound into place with the thin edging strips. The edging strip was then bound round the edges of the case itself and secured inside on the inner face of the case. It is a testament to the skill of the workers – mainly women – who applied the covers, that the joint

Quarter plate embossed paper and leather covered case, late 1840s. The face is of single sheet construction and due to narrow framing bars, there is substantial warping.

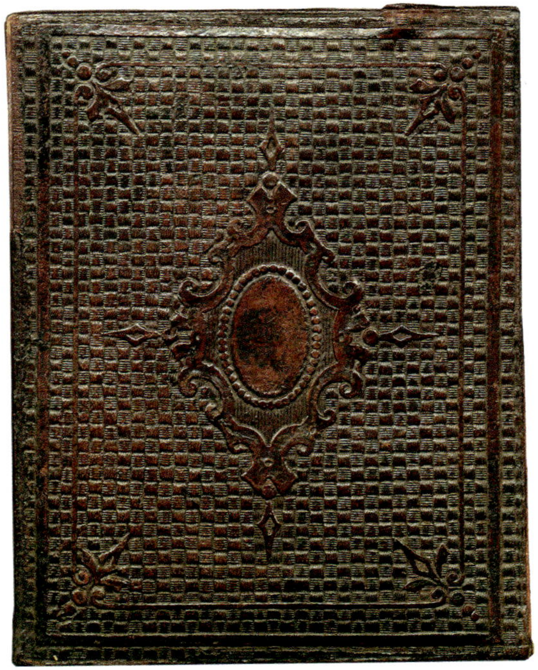

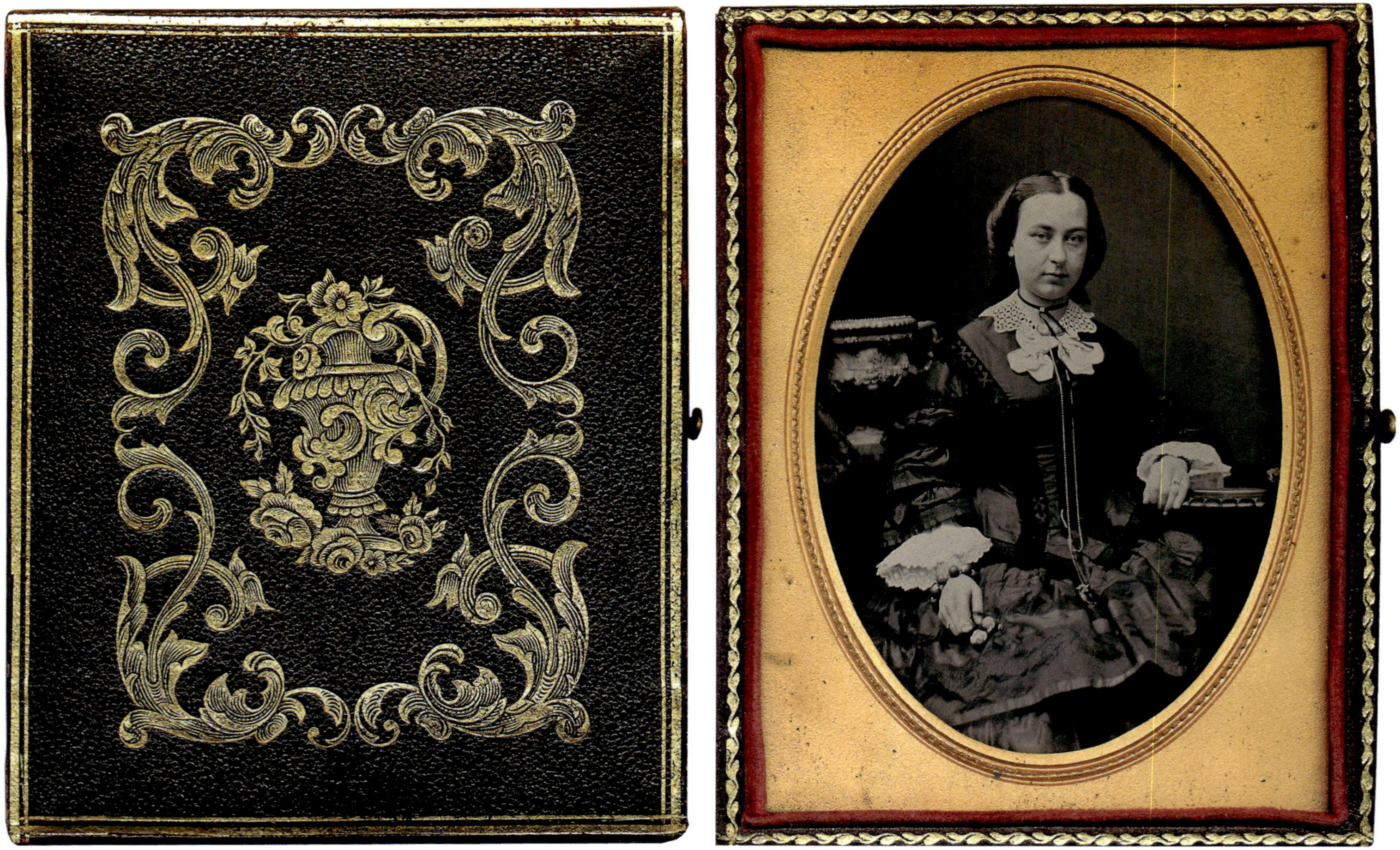

Gilded quarter plate case from the early 1850s, made of high quality leathers, embossed and gilded with an ornate scroll and urn pattern. The case is of typical 1850s construction, each half being made up of seven sections, four framing bars and three pieces of tongue and grooved wood for each face. The portrait is of an elegant lady from Southport in Lancashire, photographer unknown. It is a remarkable frustration of collecting that magnificent images and fine cases such as this have no attribution to either photographer or maker. Case shown actual size.

between embossed top and edging strip is only rarely visible. The edging strip was omitted from the edge which would become part of the hinged side of the case and here two strips of leather – one inside and one outside – were glued in place, touching in the centre to form the hinge itself. Using very thin leathers, the case could be opened almost flat, while closing cleanly and without any perceptible gap between the faces of the closed case.

The last stage was the application of any gilded decoration. According to Anthony's description '*...the gilding is performed in the usual way by means of heated rollers. The work in the covering shop is also sub-divided – each hand having a particular portion of the work to do.*[9]'

This dependence on unskilled workers carrying out repetitive tasks was being refined in Anthony's New York factory almost half a century before Henry Ford applied his novel production line techniques to making cars!

With the ambrotype and tintype offering a much cheaper alternative to the daguerreotype, a case even cheaper than the cheapest wood-framed version was sought. That demand was met by moulded papiér mâché cases – sometimes with moulded paper tops being attached to traditional wooden frames, but more often with the complete case moulded out of compressed paper. A pigment in the mixture did away with the need for a covering material, and a simple linen tape strip, applied before the case dried and hardened, produced a strong and reliable hinge. Such cases were in widespread use by the mid 1850s, and hardly surprisingly, none so far identified has carried the name of the photographer who used it to present his work.

The introduction of paper and papiér mâché cases required a change in manufacturing techniques – but also brought about a separation of the market into two quite separate categories. Moulded papiér mâché as a basis for case design and manufacture spawned products at opposite ends of the price range.

At the low end, pulped paper, mixed with a glue

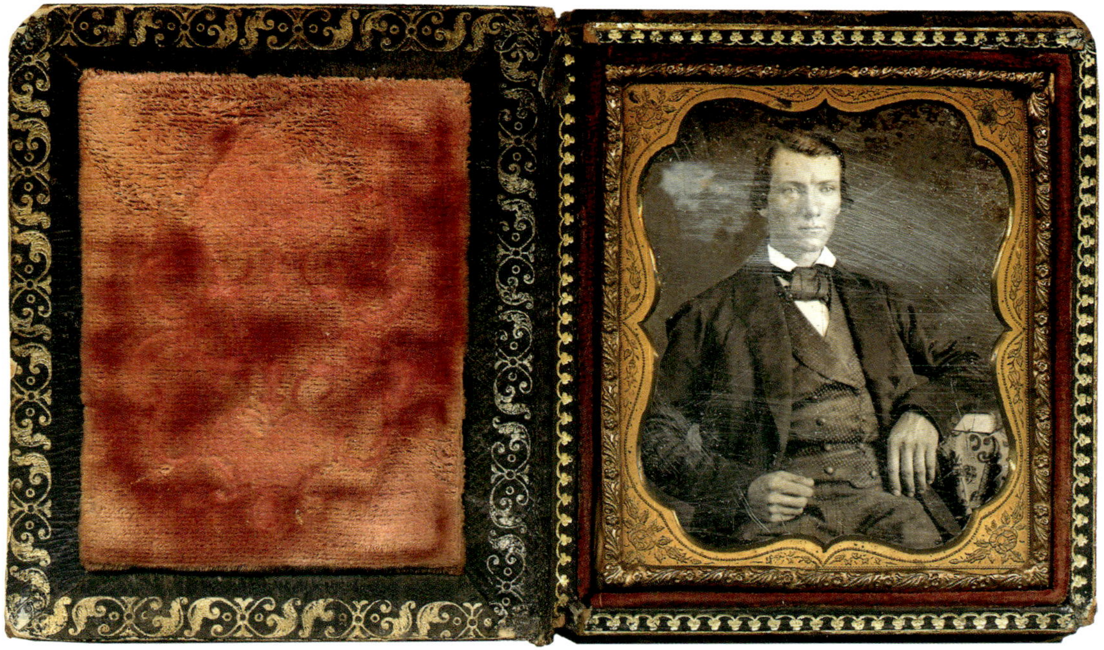

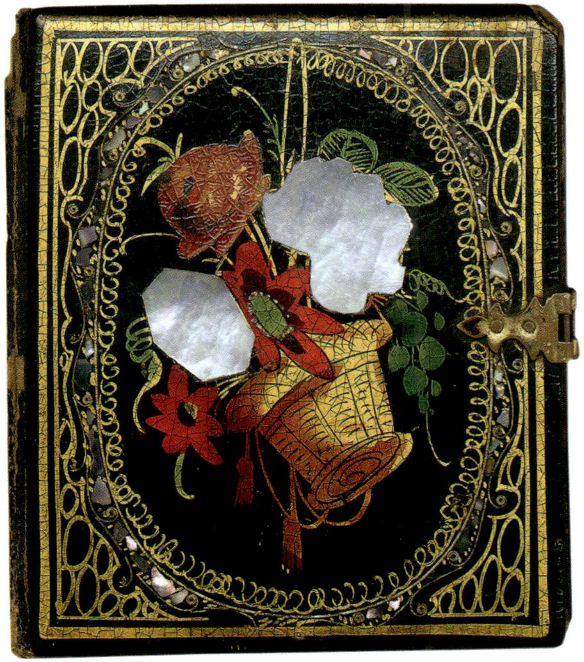

Sixth plate daguerreotype in lacquered and gilded case with inlaid mother-of-pearl. Cases like this enjoyed considerable popularity in the 1850s. Each one was hand-crafted and decorated, making this an expensive option for the packaging of that special portrait. When newly made, flower petals would have been painted over the mother-of-pearl creating flowers with a luminescent quality. Photographer unknown, case-maker unknown, early 1850s. The lid of the case is laminated paper with no framing bars, with the pink velvet pad sitting proud of the surface. The bottom of the case is undecorated japanned papier mâché. An ornate clasp is pinned through the front and rear surfaces, and closed with a chased metal strap. Of all the lacquered and painted case designs, the basket of flowers, in many variants, is the most common. The daguerreotype is showing the effects of several years withour a cover glass, having accumulated extensive abrasion to the delicate silvered surface.

Leather-covered cases sported a range of pictorial and scenic designs as well as the more common geometric and scroll motifs.
Below: The quarter plate design 'Fairy Emerging from a Rose' dates from the early 1850s. A version of this same design was marketed as a ninth plate thermoplastic case a few years later.
Right: A rare sixth plate case incorporating a portrait of the 'Swedish Nightingale', Jenny Lind, dates from the mid 1850s. Two sixth plate and one quarter plate versions of this case are known to have been produced.
Below right: Also from the mid 1850s, 'Love Birds' is another motif which was later offered in moulded thermoplastic.

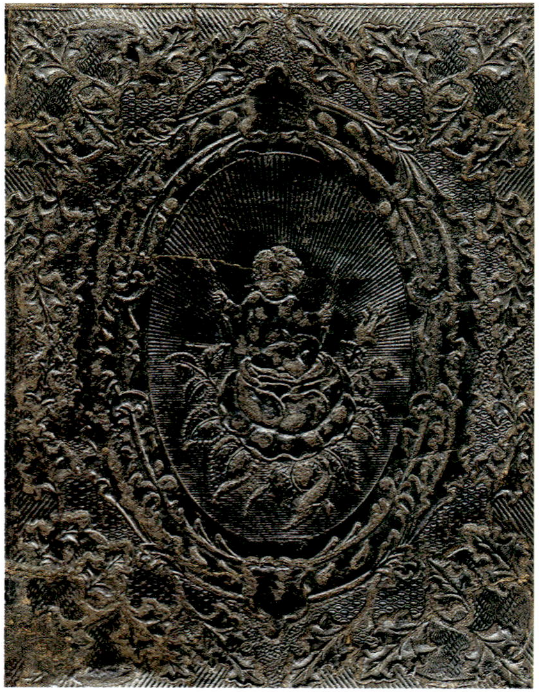

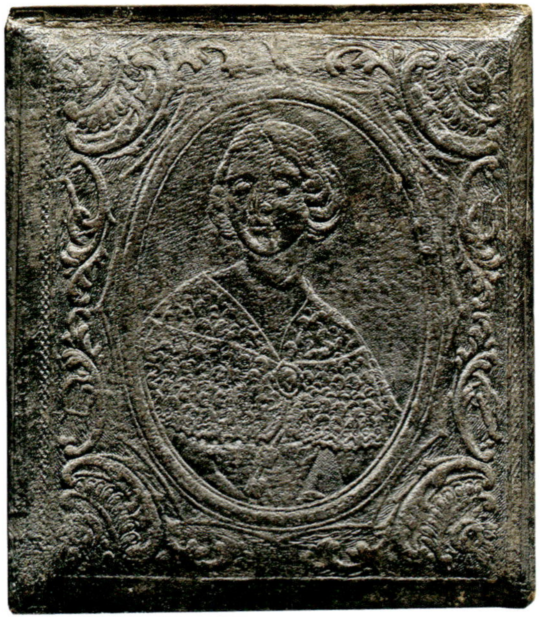

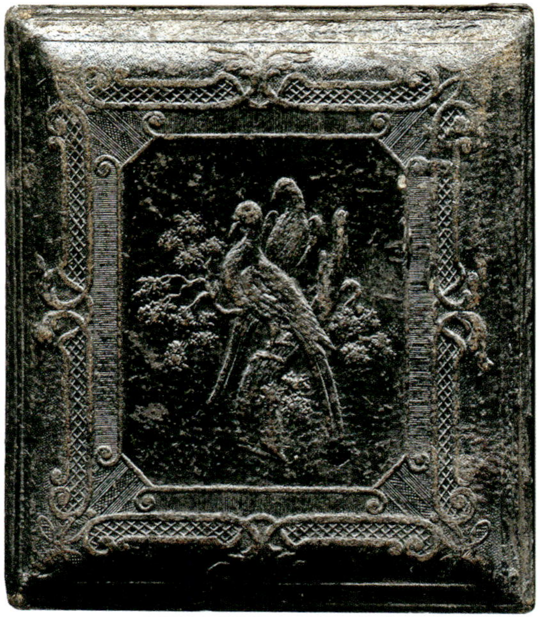

or a resin was simply stamped or moulded into shape using steam presses and simple geometric patterned dies. The majority of cases made in such a manner which have been inspected in the course of this work have been of ninth plate size and have two quite significant characteristics. Firstly they are strong and stable, and secondly the quality of the moulding often equals that of the much more expensive thermoplastic union case which is considered later in this book.

Such pressed pulp cases started to appear in the early to mid 1850s, and brought with them the innovation of a strong woven fabric hinge, adding a significant increase in strength into what had notoriously been the 'achilles heel' of cases ever since the metal hinge was abandoned.

These cases brought considerable reduction in prices at the bottom end of the market, coupled both with an increase in variety and speed of production. At the top 'designer' end of the market, however, a considerable range of individually decorated cardboard and papiér mâché cases introduced the concept of the one-off case – where a hand-painted cover gave the case the same unique quality to the case as the image it housed.

Scenes of castles, churches, landscapes and a host of others have all been found painted on to lacquered case fronts alongside, more commonly, floral designs which incorporated mother-of-pearl, silver filigree and brightly painted foliage. The use of a thin piece of mother-of-pearl as the basis of a flower – on to which petals were painted – was widespread.

The manufacture of such cases was complex. The paper pulp itself was mixed with glue and albumen and after being pressed in moulds, was covered with a number of sheets of paper to create a smooth surface. The mother-of-pearl itself was sliced into very thin sheets – sometimes highly coloured, other times white, and pressed into the paper covering while that was still soft. It was then glued into position to create a nearly-smooth top surface. A first coat of japanned lacquer was applied and then the boards were oven-dried before being buffed smooth with pumice powder – a material which had been used in photography since the introduction of the daguerreotype.

Once dried the case was painted and lacquered again – with several coats being applied until the surface was entirely smooth. A final application of gold leaf decoration completed the process.

For more elaborate designs, inlaid silver filigree was also available. Cases were also available made entirely out of mother-of-pearl, while tortoiseshell was also used. All in all, a hugely labour-intensive and time-consuming process, in stark contrast to the simplicity of manufacture at the other end of the market where keeping costs to an absolute minium was paramount.

It was not just in the methods of construction that costs were pared. Early brass mattes were made out of robust metal sheets, with finely cut edges, and bevelled where the matte met the image. The earliest examples are very plain, and have apertures which are rectangular, oval, or arch-topped. By the 1840s, American manufacturers had introduced a range of designs with ornate scalloped edges, again made out of the highest quality of materials.

It was into the flat face of the matte that photographers had their names and addresses engraved or stamped – although some examples of hand-inscribed attribution have also been found.

These early mattes were sandwiched between the image plate and the cover glass, and the package sealed with paper strips glued both to the edge of the glass and the back of the image plate. That airtight seal has protected them well.

Later examples used thinner mattes, sometimes tape-sealed, sometimes without, the whole assembly being further secured with a thin ornate brass frame and four metal flaps which folded behind the image.

A large number of different designs for mattes evolved as the market grew, incorporating geometric, scroll and floral motifs into the matte face. In America, patriotic motifs were also common.

The constant downward pressure on prices

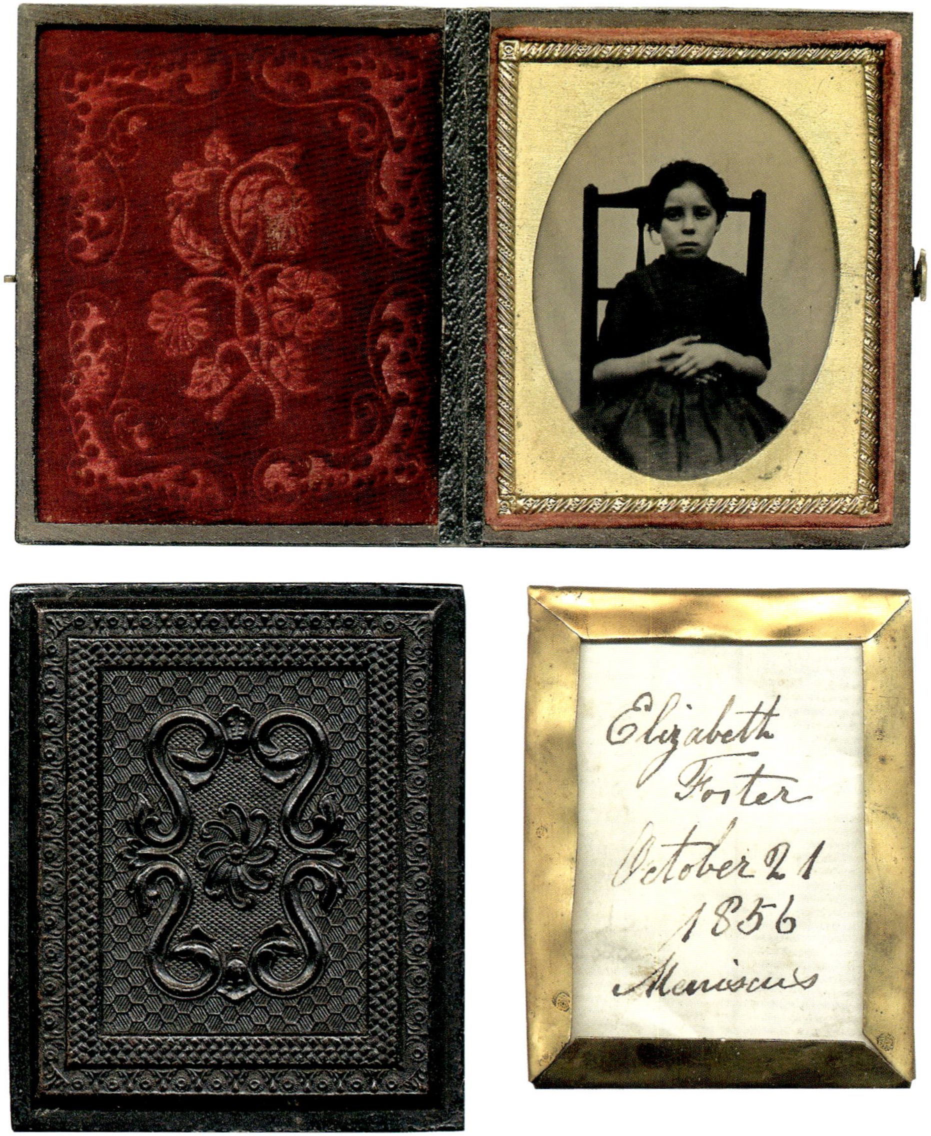

Ninth plate moulded papier mâché case from the mid 1850s, containing an ambrotype identified as 'Elizabeth Foster, October 21 1856, Meniscus'. Unusually no information on the photographer is available, yet we know what lens he used!

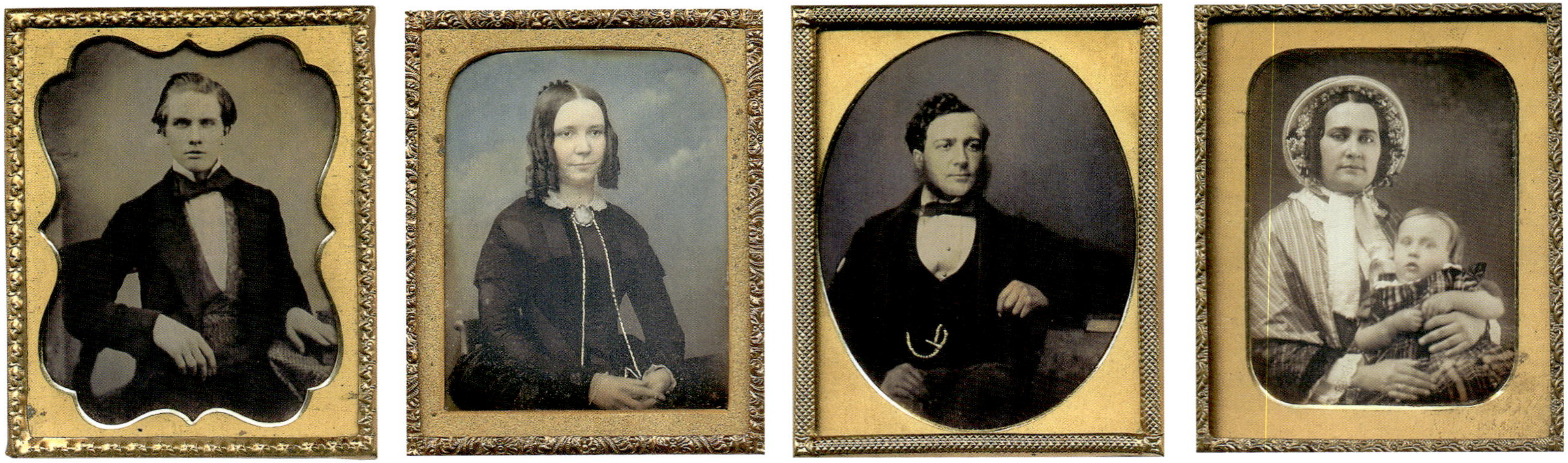

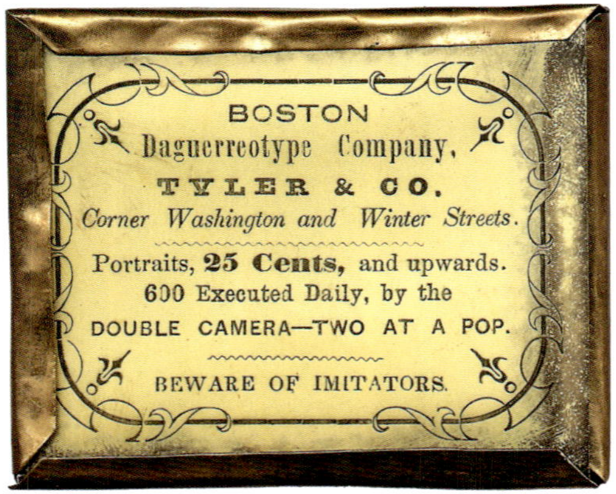

Above: Left to right, are the four most popular ninth plate matte designs according to Anthony's 1854 catalogue. They are the 'nonpareil', the 'eliptic', the 'oval' and the 'double eliptic'. In Britain, the eliptic was known as the 'dome' and the double eliptic as the 'cushion'. Three of the examples are British – the blue backed portrait being by Ross & Thomson of Edinburgh. The mother and child in the 'double eliptic' matte is by Tyler & Co, of Washington and Winter Streets in Boston whose trade card is above.

provoked the introduction of thinner metals, often heavily embossed – with the embossed design serving both to enrich the appearance of the cheaper materials, and add a level of rigidity to the matte itself.

Edward Anthony's catalogue of 1854 announced that *'Mats' and 'preservers' are formed of sheet brass. The 'mats' are known by various terms, as 'common', 'fire-gilt', 'engraved' or 'stamped'; the difference consisting in the value of the metal, or the cost of style of finishing. The work is done by means of powerful presses, driven by steam. The brass, manufactured in rolls of the proper width, is first cut into 'blanks' of perfectly uniform size by means of a punch and die operated in one of these presses. It is next pierced, that is, perforated with an opening of the shape desired, of which there are three styles generall used, viz., the 'oval', the 'fancy nonpareil,' and the 'double elliptic'. They are then straightened and passed to the 'dipping room' where by the action of strong acids the surface of each is made to assume a 'frosted' or 'marked' appearance. As soon as possible after being dipped, the mats are lacquered and dried rapidly on a table of copper heated by steam. They are then finished by having the edge and the opening champered and burnished.*[10]'

One way of dealing with that huge market growth was to reduce the number of different components required for a case – despite the fact that the quest for stability suggested otherwise – and then in the mid 1850s, to begin to automate the processes involved in case manufacture.

Early cases, despite their plainness, were complex units to construct. They were designed to look at home in high quality surroundings, on high quality furniture. Therefore their production quality had to be uncompromising. They were also designed to lie flat – and that is perhaps the major difference between early better quality cases and their poorer later counterparts. The lower half of the case – that which contained the image – was originally constructed with a flat face to lie on a table or mantelpiece, while the upper half was covered with bevelled wood, carefully shaved to give a softer rounded contour. In cases of this design, therefore, only the upper face, if any, was embossed or decorated. The lower face if it was embellished at all would contain only the photographer's blind stamp.

It is interesting to observe that very early cases such as those produced by the Photographic Institution, Salop, *(page 12)*, have the photographer's gilt stamp on the lower flat face, while those produced in the early 1850s by leading photographers such as Kilburn and Mayall, boldly display their gilded logo on the bevelled upper face. Perhaps ten years on, the evidence of wealth demonstrated by the trademark of an expensive studio was worthy of display even in households not normally known for such obvious ostentation.

In the absence of accurate records, there is no way of ascertaining exactly how many different leather, paper or cloth covered case designs were actually available during the 1850s – but it was clearly a considerable number.

The complexity of case manufacture actually made the production of 'bespoke' cases more commercially viable, reconciling the improbable partners of low cost and individual preferences. There were so many individual elements in the case's construction, and so many of them were of 'standard' sizes, that they could readily be interchanged.

There was fairly widespread agreement on the required dimensions of cases for each specific plate size, allowing a degree of interchangeability. Thus the skeleton of a ninth plate case from a particular manufacturer could be fitted out with a range of pre-stamped tops, a range of coloured velvet pads and be covered with materials at whatever quality was required.

As demand for cases grew, many casemakers sub-contracted out the making of embossed or tooled tops, and the embossed velvet pads which lined the interiors.

Just as with the stamps for photographers' names and addresses, the die, once made, could be used countless times. When applying photographers' names, addresses and logotypes, many casemakers charged only for the production of the original stamper die, thereafter offering their customers a free overprinting service for their studio details.

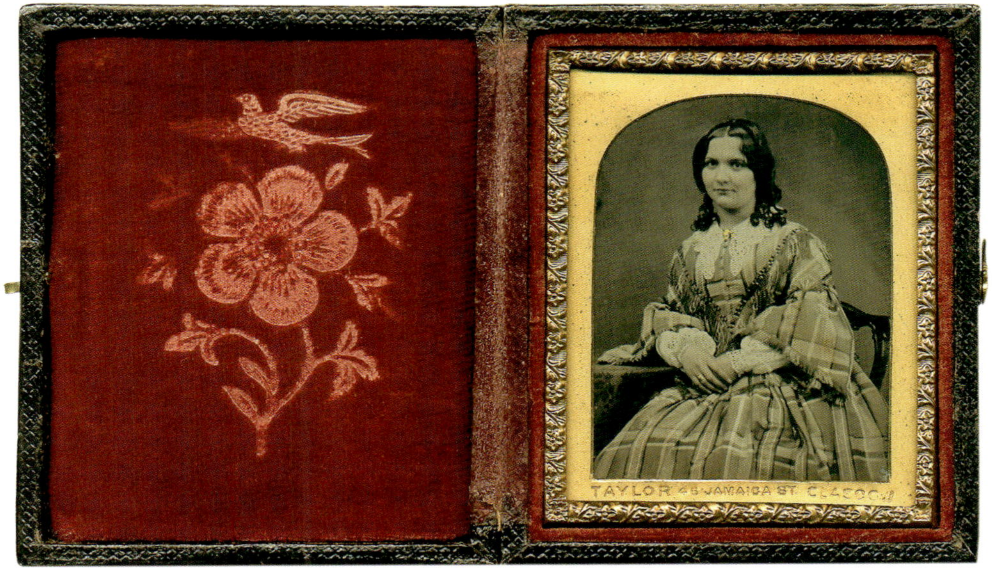

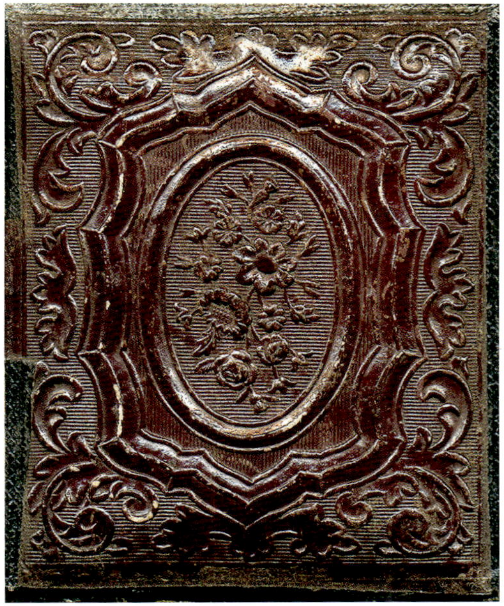

Ninth plate ambrotype by Mrs. Taylor, 46 Jamaica Street, Glasgow, in eliptic matte with photographer's stamped name and address. Mrs. Taylor was at that address from 1861 to 1864. By that time, photographers were generally using thinner and much more elaborate stamped or pressed mattes to frame their ambrotypes, suggesting that Mrs. Taylor either produced a very high quality product, or was using old stock. As the image is in a case with a pressed paper top, left, the latter is the more likely explanation. All the illustrations on these two pages are reproduced at actual size.

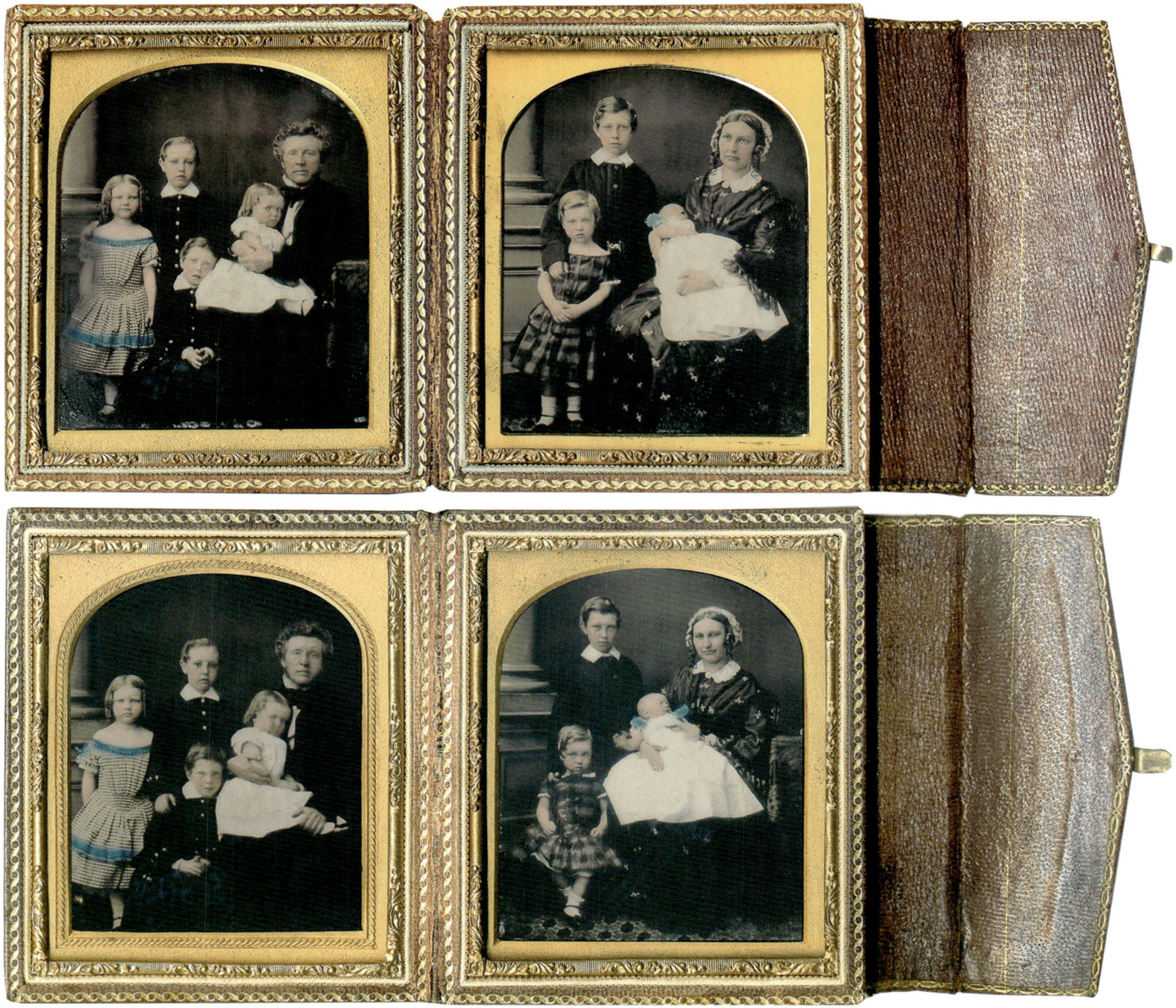

An unusual set of two pairs of ambrotypes, depicting the family of John Patten WS in 1859. Patten was a 'Writer to the Signet', the Scottish equivalent of a barrister. He is seen here with his wife Jane, and their children James, John, Henry, Hugh, Margaret, Mary and Dougald. The images are contained within a pair of leather wallet-style fold-over cases. The double, sixth plate cases each measure 82mm x 93mm closed. These cases were produced in the mid 1850s, and while most were closed with a metal slot and bar on the front, some had tiny locks fitted. They were available with both leather and velvet covers.

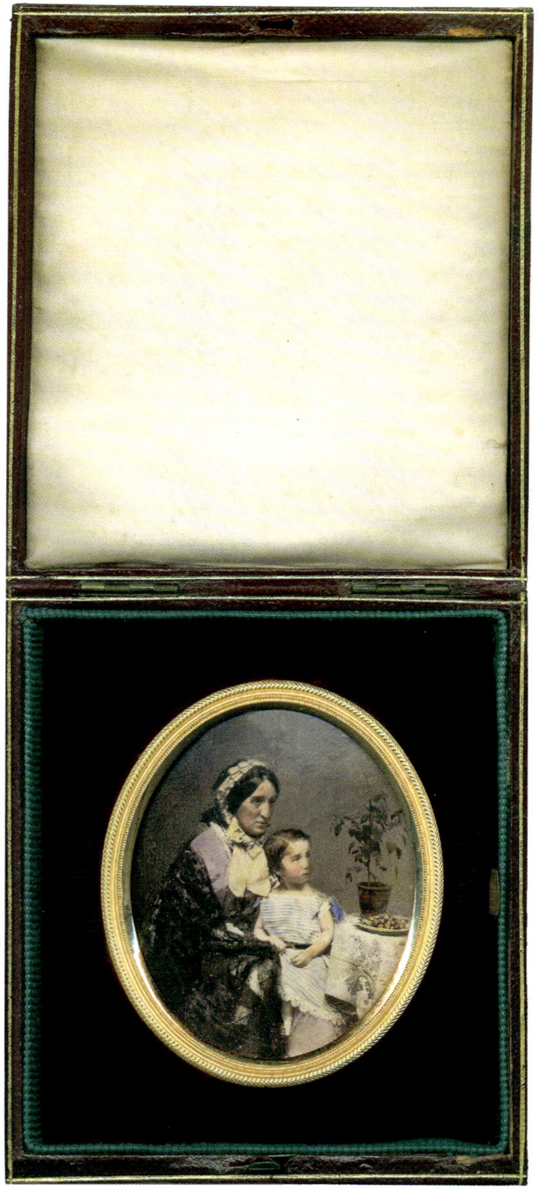

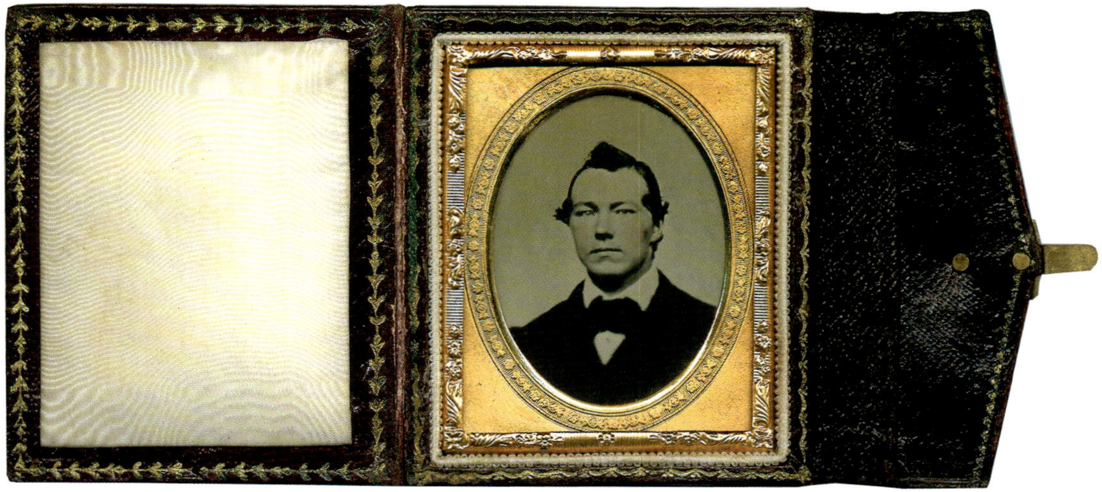

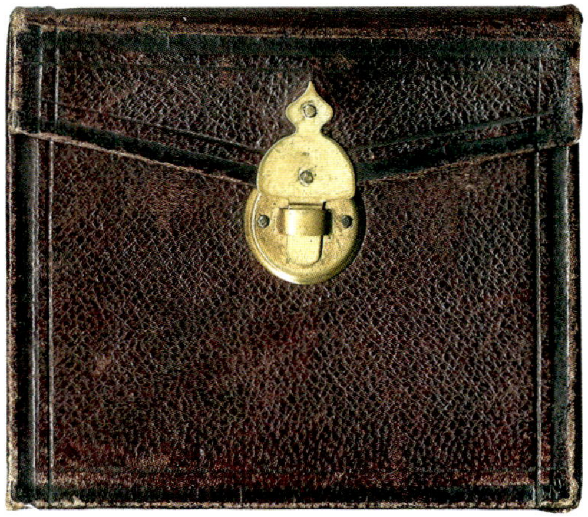

Left: Mother and daughter, photographed by James Mudd, 10 St Ann's Square, Manchester, 1860s. Hand-coloured paper print in silk-lined top-hinged leather case. Image size 60mm x 75mm. Case size 117mm x 122mm. The case uses metal hinges and a push-button closure, and in the tradition of early deep cases, it has a bevelled top and flat base. Photographer's gilt stamp on base. The image is protected by a bevelled glass, set in deep burgundy velvet and trimmed with blue-green tape. Mudd's studio was at this address from 1861 until at least 1899. Earlier, from an address in nearby Cross Street, he had earned a considerable reputation as an industrial photographer, photographing the many steam locomotives designed and built at Beyer-Peacock in Gorton, Manchester.

Above: Ninth plate ambrotype in leather covered wallet-style case with fold-over closure flap and cream silk pad, photographer unknown. Right: case shown closed, late 1850s. Case size 65mm x 76mm.

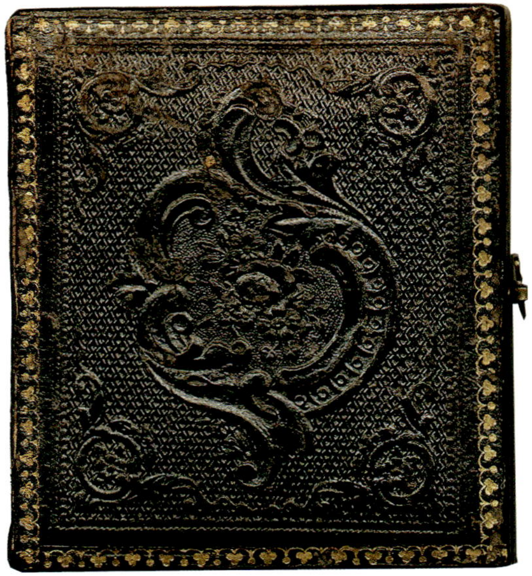

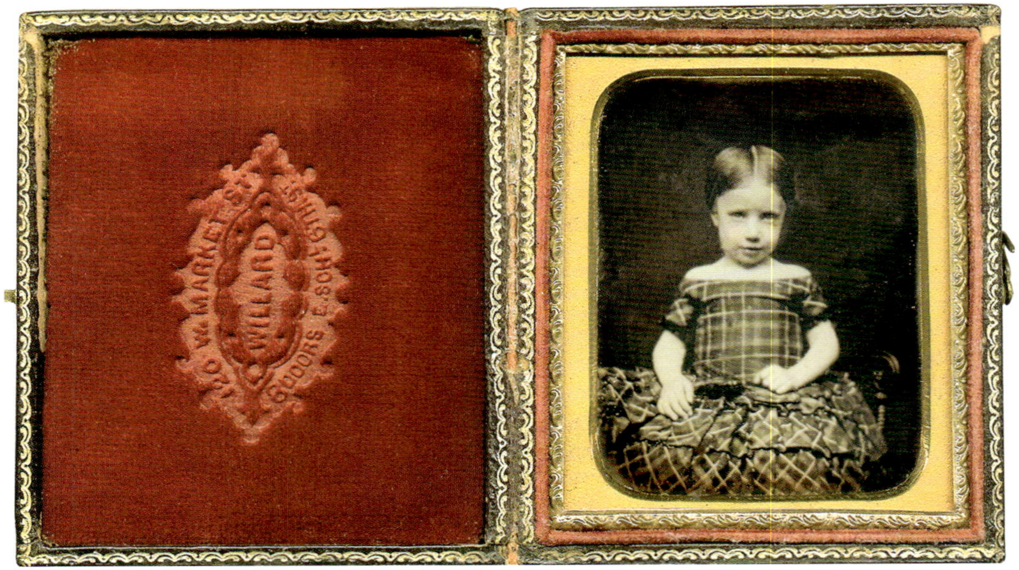

Above: Ninth plate daguerreotype by Willard, 120 W Market Street. 8 doors E Sch^{l} St and 6th St, Philadelphia. In double elliptic matte with photographer's name and address embossed into the red velvet pad. The case is finely embossed leather with gilt decoration.

Right: The same rococco design used on both ninth and sixth plate leather cases.
The sixth plate case, which is fitted with a piano hinge and a button closure, contains a fine British ambrotype of a gentleman by Ross & Thomson and set in a plain elliptic 'dome' matte. The ninth plate case contains an ambrotype of a woman, set in an oval by William Andrews' Photographic Gallery, 29 Westmorland Street, Dublin.

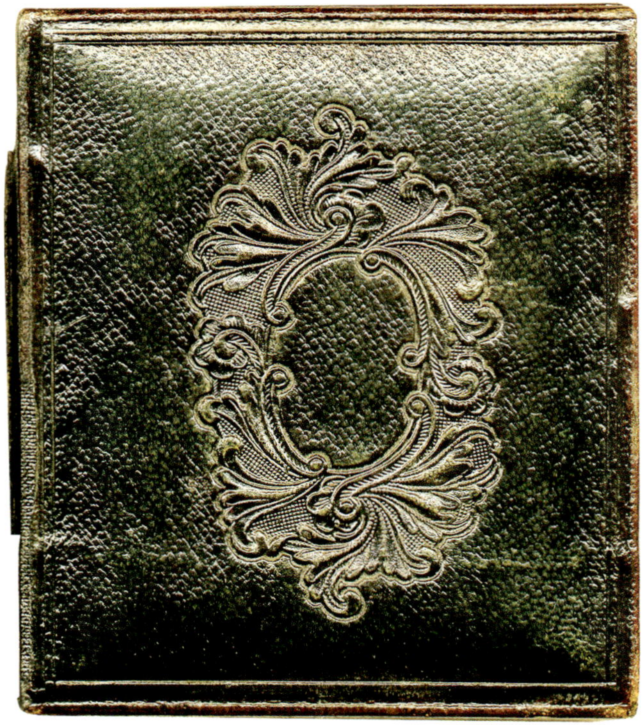

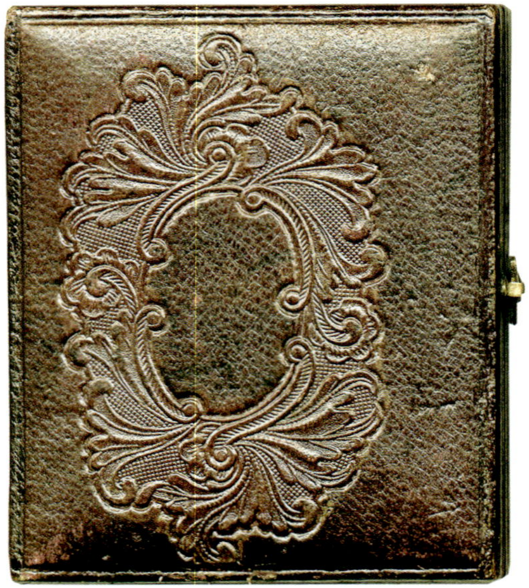

Once dies had been made for the ornate embossed patterns on the face of the cases, often at considerable cost, the makers themselves also preferred to make full use of their investment. Thus we find the same embossed motif appearing on several different case sizes. An interesting rococo design appears, for example, on a ninth plate case from the Photographic Gallery of 29 Westmorland Street, Dublin, and also on a sixth plate case in blue leather containing a fine male portrait by Ross and Thomson of Edinburgh. Interestingly, in the ninth plate example, the motif is embossed off-centre towards the hinge (see opposite).

Amongst the other more unusual coverings for cases, the so-called 'Eureka' case used leather faces and zinc edges, or even full pressed zinc covers.

Reference has already briefly been made to velvet cases, and these were available in a variety of styles. In addition to the lockable flap cases in velvet and leather, some very attractive oval designs in deep coloured velvets were available for both tintypes and carte-de-visite prints.

In addition to leather-covered, paper-covered and embossed or moulded paper cases, an even cheaper alternative was a wooden-edged and card-backed frame, available in ninth, sixth and quarter plate sizes, the latter two being the most common. This, together with thinner and cheaper mattes reduced unit costs even further.

Many ambrotypes, especially outdoor ones taken presumably by itinerant photographers, survive packaged in this way. While some of these cheaply framed images were supplied behind thin metal embossed mattes, the majority dispensed with the matte completely, relying on the metal frame alone for decoration.

So, as can be understood, the enormous expansion of the market for photography, which downward prices generated, brought with it quite considerable problems for manufacturers and suppliers. In a matter of a very few years, case manufacture had moved from what was little more than a cottage industry to a level requiring mass

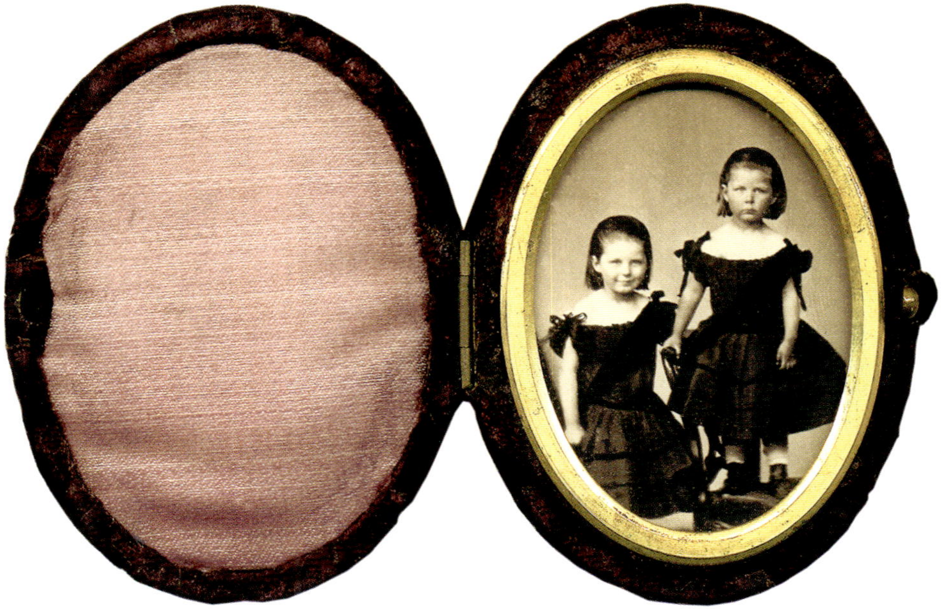

Above and left: Ninth plate velvet-covered wooden case, maker unknown, containing a carte-de-visite by J.G. Tunny, 93 Princes Street, Edinburgh. The case has a metal hinge and a push button closure. The faces are each made of a single piece of bevelled pitch pine and the edge bars are each made of steamed and shaped pine strips. The case is covered with deep purple velvet and contains a lilac silk pad. As is typical of this type of case, the velvet is showing some signs of wear in the centre of the face.

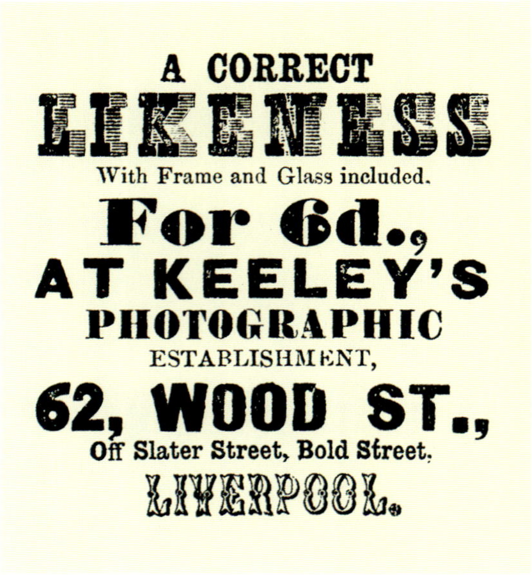

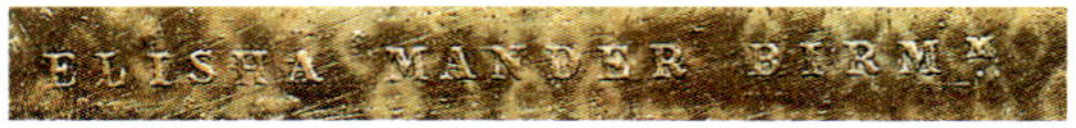

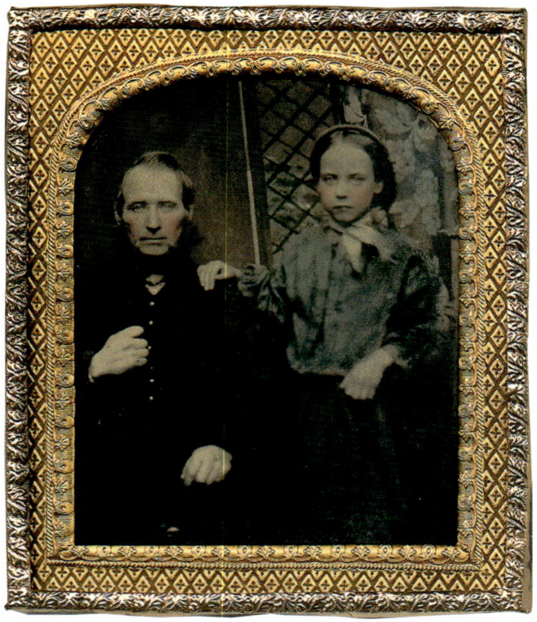

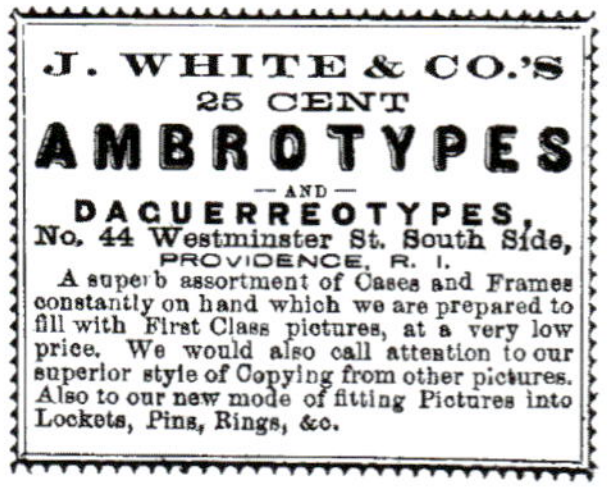

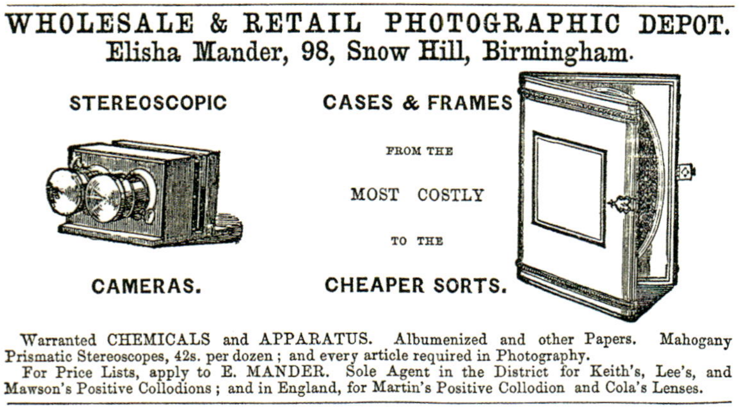

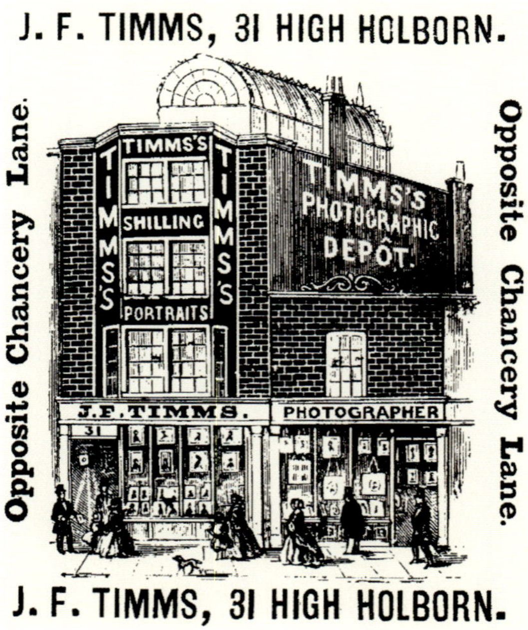

Elisha Mander of 98 Snow Hill Birmingham was a manufacturer and importer of a wide variety of cases and case fittings in the 1850s and 1860s. The tinted ambrotype above is in an embossed dome-topped matte c.*1860 with Mander's stamp embossed on the reverse. Finding the maker's name on a matte is just as unusual as finding a maker's name on a case – if not more so. The case illustrated in his 1860 advertisement is an imported Eichmeyer design with typical raised banding and round edged profile, imported from Philadelphia. Also illustrated here are trade cards from J. White & Co. of Providence, Rhode Island,* c.*1855; Keeley's of Liverpool.* c.*1862, and J. Timms of 31 High Holborn. Timms was at this address from 1857 until 1873. This card, with the glasshouse built on the roof, dates from the late 1850s, while the version opposite is a little later.*

production. It is a testament to Victorian ingenuity that such a sudden and dramatic growth was achieved apparently without the sort of shortages and back orders which might have been expected.

Prices varied considerably, but low quality cases complete with velvet pad, mats and cover glasses could be purchased wholesale for as little as 4/- (20p) per dozen for ninth plate, up to 8/9 (44p) per dozen for what were described as 'extra best quality'. Quarter plate cases of that same high quality cost 17/6 (87p) per dozen, or just over 7p each in today's currency. Given that some studios were charging as little as 1/- (5p) for taking a portrait in 1860 and supplying it in a case, profit margins must have been very low for a portrait photographer working at the cheap end of the market. At 6d (2.5p) for an ambrotype in a simple frame, they were even lower. Like many of today's studios, a living wage was only possible with a high throughput of customers and orders.

MOROCCO CASES.

Morocco Leather Cases, fig. 1464, are lined with silk or cotton velvet, fitted with dome, oval, or cushion-shaped gilt mats, best white glass and hinged cover, for receiving and preserving Daguerreotype, Talbotype, and collodion pictures.

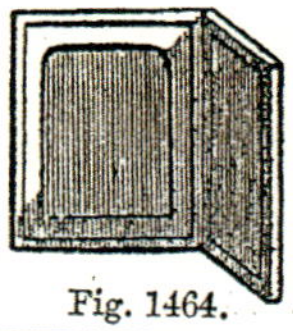

Fig. 1464.

		Sizes to receive Plates.				
		2½ by 2 s. d.	3¼ by 2¾ s. d.	4¼ by 3¼ s. d.	5 by 4 s. d.	6½ by 6¾ s. d.
1460	Morocco leather Cases, fig. 1464, with embossed leather top, lid lined with embossed cotton velvet, fitted with mats and glasses ... ... per doz.	4 0	6 6	10 0	16 0	25 0
1461	Ditto, gilt edges to rim, per doz.	4 6	7 6	11 0	17 6	27 6
1462	Morocco leather Cases, with embossed leather top and bottom, lid lined with embossed silk velvet, gilt edges to rim, mats and glasses, ... per doz.	6 6	10 6	16 0	27 6	45 0
1463	Morocco leather Cases, *extra best quality*, with mats and glasses ... ... per doz.	8 9	13 9	17 6	—	—

MOROCCO FRAMES.

Morocco Leather Frames, fig. 1475, lined with velvet, gilt edges, fitted with dome, oval, or cushion-shaped gilt mats, and best white glass, for containing Daguerreotype, Talbotype, or collodion pictures.

1465	For plates 2½ inches by 2 inches	... per dozen	£0	3	0
1466	" 3¼ " 2¾ "	... "	0	4	3
1467	" 4¼ " 3¼ "	... "	0	6	6
1468	" 5 " 4 "	... "	0	12	0
1469	" 6½ " 4¾ "	... "	0	17	0

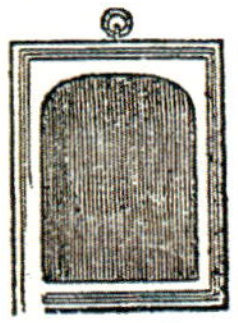

Fig. 1475.

Left: A page from a catalogue produced by Frederick J. Cox, in the late 1850s, giving prices for some of the most commonly used case sizes. It is interesting to note that in addition to casing daguerreotypes and 'collodion pictures' the advertiser suggests that 'talbotype' or calotype paper prints might be marketed in this way. While the albumen print, richly hand-coloured, was offered in leather cases by some eminent studios, there is no evidence of cased calotypes ever achieving much popularity. The 5" x 4" case seems to have been almost uniquely British, while the largest case offered in this advertisement is so uncommon that only a single example has been inspected during the course of the research for this book.

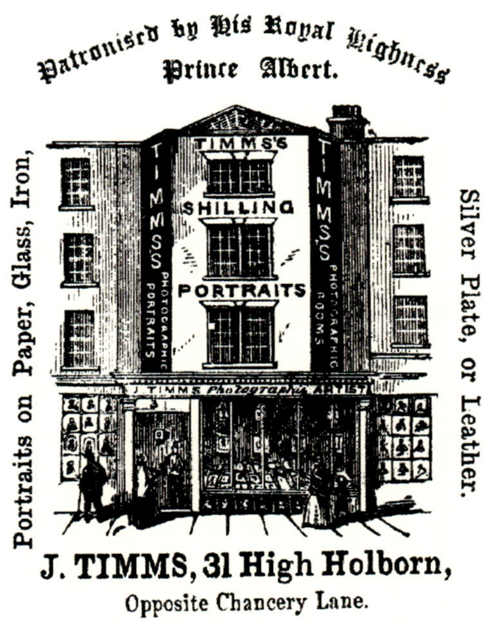

Footnotes

1. Philip Delamotte, *The Practice of Photography - a Manual for Students and Amateurs*, second edition, London, The Photographic Institution, and Low & Son, 1855. p.83.
2. Carl Gustav Oehme styled himself simply as 'Gustav Oehme' on the labels affixed to his daguerreotypes. Trained originally as a mechanical engineer, Oehme learned the rudiments of the daguerreotype process direct from the inventor while in Paris in 1840. Together with a friend, optician and photographer L.P. Graff, he presented one of the earliest exhibitions of photography in Berlin in 1841. His studio at 20 Jagerstasse, Berlin, was opened in 1843.
3. While most of the surviving examples of the Wharton pan and preserver bear the legend 'Beard Patentee', the example illustrated in this work (pp.30-31) does not.
4. Floyd & Marion Rinhart, *American Miniature Case Art* A.S.Barnes and Company, South Brunswick & New York, and Thomas Youseloff Ltd, London, 1969.
5. High quality studios such as William Kilburn used leather hinges on the majority of their smaller cases, and double metal hinges on their quarter plate cases. The two quarter plate examples illustrated on page 5 are both houses in such cases
6. Henry A. Eichmeyer was both a photographer and a casemaker. An accomplished daguerreotypist in his own right, he was based in Philadelphia with a studio at 62 Walnut Street. His design patent No.694 for the miniature case style which bears his name was issued on February 27th 1855.
7. Edward Anthony, *A Comprehensive and Systematic Catalogue of Photographic Apparatus and Material, Manufactured By E. Anthony*, Henry H. Snelling, New York, 1854, pp v-vi.
8. ibid, *p.vi.*
9. ibid, *p.vii.*
10. ibid, *p.vii.*

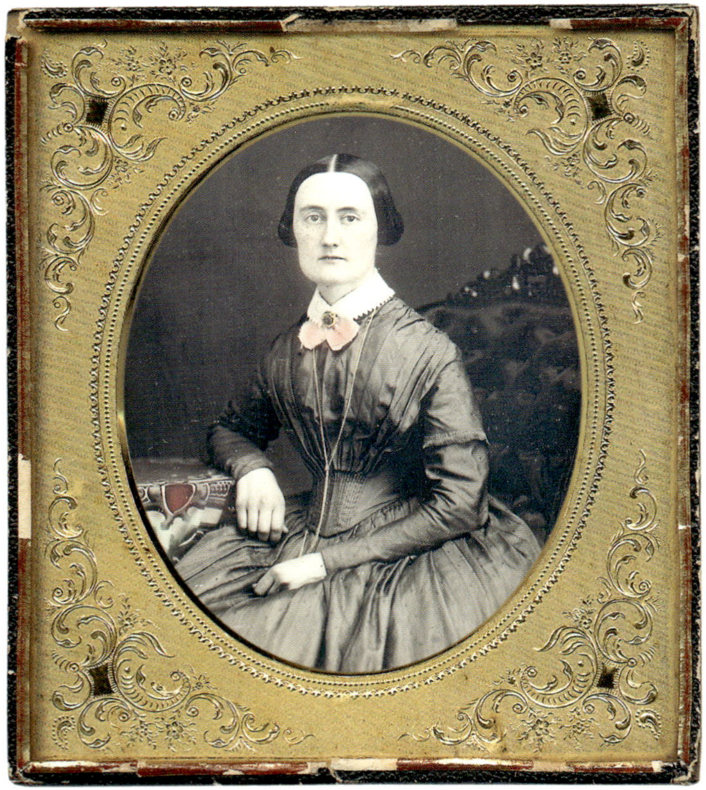

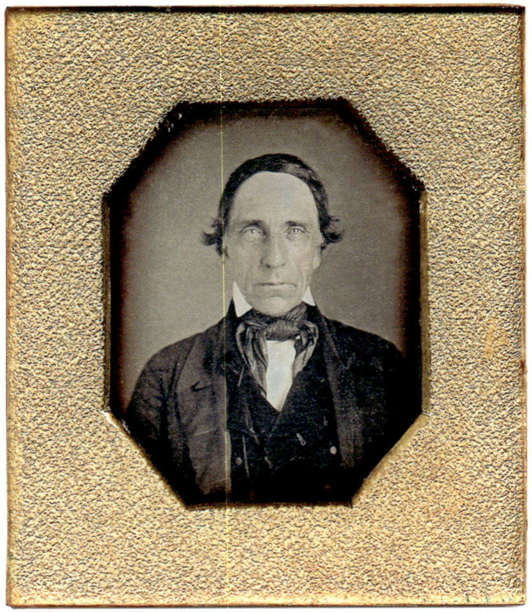

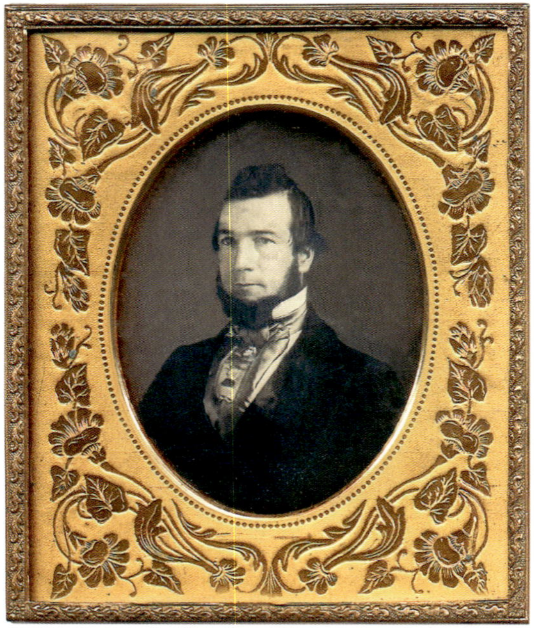

Just as the Wharton daguerreotype case enabled a small ninth plate daguerreotype to be held in a larger case, so other designers came up with ornate mattes to achieve the same effect. Above is an oversize matte and frame for a sixth plate daguerreotype. Size 92mm x 103mm, compared with the normal sixth plate matte and frame which measured 71mm x 83mm. This example is a wall-hanging frame probably dating from the early to mid 1850s.

Right and above right: Two mattes designed to house ninth plate images in sixth plate cases. The upper example dates from the mid 1840s, while the lower example comes from about ten years later.

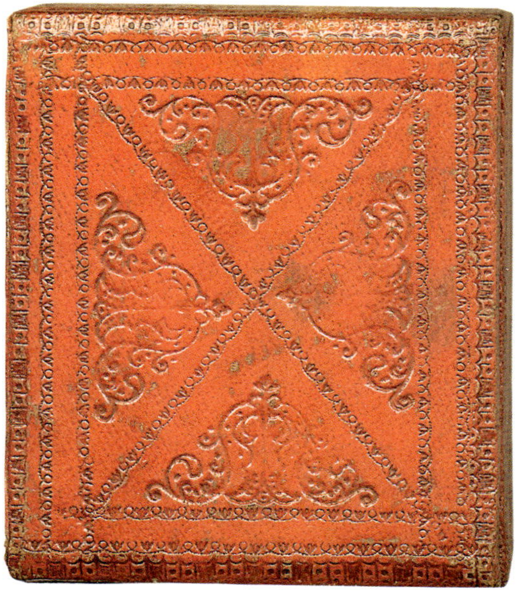

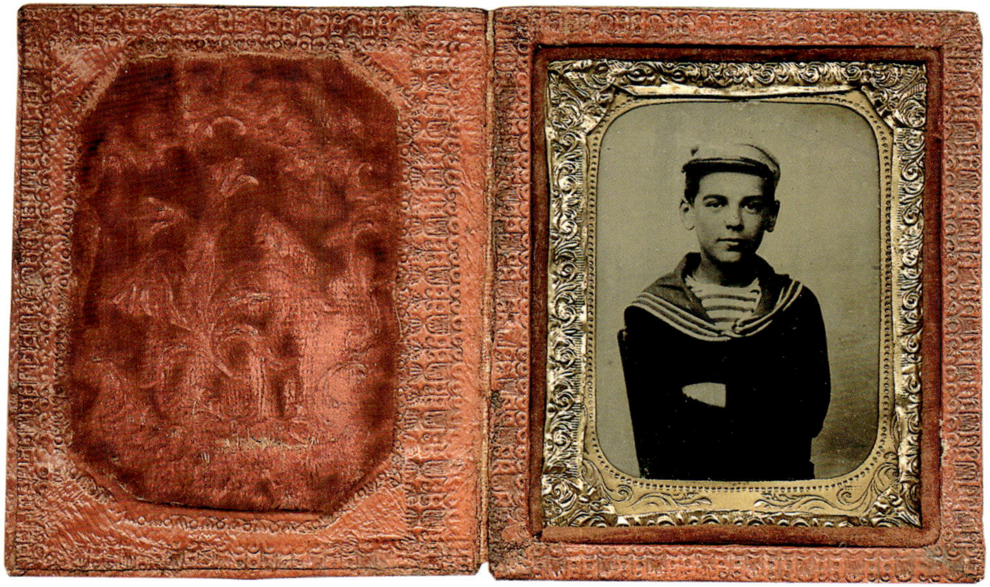

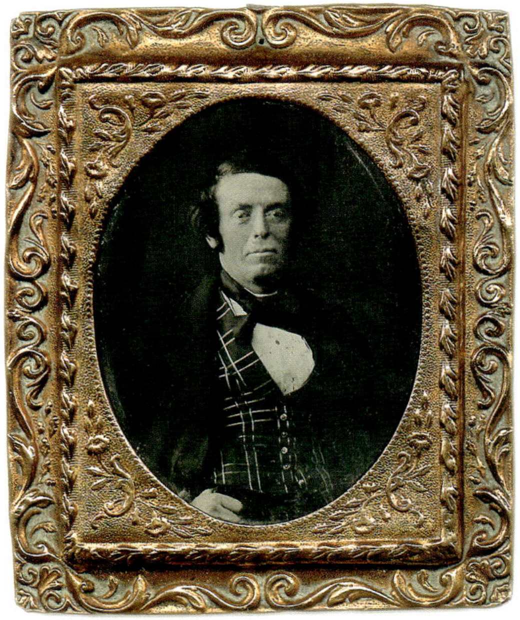

Above: A French case from the late 1860s. Cases were not the preferred method of presenting daguerreotypes, ambrotypes or tintypes in Europe. This case is of unusual design, and houses a ninth plate ferrotype or tintype of a boy in a sailor suit. The case has a hardwood base made up of a single sheet of wood, and hardwood framing bars. The top is also a single piece of thin hardwood. The velvet pad is a crudely cut octagonal shape, and lies on the surface of the image's cover glass when the case is closed. The case is covered in a bright red leather, embossed on the front, and originally had gilded decoration in the embossed cover motif. There is no clasp.

Left: The more popular methods of presenting images in France were wooden or pressed metal frames. This example, from the mid 1860s, comprises a single piece of pressed brass foil over a black japanned recessed pan. It contains a ninth plate ambrotype. The two components of the frame are held together with the matte crimped over the edges of the pan. The pan bears the legend 'JS No.3050, Breveté SGD' stamped on the inside, therefore reading laterally reversed on the back plate.

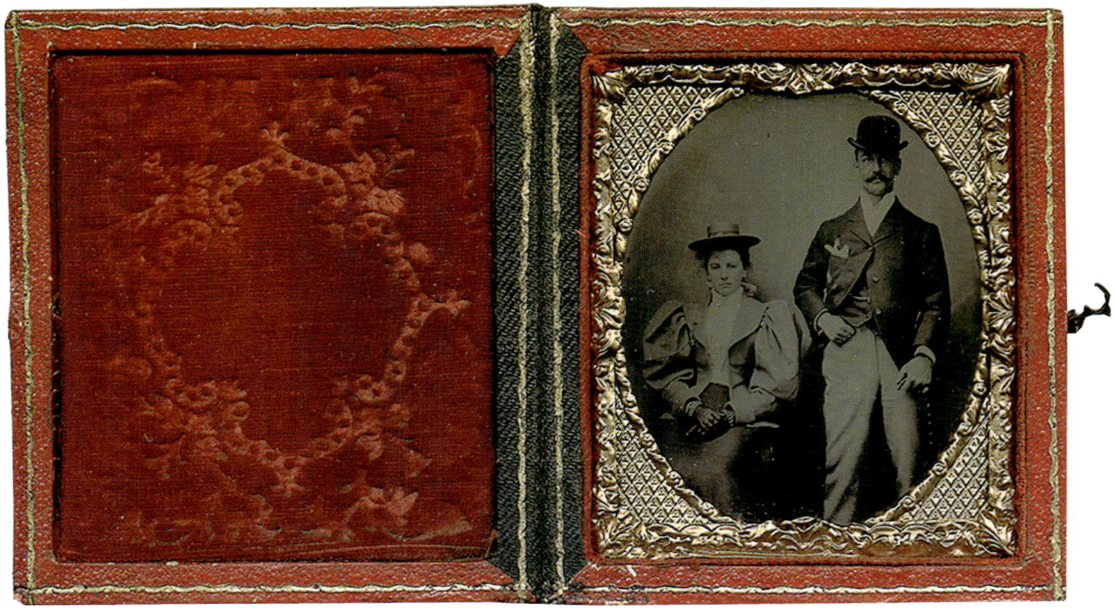

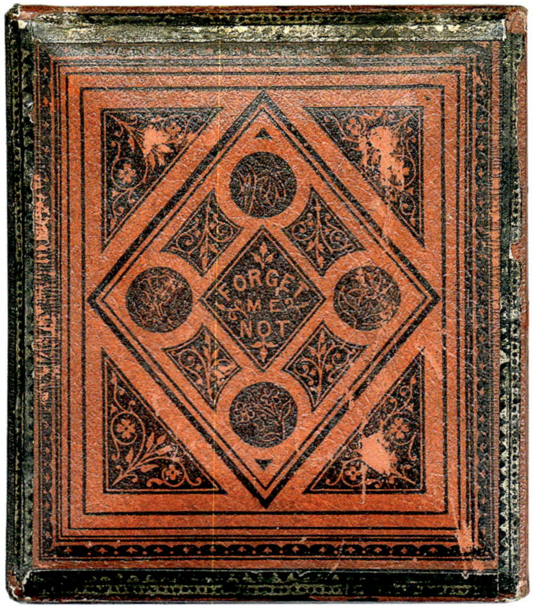

Above: The swansong of the portrait case. This example dates from about 1875-1880, with the tintype established at the bottom end of the market, and the preferred medium of the itinerant fairground photographer. The case is paper and card over a simple wooden frame, two colour printed in red over black with the motif 'forget me not'. A very thin pressed foil matte is used to keep cost down, as this sort of portrait was an impulse buy on a day out. The tintype, taped to cut-out paper mounts, continued to be popular well into the twentieth century.
Right: A pressed metal French-made case, velvet-covered and silk-lined. It is fitted with a single short piano hinge and a push-button closure and dates from about 1870. It houses an oversized ninth plate ambrotype of a young man set in a gilded twisted rope border. The image measures 52mm x 63mm, compared with the typical ninth plate image at 49mm x 62mm. The overall dimensions of the case are 65mm x 75mm. The purple velvet has faded somewhat over the years, but the cream silk is still in remarkably good condition.

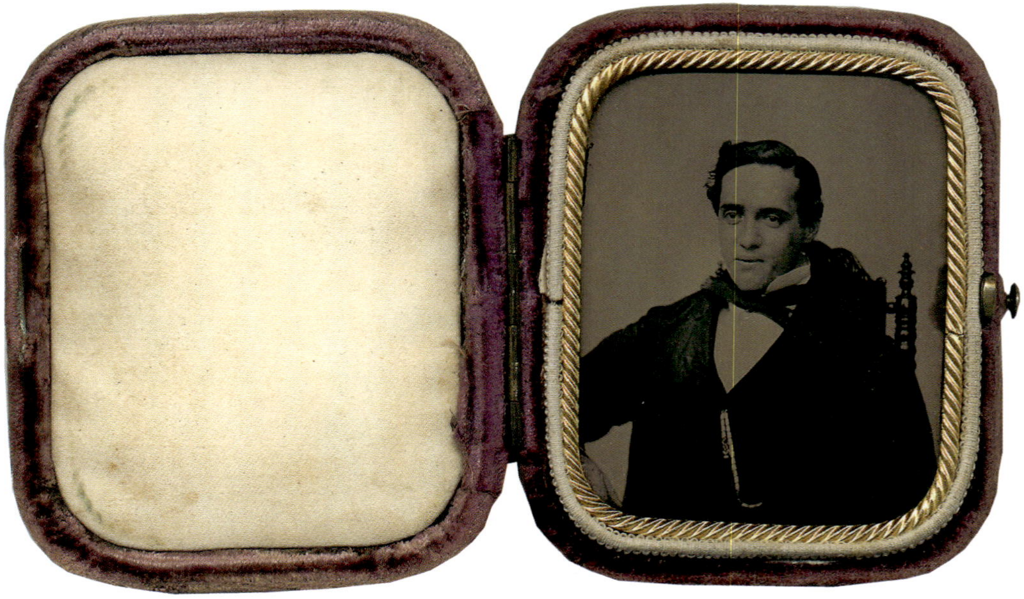

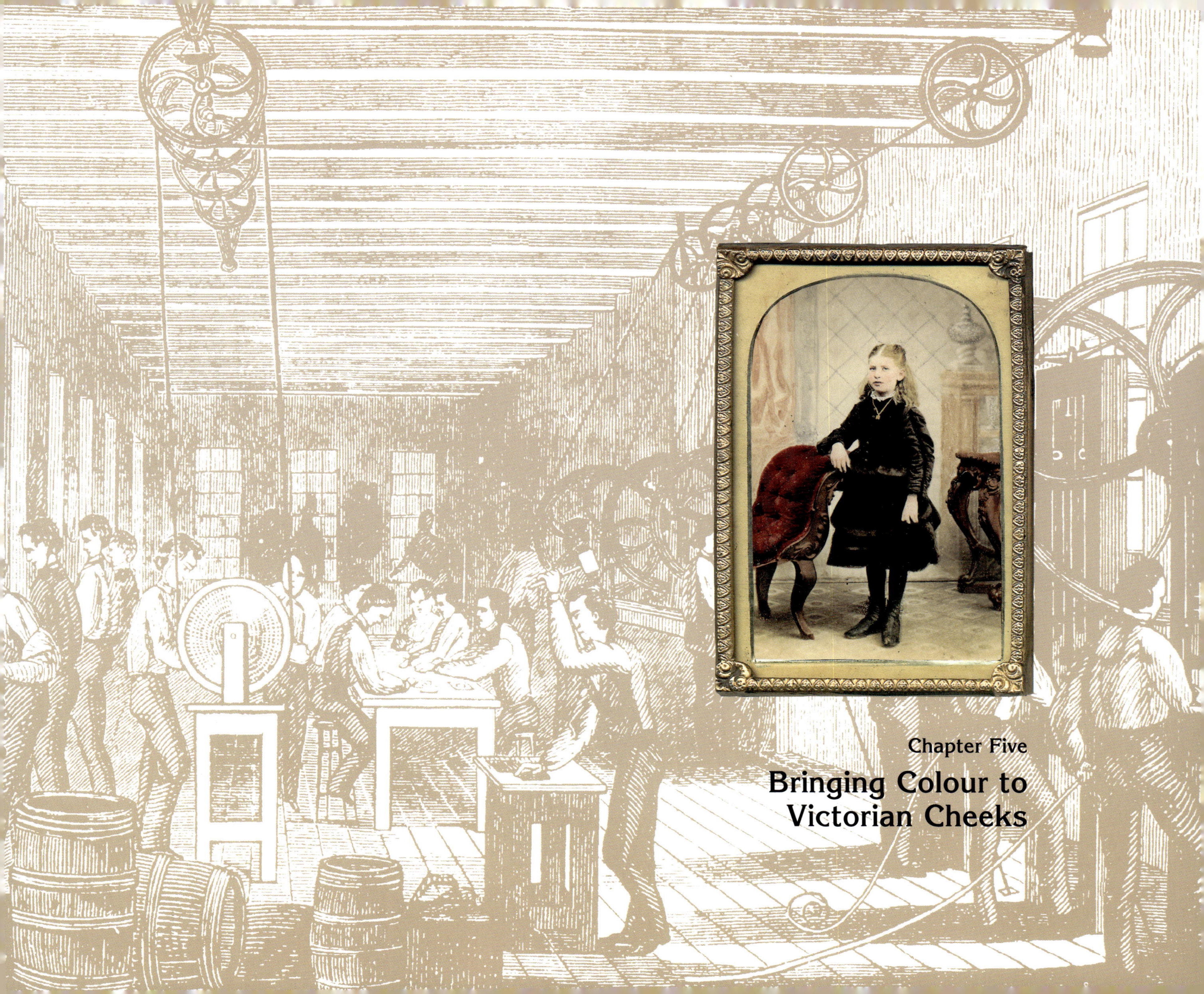

Chapter Five

Bringing Colour to Victorian Cheeks

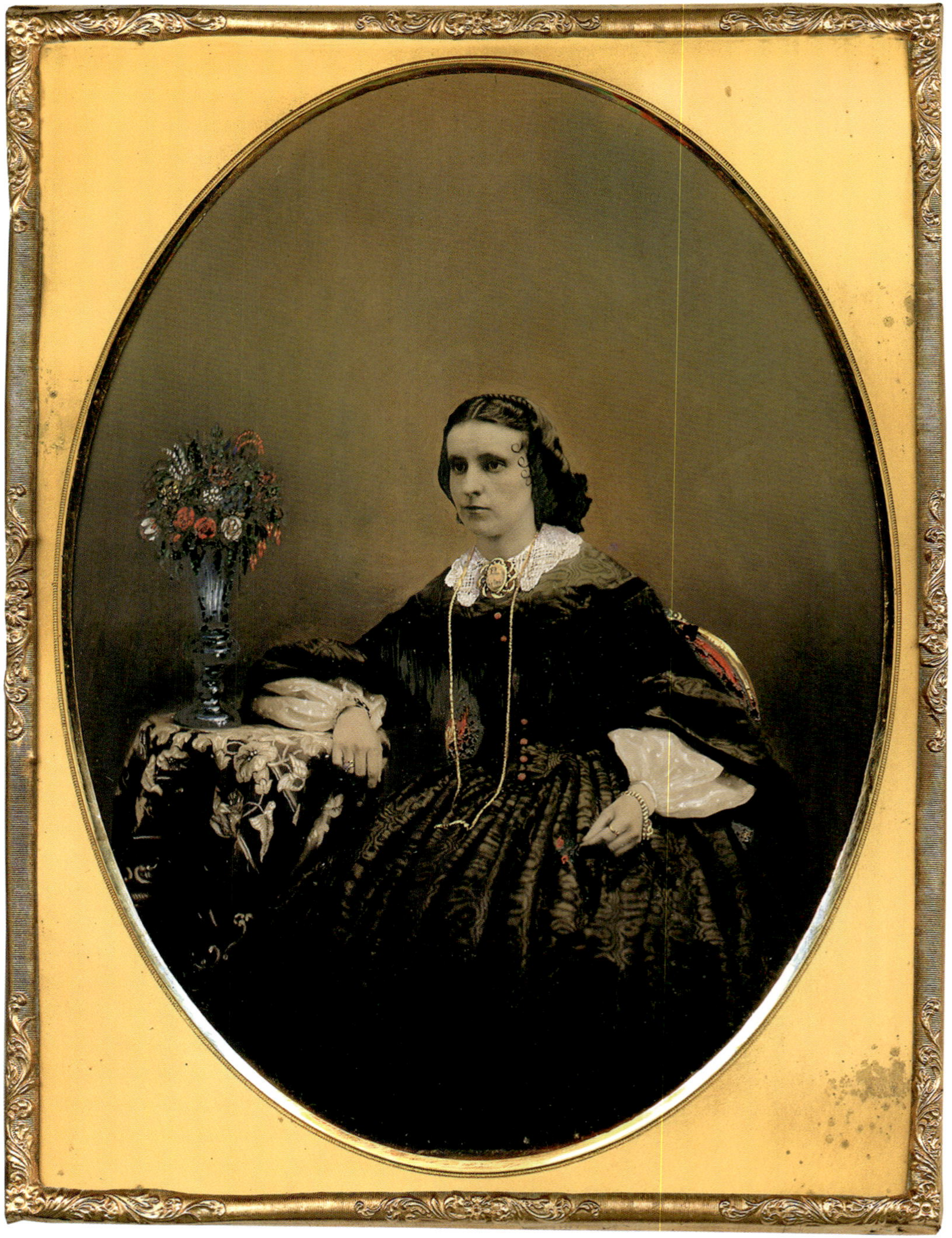

The art of the mid-Victorian photographic colourist is seen at its best in this superbly tinted and gilded whole plate ambrotype, photographer unknown, late 1850s. The decoration on this fine image is a mixture of applied powder colour, with painted colour on the flowers. Whole plate ambrotypes thus decorated were the ultimate achievement of the medium, and are as highly prized by collectors today as they were by their owners more than one hundred and forty years ago. Actual image size 158mm x 211mm.

Chapter Five:

Bringing Colour to Victorian Cheeks

When the first public announcements of photography appeared, the monochrome image of the small silver daguerreotype plate was heralded by a society obsessed with invention and innovation as being so close to perfection that nothing could be expected to improve upon it! As one newspaper eloquently described it, nature was the artist, and the photographer was merely a secondary agent, able neither to flatter nor detract from the subject placed before the camera.

Nature however needed a helping hand if she was to perform her task properly. For a start, the daguerreotype process was sensitive only to blue light, so advice had to be given to sitters as to what they ought to wear for their ordeal. The major problem was the length of exposure – the longer it was the less happy the subjects looked in their 'likenesses'. The speed of early lenses was a major governing factor in keeping exposures long, until, as has already been mentioned, the fast Petzval lenses were introduced. One solution to this in the earliest days of the process, proposed and developed by the American Alexander Wolcott[1], was to replace the camera lens with a round hole and a large concave mirror which reflected the image back on to the daguerreotype plate. This had two advantages – firstly it considerably reduced exposure (or allowed larger images to be produced at the same exposure as had formerly been needed for smaller ones) and it overcame the lateral reversal of the image which was created by a lens system exposing on to a metal plate. This difference separated images produced by Daguerre's system in the early days from those produced by the American system. Later, a reversing prism attached to the front of the camera – pioneered in Britain by Antoine Claudet[2] – corrected the reading of the image.

Early on in the use of the process, the limitations of its blue sensitivity had been noted. Outdoors, it was remarked, the sky was 'done' long before the trees were 'ready'! In the studio, several ingenious solutions to this problem were introduced. In America, one idea was to filter sunlight through a blue copper sulphate solution to increase its actinic qualities – and despite the fact that no such increase in actinic light could have thus been created, great improvements were claimed for the innovation. Another, used by the American John Draper, was to apply white flour make-up to the faces of the sitters to lighten their complexion and reduce exposure further.

Faster lenses, and the use of bromine and chlorine as well as iodine, gave the process a sufficient increase in sensitivity to render many of these innovations unnecessary within a very few years.

Other more useful – and lasting – ideas included Richard Beard's advice to sitters as to what they should or should not wear when posing for their miniature portraits[3]. Sensibly, they were advised not to wear extremes of tone – black or white – as the process could not cope with such a range. The best results were achieved when the tonal values of face, clothes, props and background were all within a very carefully controlled range. Similarly with colour, advice was offered, and more suitable clothes were often available if the advice was not taken or not fully understood!

The early honeymoon period – in which criticism of photography was hardly heard – was short lived, and very quickly replaced with recurring concerns about whether or not photography, limited to the silver and white of the daguerreotype, could ever really satisfy the ever increasing demands of its customers!

As early as September 1841, the pages of *The Spectator* carried critical appraisals of the 'new art' – '*Miniatures of persons who had very red faces which looked black and heavy from which we infer that redness of the lips contributes to give the mouth the dark tint that, added to the strong shadow between and below the lips, makes this feature look larger and coarser than in life. The grave and formal attitude commonly assumed by the sitter, being faithfully reflected in the miniature portrait, the sombre effect of the strong shadows and colourless lights of the photograph is increased to an unpleasing degree of sternness occasionally amounting to a repulsiveness...*

Sixth plate ferrotype or tintype portrait of a Mexican or Spanish-American lady in oval matte, with tinted skin-tones and gilded rings, earrings and brooch, late 1850s. This image was sold in an octagonal thermoplastic union case.

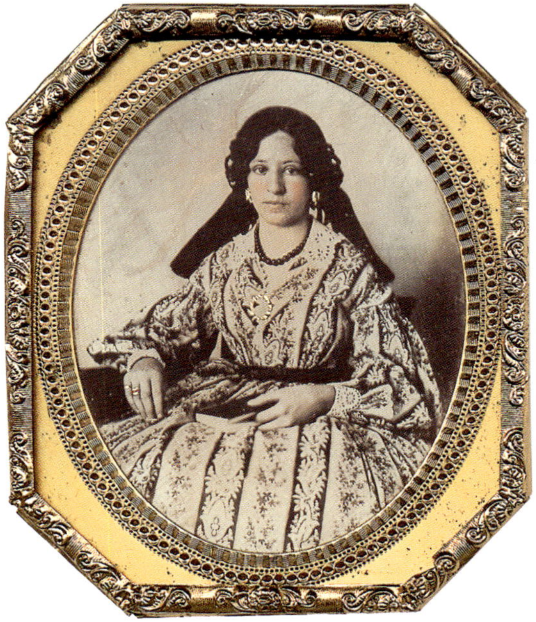

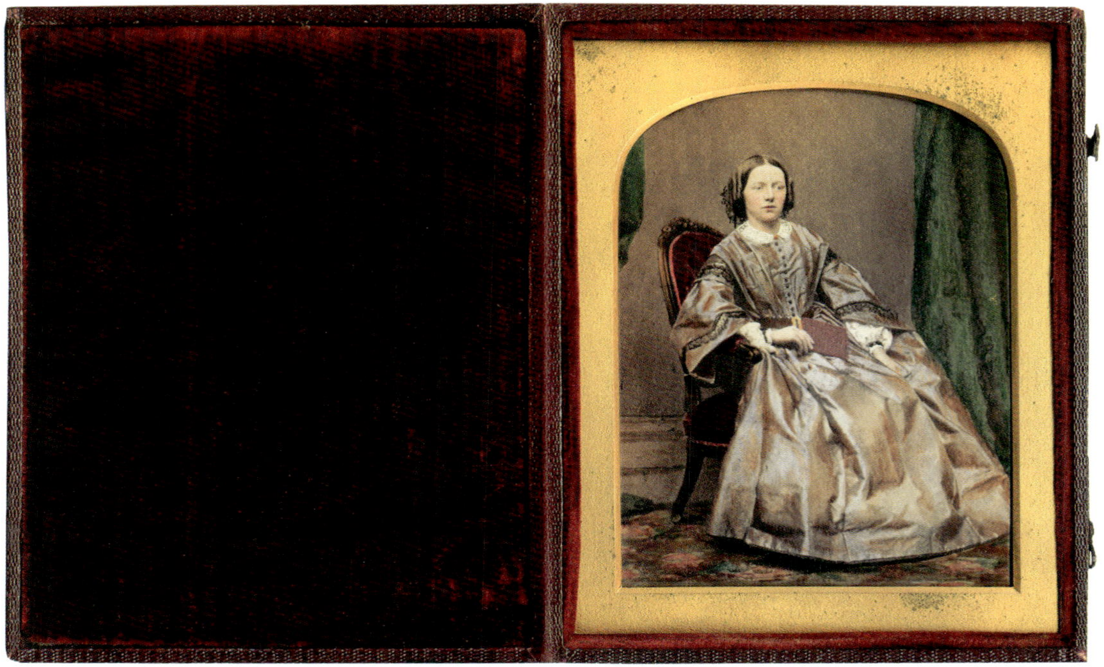

Cased tinted paper print by the Liverpool Institition of Photography, Lord's Chambers, 87 Lord Street, Liverpool, 1860s, set in burgundy leather case, with photographer's gilt stamp on base. Burgundy velvet pad and trim. The sitter is holding a half plate cased photograph. This image is in the rather unusual 5in. x 4in. case, 112mm x 138mm, a popular British size. The Liverpool Institution of Photography was at this address from the mid 1850s through to the early 1860s. From 1862 the studio traded under the name of the proprietor William Keith. Under a variety of other names, there was a studio at this address until the end of the nineteenth century.

...The photographic likenesses are deficient in two of the most attractive features of a painted resemblance – colour and vivacity, They are miniatures in chiaroscuro, adumbrating the forms of the face, only the expression is cold, severe and gloomy.[4]'

Such criticism clearly did not reach far beyond the boundaries of London initially, for provincial newspapers still eulogised about the process well into 1843. Eventually they too openly questioned photography's once-acknowledged 'perfection'. The issues as to whether or not photography was an art began at the same time, and are still to an extent unresolved today!

Photography was, after all, the replacement for the miniature painter's brush, and although photography was unquestionably better suited to the reproduction of fine detail than had been the painter, there was no doubt that the painting had one characteristic that the daguerreotype did not.

Central to the growing dissatisfaction with photography by the end of the 1840s was that the 'art' was already a decade old and still there was no suggestion that inventors were any closer to being able to photograph nature in all her true colours! Those staunch advocates of the processes then in common use – the daguerreotype and the calotype primarily – still clung to the claim that colour was superfluous, but the public had for some years demonstrated that this was not the case.

As photography had, from the outset, been described variously as an extension of painting, it was hardly surprising that it was to the art of the painter that photographers turned in the quest for the elusive colour. Photographic premises were described as studios to establish a link with painting. The delightful newspaper account with which Chapter One was opened used the phrase *...has established his painting rooms – to speak in the old phrase*, and continued to describe how the photographer used *light, which to him acts the part of a pencil.*[5]

Turning to the long developed skills of the painter to introduce colour to the 'new art' of photography was simply logical.

A number of suggestions for colouring photographs by hand had been proposed since the mid 1840s, and Richard Beard actually patented a colouring method in 1852 – Patent No.9292 'Improvements in the Means of Obtaining Photographic Likenesses'. The 'improvements' in question may have originated in experiments carried out in 1840 by a Swiss engraver, J.B. Isenring,[6] but the processes Beard patented were far from easy or even practical. The 'process' involved making several very careful tracings of the image, one for each required colour, and cutting a hole in each to the exact size of the area to be coloured. A mixture of finely particled pigment and gum – the colour having first been dissolved in isinglass, gum or gelatine and then dried and ground – was carefully sprinkled on to the plate through the hole cut in the tracing, and then breathed on to slightly melt the gum and create adhesion. In the earliest days of the daguerreotype before gold toning was commonplace, the image surface was too delicate even to withstand the gentle application of colour with a sable brush.

Beard also proposed colouring the cover glass, carefully matching the positioning of the colour so that it married up with the image when the 'sandwich' was assembled for casing. Just how successful or widespread his methods were is impossible to ascertain. What seems certain is that colouring of daguerreotypes did not really enjoy any widespread popularity until much later in the 1840s. Perhaps the fact that colouring in the early days doubled the price of the portrait acted as a severe restriction on sales.

When sophisticated colouring did become possible, studios offering the service were both profitable and popular. Purists – if such they can be called – did not approve of colouring at all, and the American photographic writer Henry Snelling, in his 1849 volume *History and Practice of the Art of Photography*[7] made his views well known early in his text –

'I very much doubt the propriety of colouring the daguerreotypes, as I am of opinion that they are little, if any, improved by the operation, at least as it is now generally practised. There are several things requisite in an artist to enable him to colour a head, or even a landscape effectively, and correctly, and I must say that very few of these are possessed by our operators as a class. These requirements are, a talent for drawing – taste – due discrimination of effect – strict observance of the characteristic points in the features of the subject – quick perception of the beautiful, and a knowledge of the art of mixing colours, and blending tints.

'The method now pursued, I do not hesitate to say, and have no fears of being contradicted by those capable of criticising, is on the whole ruinous to any daguerreotype, and to a perfect one absolutely disgusting!'

Snelling, a highly respected figure on account of his writings, was somewhat at odds with the general public who bought commercial portraiture, both in his condemnation of the idea of colouring daguerreotypes, and by his assumption that a good daguerreotype was destroyed by the practice. A few years later, with colouring the norm rather than the exception, he was in a very small minority! When colouring was first introduced, however, he was not alone in his condemnation, as the American studio of Southworth and Hawes, amongst others, initially completely refused to tint, although they eventually relented – perhaps under pressure from their customers – and some exquisite large whole plate tinted examples of their work survive in American collections. The Frenchman Arago is on record as describing the process in even less complimentary terms than Snelling!

...to hand tint a lovely image, even by the hand of a reputable artist, is as if to set a signwriter to retouch the wings of a butterfly.[8]

There were two quite distinct schools of thought as to how the colour might most effectively be applied. The most widespread approach with daguerreotypes was carefully to paint the areas of the plate to be covered with a thin layer of gum arabic, or isinglass – so thin as to be invisible, and to then let it dry. The artist – often a miniature

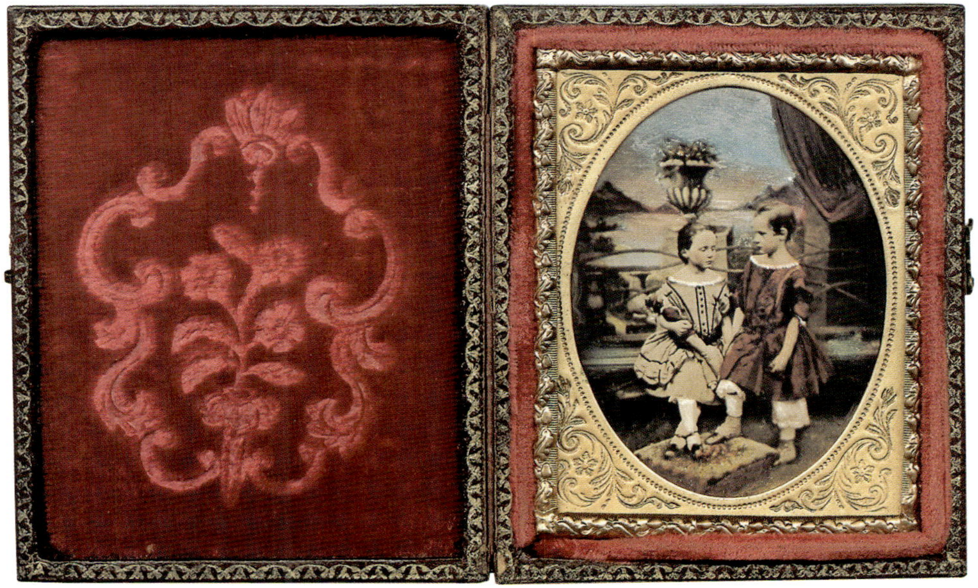

Cased ninth plate tinted ambrotype by W. H. Franklin of Deal, Kent, c.1860. This image is one of a pair, the other is illustrated on page 39. The line between photograph and painting is almost lost in an image as heavily overpainted as this. The image is set in an embossed leather case with cerise velvet pad and trim. Subtle colour has been applied to the faces and clothing of the children, with a more painterly approach having been taken to the landscape backdrop.

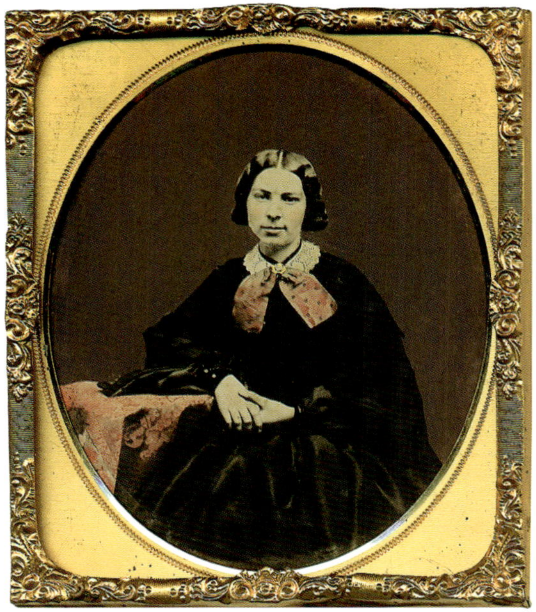

Above: Tinted sixth plate ambrotype by Eccles of Agur Street, Bury, Greater Manchester, 1860s, set in brown leather Eichmeyer case, with photographer's gilt stamp on base. The case is fitted with brown velvet pad and trim. The subject has tinted skin tones which have almost completely faded with time. Her brooch has been gilded, and the background has been overpainted in deep purple/brown, while the tablecloth and the subject's scarf have been picked out in reds.

Opposite page: Tinted sixth plate ambrotype by George Coulder, Photographic Artist, Scarborough, probably mid 1850s. The case has a deep red/brown pad and trim, and the image is housed in a high quality embossed matte and frame. Interstingly, the trade directories of the time do not list a photographer by this name, yet he was obviously sufficiently well established to use cases with his gilt stamp on the base, albeit listing his name and profession only, not his address.

painter by training and preference – would then apply the colour using dry powder pigments and a dry soft sable brush a with fine point. The gum was first rendered 'tacky' by breathing lightly on it, ensuring that the pigment powder would stick. The surface remained very delicate and susceptible to abrasion.

The whole process was carried out with the aid of a powerful magnifying glass, and the best colourists were so good that their work shows absolutely no brush strokes whatsoever.

Central to their success, of course, was an ability to mix realistic colours and to apply the essential tints, tones and shading necessary to make the colour lifelike. In that respect at least, Snelling's words of caution were appropriate – done badly, the effect was terrible!

However, executed well, the effect was stunning, and in many instances, surprisingly realistic. The flesh tones applied to faces and hands – and the rouged effects on cheeks – were the result of considerable experience both in colour mixing and application. Clothing was not just coloured but shaded, and jewellery highlighted with either gold leaf, or a gold paint applied with considerable care. The ability of the artists to colour large areas was particularly noteworthy. Indeed, the tinting on some celebrated daguerreotype nudes – where entire bodies were tinted and graduated with remarkable artistry – was so convincing that the casual viewer could be forgiven for thinking momentarily that the colour was natural!

Snelling offered considerable advice on colour mixing and colour preparation in his 1849 book – although still with a disapproving sting in the tail –

'The method of laying colours on daguerreotypes is one of considerable difficulty inasmuch as they are used in the form of perfectly dry impalpable powder... The writer is confident that some compound, or ingredient may yet be discovered which, when mixed with the colors, will give a more delicate, pleasing, and natural appearance to the picture than is derived from the present mode of laying them on, which in his estimation is more like plastering than coloring... In colouring Daguerreotypes, the principal shades of the head are made with bistre, mixed with burnt sienna, touching some place with a mixture of carmine and indigo... The flesh tints are produced by the use of light red, deepened towards the shaded parts with yellow ochre, blue and carmine mixed with indigo, while the warmer more highly coloured parts have a slight excess of carmine or lake.[9]'

If the sitter was wearing diamonds, some finishers created pinpricks through the image to the silver of the plate itself, that slight scratch causing the 'jewels' to appear to sparkle when the image was moved near a light.

In his book *Theory and Practice of the Photographic Art*[10] William Sparling, Roger Fenton's assistant in the Crimea, gave a good and very full account of the best advice for colouring daguerreotypes, including a list of the range of colours considered necessary. It is sometimes easy to forget, in reading this wealth of detail, that here we are talking about the colouring of a portrait photography or which the figure may be only a little over an inch in height!

'Nearly, if not quite all the various colours used in painting may be made from the five primary colours, black, white, blue, red, and yellow; but for the Daguerrean artist it would be the best policy to obtain such as are required by their art already prepared. In a majority of cases, the following will be found sufficient, viz., carmine, Prussian blue, white, chrome yellow, gamboge, for drapery; yellow ochre for the face, or all three; light red; indigo; burnt sienna; bistre or burnt umbre.

If, in colouring any part of a lady's or gentleman's apparel, it is found necessary to produce other tints and shades, the following combinations may be used:

Orange – Mix yellow with red, making it darker or lighter by using more or less red.

Purple – This is made with Prussian blue, or indigo and red. Carmine and Prussian blue produce the richest colour, which may be deepened in the shadows by a slight addition of indigo or brown.

Greens – Prussian blue and gamboge makes a

very fine green, which may be varied to suit the taste of the sitter or operator, by larger proportions of either, or by adding white, burnt sienna, indigo, and red, as the case may require. These combinations, under different modifications, give almost endless varieties of green.

Brown – May be made of different shades of umber, carmine and lamp-black.

Neutral Tint – Is composed of indigo and lamp-black.

Crimson – Mix carmine and white, deepening the shaded parts of the picture with additional carmine.

Flesh colour – The best representative of flesh colour is light red, brightened in the more glowing or warmer parts with carmine, softened off in the lighter portions with white, and shaded with purple and burnt sienna.

Lead colour – Mix indigo and white in proportions to suit.

Scarlet – Carmine and light red.

For jewelry – Cups of gold and silver preparations accompany each box for Daguerreotypists, or may be procured separately.

The method of laying colours on Daguerreotypes is one of considerable difficulty, inasmuch as they are used in the form of perfectly dry impalpable powder. The rules we shall give for colouring Daguerreotypes depend, and are founded, upon those observed in miniature painting, and are intended more as hints to Daguerreotype artists in hopes of leading them to attempt improvements, than as instructions wholly to be observed.

The writer is confident that some compound or ingredient may yet be discovered which, when mixed with the colours, will give a more delicate, pleasing and natural appearance to the picture than is derived from the present mode of laying them on, which in his estimation is more like plastering than colouring.

In colouring Daguerreotypes, the principal shades of the head are to be made with bistre mixed with burnt sienna, touching some places with a mixture of carmine and indigo. The flesh

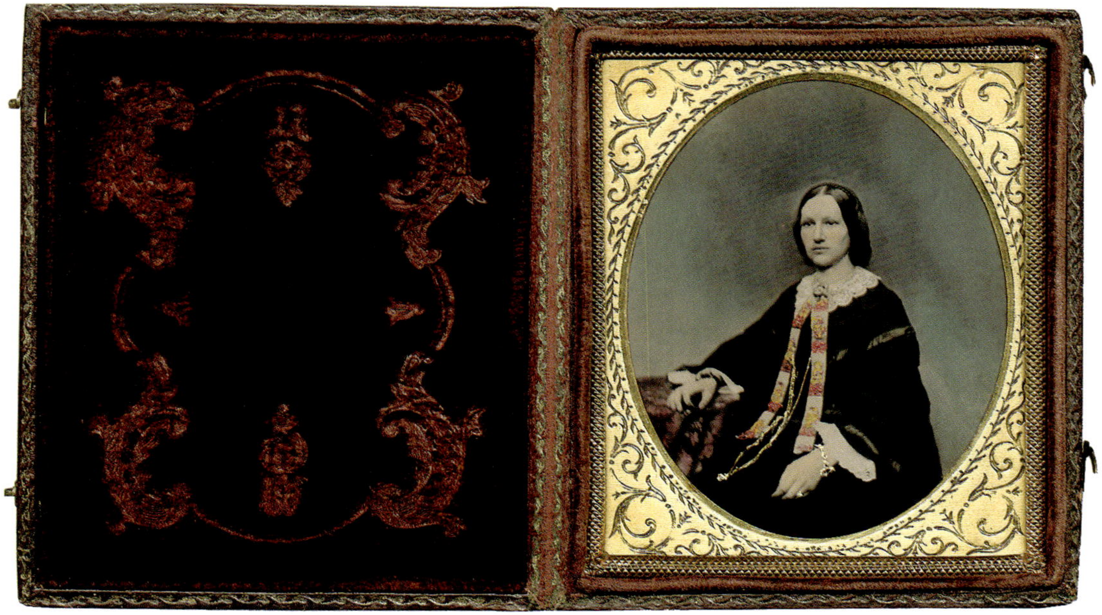

tints are produced by the use of light red, deepened towards the shaded parts with yellow ochre, blue and carmine mixed with indigo, while the warmer or more highly coloured parts have a slight excess of carmine or lake. Colour the shades about the mouth and neck with yellow ochre, blue, and a very little carmine, heightening the colour of the lips with carmine and light red, letting the light red pre-dominate on the upper and the carmine on the lower lip; the shades in the corner of the mouth being touched slightly with burnt sienna mixed with carmine.

In colouring the eyes, the artist will of course be guided by nature, observing a very delicate touch in laying on the colours, so as to preserve as much transparency as possible. A slight touch of blue – ultramarine would be best if it would adhere to the Daguerreotype plate – in the whites of the eyes near the iris, will produce a good effect.

In colouring the hands of men it will be necessary to use the darker tints with more freedom, according to the complexion of the sitter. For women, the warmer tints should predominate, and in order to give that transparency so universal with the softer sex – and which gives so much loveliness and beauty to the face – a little white may be judiciously intermingled with the red tints about the lighter portions of the face.

In taking the likeness of a lady with light or auburn hair, by the Daguerreotype process, much of the beauty of the face is destroyed, on account of the imperfect manner in which light conveys the image of light objects to the spectrum of the camera; and this, I conceive, is an instant where the defects may be obviated in some measure by proper colouring. To do this touch the shaded parts with burnt sienna and bistre, filling up the lighter portions with yellow ochre, delicate touches of burnt sienna, and in those parts which naturally have a bluish tint, add very delicate touches of purple – so delicate in fact as hardly to be perceived. The roots of the hair at the forehead should also be touched with blue, and the eyebrows near the temples made of a pinkish tint. The chin of a woman is nearly of the same colour as the cheeks in the most glowing parts. In men it

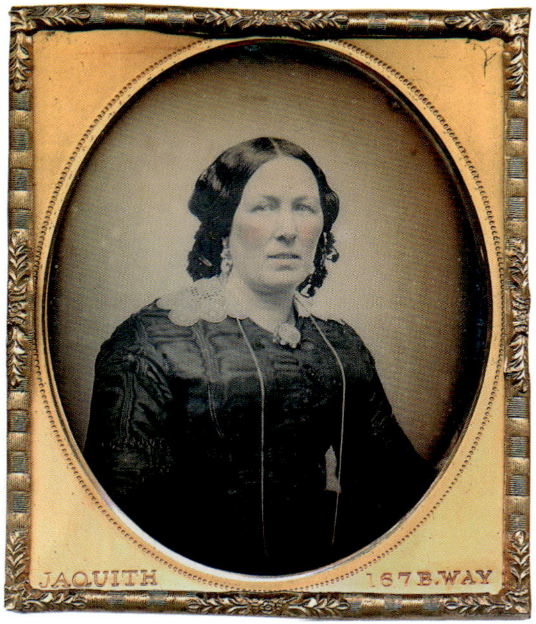

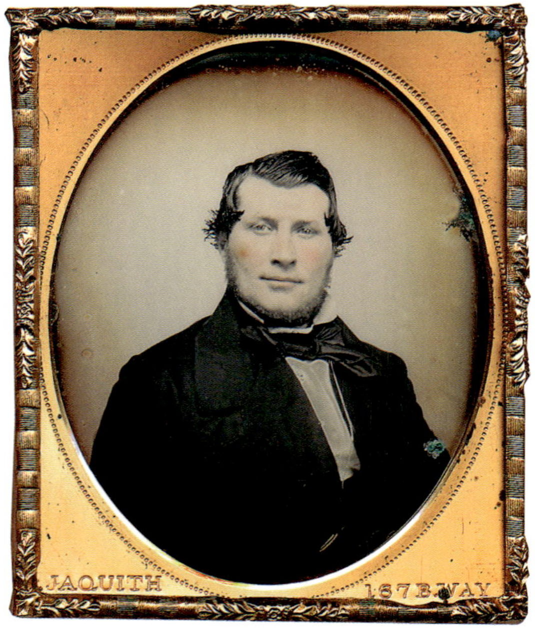

Two delicately tinted sixth plate daguerreotypes by Jaquith of 167 Broadway, New York, 1850s.

is stronger and of a bluish tint, in order to produce the effect given by the beard.

In portraits of women – the middle tints on the side of the light, which are perceived on the bosom and arms, are made of a slight mixture of ochre, blue and lake, (or carmine), to which add, on the shaded side, ochre, bistre, and purple; the latter in the darker parts. The tints of the hands should be the same as the other parts of the flesh, the ends of the fingers being a little pinkish and the nails of a violet hue. If any portion of the fleshy parts is shaded by portions of the dress, or by the position of the hand, this shade should be coloured with umber mixed with purple.

TO COLOUR THE DRAPERY. – Violet velvet. – Use the purple made of Prussian blue and carmine, touching up the shaded parts with indigo blue.

Green velvet. – Mix Prussian blue and red orpiment, shaded with purple, and touch up the lights with a little white.

Red velvet. – Mix a little brown with carmine, shading with purple, marking the lights in the strongest parts with pure carmine, and touch the most brilliant slightly with white.

White feathers. – May be improved by delicately touching the shaded parts with a little blue mixed with white. White muslin, linen, lace, silk, &c., may also be coloured in the same way, being careful not to lay the colour on too heavily.

FURS. – Red furs – may be imitated by using light red and a little masticot, shaded with umber.

Gray furs – black and white mixed and shaded with bistre.

Sable – white shaded lightly with yellow ochre.

These few directions are quite sufficient for the art, and it is quite unnecessary for me to pursue the subject further. I would, however, remark that the Daguerreotypists would find it greatly to their advantage to visit the studios of our best artists, our public galleries of paintings and statuary, and wherever else they can obtain a sight of fine paintings, and study the various styles of colouring, attitudes, folds of drapery, and other points of the art. In colouring Daguerreotypes, artists will find the magnifying glass of much advantage in detecting imperfections in the plate or in the image, which may be remedied by the brush. In selecting brushes choose those most susceptible of a fine point, which may be ascertained by wetting them between the lips or in a glass of water.'

The Kilburn quarter plate daguerreotype portrait of a young man illustrated at the beginning of this book, (page 7), is a fine example of this careful and sensitive application of colour.

When the ambrotype, or collodion positive, came into vogue in the early 1850s, the methods used varied from photographer to photographer. The same technique of applying dry powder pigment was used by many photographers, as 'BH' describes in a June 1854 letter to the *Journal of the Photographic Society*. Letter writers often hid behind anonymous signatures, initials, or names which described their state of mind!

'SIR, Your correspondent Nil Desperandum requires a method of colouring collodion positives. I have found the following to answer very well; very beautiful effects indeed may be obtained by any one who has a light hand and some idea of colour. In a perfectly clean and well-glazed pipkin, put distilled water 4 ounces, 30 grains of best isinglass or gelatine, boil for a few seconds, and strain through fine clean linen into a bottle for use. When wanted, place the bottle in hot water and use the same as collodion; do this as quick as possible, and set the plate by to dry, or the heat of a spirit lamp may be applied to the back, holding the plate in a slanting position and blowing on to the plate; it must not be more than slightly warmed; when cool it is breathed on, and the dry colours, as sold for the purpose, applied in the smallest possible quantity, using only sable brushes for flesh, and a larger soft camel hair for the back ground; or another plan is to varnish them and apply the colour before the varnish is quite dry, taking care not to touch the shadows too much, as it will produce a misty appearance anything but pleasant.[11]'

Some workers applied the colour directly on to the collodion image, the stage of applying a coating of gum arabic apparently discarded as breathing on the collodion itself could easily render it tacky enough to accept the pigment. Sadly with time, this has proved not to be as permanent in many instances, and the colours have lost their adhesion to the image. With a lot of ambrotypes, all that is left to identify the image has having once been coloured is the gilding (gold leaf ground into a gum, Isinglass or gelatine mixture) applied to rings, necklaces and watch chains. It is ironic that the better coloured portraits are often from the older process.

An alternative method was to paint the colour on to the image surface using gum-based paints. This gave stronger colour, but the brush strokes were impossible to conceal, and the colour can clearly be seen under some lighting as a surface application. In some fine examples, faces and clothing were coloured using the more subtle approach, while the vibrancy of flowers was achieved with the stronger colours.

There is no doubt that the photographic studios which provided this service saw themselves as artists, every bit as much as those who used paint exclusively. Indeed many photographic portrait studios also offered a 'traditional' painted portrait as an alternative to a photograph. They all offered a service to paint a portrait from a photograph.

Major studios employed painters both to carry out this exacting task, and to tint originals. In an advertisement in *The Times* on August 4th 1846, an advertisement for Antoine Claudet's studio promised quality with the utmost decorum –

'CLAUDET'S DAGUERREOTYPE PORTRAITS, lately so much eulogised by the leading papers, and particularly by the journals of the fine arts, are all non-inverted, and when coloured by Mr. Mansion, an artist of ability, are the most exquisite miniatures. Mr Claudet operates himself, and never allows an inferior portrait to leave his establishment. Ladies have the attendance of a respectable female. Open from 9 o'clock. - 18 King William Street near the Adelaide Gallery.'

It was followed by selected quotes from journal coverage of Claudet's services.

'THE JOURNALS of the FINE ARTS on PHOTOGRAPHY – "A Daguerreotype portrait that could truly be pronounced a flattering likeness we certainly never expected to see: that phenomenon, however, was presented to us recently visiting the establishment of Mr Claudet" - Athenaeum July 4. "We confess we had no idea of the possibility of producing anything so artistic and elegant on a metal plate." - Art Union July 1. "Mr Claudet's productions approach more nearly to the highly finished miniature than anything we have yet seen." Literary Gazette July 4.'

By good luck or good planning – we will perhaps never know which – the advertisement immediately below Claudet's was placed by Richard Beard, preeminent amongst his competitors, one of whose studios was at the opposite end of the same street.

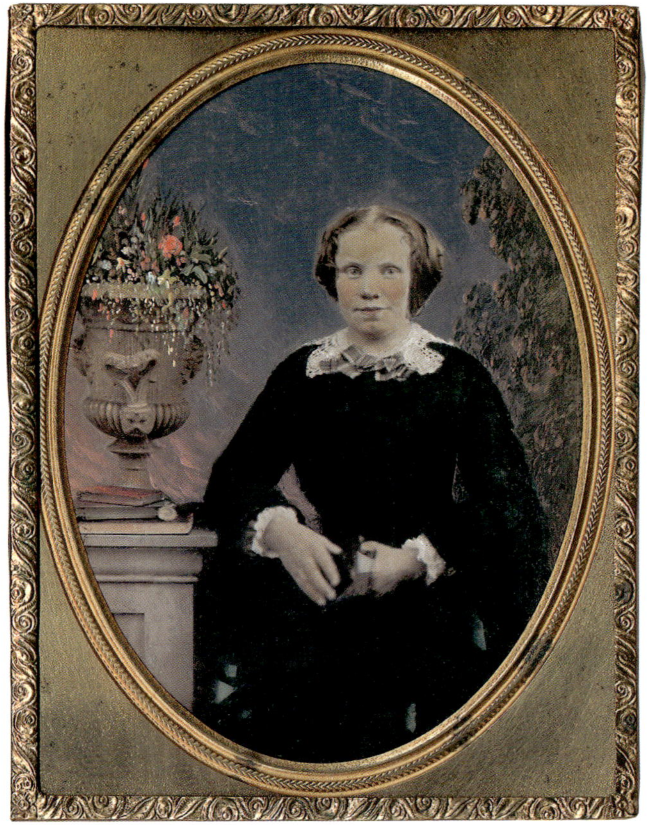

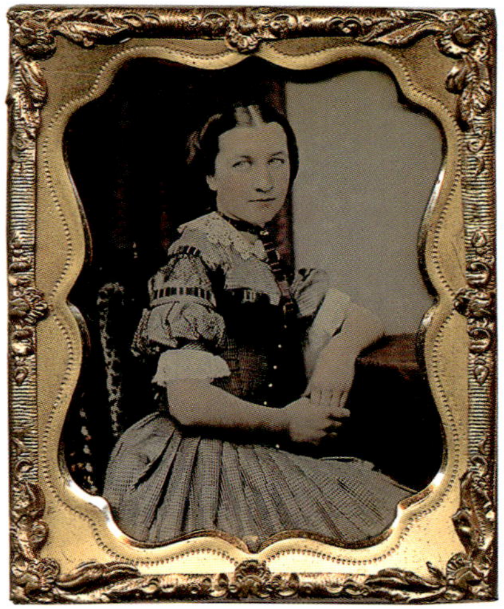

Above left: Quarter plate ambrotype from the mid 1850s, heavily overpainted with thickly applied paint – leaving almost none of the original photograph visible through the paint except the sitter's face. The style in which colour has been painted on to the flowers is very similar to the painting technique used in the whole plate example on page 78.

Above: Ninth plate tinted ambrotype, c.1860. Despite the detailed instructions on colouring given by Sparling (see previous pages), the tinting on this image is restricted to a flesh colour lightly applied to the subject's face and arms, and a deep burgundy for the curtains and tablecloth. Her buttons have been picked out in gold. The case in which the image was sold has a matching burgundy pad and trim.

Both these images are reproduced at actual size.

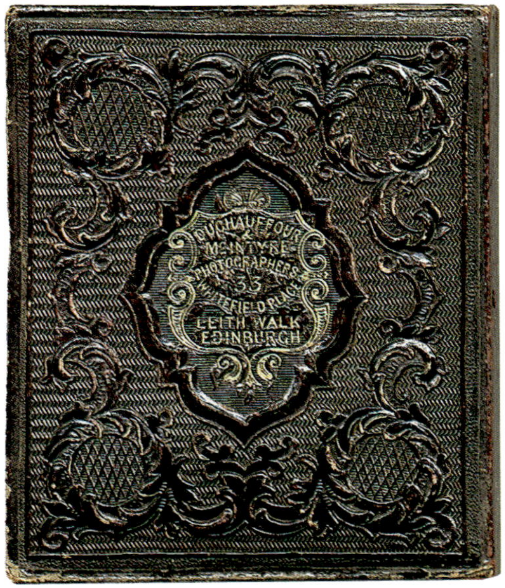

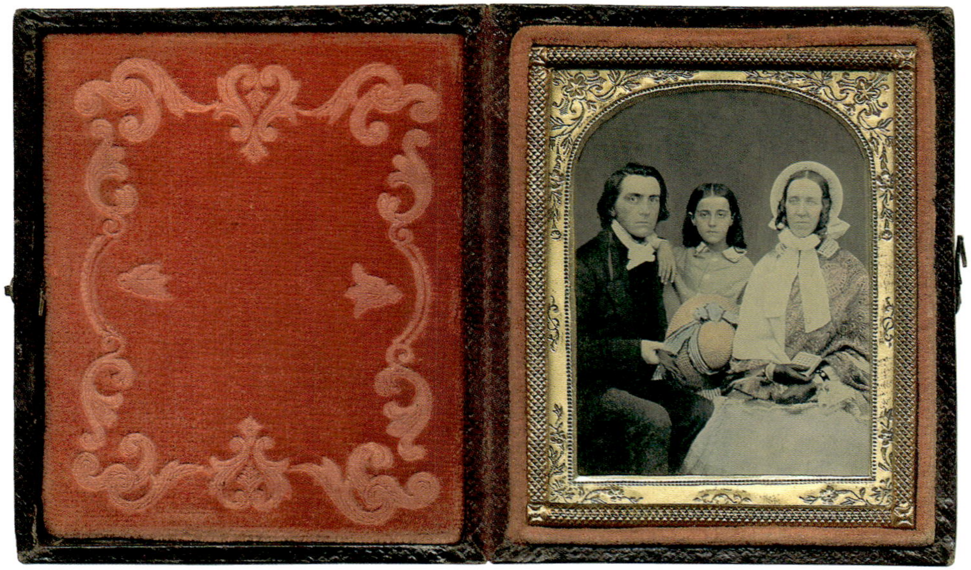

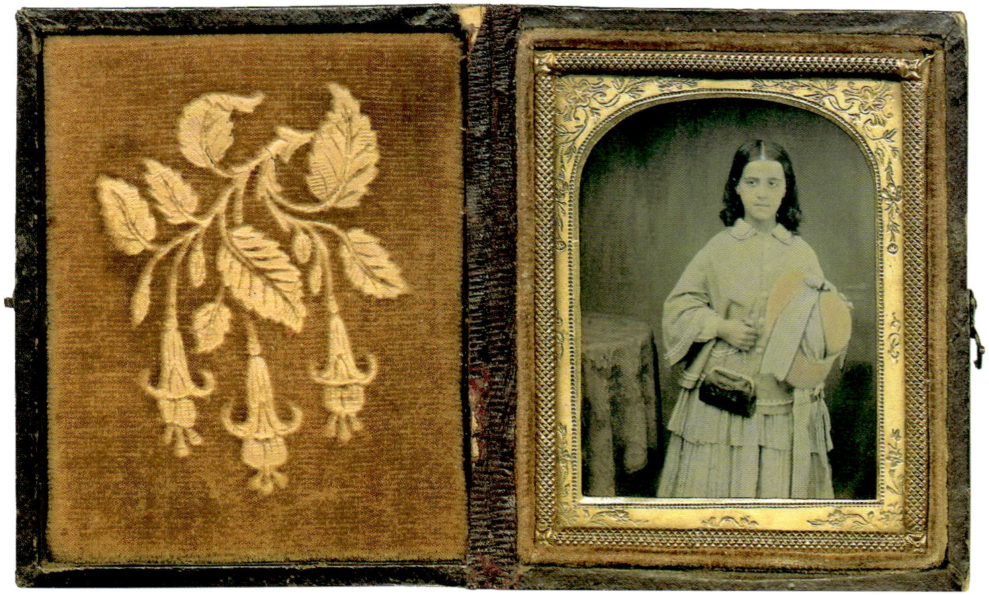

Two lightly tinted ninth plate ambrotypes by Duchauffour & McIntyre of 33 Whitefield Place, off Leith Walk, Edinburgh, late 1850s. Interestingly, for two portraits taken at the same time and tinted with exactly the same palette of colours, the decoration within the two cases is quite different. While the family group portrait is set in a pink trim and the case is fitted with a pink velvet pad, the portrait of the little girl is set in beige trim and has a beige pad. Neither is particularly appropriate for the colouring on the images themselves. These two portraits appear to have lost considerable colour over the years – there is still a hint of a blue colouration on the girl's dress. Only the flesh tint and the pink applied to the bonnet ribbon seem to have been a sufficiently stable pigment to endure the passage of time. The fuschia embossed on to the beige pad was a popular motif in the 1850s and 1860s, and has been found on a considerable number of cases. It has also been found in pink and deep red, with pink appearing to be the most popular.

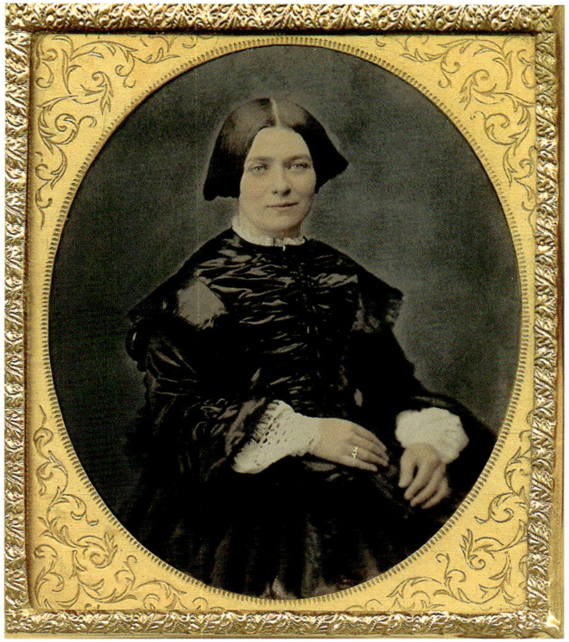

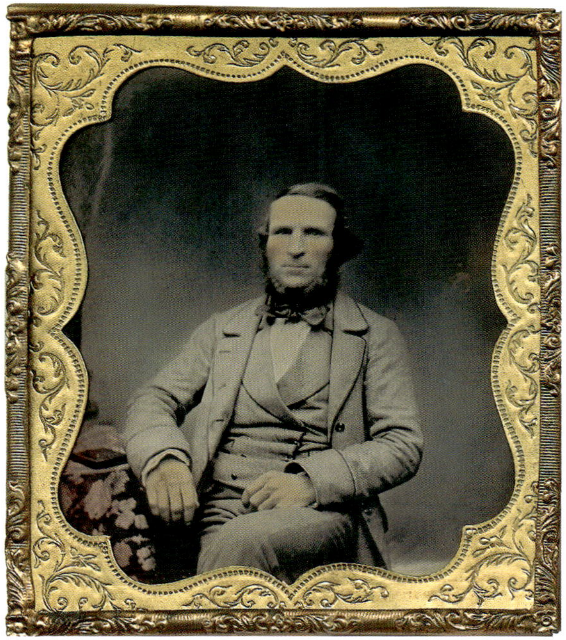

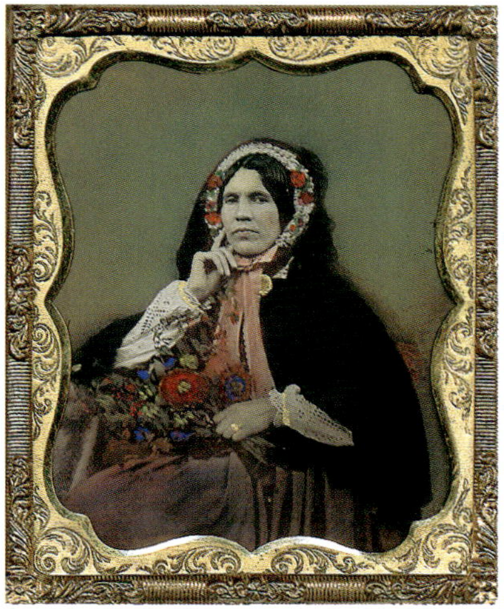

'MR. BEARD'S COLOURED PHOTOGRAPHIC PORTRAITS are taken daily at 85 King William street, City, 34 Parliament street, Westminster, and at the Royal Polytechnic Institution, Regent street. "The likeness obtained after the late improvements is indeed a veritable reflection of the face." – Morning Post.

"The portraits in colours, by their singularly close approximation to nature, no less delighted than astonished us" – Morning Herald. *"The resulting tableau will bear comparison with the best miniature."* – Morning Chronicle.'

Below, appearing to be a separate advertisement, Beard repeated further favourable comment on his work.

'THE TIMES *on PHOTOGRAPHY. - "We have been much pleased with the inspection of some portraits by Mr. Beard. A great improvement has been effected. The portraits now exhibit a degree of boldness, and stand out with a relief greatly desiderated in all the earliest specimens of the art, while the method of colouring renders them agreeable and life-like." Mr. BEARD's establishment, 85, King William street, City: 34 Parliament street Westminster: and the Royal Polytechnic Institution.'*

(In both – or all three – advertisements, the use of a lower case 's' in street names typifies the style of the period.)

With the advent of colouring on a widespread scale, the presentation of the nineteenth century photographic portrait seems to have taken on a new dimension. Initially available with white or pink silk pads, the miniature case soon sported a wide variety of pads, in a range of materials, patterns and colours.

With first quality velvet, cotton velvet, silk or satin available, and the possibility of colour matching the pad and surround to the colours of the sitter's clothing, the case interior became as much a part of a personal statement as the pose adopted for the camera.

With, for example, a deep green velvet pad echoing a green checked dress, and a gold dog-tooth paper edging around the case edge echoing

Above left: Sixth plate tinted ambrotype of a lady, with gilded ring. Only the skin tones appear to have been tinted in this fine image, yet the effect is surprisingly realistic.

Above centre: This sixth plate ambrotype has had tints applied to the gentleman's skin and to the tablecloth, as well as a shaded blue wash to the background.

Above right: Heavily painted ninth plate ambrotype of a lady with a rose bonnet. The decision to paint a green ground behind the subject is a curious one.

The two sixth plate images are both laterally reversed – note the wedding ring on the lady and the jacket buttons on the gentleman's suit – while the ninth plate image is right-reading. All three of these images date from c.*1860 and are housed in thermoplastic union cases.*

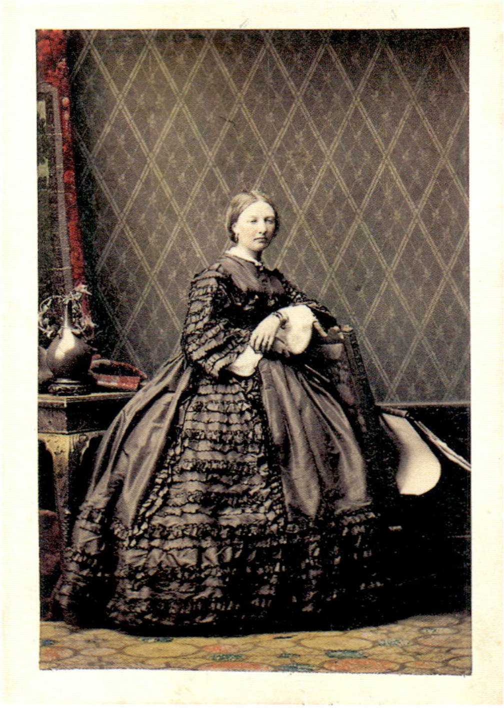

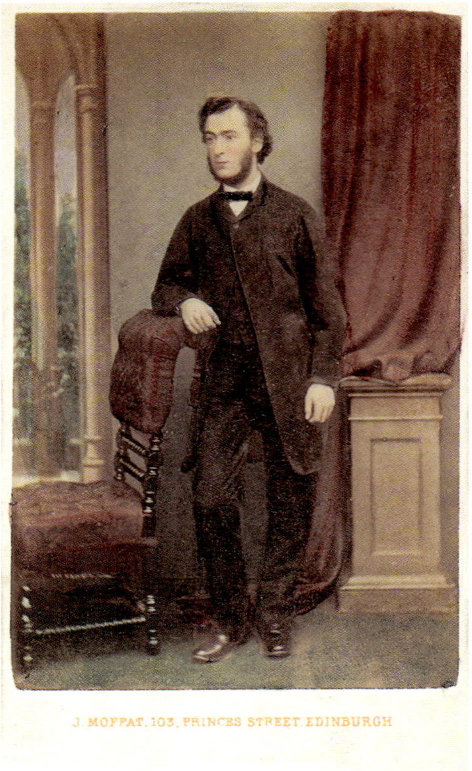

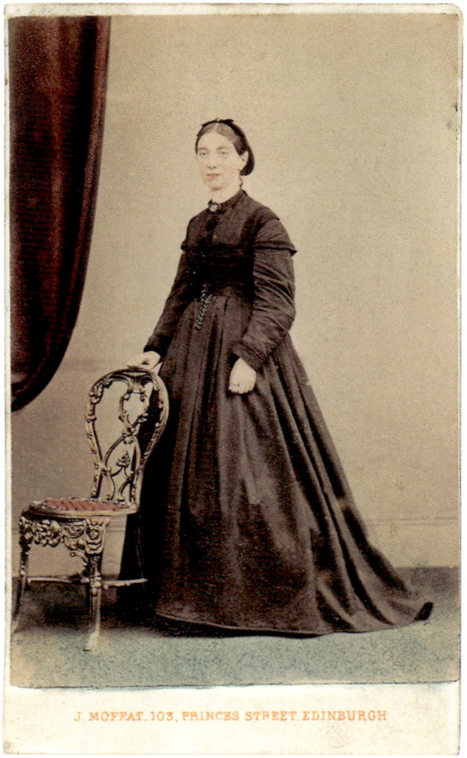

Left: Tinted portrait of an unidentified lady by Camile Silvy, 38 Porchester Terrace, Bayswater, London, mid 1860s. Silvy is reputed to have been the first photographer in London to take up the carte-de-visite format in 1859, the date coinciding with his acquisition of the Caldesi studio. He was an acclaimed portrait photographer, with a sensitivity for posing and for lighting. Technically, his carte-de-visite prints are of the highest quality, and show little deterioration over the years. While the work of other photographers has faded, Silvy's cartes are as rich and luxurious today as they were one hundred and forty years ago. His portrait clients were London's rich and famous, and his Porchester Terrace studio enjoyed considerable popularity over more than a decade. He operated the studio from 1859 until perhaps no later than the summer of 1868. Silvy carte-de-visite portraits are typically mounted on shorter cards than the standard used by other photographers.

Centre and right: A pair of tinted carte-de-visite portraits by John Moffat of 103 Princes Street, Edinburgh. Moffat moved to this address from his earlier studio at 60 Princes Street in the summer of 1860, and he continued to operate there until 1875. During his long professional career he occupied premises at four different addresses on Edinburgh's premier street. These portraits date from c.*1870. An accomplished watercolour artist as well as a photographer, it is perhaps not surprising that Moffat's carte-de-visite photographs were available tinted.*

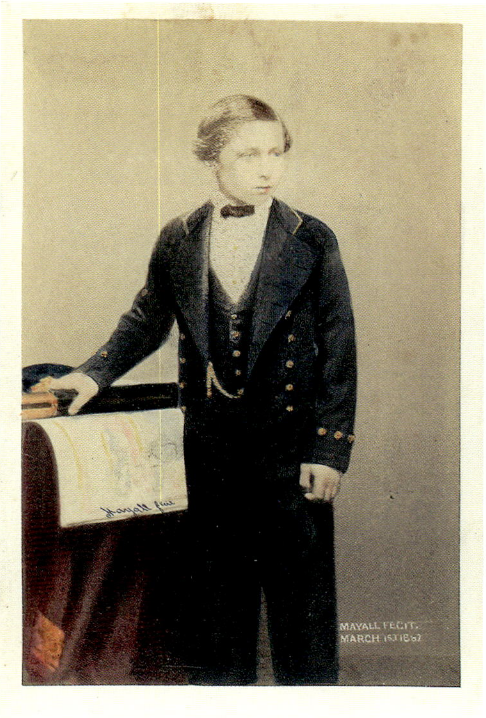

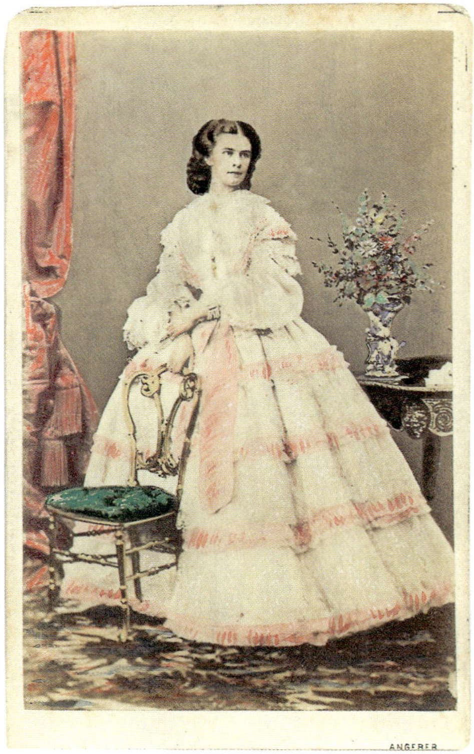

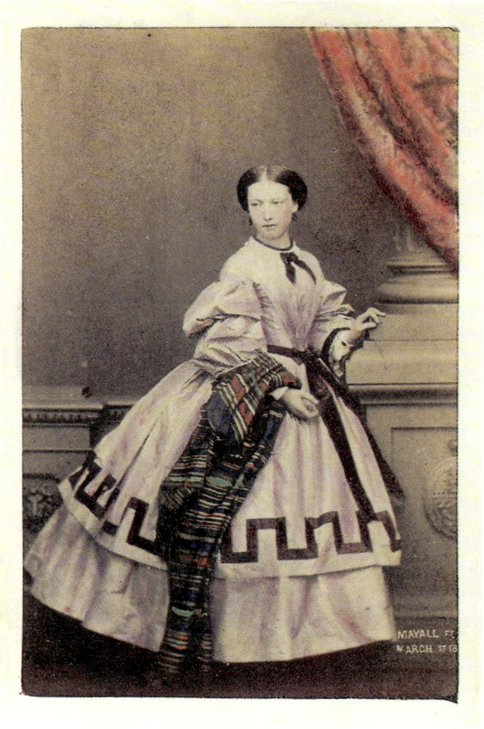

Tinted carte-de-visite prints of Royalty, both British and European, were sold widely through photographic studios and print sellers. Perhaps the most successful images, Mayall's pictures of Queen Victoria and her children, could be acquired either coloured or plain.
Left: Tinted portrait of Prince Arthur, Duke of Connaught, photographed by J.E. Mayall on March 1st 1862. The legend 'Mayall fecit' is written in script on the coloured cloth to the Prince's left – probably scribed on to the glass plate negative, while 'Mayall fecit, March 1st 1862' appears in white bottom right, having been printed in black ink on to the negative. Perhaps no more than three colours, and some gilding, have been used to create the effect here.
Centre: The Empress of Austria, photographed by Angerer, early 1860s. Despite looking richly coloured, only three or four tints have been used to create this portrait. Each is added relatively crudely, typical of a print produced in large numbers and coloured on a 'production-line' basis.
Right: The Princess Helena, March 1st 1862, also by J. E. Mayall. Blue, red, green and a flesh tint have been used very cleverly to create the illusion of many more colours. The brown is the colour of the albumen image itself, and the yellow/cream the base colour of the paper.
All the images on these two pages are reproduced here at actual size.

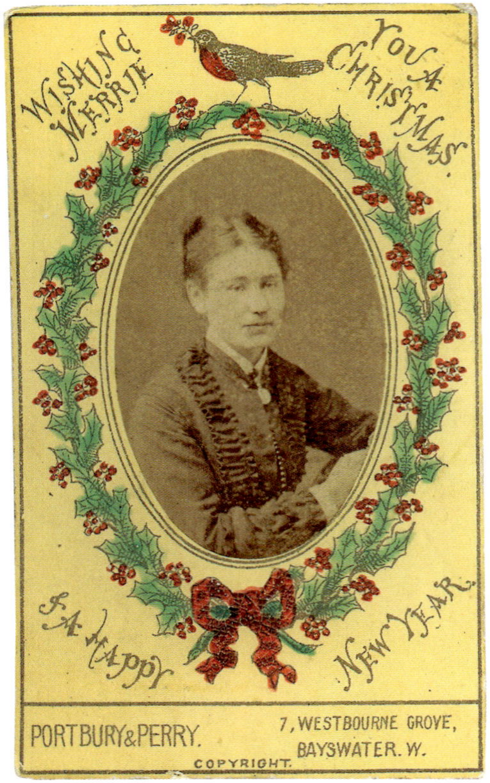

Coloured cartes, coloured enlargements – made with the solar enlarger – and life size paintings based on cartes were all available from High Street studios. William Portbury and John Perry ran their studio, the Photographic Art Union, in Piccadilly from 1863 until 1867, opening in Westbourne Grove, probably in 1866. Portbury operated the studio alone from 1868. Interestingly, here it is the decoration surrounding the portrait rather than the portrait itself which has been coloured.

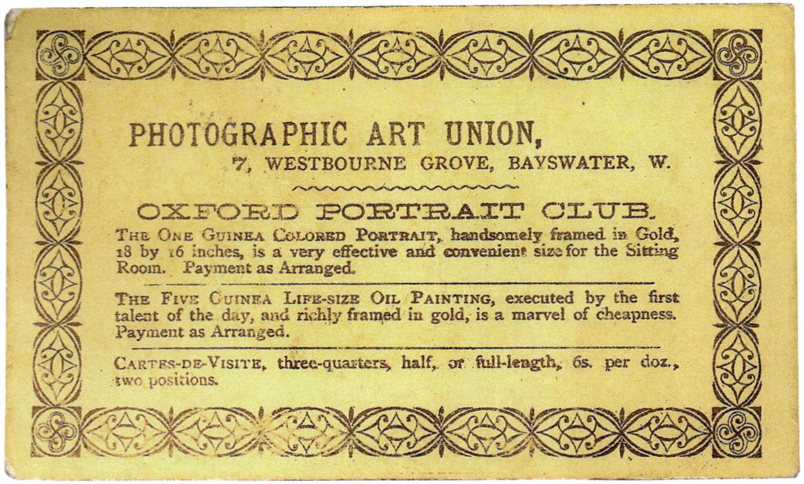
PHOTOGRAPHIC ART UNION,
7, WESTBOURNE GROVE, BAYSWATER, W.

OXFORD PORTRAIT CLUB.

THE ONE GUINEA COLORED PORTRAIT, handsomely framed in Gold, 18 by 16 inches, is a very effective and convenient size for the Sitting Room. Payment as Arranged.

THE FIVE GUINEA LIFE-SIZE OIL PAINTING, executed by the first talent of the day, and richly framed in gold, is a marvel of cheapness. Payment as Arranged.

CARTES-DE-VISITE, three-quarters, half, or full-length, 6s. per doz., two positions.

the sitter's rings and necklaces, a luxurious 'bespoke' effect was created.

By the time the carte-de-visite was in the ascendancy, almost every portrait studio offered to enlarge or reduce photographic portraits, and to have them coloured or painted in every size from the tiny image used in a brooch or a locket right up to life size portraits and larger! The colourists used water based dyes which penetrated the surface and gave a relatively permanent coloured finish. Thanks to the sepia on cream of the albumen print, the colourist actually had very little to do to the skin tones to make them look good. A slight warming of the cream/sepia skin on the print produced a surprisingly realistic colour. The natural brown of the print looked coloured anyway, and in many portraits, it is apparent on close scrutiny, that very little colouring has actually been carried out, despite the very realistic appearance. With cartes costing as little as two shillings for half a dozen tinted prints (10p), the amount of time a colourist could afford to spend on the prints must have been very small indeed.

Bearing in mind that hand tinted prints were available on a commercial scale for 2d – less than 1p – each, it becomes apparent that adding colour had to be simple and speedy.

As the carte-de-visite became popular, leading studios such as J.E. Mayall marketed tinted carte portraits of the the Royal Family, and these were available through High Street studios nationwide. Studying them closely, the quality of the colouring can be appreciated, despite the fact that they must have been coloured on a 'production-line' basis. The commercially produced portrait, however, was rarely tinted. The additional expense of tinting what was a utilitatian low cost portrait was not widely appreciated. Other studios advertised that they painted from photographs, or even painted over photographs. Photography may have become the medium for everyman, but it had not shaken off the traditions of the miniature painting. To many, the more like a painting it looked and the less the original photograph remained visible, the higher its perceived value!

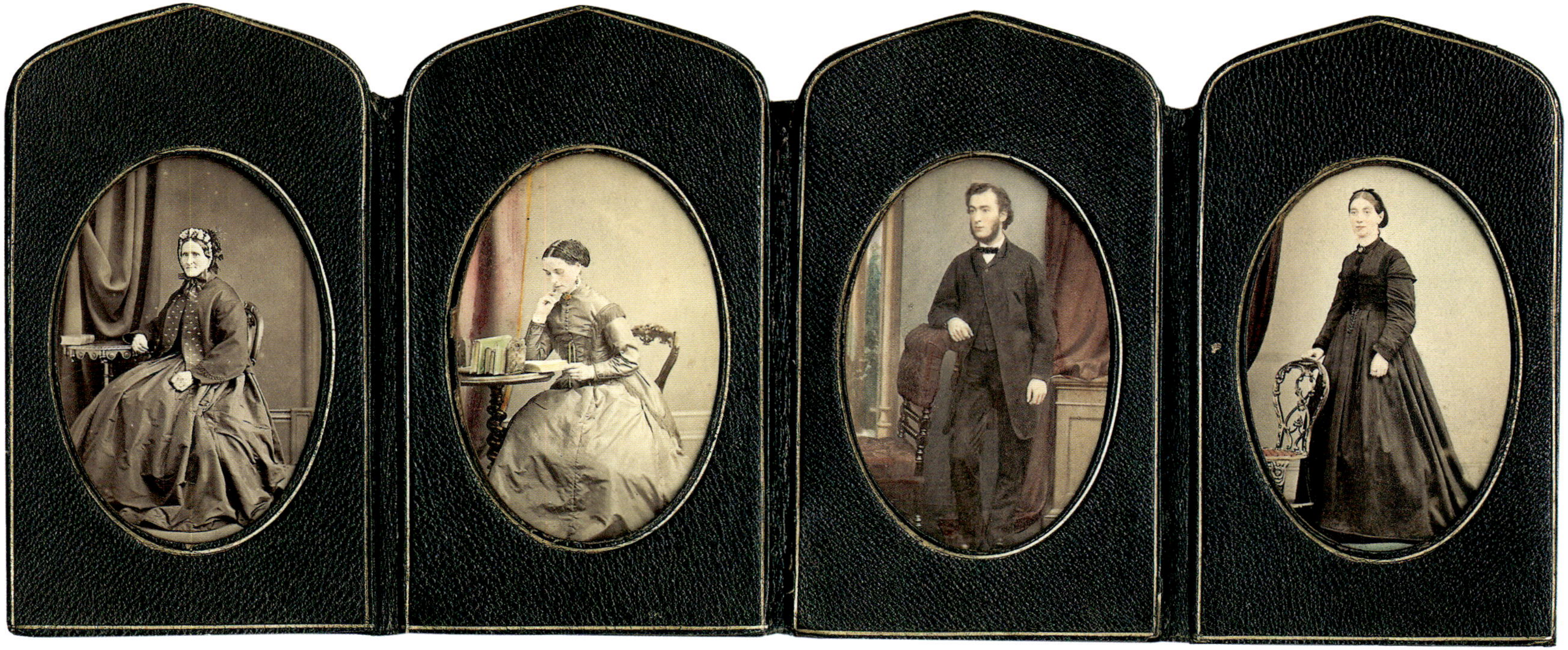

Leather folding frames for cartes-de-visite were a popular successor to the cased portrait, and ideal for display in the Victorian drawing room. This example is in fine quality black leather, with gilded decoration. The majority of cartes, however, were stored and displayed in family albums.

Footnotes

1. Alexander Wolcott (1804-44) is credited with opening the first professional photographic portrait studio in the world – in New York in March 1840, and with having taken what was probably the first successful daguerreotype portrait on October 7th 1839. Labels on the backs of some early Beard daguerreotypes confirm that the reflecting camera was used at the Royal Polytechnic Institution studio in its early days, and indeed Beard had acquired the British patent rights for the camera. Wolcott himself later moved to London, established a daguerreotype studio with John Johnson, and patented an unusual device for copying daguerreotypes, British Patent 9672, March 18th 1843.
2. Claudet advertised his studio as 'Mr Claudet's Coloured and Non-Inverted Daguerreotype Establishment' in the *Art Union* in October 1846. Inverted daguerreotypes could have their right-reading restored by copying them using either Wolcott's copying camera, or a device designed by Claudet for the same purpose.
3. Beard's advice to sitters on dress was not unique. Several contemporary magazines offered advice to their readers. In the *People's Journal*, Volume II, 11846, p.288, the writer cautioned *'Some ladies dress themselves out in snowy berthas and spotless wristbands; but many a good picture is spoiled by the spottiness occasioned by the powerful action of this colour upon the plate.'*
4. Limited understanding at the time of the narrow spectral sensitivity of the daguerreotype plate is apparent in this reference to the dark lips.
5. *Dumfries & Galloway Courier*, March 27th 1843.
6. Johann Baptiste Isenring, a Swiss painter and daguerreotypist is credited with putting together the first exhibition of photography in Europe – exhibiting 47 daguerreotype portraits, still lifes and architectural subjects – in St Gallen in August 1840.
7. Snelling, Henry, *The History and Practice of the Art of Photography; or the Production of Pictures Through the Agency of Light*, published by G. P. Putnam, New York, 1849, page pp 76-77.
8. Quoted in Stephan Richter *The Art of the Daguerreotype*, Viking Books, 1989, page 12.
9. Snelling, Henry, *The History and Practice of the Art of Photography; or the Production of Pictures Through the Agency of Light*, published by G. P. Putnam, New York, 1849, pp.130-131.
10. W. Sparling, *Theory and Practice of the Photographic Art* Houlston & Stoneman, 1856, pp.204-206.
11. *Journal of the Photographic Society* No.18, June 21st 1854, p.224.

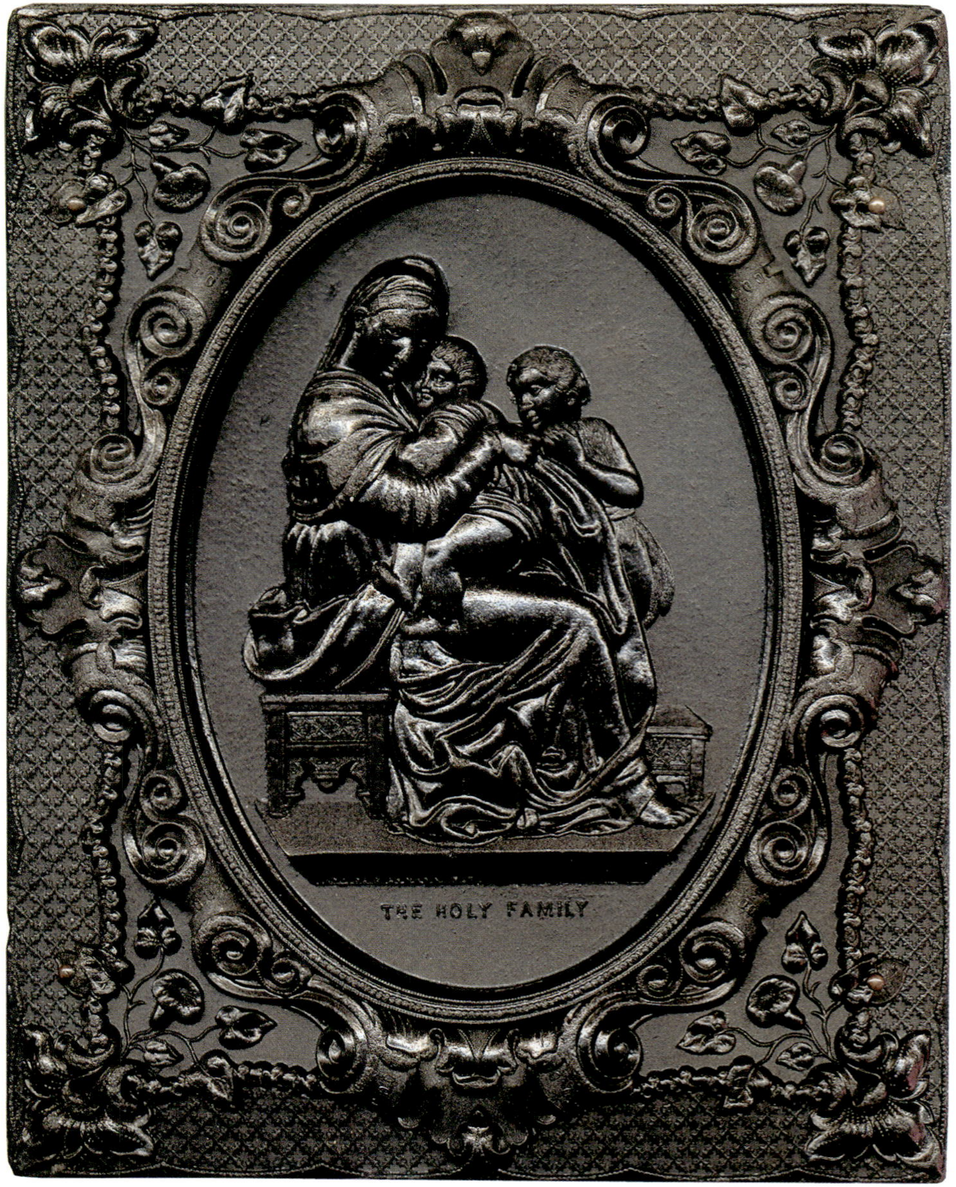

'The Holy Family', a half plate thermoplastic union case by Holmes, Booth & Hayden, 1859-60.
The pictorial union case is today highly prized by collectors, although in their day they carried no price premium over the simpler and cheaper to produce geometric designs.
Almost one thousand different designs were realised in thermoplastic between 1852 and 1862, many of them the height of the die-maker's art. This case is based on Raphael's painting 'Madonna della sedia' completed in 1515 and the die from which it was moulded was created by Henning and Eymann of New York. Henning and Eymann created the half plate case, 'The Vision of Ezekiel', also derived from a Raphael painting, illustrated on page 98.

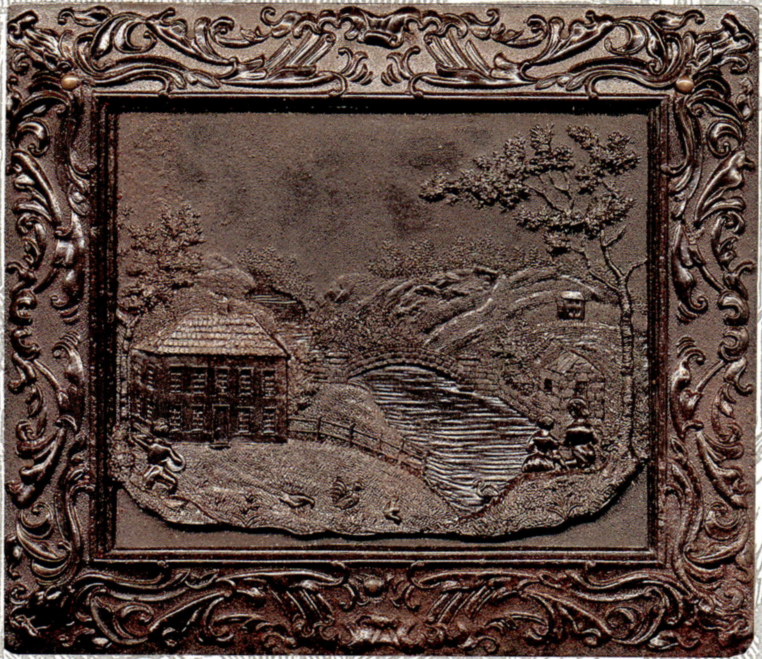

Chapter Six

The Thermoplastic Case and the Art of the Die-Maker

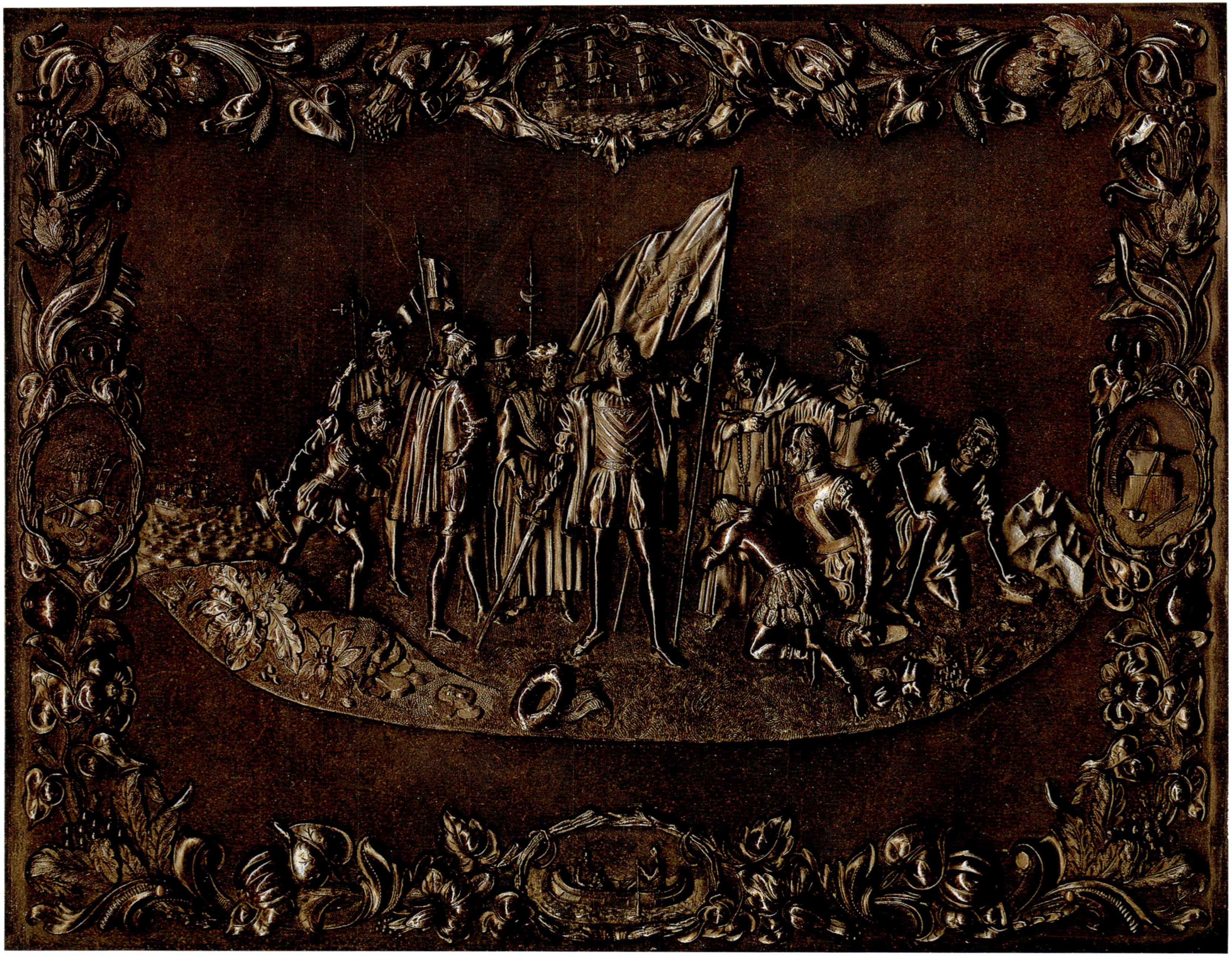

'The Landing of Columbus' is one of only three known whole plate union case design. The case measures 237mm x 186mm and holds the tinted ambrotype portrait on page 78.

Chapter Six:

The Thermoplastic Case and the Art of the Die-Maker

If the development of the photographic case had been restricted to leather, paper and papier mâché examples, it would still have left us with a rich inheritance. However, with the introduction of the thermoplastic case in the early 1850s, the casemaker's art changed out of all recognition. Plastic, thought of by so many as a modern innovation, brought to the presentation of the Victorian photographic portrait a degree of skill and sophistication which only a very few years before would have been unthinkable.

It brought casemaking out of the realms of hand-crafted industry into 'modern' mass production.

It turned the case – once merely the outer protection for the photograph – into an *objet d'art* in its own right and, in doing so, expanded the market considerably by raising the selection of case – or at least of the design, motif or image moulded on to the case – to a level of importance equalling that of the picture it contained.

The introduction of the union case has often been written of as a logical evolution from the moulded papier mâché product, but this is incorrect. The two are generally contemporary. Papier mâché cases started to appear at the turn of the decade, and the first union cases appeared as early as 1852.

The two products have a lot in common, however – the most important being that both removed casemaking from the traditional procedure of fixing covers to wooden frames. Neither the papier mâché case nor the union case were based on wooden frames, although one design reputedly used a metal frame, and some patented designs were reinforced with metal strips. Both types of cases were moulded products. Both methods of manufacture also allowed the casemaker to incorporate sophisticated and often delicate design motifs into the faces of their products, although as will be seen, the union case soon left the moulded paper case far behind in terms of the complexity and delicacy of the patterns which could be produced.

Where they differ fundamentally – apart from the moulding material – is in the hinging. While the papier mâché case used a ribbon hinge and conventional fasteners, the union case used riveted or embedded brass hinges and closures.

Portrait of a lady, ninth plate ambrotype with tinted background, housed in a simple geometric union case by Samuel Peck & Co, c.1857. The label inside acknowledges Peck's patent of October 3rd 1854, Halvorson's patent of August 7th 1855 assigned to Peck, and Peck's third patent of February 5th 1856. The union case, its moulding and its hinges, was the subject of fierce rivalry between the major manufacturers, and most defined their patent rights on labels inside each case.

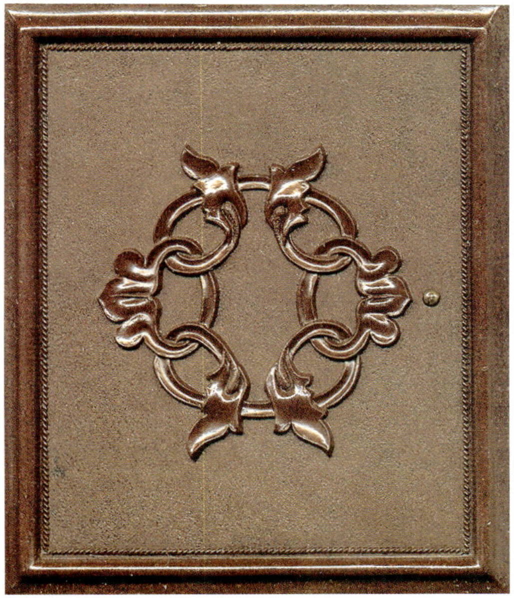

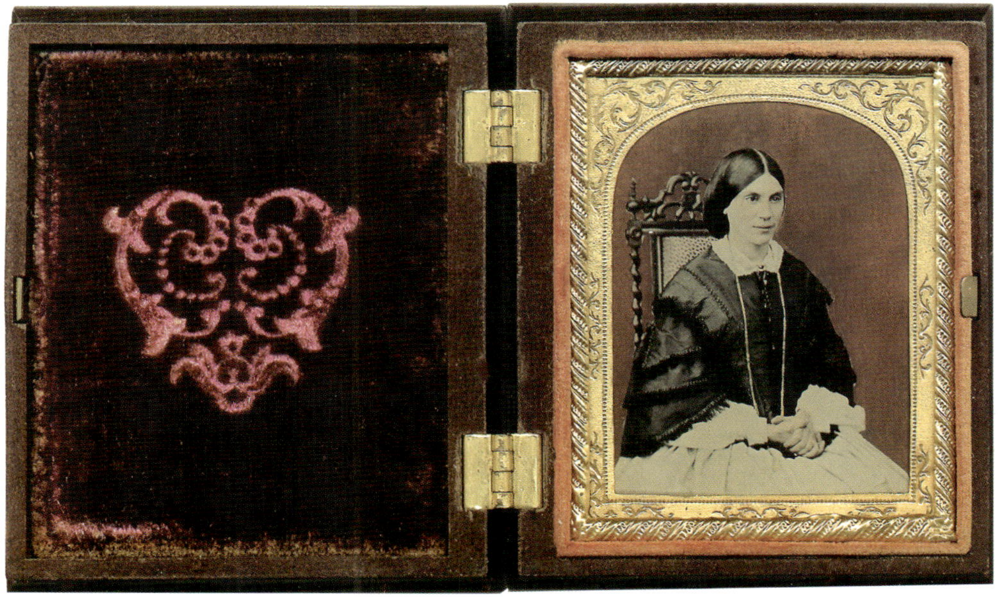

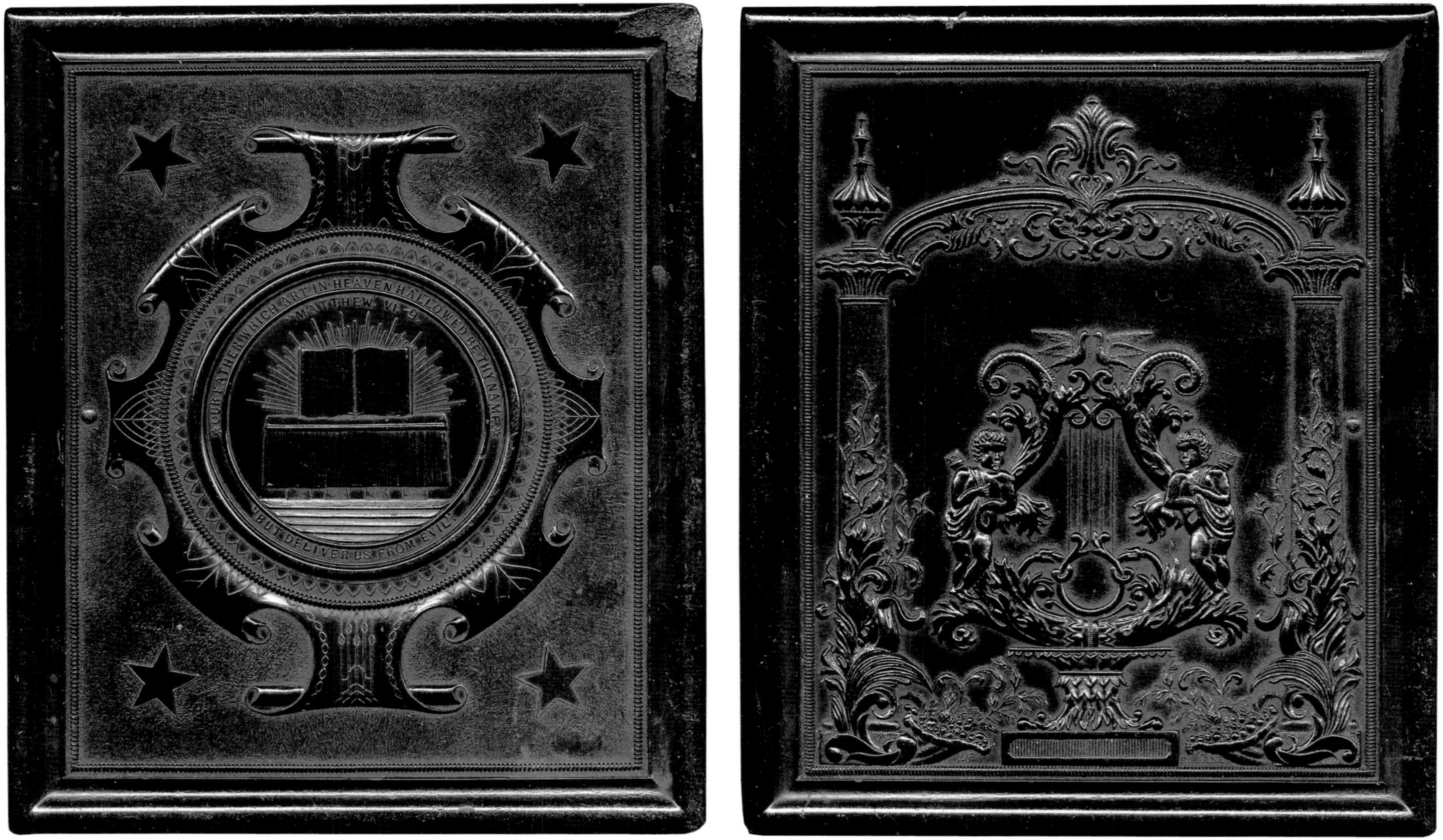

Quarter plate thermoplastic union case, reproduced actual size. One face bears a design known as 'the Memorial' while the other contains the words of the Lord's Prayer, surrounding an open book (Bible?) on an altar. This case, in black plastic, was produced as a proper housing for a deathbed portrait, or a portrait of a loved-one now deceased. Many union case designs celebrated religious motifs and ideals. This case is believed to have been one of the first produced by Samuel Peck, as a letter concerning the evolution of the design survives, dated 1853.

It is perhaps worthwhile at this stage, before examining the range and quality of the union case, to define the word *plastic*. While most dictionaries today offer two definitions of the word, the Victorians knew only one. Plastic, to them, meant *produced by moulding or capable of being moulded*. Today a second definition is offered to define the synthetic and polymer materials which are such an integral part of our lifestyles. So, by that earlier definition, a wide range of materials were and are plastic rather than plastics.

Thus to Victorians, gutta percha[1] was plastic – a natural rubbery material which became pliable when heated and could be crudely moulded. When cool, it became rigid and impermeable. Gutta percha was used for a variety of products from the 1840s – from knife handles to small dishes and ornaments. As far as photography was concerned, its resistance to acids made it an ideal substance out of which to fabricate processing dishes and vessels. Union cases are often mistakenly described as 'gutta percha' which they are not.

By the modern definition, only polymer materials would be described as 'plastics' rather than 'plastic'. It is a fine distinction. To those who believe that the first true plastics grew out of an understanding of polymer science, a lot of earlier materials such as the shellac-based thermoplastic of which union cases were made, gutta percha, bois durci[2] and others would be excluded from a list of so called 'true plastics'.

The currently understood distinction is between natural and synthetic materials. The materials used in the manufacture of union cases were natural materials, moulded under heat and pressure. Today's plastics are synthetic materials produced as a result of strictly controlled chemical reactions.

In that respect, the first true plastic – by the second definition – is widely recognised as being cellulose nitrate, later patented in the USA by John Wesley Hyatt, and later given the generic name of 'celluloid'. The first patents for celluloid were granted in 1869, some seventeen years after the introduction of the material from which union cases were made, although nitrocellulose itself had been used as the basis for Parkesine by British manufacturer Alexander Parkes of Birmingham[3] as early as 1862 in the manufacture of frames, boxes, moulded medallions and even piano keys!

It cannot just be as a result of scientific advance that this distinction has been arrived at. Indeed just why there should be an almost universal assumption that plastics are 'modern' is difficult to explain – given that polystyrene, that most ubiquitous of plastic materials, was actually first produced in England about the same time that Queen Victoria acceded to the throne!

The thermoplastic material of which union cases were made, however, was first identified in 1852, and patented in 1854 by Samuel Peck[4], onetime photographer himself, and in the years immediately prior to 1852, manufacturer of both leather and papier mâché photographic cases.

Peck was not alone and, like so many other pioneering innovations, thermoplastic materials were produced along almost identical lines by several other contemporary workers, each experimenting in apparent ignorance of the others.

Peck does, however, appear to have been the first to produce and market cases, with his first designs apparently available widely from mid 1853. One of the first of these designs – a light relief moulding by comparison with later and more ambitious designs – depicted a funereal memorial on one side and the Lord's Prayer contained within a circular motif on the other. If not the first, it was certainly a very early Peck design, and both faces of it are illustrated here.

Indeed as the nineteenth century was more able to come to terms with death – particularly infant death – than we are today, a considerable market was developed by the production of suitably religious subjects with which to encase deathbed portraits, or recase portraits of loved ones now deceased. This particular theme in union case decoration will be dealt with in greater depth later in this chapter.

Within a very few years of its introduction, the union case evolved into one of the most elaborate

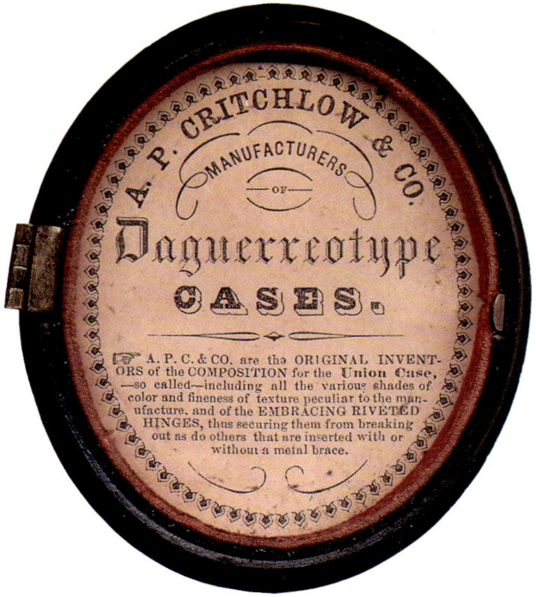

The interior of a union case by A. P. Critchlow, claims that – 'A.P.C.&Co. are the original inventors of the composition for the union case – so called – including all the various shades of color and fineness of texture peculiar to the manufacture, and of the embracing riveted hinges, thus securing them from breaking out as do others that are inserted with or without a metal brace.' *This label comes from a rare case known as 'The Serenade', one of a small number of oval cases produced in the late 1850s.*

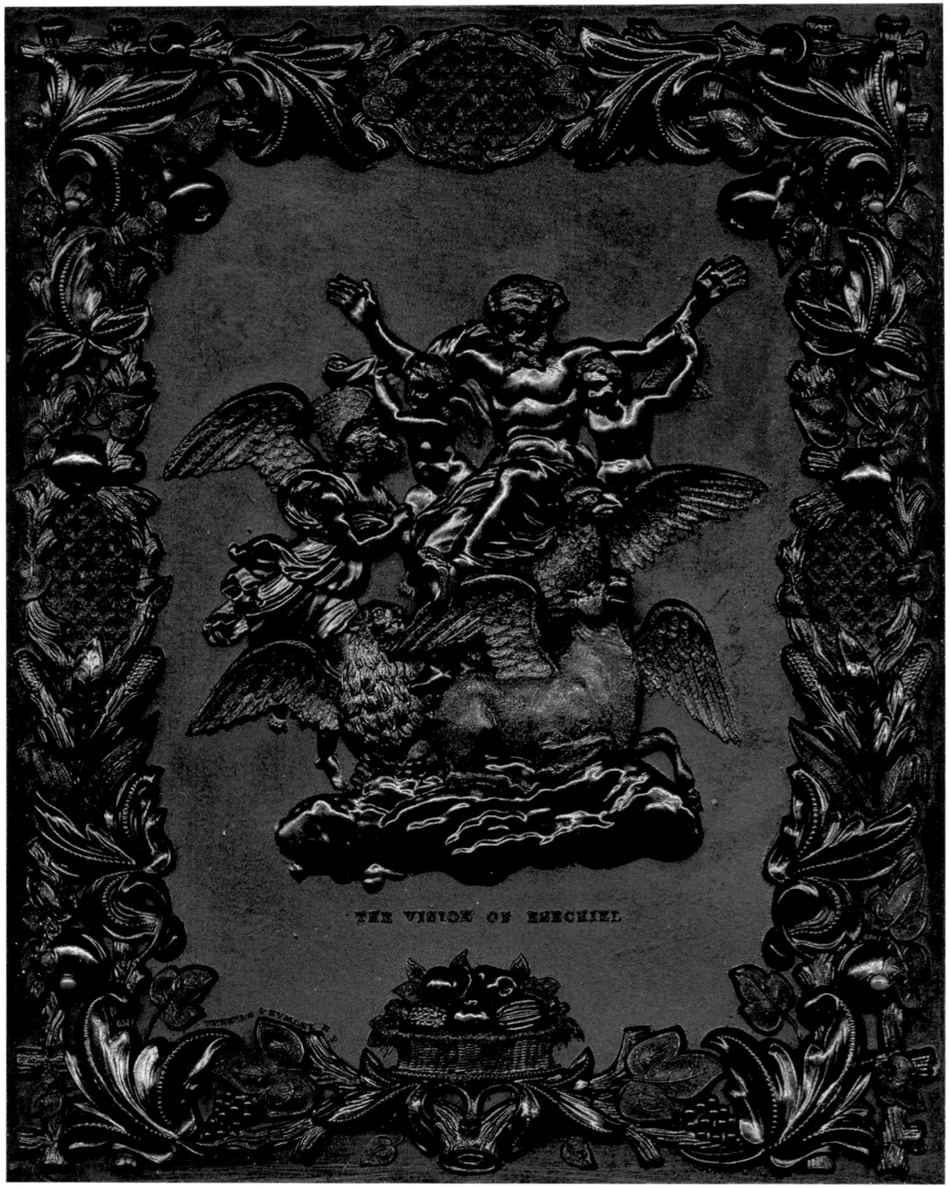

'The Vision of Ezekiel', engraved by Henning & Eymann, and manufactured by Holmes, Booth & Hayden, half plate union case, 1859-60. Raphael painted 'The Vision of Ezekiel' in 1518, drawing on the story of Ezekiel from the Old Testament. This case is highly prized by collectors because of the intricacy of its decoration, although it is available in some numbers. The basket of fruit at the bottom of the case design appears in over a dozen Holmes Booth & Hayden cases, sometimes as the primary motif, and also as part of the border decoration as here. It appears on cases from half plate down to sixteenth plate size. Variants use the same style of basket filled with flowers.

and sophisticated means of packaging photographs either before or since. It is unknown just how many designs were available – but it certainly exceeds nine hundred. And given that cases bearing the same or similar design motifs were available in a range of sizes and a (limited) range of colours, the choice must have been considerable. Leading American collectors have identified and catalogued over nine hundred variants and some of the cases illustrated here are very recent additions to those American listings. There will be many others as yet unlisted.

At least a dozen manufacturing companies were involved in their production at one time or another. Some of the most common were those produced by Samuel Peck - under the 'S. Peck & Co' banner. Peck acquired Halvorson's patents early on in the life of the case. The Scovill Manufacturing Company had been in partnership with S. Peck & Co since the early 1850s, later taking over the production of Peck cases when Peck himself left the business. A formal merger of the two companies' interests in union case manufacture in 1855 led to their joint output being marketed under the Peck name. A number of smaller companies arrived late on the scene – including onetime die-makers Frederick Key, Smith & Hartmann and several others.

John Smith – die engraver and Morocco case maker of New York – had a long tradition of leather case manufacture before becoming a somewhat late entrant into the plastic manufacturing scene. He had also been responsible for the engraving of dies for Peck cases in the mid 1850s, and he is believed to be the Smith whose name appears on several fine designs both by Peck and by Littlefield, Parsons & Co.

Another John Smith, this time of Birmingham in the English Midlands, a onetime horn button-maker, took up thermoplastic case manufacture in

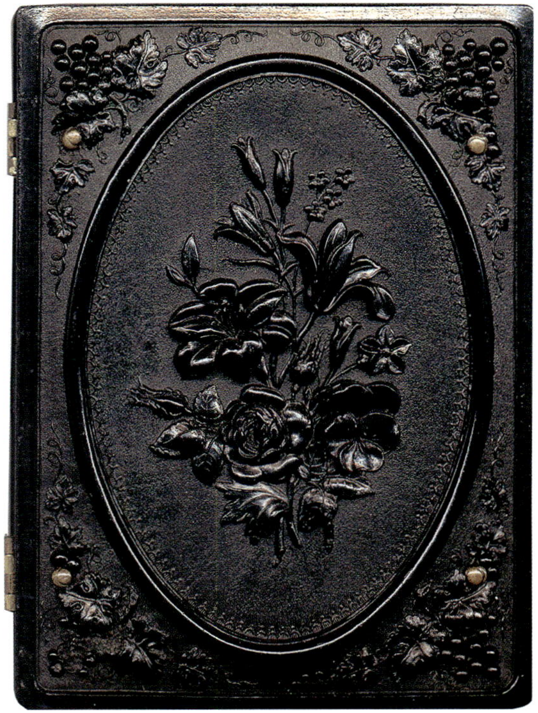

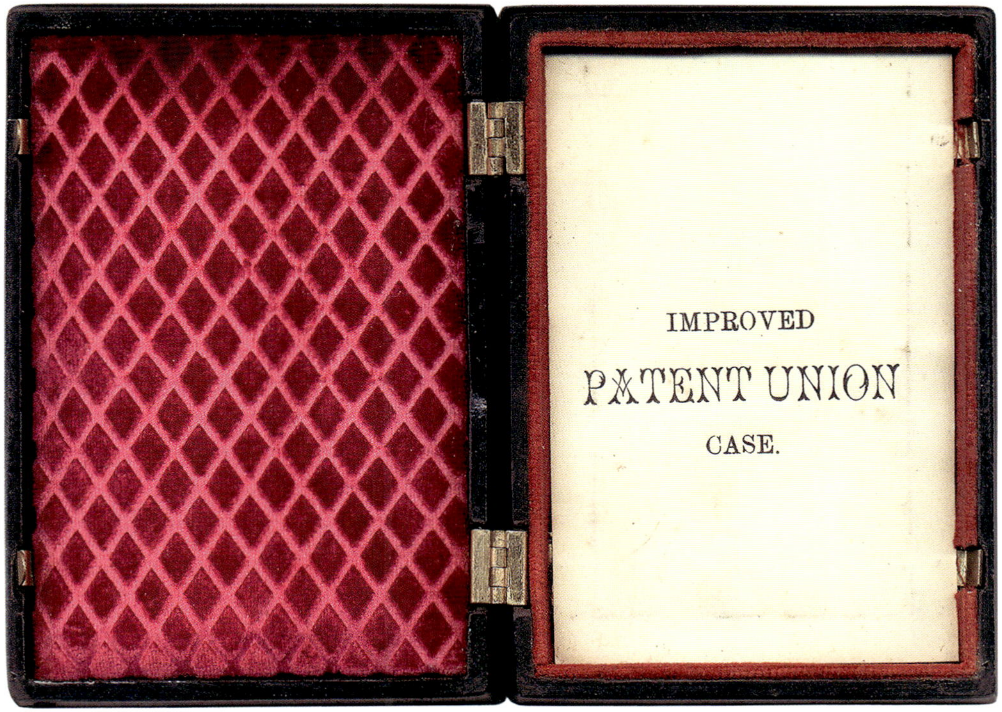

Union case for the carte-de-visite made by the British maker John Smith. The distinctive diamond-hatched purple velvet pad is unique to cases made by Smith and his successors, James and Edwin Gyde. While labels in early Smith cases bear the legend 'Smiths Patent Improved Union Case', research suggests that the label seen here dates from post-1862 when the Gydes operated the business. Actual case size 78mm x 107mm.

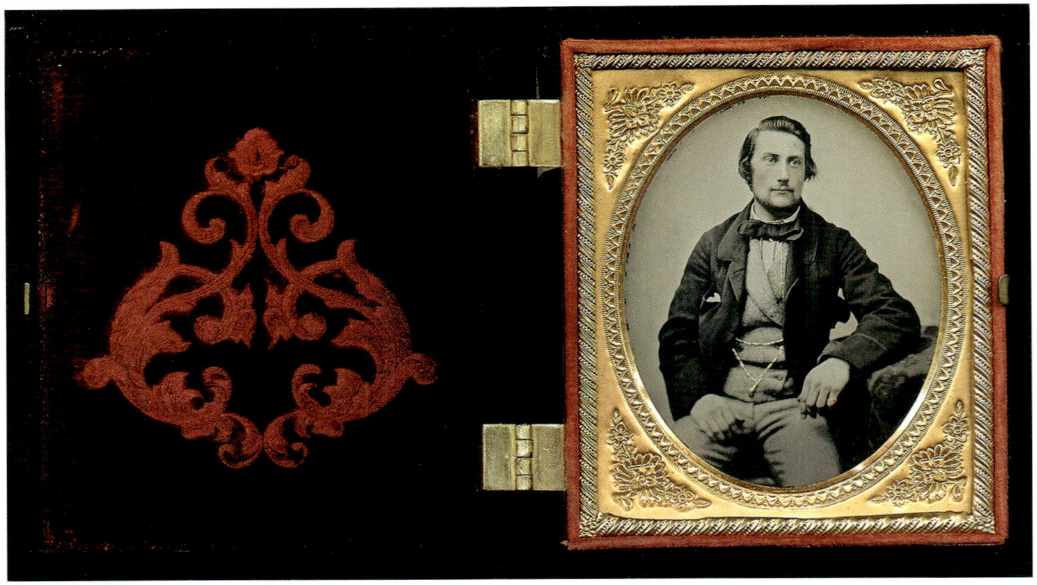

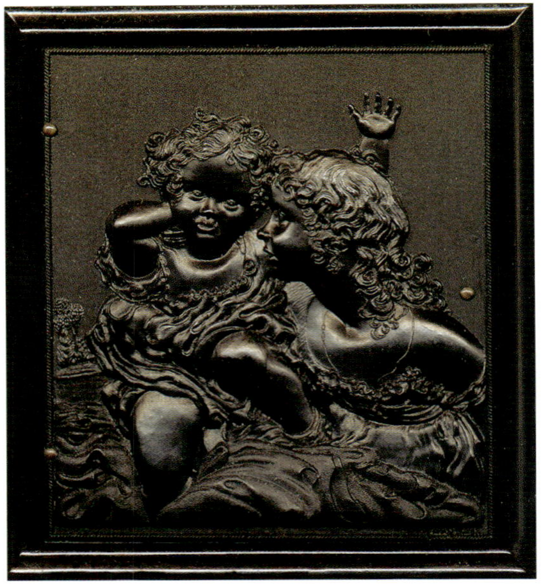

'The Calmady Children', a sixth plate union case based upon a painting by Sir Thomas Lawrence. The original painting is in New York's Metropolitan Museum of Art. Despite being relatively common, this case is prized by collectors on account of the beauty of its execution. The die was made by Hiram W. Hayden and the case produced by S. Peck & Co. Hiram Hayden went on, with his two brothers, to become part of Holmes, Booth & Hayden, creators of almost fifty very fine union cases after 1857. Actual case size 88mm x 97mm.

1859, and produced some highly detailed cases. He and his successors James and Edwin Gyde, remain the only British plastic casemakers yet identified.

There were a lot of Smiths involved in die making, engraving and case manufacture. Frederick B. Smith with Hermann Hartmann produced some fine designs, and an F.H. Smith is also mentioned in contemporary accounts. Hiram W. Hayden, of Holmes Booth & Hayden, was also a die-maker working at one time for Peck – during which period he produced the superb case design 'The Calmady Children' after a painting by Sir Thomas Lawrence which is illustrated in this chapter.

Alphabetically, the makers were as follows:-
J. Lewis Baldwin, A. B. Chapman, A.P. Critchlow (later incorporated into Littlefield Parsons & Co.), the Florence Manufacturing Company. Halvor Halvorson, Holmes Booth & Hayden, Frederick Key, Kinsley & Parker, Littlefield, Parsons & Co., Patent American Union Case Co., Samuel Peck & Co., Scovill Manufacturing Company, John Smith (British), and Wadhams Manufacturing Company. The Patent American Union Case Company may not, however, have been a manufacturer. There is strong, albeit circumstantial, evidence to support the opinion that this was simply the name under which some American cases were imported and marketed in Great Britain

The composition of the materials used for making union cases varied slightly from manufacturer to manufacturer. In his original American Patent (No.11758, October 3rd 1854) Peck gave full manufacturing details. He used a mixture of shellac and ground wood fibres (sometimes referred to as 'wood flour') together with a dye – unspecified – ground to the finest possible powder between rollers and under considerable pressure. When heated, this mixture became plastic.

Again under great pressure, it was pressed into moulds bearing the engraved design, motif or picture which would form the upper surface of the case.

Not long after Peck's patent had been filed,

news came back to him that a similar patent specification had been filed by one Horace Barnes on behalf of Halvor Halvorson. The patent specifications became the subject of extended discussions before Halvorson's patent was finally granted on 7th August 1855. Behind the scenes dealing seems to have been going on between the two parties, however, for not long afterwards and for an undisclosed sum, Halvorson's patents were assigned to Peck.

Several case labels bear the triple patent details:- *Genuine Union Case, improved, S. Peck's Patent Oct.3rd 1854, H. Halvorson's Patent Aug.7th 1855 Assigned to S. Peck, S. Peck's Patent Feb 5th 1856.*

The first case designs were moulded in plain black, but later designs were available in various shades of browns. Some even use a mottled brown more reminiscent of bakelite radios of the 1920s! Smaller cases were subsequently available in a selection of pastel colours as well and these, by virtue of their rarity, are highly prized by collectors.

Perhaps more than any other photographic product, the union case was the subject of a multitude of patents. Although the basic case composition and manufacture seems to have been fairly effectively covered by Peck and Halvorson's patents, the Englishman John Smith took out three patents in the UK to cover his composition, and his processes for producing coloured cases.

If the composition of the plastic material was fairly straightforward, the hinges and the means of attaching them to the case were the subject of several other patents by a variety of companies. The latter problem was quite complex. The case was made of a brittle plastic. Hinging the upper and lower halves of the case together could have been relatively simply achieved with a linen strip – such as was often used in papier mâché case construction – but the fixing of an effective closure was a different problem altogether. All union case manufacturing companies seem to have approached the problem from the same direction – using metal hinges and closures both to avoid stresses on the plastic as the case was opened and closed, and to ensure that when open, the case lay flat – lay flat, that is, except where high relief designs made such a plan impossible.

Ironically, while the use of metal hinges and closures was marketed as a strength, they have turned out to be the areas of greatest stress and most frequently found damage in union cases today.

Fixing the metal to the plastic was a considerable problem – and was solved by a variety of methods, almost every one of which was covered by a patent.

Most typical is the face riveted hinge – with several design differences in the hinge shape defining which manufacturer was responsible for it. Face riveted closure devices were also standard. This gave each half of the hinge the basic shape of an L with an additional arm at the bottom of the toe. The toe of the L was fitted against the spine of the case, with the downward extension set against the thickness of the case spine. In place, the hinge was flush with the edge of the spine. The vertical arm of the L therefore lay

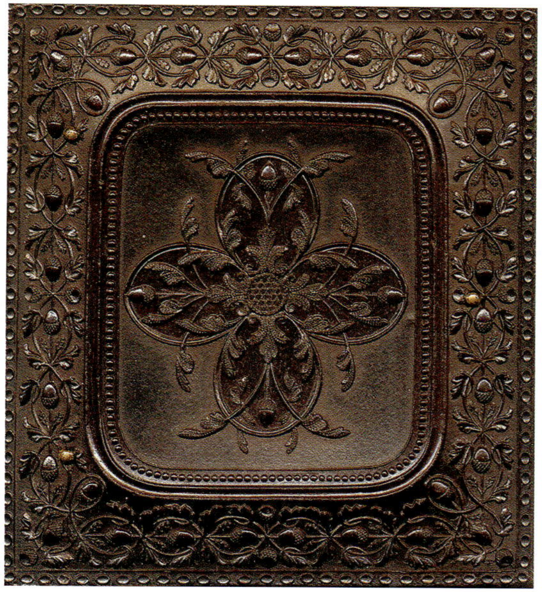

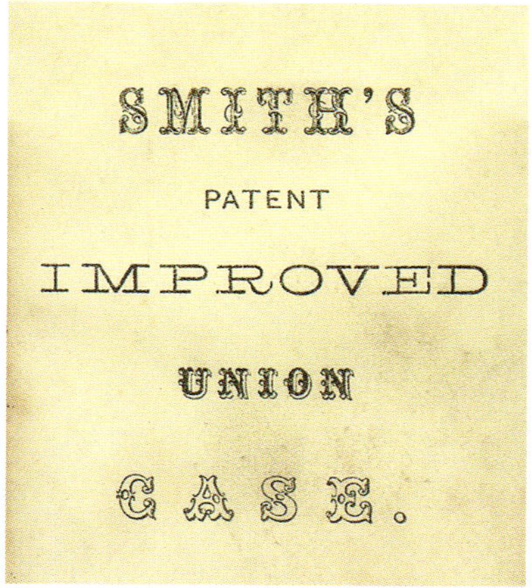

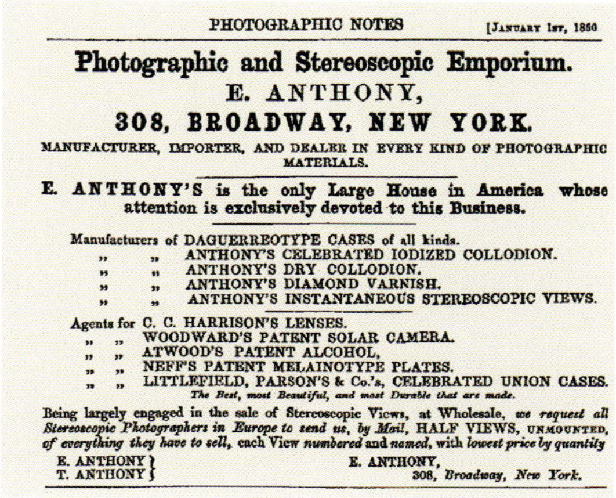
PHOTOGRAPHIC NOTES [January 1st, 1860

Photographic and Stereoscopic Emporium.

E. ANTHONY,

308, BROADWAY, NEW YORK.

MANUFACTURER, IMPORTER, AND DEALER IN EVERY KIND OF PHOTOGRAPHIC MATERIALS.

E. ANTHONY'S is the only Large House in America whose attention is exclusively devoted to this Business.

Manufacturers of DAGUERREOTYPE CASES of all kinds.
" " ANTHONY'S CELEBRATED IODIZED COLLODION.
" " ANTHONY'S DRY COLLODION.
" " ANTHONY'S DIAMOND VARNISH.
" " ANTHONY'S INSTANTANEOUS STEREOSCOPIC VIEWS.

Agents for C. C. HARRISON'S LENSES.
" " WOODWARD'S PATENT SOLAR CAMERA.
" " ATWOOD'S PATENT ALCOHOL,
" " NEFF'S PATENT MELAINOTYPE PLATES.
" " LITTLEFIELD, PARSON'S & Co.'s, CELEBRATED UNION CASES.
The Best, most Beautiful, and most Durable that are made.

Being largely engaged in the sale of Stereoscopic Views, at Wholesale, *we request all Stereoscopic Photographers in Europe to send us, by Mail*, HALF VIEWS, UNMOUNTED, *of everything they have to sell*, each View *numbered* and *named*, with *lowest price by quantity*

E. ANTHONY }
T. ANTHONY }
E. ANTHONY,
308, *Broadway, New York.*

Top: Acorn motif case by the English John Smith c.*1860, and the label he affixed inside. Actual case size 88mm x 98mm.*

Above: In January 1860, Anthony's of New York advertised direct importation of Littlefield, Parsons & Co's union cases in the British press.

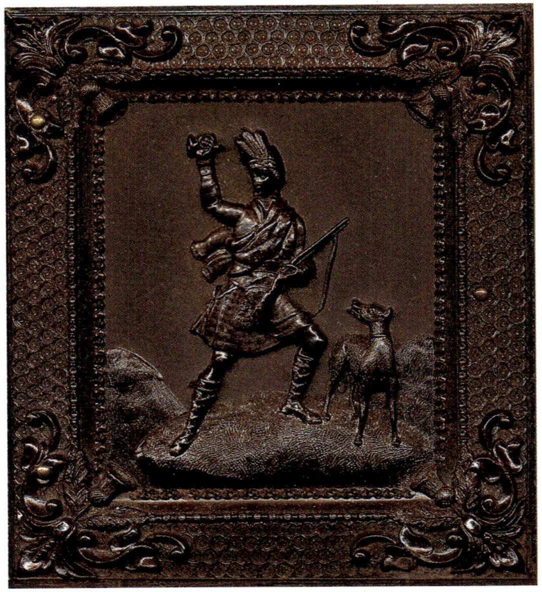

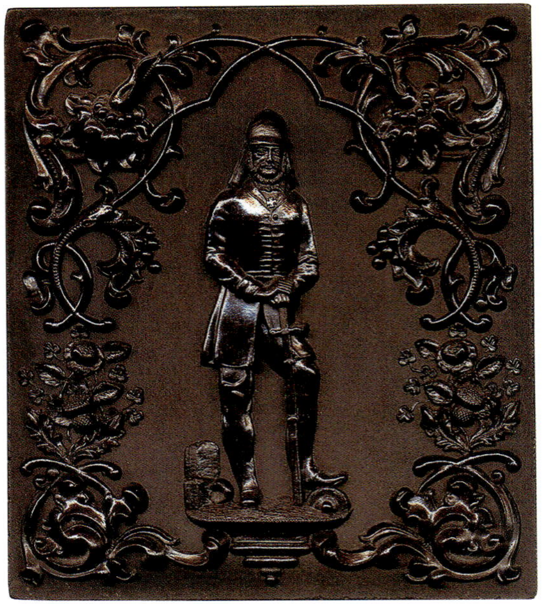

Above left: 'The Highland Chief', sixth plate union case by Holmes, Booth & Hayden, c.1859, depicts a highlander wearing a kilt and sporran with an outrageous head-dress. Scottish thistles decorate each corner of the design. Actual case size 84mm x 94mm. Above right: 'Sir Henry Havelock' hero of the Indian Mutiny, featured on both a sixth plate case (here) and a quarter plate variant. He also featured on a brand of Cuban cigars which bore his name! This union case was made by Littlefield, Parsons & Co. Actual case size 83mm x 95mm. As with so many of these beautiful cases, the die-makers did not sign their work, so we do not know who was responsible for either of these detailed designs.

along the inside of the case face and was riveted through the case top or bottom. When geometric patterns were used, the rivet head was usually worked into the design of the case, making it largely invisible. For pictorial designs, the small rivet head was often coated with black shellac making it as inconspicuous as possible.

Although this would seem to be a fairly weak design – with considerable stresses being placed on the rivet – it worked extremely well, avoiding any stress whatsoever on the weak spine of the case. Considerable stresses were placed on the rivet itself, however, and loose rivets are common in surviving cases.

The face riveted hinge, however, was not the first attempt at the union of brass and plastic. Indeed, using the Lord's Prayer case as an example of very early Peck design, the hinge is seen as the case's major weakness. In such cases both the hinge shape and the method of fixing are totally different. For this first example of the product, a much-shortened basic L shape was used, with the upright of the L being set into a slot within the thickness of the case spine, and glued into place. It was then pinned rather than riveted from the inside of the case. The pin holding the hinge in place was then concealed by the facing pad or the velvet trim which would eventually hold the picture in place. The example of the case used in this book has only one of the four hinge fixtures still intact. Two are cracked but still 'holding' while the fourth has broken away completely to reveal both the remains of the glue and the single hole through which the pin was once driven to hold the case together. It has hitherto been assumed that the absence of visible rivets meant that this type of hinge was either simply glued or moulded into a slot in the plastic thus producing an inherently weak link in the construction. The evidence of a pin hole in the exposed hinge suggests that the additional security of pins is in fact a weakness of the design rather than the inserted hinge itself. However, a later Peck patent (14202, February 5th 1856) allowed for the incorporation of metal strips into the actual plastic during the moulding process and, presumably, the side pin was fixed through both the hinge and this reinforcing strip to spread stresses better and reduce cracking.

Even in these early examples, however, face riveting has been used to hold the closure in position.

Examples of the reinforced case bearing labels which include the 1856 Peck patent have survived in several sizes – and survived intact. Of course the case wall thickness needed to be considerably greater if the inserted hinge and moulded reinforcing bars were being used and cracking of the brittle plastic during assembly was to be avoided. Thus the case was heavier and a little bulkier than many face riveted designs. The thickness of the plastic edging round the picture rather detracted from the 'fineness' of the picture and must presumably have been considered a detracting influence. Cracking had, at one time, apparently accounted for a 30% production loss.

Examples of the inserted hinge fall into two groups – those with a glued and side pinned fixture as used on the Lord's Prayer, and some which were side riveted – where the brass rivet heads are clearly visible on the case spine.

Indeed one fine oval case, dating from 1856 or 1857 – and clearly without reinforcing bars by the very nature of its design and shape, is held together with a single side-riveted hinge using the slot system and has survived absolutely intact. Two brass rivet heads are clearly visible on the small squared plastic moulding which carries the hinge itself. A single rivet head on the case faces – outside the area of the geometric design – marks the closure.

The plain face-riveted version is, however, by far the most common. In a few instances the rivet head is decorated – sometimes with a small rosette pattern – but the majority are plain brass with or without a black shellac coating. While most originally had a black finish, some were actually produced with a polished – or even gilded – rivet head.

The rosette-headed rivet was not purely decorative. It too was designed to spread the stresses more evenly and prevent cracking. While many round-head riveted cases are now showing some looseness in the hinges, surviving examples of the rosette headed rivets have remained very tight.

Gilded and polished hinges were also used in some designs – notably by A.P. Critchlow and later by Littlefield & Parsons, who had several patents covering their hinge design and method of insertion.

Peck actually patented a method of producing a completely gilded case – placing a small sheet of gilded paper in the mould before the plastic was pressed into place. The result was a perfect gilt finish to the face of the case. In such cases a gilded rivet head was the least that could be expected! That technique was further refined to incorporate a small gilded cameo head in the centre of the design on an otherwise black case, and such designs are both rare and highly treasured by collectors today.

Amongst the rarest of all the cases – certainly in the UK – are Wadham's, with a totally different hinge design to all the rest. Their hinge used long arms running up the inside of the top and bottom edges of the case halves. The theory was that by using the Kinsley & Parker patent external case hinge[5], there would be a dispersal of the stresses away from the spine. In reality, the stresses along the upper and lower edges of the case were even greater, and many Wadham's cases show signs of extensive damage and subsequent repair.

Union cases were available to take all the standard sizes of portrait available at the time, with the number of variants in each size reflecting the popularity of each particular format. The cheaper portrait sizes of sixth and ninth plate are represented by the largest number of known designs. There are many fine examples of quarter plate cases, a smaller number of half plate designs, and only three known whole plate examples. Almost all the sizes available were fractions of the whole plate, although a small number of photographers used the increasingly popular 5in. x 4in. (125mm x 100mm) format which survives as today's large-format standard.

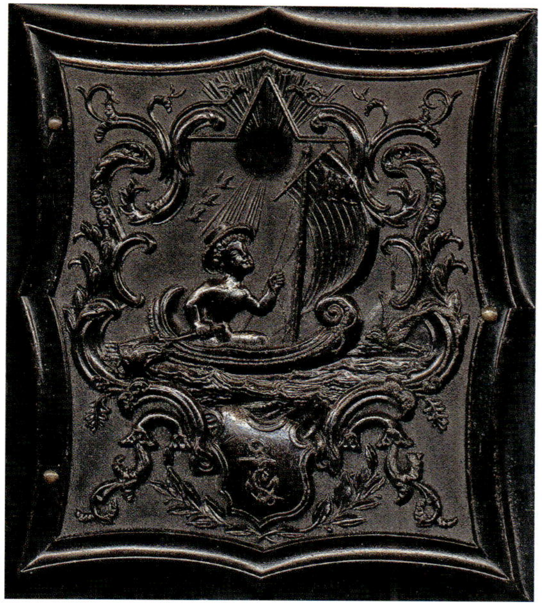

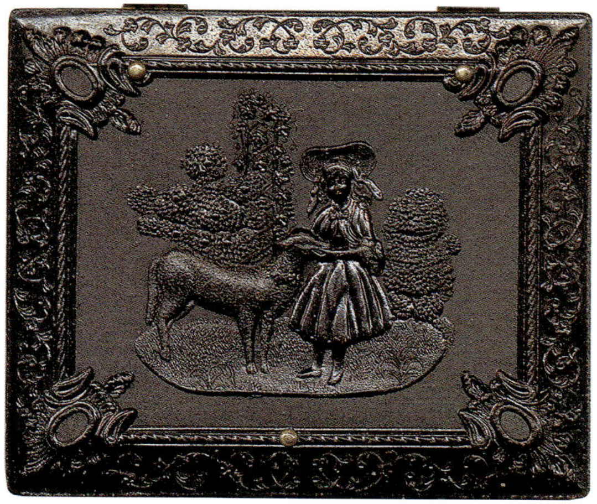

Above left: 'Bobby Shafto', sixth plate case by Alfred P. Critchlow & Co., containing the two daguerreotypes by Jaquith of Broadway which are illustrated on page 84. Actual case size 83mm x 95mmm.

Above: 'Mary had a Little Lamb', ninth plate case by Littlefield, Parsons & Co. Actual case size 75mm x 65mm. There is also a ninth plate octagonal version of this case. At least one other case is known to be based on a nursery song, entitled 'See-saw Margery Daw'.

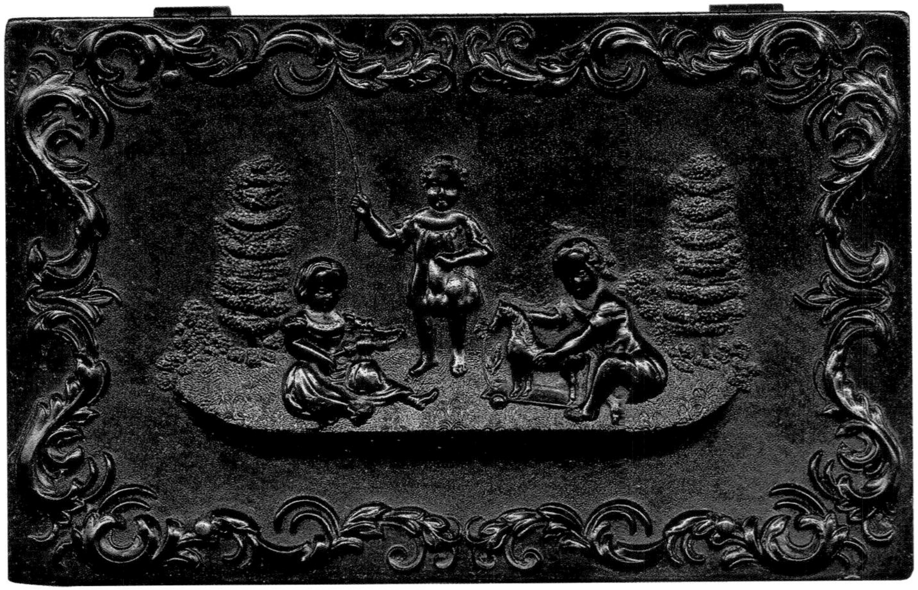

'Children with Toys', a double ninth plate union case by Littlefield, Parsons & Co. A double sixteenth plate size also exists with the same central motif.

The author's collection contains only one case design in this format, designed by Frederick Key for Samuel Peck & Co.

It is worth comment at this point that that case was clearly produced for a British market – its motif being intertwined thistles, roses and shamrocks. Many other 'British' subjects have also survived including cases using the design of *Sir Henry Havelock* (see page 102).

There is no record of the full range of colours in which union cases were manufactured. At least four different shades of brown have been identified, together with black and a small number of pastels. The ratio of brown to black is also difficult to ascertain but if the collection from which these illustrations have been drawn can be assumed to be typical – an unsound basis for any serious analysis – the ratio is about three to two in favour of brown of one shade or another.

The British casemaker, John Smith patented a process in 1860 for producing highly coloured cases, and one example in a vivid red survives in a private collection in the UK. Smith's patents referred to several colours, and compounds resembling marble in appearance, but this one red example remains the only one yet seen.

Manufacture of the cases followed fairly similar processes with regard to the preparation of the mixture of materials and the actual moulding of the case 'shells'.

While all the brown cases were probably based on wood fibres plus dye, the composition of the black cases did vary from one manufacturer to another. Variations from Peck's original patent – which had always been rather vague in its terminology of 'woody fibres or other suitably fibrous materials' ranged from soot or lampblack with wood resin and shellac, to crushed cannel-coal and shellac.

Cannel-coal was characterised by its ability to be crushed into very fine particles indeed, a characteristic which also made it burn very well with little or no ash, and played a major role in the success of the Wigan coalfield in England and several of the coalfields in the northern American states. This material gave cases with a very rich black and highly detailed finish.

Given the tastes of the time, it is surprising that the range of colours is so limited. While velvet and leather cases were available in a wide variety of colours, union cases appear to have been so only on a very limited scale, and with coloured examples generally limited to the smallest sizes. Green, red and blue leather cases are not uncommon, and velvets in a variety of surprisingly bright colours were produced. Their plastic equivalents are much less easily obtained.

Union case designs fall into a number of clearly definable groups. Being American in origin, a body of cases exists which celebrates America and its history. Understandably these cases are rarer in Britain than in the United States. Many have made their way across the Atlantic over the years, containing images which are obviously American in style, dress and origin, but very few have been found containing an obviously British portrait. Classic amongst these is the magnificent whole plate case – one of only three known large designs

– depicting *The Landing of Columbus*, (page 94).

A second body of cases depict scenes or figures of European origin – the fine cases bearing the figure of *Sir Henry Havelock* (page 102), the *Calmady Children* (page 100) and the *Highland Chief* (page 102) being notable examples. There are also a pair of quarter plate cases bearing the scene of *General Marion Sharing Yams with a British Officer*, which have links with Britain if only indirectly.

Group three depict childhood memories, and cover illustrations from nursery rhymes, children at play, pets and the like. Several from this group are illustrated on pages 103 and 104.

A fourth group illustrate scenes from nature – animals, birds, flowers, landscapes and other rural themes.

The largest group – making about three-quarters of all known case designs – are geometric and scroll motifs. Although these were probably much quicker and cheaper to make – and probably did not demand the services of a highly skilled die-maker – there was, surprisingly, no difference in price between these and the scenic cases. Today's collectors prize the scenic cases much more highly than all but a few of the geometrics.

Most interesting are a group of cases based around religious motifs, of themes of death and the 'hereafter'. Several of these have already been illustrated in this chapter – *The Lord's Prayer, The Memorial, The Holy Family*, and the *Vision of Ezekiel.*

There was also a range of interpretations of a pair of sculpted marble medallions entitled *Day – Aurora with the Genius of Light*, and *Night with her Children Sleep and Death* both created in 1815 by the Danish sculptor Bertel Thorvaldsen[6]. Of especial interest in considering these case designs is the fact that *Day, Aurora with the Genius of Light* was an inspiration to three casemakers, both British and American, although interpreted in quite different ways.

Both medallions were used as the basis of a trio of ninth plate case designs by Samuel Peck, while

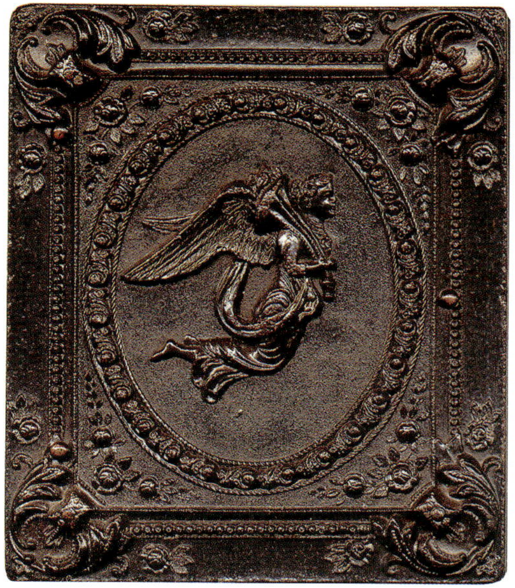

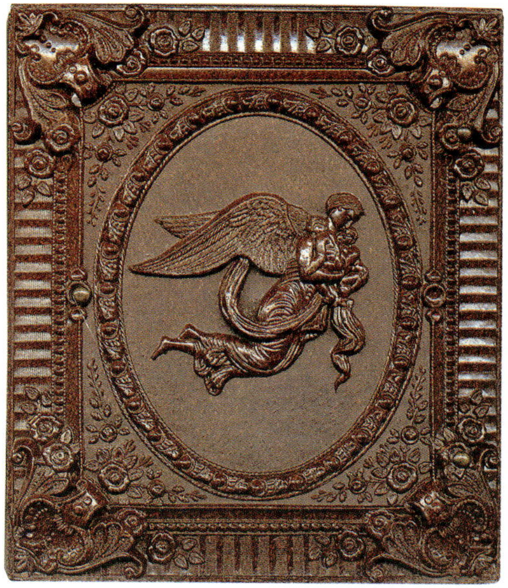

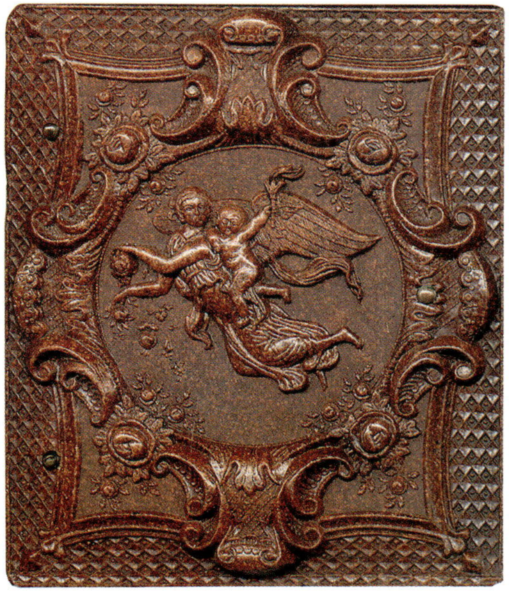

Above left: 'Angel with Cornucopia', ninth plate case by Littlefield, Parsons & Co. Actual case size 65mm x 75mm.
Above right: 'Night with her Children, Sleep and Death', ninth plate case by S. Peck & Co. Actual case size 65mm x 75mm.
The similarities between these cases strongly suggest that the diemaker was the same for both – note particularly the oval border, the flower details in each corner, and the flowing robe hanging from the angel. All are too similar to be the creations of different craftsmen.
Left: 'Day, Aurora with the Genius of Light'. ninth plate union case by S. Peck & Co., containing Peck's 'Genuine Union Case Improved' label. Actual case size 65mm x 75mm.

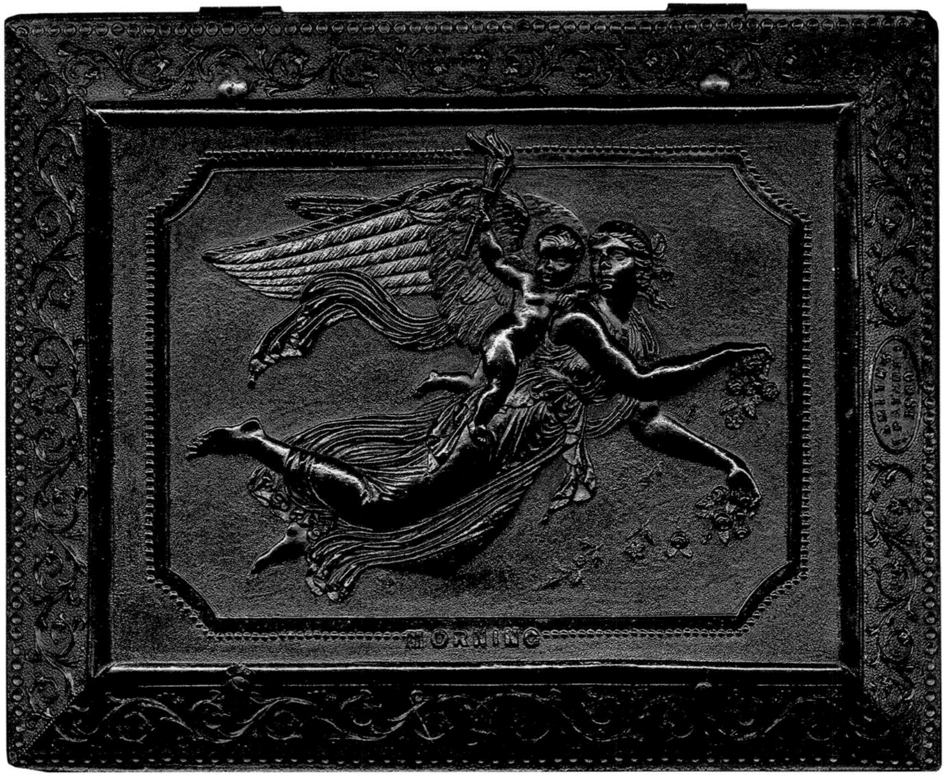

'Morning', a quarter plate union case by John Smith of Birmingham. This case uniquely carries a patent date in the margins. Two other versions of the same design, but with different borders, omit the patent date, and carry either the names of the die-makers, Brookes and Adams, or the single word 'patent' in the inner border. Brookes and Adams operated in Great Charles Street, only a very short distance from Smith's factory at 62 Constitution Hill.

Birmingham's John Smith produced two magnificent quarter plate cases using *Day*.

Peck produced two cases based on *Day*, and one on *Night*. While in Thorvaldesen's original medallions, and in John Smith's cases, Aurora is flying from left to right, Peck had her flying in the opposite direction.

One of Smith's cases is also the only case so far discovered to have the casemaker's name and patent as part of the moulded design.

Thorvaldsen's angel theme, based on *Night with her Children* was also picked up by Littlefield Parsons & Co, who replaced the children with a cornucopia for two ninth plate cases and one sixth plate.

It is assumed that many of these cases were used for housing portraits of the deceased. Other biblical themes included scenes such as *Rebekkah at the Well* and *Daniel in the Lion's Den*, often drawing on well-known illustrations as reference.

Several of the die-engravers marked their work – 'Brookes & Adams fecit' can be found in one version of the case design which Smith entitled *Morning* while another variant simply has the word 'patent'. The case which bears the legend 'Smith's Patent 1860' must also clearly have been engraved by Brookes and Adams, but is unsigned.

Smith & Hartmann included their names on several case designs, as did Frederick Goll, while Frederick Key either included 'Key' or 'K' in his designs – sometimes cleverly incorporated into the design itself so rather less than easy to find!

An American John Smith included 'Smith' on several designs, while R. Paine's name appears only on one case as far as current research can ascertain – *The Memorial*. A. Schaefer's name appears on a small number of pictorial designs – notably *The Fire Chief* illustrated on page 110 where his name is included in letters large enough perhaps to persuade the viewer that Schaefer was the name of the fire chief rather than the die engraver!

Surprisingly, some of the finest and most delicate of designs are not identified in any way. *Sir Henry Havelock*, one of the crispest of designs yet found has already been referred to, and *The Beehive* with its plethora of detail are both apparently anonymous, while Frederick Key applied his name to several quite basic geometric motifs!

While the names of Peck, Littlefield Parsons & Co., and A.P. Critchlow are well known to case collectors, the name of John Smith, Britain's sole maker of thermoplastic union cases so far identified, is much less familiar. His name is recorded on three patents and in only one other published reference. That single reference, in an 1862 Birmingham Trade Directory, merely records his name and gives his address as 'rear of 65 Constitution Hill'.

Measured numerically against the most prolific makers, Smith's contribution to the thermoplastic case market was tiny. There are over 350 known cases with the Littlefield, Parsons & Co. label for example, while Smith's known output sits comfortably between that of Wadhams (18 cases identified) and Frederick Key (5). Measured qualitatively, however, he deserves great respect. Using a unique – and patented – thermoplastic, he produced a very high quality product.

Smith came to casemaking from the manufacture of horn buttons – the name was a commonly used euphemism for plastic imitation horn. Birmingham was a centre for early plastics manufacture, and several dozen button-makers were operating within the area.

The plastic material he used was very fine – presumably modified from the hard plastic used in button-making – and his cases were cast in dies of the very highest quality, at least some of which were made by Brookes & Adams, also of Birmingham. The artistry shown in both his pictorial and geometric designs is considerable.

Smith's known output to date comprises one ninth and two sixth plate frames, four quarter plate, three sixth plate, five ninth plate cases and, unusually, five cases designed for the humble carte-de-visite. Three of those five were of a small format almost unique to this maker. Whereas the American tradition seems only rarely to have accorded such lavish framing to the paper print – preferring to fill thermoplastic cases with daguerreotypes, ambrotypes and tintypes – the British tradition did endow cartes-de-visite made by society photographers with much the same value.

Smith's small carte-de-visite cases were not only of compact dimensions across their faces, they were also unusually slim giving the case a profile less than 70% of conventional thickness. It can be argued that the high quality of the thermoplastic used by Smith, and its resistance to warping, made such slim designs in a relatively large size a practical proposition. None of the Smith cases so far identified – and now in collections in Britain and the United States – show any marked tendency to warping.

The two carte-de-visite case sizes produced by Smith were quite substantially different, the smaller requiring a trimmed carte-de-visite to be inserted. Both these case sizes were moulded out of very thin profile thermoplastic, confirming that by his 1860 patent Smith had created a composition which was both light and dimensionally stable. That stability is demonstrated by the fact that the smaller case is a mere 17mm in thickness. The larger case measures 78mm x 107mm x 18mm thick, while the smaller case measures 64mm x 96mm.

At the time Smith began manufacturing thermoplastic objects, there was a widespread view in Victorian Britain that American photographic frames and cases were of superior quality to the home-made examples. Thus it was that British companies incorporated American references into their catalogues, and in some cases, even incorporated the word 'American' into their names.

John Smith was no exception. What may well have been his first photographic products in moulded thermoplastic – ninth and sixth plate frames – bear the legend 'Smith's American Patent Composite'. These frames, which will be discussed later, are moulded from rather crude moulds, well short of the finely detailed relief evident in all his later union cases. The material itself, however,

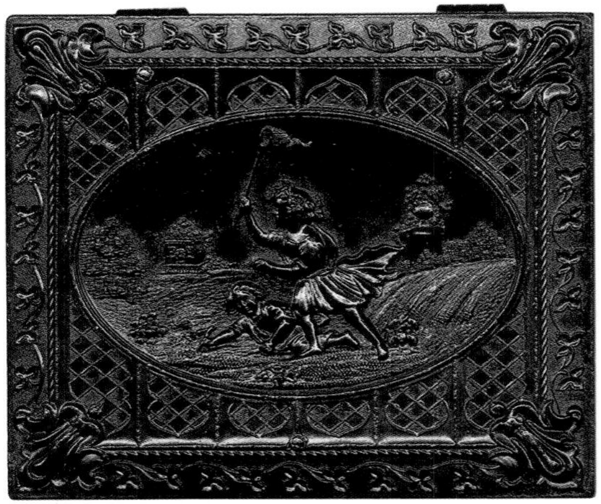

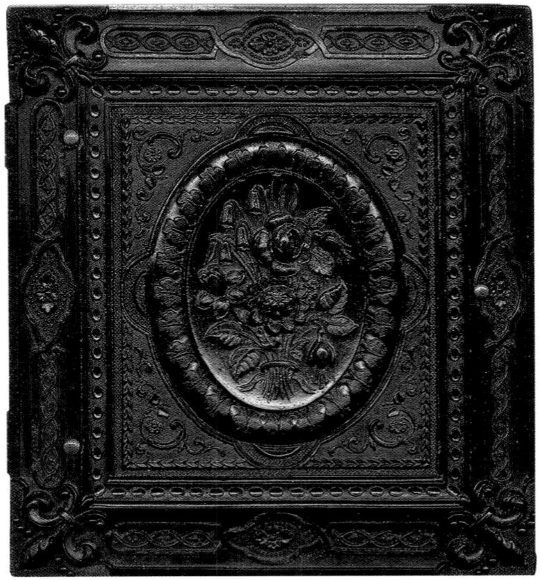

Above: 'Catching Butterflies', ninth plate case by Littlefield, Parsons & Co. Actual case size 75mm x 64mm.
Above right: 'Bouquet of Flowers', a very rare sixth plate union case design by John Smith, bearing an 'Improved Patent Union Case' label from the post-1862 period. Actual case size 89mm x 99mm.

shows many of the qualities which were used to great effect in later productions – rigidity and resistance to warping, and fine consistency giving a smooth finish.

Early on in research into John Smith, it was assumed that this material was probably that covered by Smith's first patent[7]. That first patent described a thermoplastic material produced by taking –

'... one pound of shell-lac and dissolving it by heat on an iron slab; I then mix with it an equal quantity by bulk of ebony dust, produced either by sawing, turning, or pulverisation, or otherwise, after which I add the colouring matter; this for an intense black composition would consist of three ounces of black asphaltum reduced to a fine powder, three ounces of ivory black, or charcoal powder, or lamp black, the ivory black being used for the purpose of hardening the composition, or if hardness be not desirable, then I employ charcoal or lamp black.'

From his first patent, therefore, it is clear that Smith understood the need for a very hard compound for his photograph cases, giving rigidity without being brittle. This compound differs materially from those cited in the several American patents relating to the union case.

Peck acknowledged that the recipes for a thermoplastic material were already in the public domain and merely recorded that –

'The composition of which the main body of this case is made and to which my invention in applicable, is composed of gum shellac and woody fibers or other suitable fibrous material dyed to the color that may be required and ground with the shellac and between hot rollers so as to be converted into a mass, which when heated becomes plastic...'

To overcome the tendency of moulded plastics to fracture, Peck patented – amongst other things – the idea of embedding a piece of card or paper in the mould in such a way that it bonded permanently with the plastic material. In this manner, he claimed a significant improvement in the material's resistance to either splitting or warping.

Mark Tomlinson[7] described his material – for which, like Smith, he claimed great rigidity, and reduced liability to chip or fracture – in a little more detail –

'This composition consists of equal parts, by weight, of shellac, Breckenridge or cannel-coal, and ivory black... ...and this composition possesses a greater degree of tenacity or less degree of liability to fracture...'

By the time of his 1860 Patent – No.1503, dated 21st June 1860 and sealed on November 1st – Smith's researches into the robustness of his plastics had led him to several important modifications.

'This invention consists of certain improvements upon a former Invention having the same object for which her Majesty's Letters Patent bearing date the Nineteenth day of December, in the year of our Lord One thousand eight hundred and fifty-nine, having been granted to me, and this present Invention has arisen in the course of

experiments made by me for the purpose of ascertaining whether any, and, if any, what other ingredients could be advantageously added to the composition, my object being the attainment of greater density, tenacity, lightness, and delicacy of tint in colouring, than I am enabled to produce with the materials named in the Specification of my former Invention.'

In Victorian parlance, tenacity was used to describe a cohesive strength in the material, so Smith was clearly intent on producing a much more robust material than that possible with his earlier compositions.

Victorian patents were written in a notoriously imprecise and repetitive manner. Thus, in some respects, the wording of the recipe for the basic black composition is identical in both the 1859 and 1860 patents. Slight variations in other aspects of the language used in the descriptions suggest that the 1859 patent covered theoretical possibilities, while the 1860 version actually reflected achievements.

Certainly the 1860 patent seeks to overcome problems in the construction of the cases which could only have been recognised by manufacturing experience. Issues of rigidity, robustness, weight and density of material, as well as purity of colour, could only really have been appreciated by practical experience.

It is of interest to note that Smith avoids any consideration of hinges and clasp in either of his patents, merely acknowledging in his 1859 patent that –

'In manufacturing double-sided articles such as the cases alluded to in my title, each shell or side is moulded separately, and afterwards suitable connected by hinges or rivets, which, together with any locks or fastenings that may be necessary for such cases, can be attached by any of the ordinary modes used in wood or papier mâché cases.'

This is an unusual reference, as by 1859, no union cases had locks or fastenings attached in the same way as those on wooden or papier mâché cases – perhaps another pointer to his lack of case making experience at that time.

Both patents make reference to the production of coloured cases, in a remarkable variety of colours. From the 1860 patent, Smith offered a full description of his methodology –

'In making the composition of a chocolate or brown tint I use with the lac three ounces of brown asphaltum and about one ounce of rouge, more or less, according to the tint required.

For green tints or other darker tints, I employ any suitable colouring matter to produce the tint required.'

His 1859 patent referred to powdered coloured pigments being added – is it perhaps possible that when he tried such an approach he discovered that powder pigment weakened the material, or failed to produce the smoothness of colour required? He continued –

'To produce light colours I take the dust of boxwood (produced by any of the means aforesaid) as a colouring matter of itself, to which if a still lighter tint be required, I add an intense

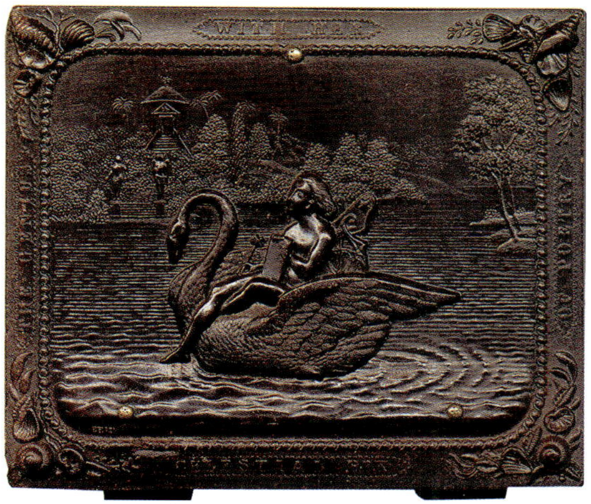

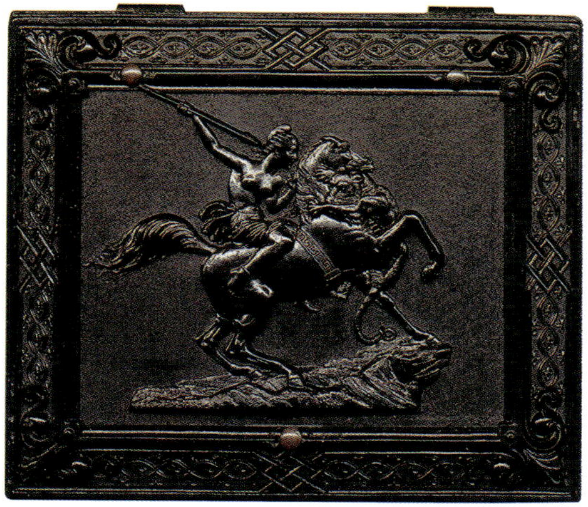

Two of the most highly prized examples of ninth plate union cases.

Above left: 'The Genius of Poetry with her Celestial Pen', ninth plate union case engraved by Frederick Seiler – whose name appears reversed in the water at the bottom left of the case. None has yet been found with a maker's label in it! Case measures 75mm x 65mm.

Above: 'Amazon on Horseback being Attacked by a Tiger', ninth plate union case attributed to John Smith and based on a sculpture by Adolphe Kiss which had been exhibited at the 1851 Great Exhibition at the Crystal Palace. Certain features in this case are strongly reminiscent of known Smith case designs, although no example of this case has yet been found with a maker's label in it. So far cases from two distinctively different moulds have been identified, one incorporating the legend 'patent' in the bottom margin (here) and the other without. Case measures 76mm x 65mm.

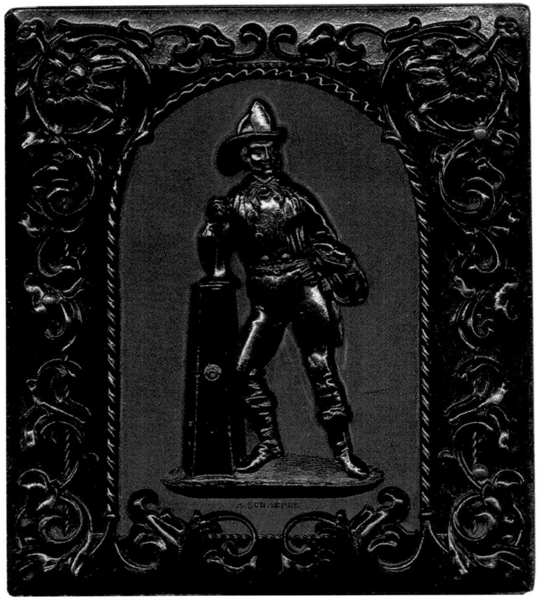

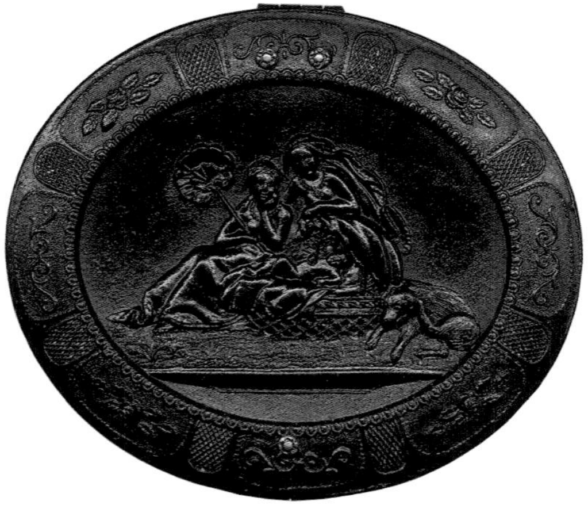

Top: 'The Fire Chief', sixth plate case by Littlefield, Parsons & Co. Actual case size 83mm x 95mm.
Above: 'Moses in the Bullrushes', one of three ninth plate union cases using variants on this design by Littlefield, Parsons & Co., shown here at actual size 66mm x 55mm.

white in the shape of barytes or any other suitable colouring. The whole of these ingredients must be well amalgamated until the mass shall appear thoroughly homogeneous in its nature when homogeneity is desired, but if streaked or veined composition is required this may also be produced by twisting or rolling together two or more masses of different coloured compositions. In this way imitations of marble, onyx, malachite, or other stones and gems may be obtained.'

It is presumed that these streaked mixtures were used for his composition jewellery, rather than union cases. Certainly none has yet been located which employs this technique.

As already mentioned, one red case has been identified, so Smith's ideas about colouring his composition certainly went well beyond mere theory!

It is not unreasonable to read Victorian patents literally, so perhaps Smith's *modus operandi* can be revealed by investigating the instructions he offers.

Whereas Peck and Tomlinson record the constituents of their composition – in Tomlinson's case *'equal parts, by weight, of shellac, Breckenridge or cannel-coal, and ivory black'* – Smith gave actual quantities.

An appropriate reading of that distinction might lead to the conclusion that for Peck and Tomlinson production was on a large scale, whereas for Smith it was more of a cottage industry.

The Smith ingredients list is precise – 16 ounces of shellac, 16 ounces of ebony dust, and 3 ounces of black asphaltum, and for his hard black composition, the addition of 3 ounces of ivory black, making a total mixture of 38 ounces. For the brown thermoplastic, the 3 ounces of ivory black and 3 ounces of black asphaltum were replaced by 3 ounces of 'brown asphaltum' and 1 ounce of commercial rouge – more usually used for cleaning daguerreotype plates – making a total weight of 36 ounces. In neither instance is this a large amount, suggesting production in low numbers rather than large.

A single mixture prepared according to the patent specifications would enable the manufacture of relatively few cases.

Estimating the size of the thermoplastic slug which was placed in the die must never have been a precise art, so there must have been waste. But as the composition could, in principle, be reheated and reused, ultimate wastage would have been nil. One might assume, therefore, that to each mix might have been added the wastage from the previous mix. Indeed such a proposition might account for local areas of different colour in several Peck brown cases.

With one face of a small carte-de-visite size case weighing fractionally under an ounce, a single mix of the black composition would have produced no more than three dozen 'shells' as Smith called them, or eighteen cases.

The quarter plate *Morning* case weighs just under 3 ounces per shell – yielding perhaps just six complete cases per mix.

These figures sit comfortably alongside the very small numbers of each of Smith's cases known to be in collections today. The moulds from which American cases were made are known to have been easily damaged, and to have suffered wear with repeated use – and there can be no justification for believing the British ones would have fared any better.

What is true of Smith cases is that none of the surviving examples shows significant signs of wear or damage to the moulds. What is also known is that there are surviving examples of *Morning* which come from four different moulds, and surviving examples of *Amazon on Horseback being Attacked by a Tiger* which come from two.

The one factor which might raise the estimated output – either up or down – comes from a later statement in Smith's 1860 patent, where he talks first about increasing density, and presumably weight, and also about combining rigidity and robustness with lightness –

'In cases where it may be desirable that the composition should possess greater density of material than the above described, that quality may be produced by the addition of mineral

substances, such, for instance, as barytes or oxide of magnesium, the proportions of which may be governed by the requirements of the case, and when greater tenacity than the above is desired, that quality may also be obtained by the admixture of a due proportion of vegetable fibre other than wood dust, as for instance the shearings of cottons, velveteens, or hemp, flax, or other such like materials, and for the purpose of obtaining a light and strong composition, paper pulp mixed with the other ingredients will be most advantageous.'

It is reasonable, perhaps, to assume that with a relatively small output from each mould – to ensure no evidence of wear – and several moulds of popular designs, the actual production quantities per design and per mould were relatively small, perhaps amounting to no more than two or three dozen shells at a time.

The relative scarcity of Smith cases today must be as a result of relatively small-scale production, or a relatively short production period. Smith appears as a photographic casemaker in only one of the local trade directories of his day, and on only one occasion – *Kelly's Directory* for 1862.

The information contained in that directory would have been prepared in 1861 – and even that is late for a new entrant into the union case market. That lateness may in itself explain the disproportionately large number of carte-de-visite case designs in Smith's œuvre. By the early 1860s, in Great Britain at least, the daguerreotype was almost obsolete, the ambrotype was in decline, and the carte-de-visite was being exploited by photographers at all levels of society – from the cheapest in working class areas, to society photographers such as Camille Silvy, Antoine Claudet and others.

The question remains, however, as to why John Smith, with important manufacturing patents to his name apparently only advertised himself as a maker of union cases for one year.

Before seeking an answer to that question, it is worthwhile to review the labelling of Smith's cases. Significantly, Smith cases seem to have been

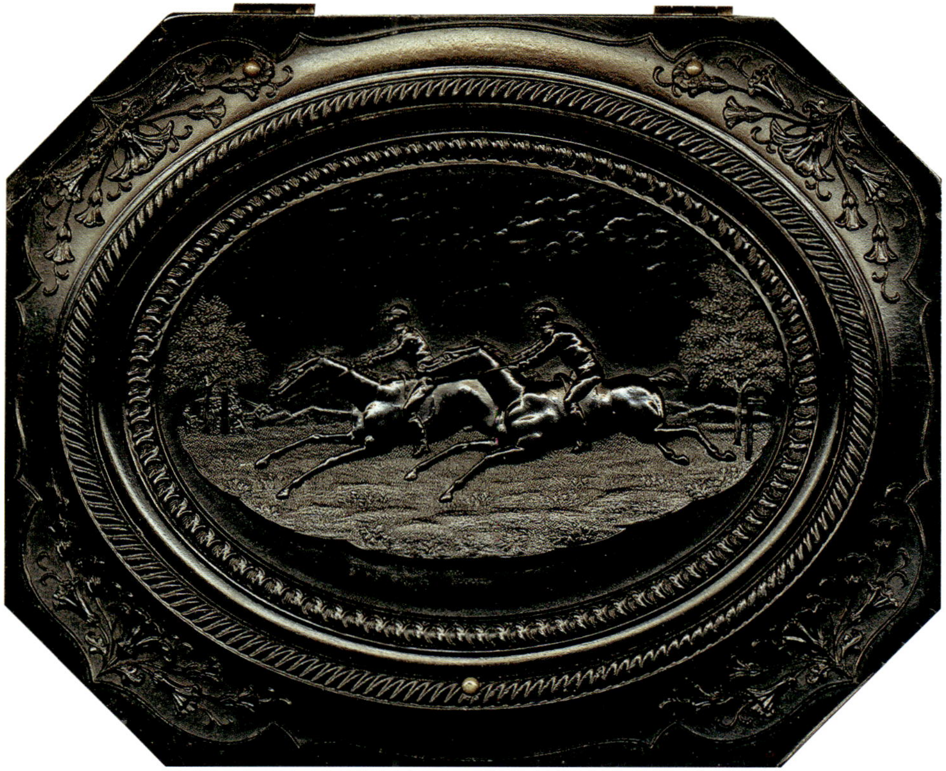

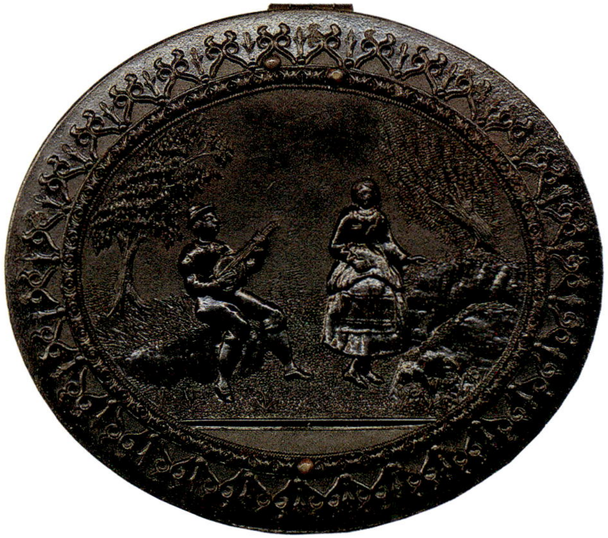

Above: 'The Horse Race', octagonal quarter plate union case by Littlefield, Parsons & Co, highly prized by collectors and found in both brown and black thermoplastic. The case, shown here actual size, measures 122mm x 99mm.

Left: 'The Serenade', a sixth plate oval union case by Littlefield, Parsons & Co, possibly based on a European painting or print. Case size 79mm x 69mm. Single hinge slim profile cases like this were highly prone to damage, and many show shearing of the fine plastic mouldings inside.

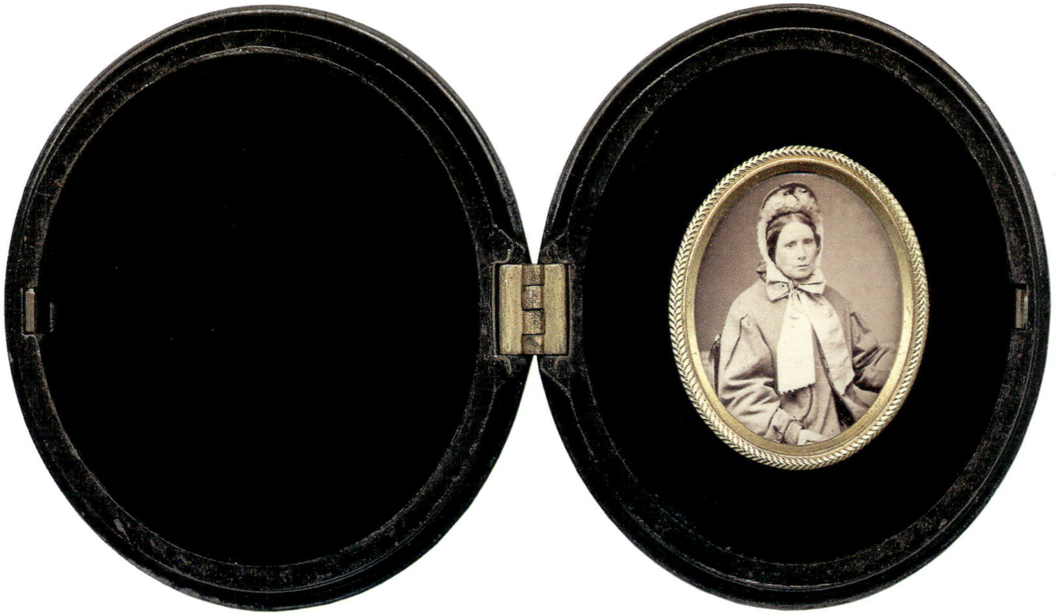

Oval sixth plate union case by Peck and Halvorson, fitted with black velvet pad and black velvet surround to take a sixteenth plate paper image with gilt surround. This is a typical interior decoration for housing an image of a recently deceased relative during mourning. Case and image shown here at actual size 72mm x 82mm.

labelled in one of three different ways.

A significant number of surviving examples seem never to have contained a maker's label at all – the 'image side' being faced with a plain deep blue/grey paper – others were sold with one of two 'brand' labels inside them. The easiest to associate with John Smith is the label which bears his name – within the brand-name of 'Smith's Patent Improved Union Case'.

Although John Smith is registered at 'rear of 65 Constitution Hill' only in 1862, the same address is listed in subsequent years under different ownership. In 1862 Smith is registered at the address, while James and Edwin Gyde, listed as *general factors* are listed at 95 Northwood Street. By the following year, James and Edwin Gyde are listed at both addresses, and are identified as *photo case makers*. That listing continued until 1866. It is not unreasonable, therefore, to hypothesise that James and Edwin Gyde were successors to John Smith in his casemaking business.

As several of the known examples of Smith cases which contain the 'Improved Patent Union Case' label can be identified as being post-1863, it is also not unreasonable to conclude that this variant on the label may very well relate to the Gydes' period of manufacture. While by no means an exhaustive survey, reference to other collections containing Smith cases has suggested that the 'Improved Patent Union Case' label is more common than 'Smith's Patent Improved Union Case' – reflecting perhaps Smith's short engagement with the product.

For a period approaching twenty years, the union case enjoyed considerable popularity, despite the cost of some of the more elaborate designs.

The union case was a product of its age and for its age. It was also only practical as long as photography was exclusive. As soon as cost savings in the manufacture of the photographic materials, and in the production of photographs themselves opened up the market to those who could only afford a low price product, the days of the union case – and indeed of the cased photographic portrait in general – were numbered.

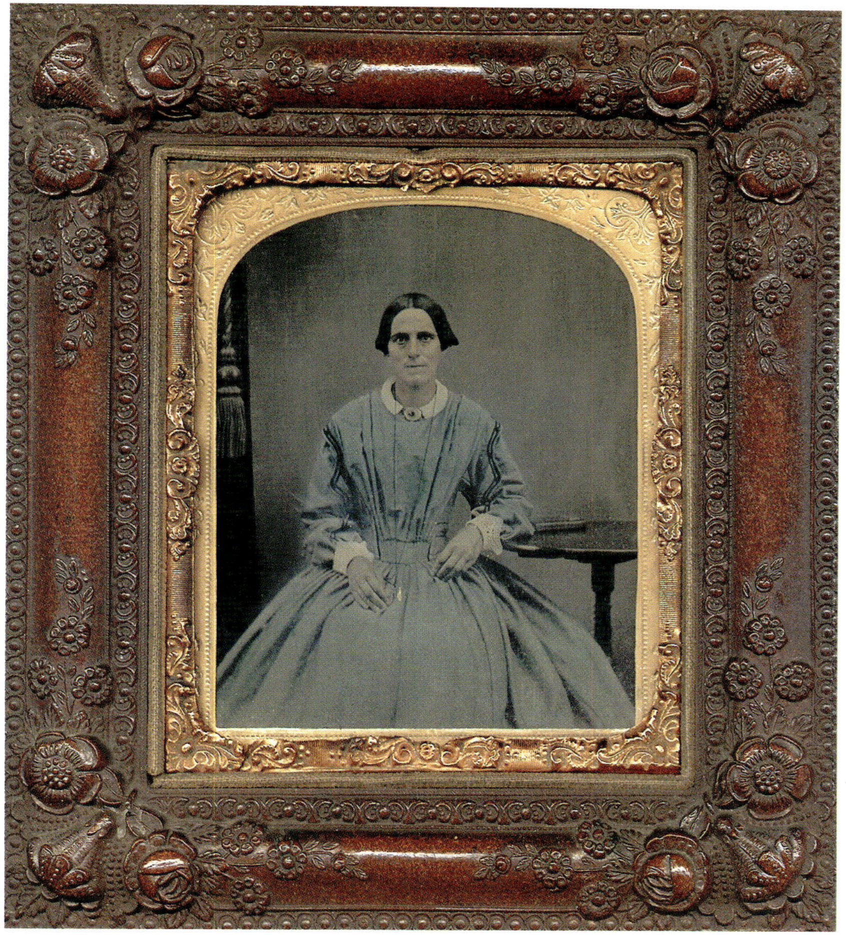

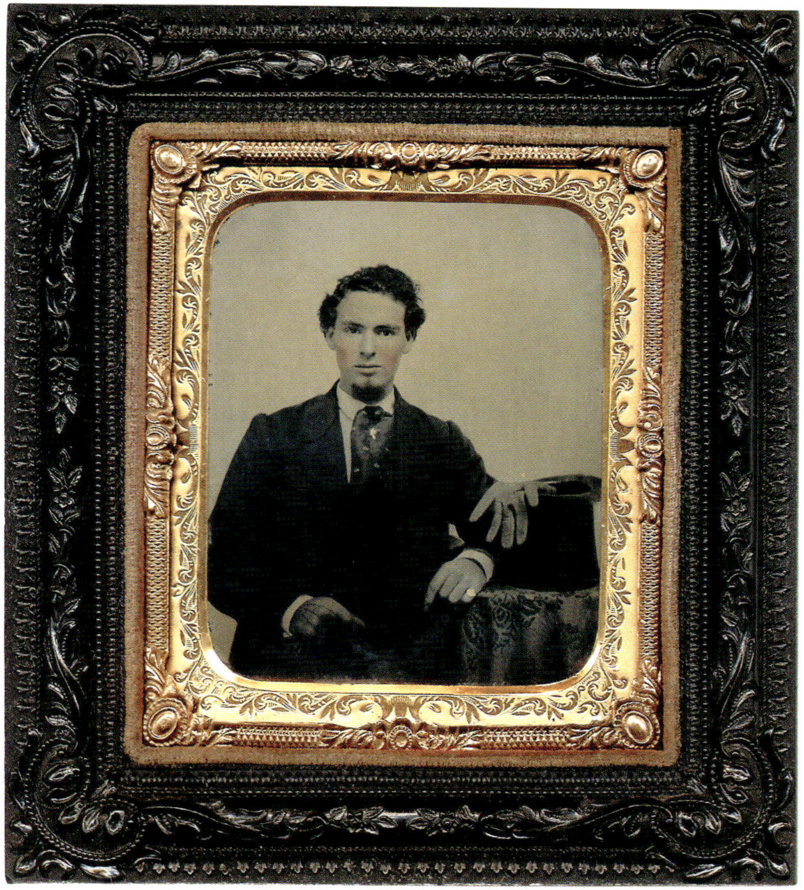

Two sixth plate thermoplastic frames, mid 1860s, each housing a tinted ambrotype. Photographers unknown. The black frame was manufactured by Wadhams Manufacturing Company, but no maker has yet been identified for the brown example. The same designs were available in quarter plate as well. Actual frame sizes are 112mm x 125mm (left) and 107mm x 119mm (right).

But it was not just cases which were made out of thermoplastic. Plastic frames were manufactured in both Britain and the United States, and in a variety of formats.

While union case makers were generally fairly assiduous in making sure that their makers' labels were inserted in their cases, all but a few of the thermoplastic frame makers chose to remain anonymous. Less than half a dozen quarter plate frames designs have so far been identified, with even fewer sixth and ninth plate. While half plate frames are very rare in Britain, several very elaborate designs were marketed in America.

Thermoplastic frames, perhaps because of cost, never achieved the popularity of their wooden and papier mâché counterparts.

The one format in which the thermoplastic frame did achieve a measure of popularity was, of course, the carte-de-visite. The carte, which came at the end of the era of the unique image, and rapidly replaced it, became the universal medium of portraiture within a very few years. It was rarely housed in thermoplastic cases – there are twelve known designs, none of them very common – but

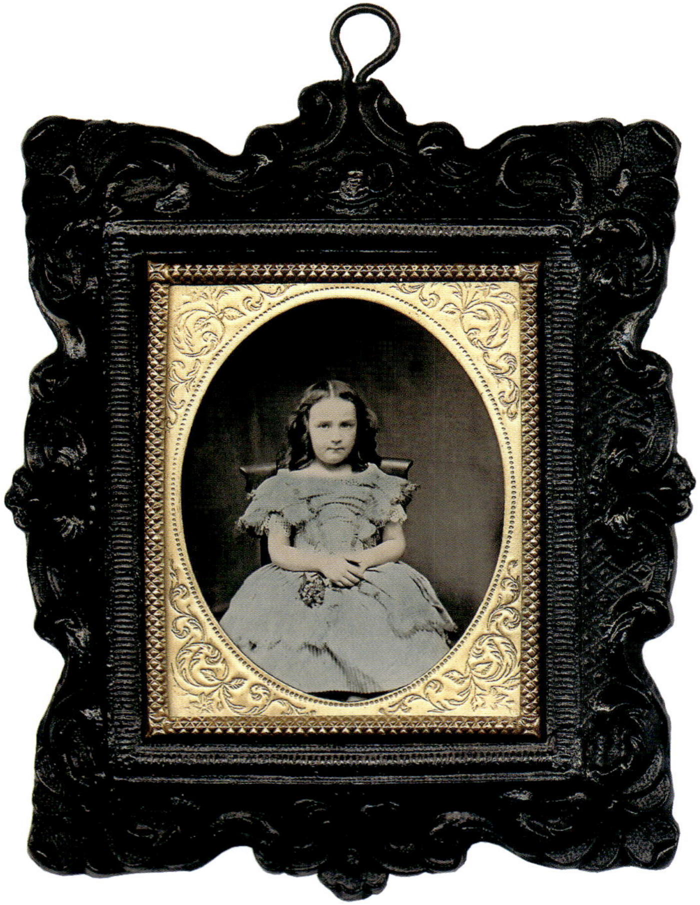

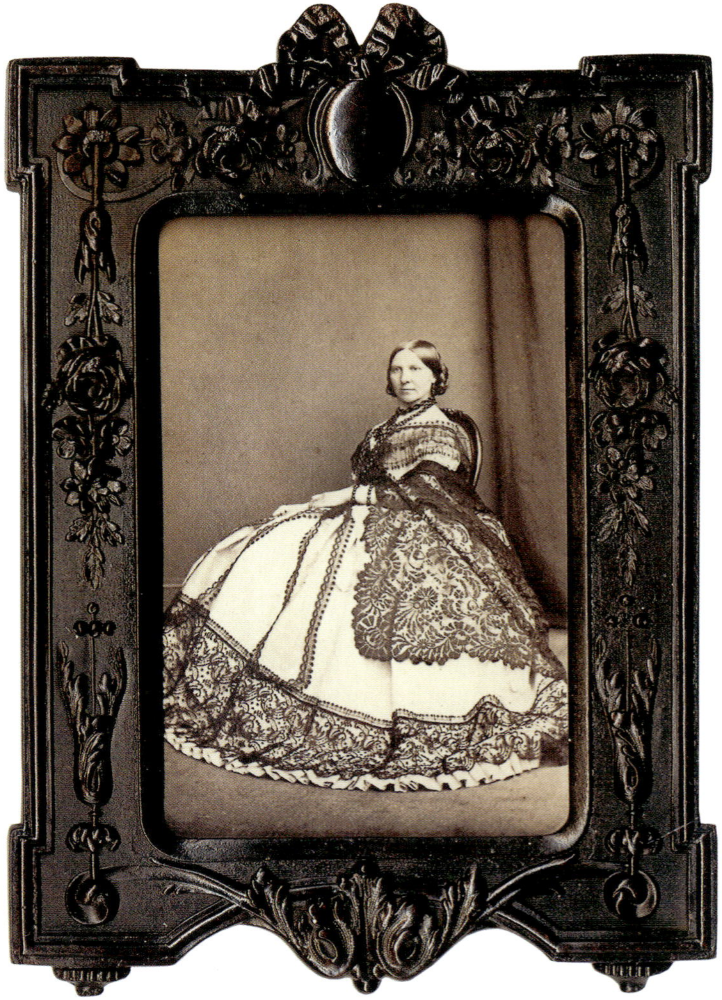

Above left: A ninth plate moulded thermoplastic frame by John Smith of Birmingham, c.*1860. Despite its British origins, the frame back bears the legend 'Smith's American Patent Composite'. The metal frame surrounding the image held it in place, with the top and bottom flaps fed through slots in the frame back, and bent up and down respectively. Shown actual size.*
Above right: A high quality thermoplastic frame for a carte-de-visite print, c.*1870. Shown actual size.*

was an obvious format for framing.

Thermoplastic frames for the ubiquitous print format continued to be made well into the 1880s.

As the quality of thermoplastic moulding became more refined, the crispness of the designs improved dramatically.

From the earliest plastic frames made by John Smith in Birmingham in 1860, through to the products of French manufacturers twenty years later, the evolution of the process was relentless.

Despite all that progress, however, there is evidence in the shapes of the surviving frames, that manufacturers could not fully overcome the tendency of the material to contract in an uneven manner as it cooled, especially in thin profile.

Eventually it became the family album and other cheaper methods of framing which won the day.

Moulded thermoplastic did not completely die out, however, finding a variety of other uses in the photographic packaging and presentation market.

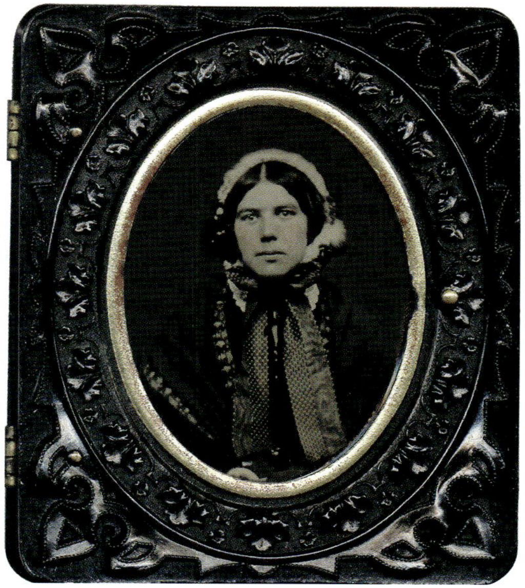

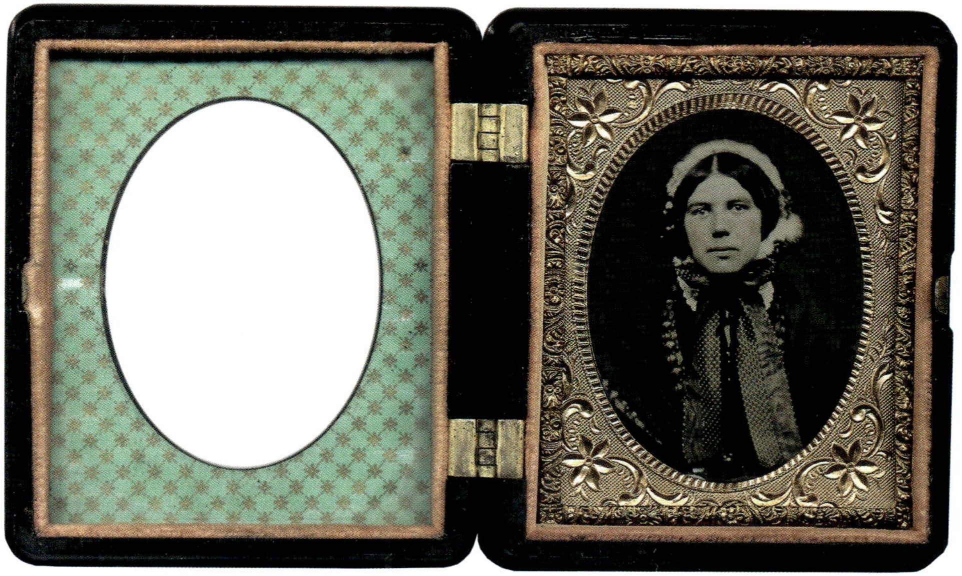

Perhaps denying the idea that the popularity of the case might have had a little to do with privacy, the 'peek-a-boo' case was clearly designed to allow the artistry of the photograph and the artistry of the case to be enjoyed together. Both ninth and sixth plate peek-a-boo cases were available, but never common. Only two designs have been identified in each size, and they remain rare and highly prized by collectors. The example here is ninth plate size, shown actual size.

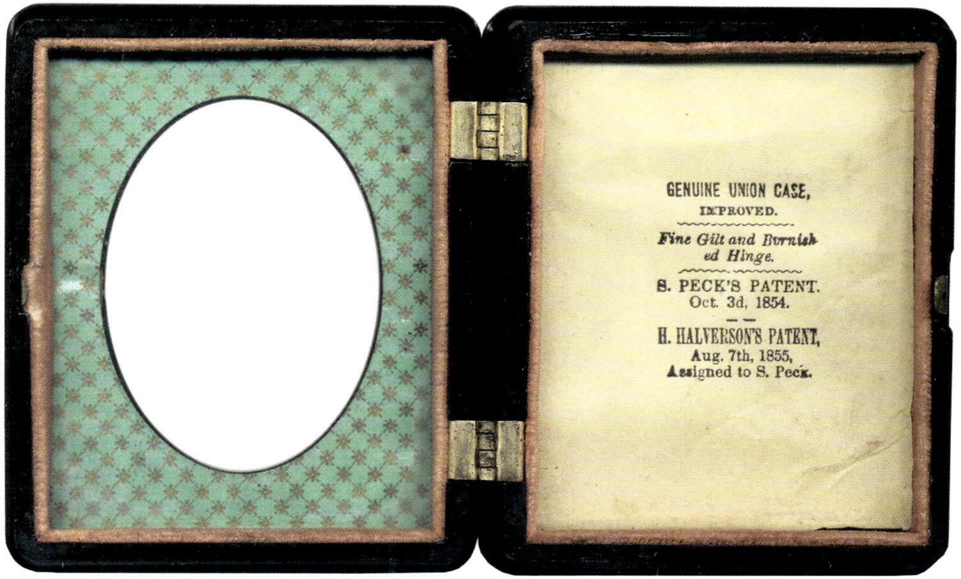

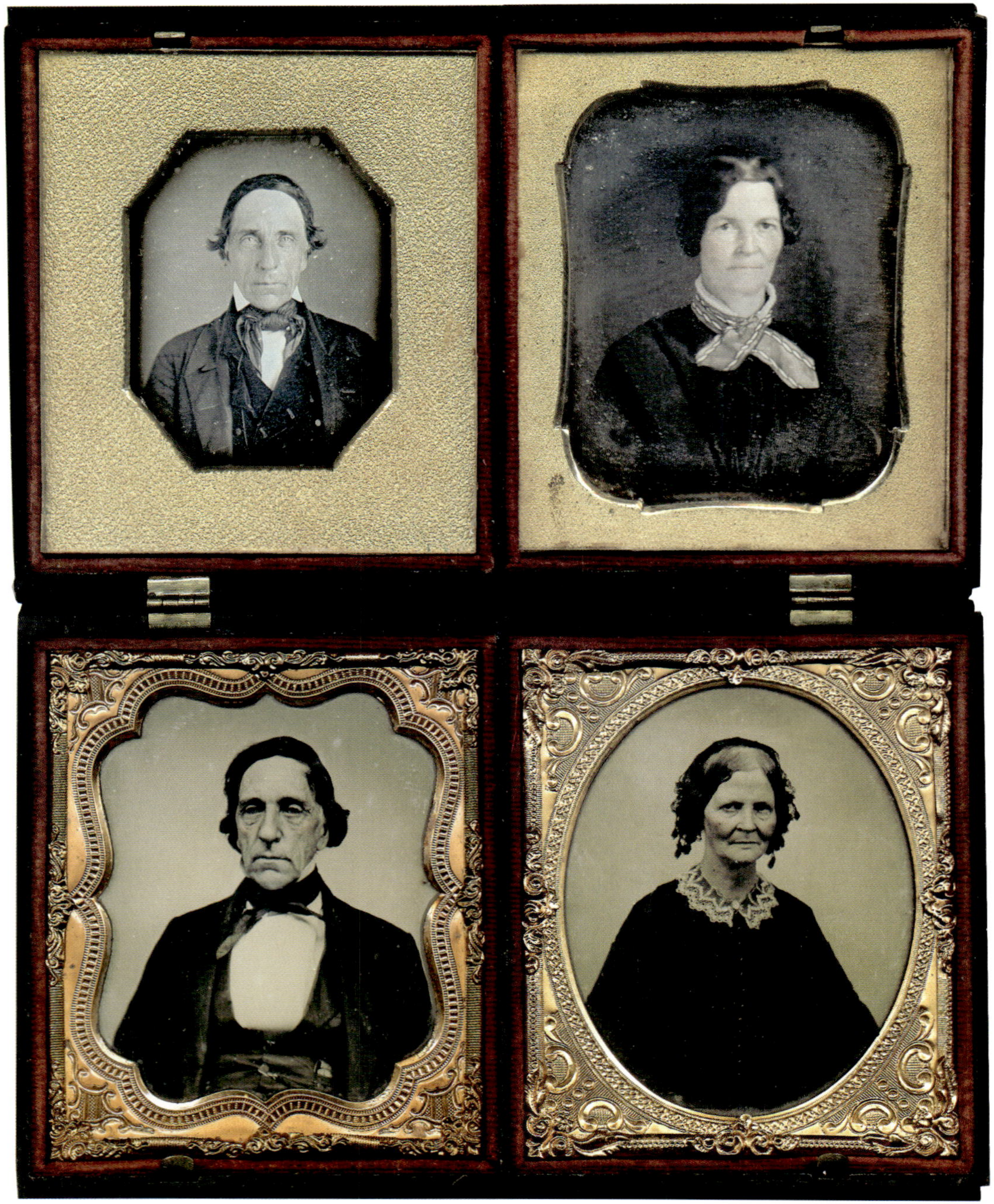

While the majority of cases took either a single image, or a pair of images, a very small number were designed to take four, and one design, known as 'Two Lovers Going to the Well' could accommodate five or ten – two ninth plate and three sixteenth plate in each side!
This design, 'Mother, Child and Dog' was available for two or four images, and the mattes and fittings illustrated here offer an interesting assortment of contemporary styles. The upper left design of matte is the oldest, followed in age by top right, bottom left and bottom right. Ten years would appear to separate the pairs of sixth plate portraits, the upper pair being daguerreotypes and the lower pair are ambrotypes.

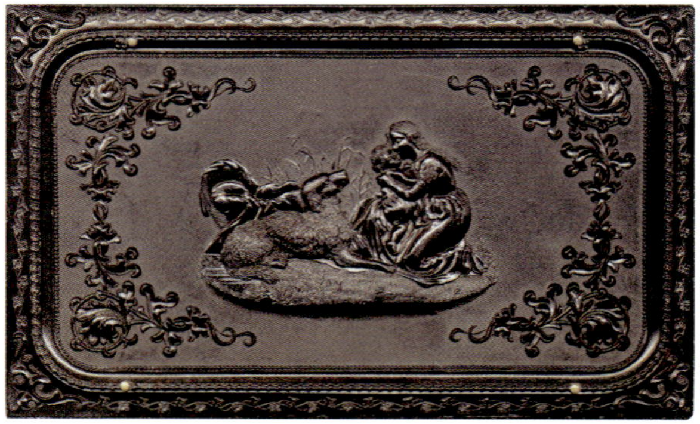

The 'Mother, Child and Dog' design appears on four cases – a variant of the case illustrated here, and two smaller sixth plate examples. There are other cases also depicting dogs, such as 'Going to Market' and 'Teasing her Dog'. Actual case size 159mm x 97mm.

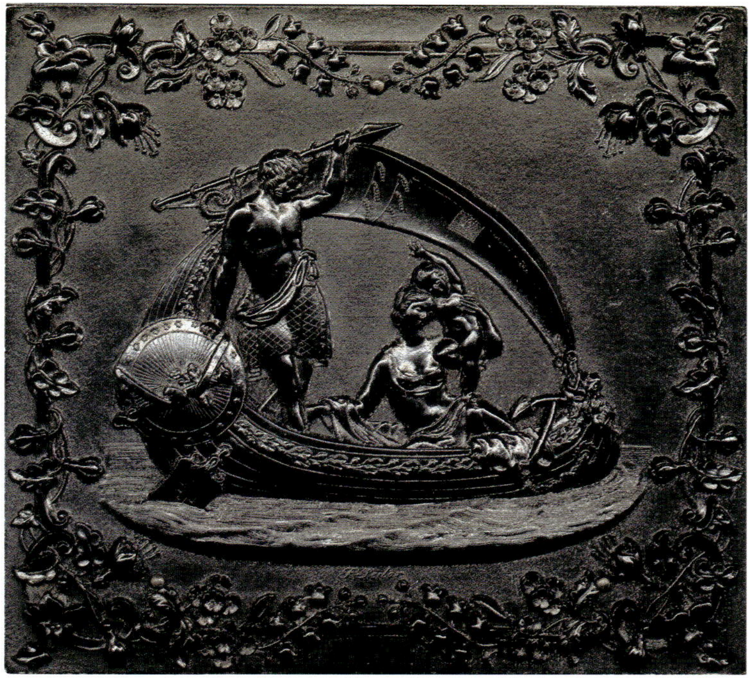

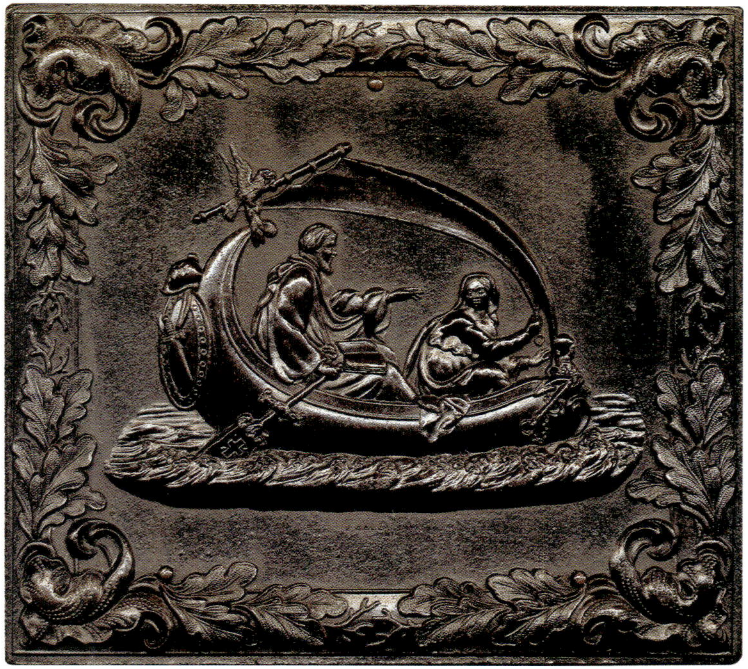

'The Voyage of Life' is a theme which is traced through no fewer than seven sixth plate case designs. Four different periods in the voyage of life have been identified – 'The Launching', 'Youth, love', 'The Family' (above left with a die engraved by Frederick Seiler) and 'Old Age' (above right from a die engraved by Frederick Goll). All are considered to be extremely rare, and are treasured by collectors. Three different versions of 'The Launching' have been identified, two of 'Youth, Love' and one each of the two illustrated here. Shown actual size.

This page: 'The Wedding Procession', a half plate case celebrating the wedding of Priscilla Mullins with John Alden as described by Henry Wadsworth Longfellow in his poem 'The Courtship of Miles Standish' written in 1858. This case must have been designed and marketed within a very short period of time after the publication of the poem. In the case design, from a die engraved by Anthony Shaefer based on one of the illustrations in the 1859 publication of Longfellow's poem, Priscilla is seen riding to her marriage on Alden's white bull Raghorn. Shown actual size.
Opposite page left: A quarter plate geometric design made the more interesting by the inclusion of a thermoplastic 'cameo' of William Shakespeare in the centre. This particular case design could be purchased with one of several different cameo inserts. Shown actual size.
Opposite page right: 'The Parting of Hafed and Hinda', a quarter plate case by Holmes, Booth and Hayden, from dies engraved by Henning and Eymann.

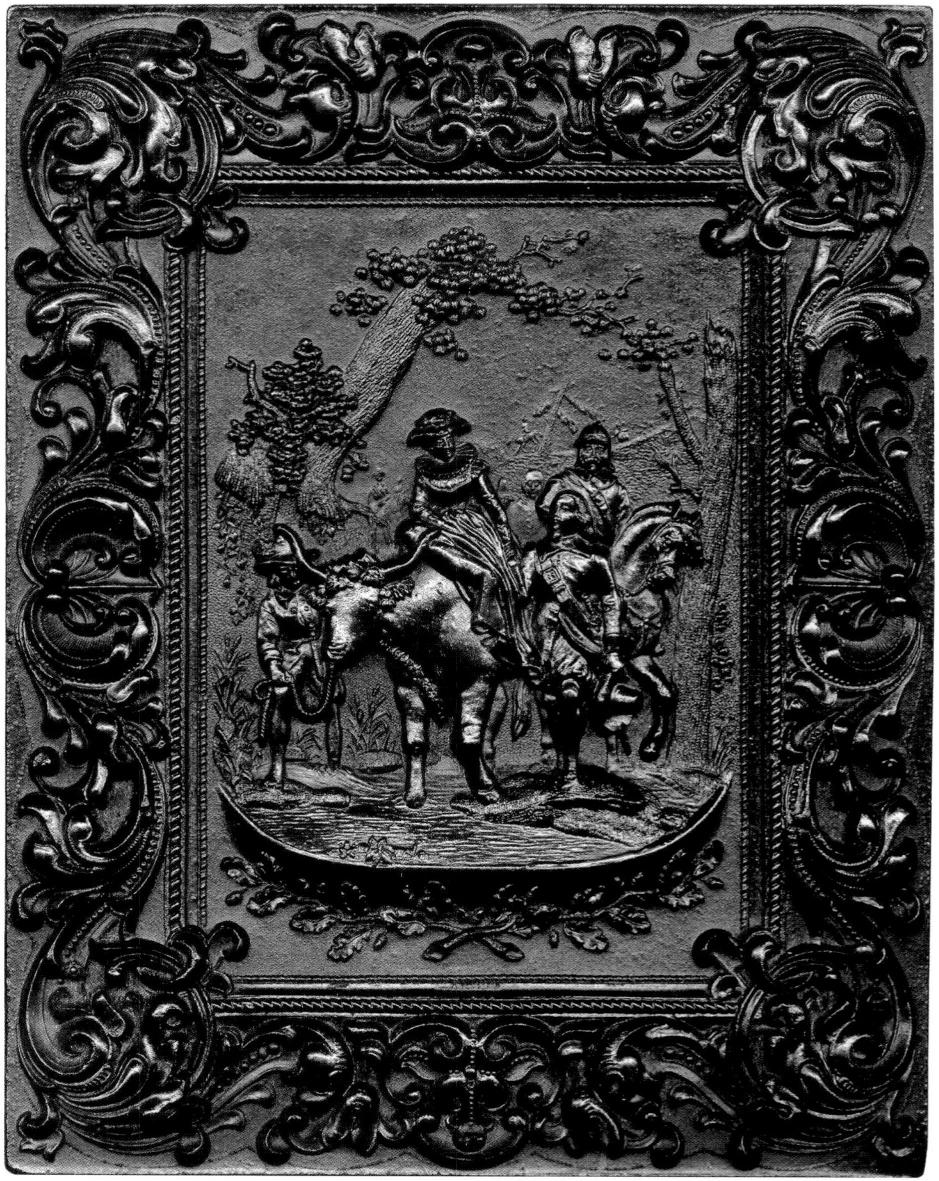

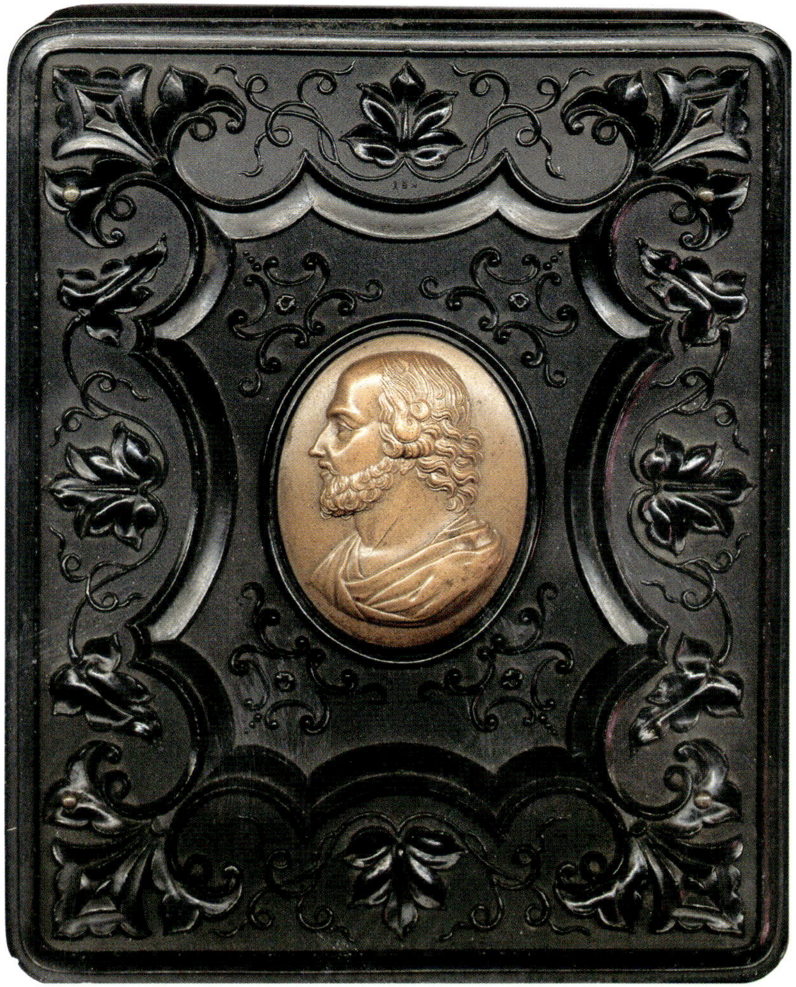

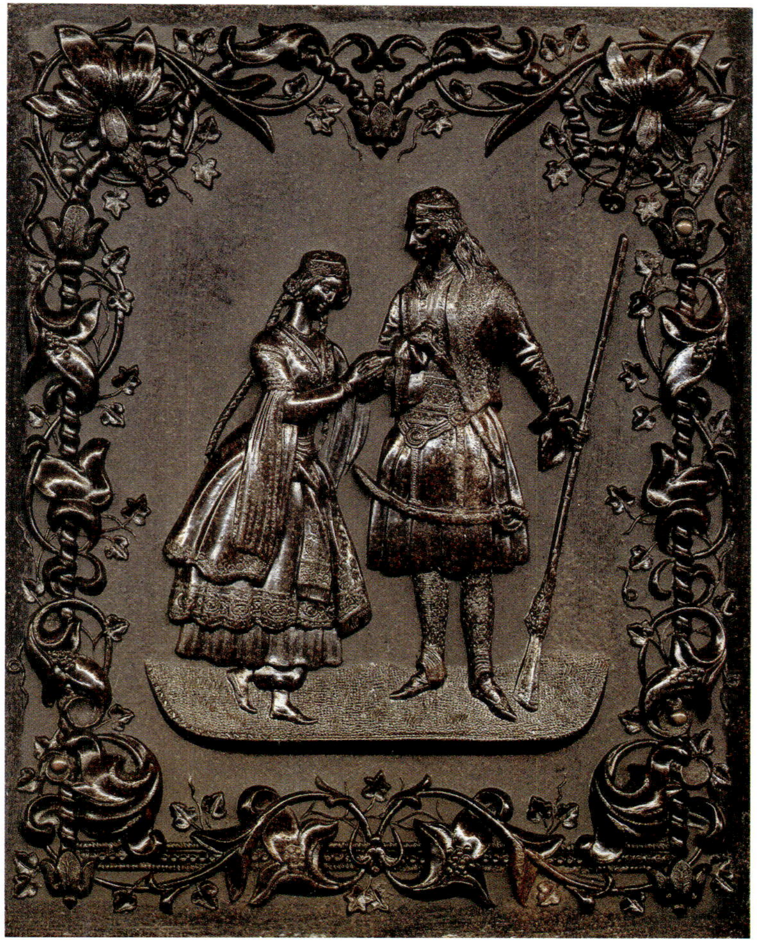

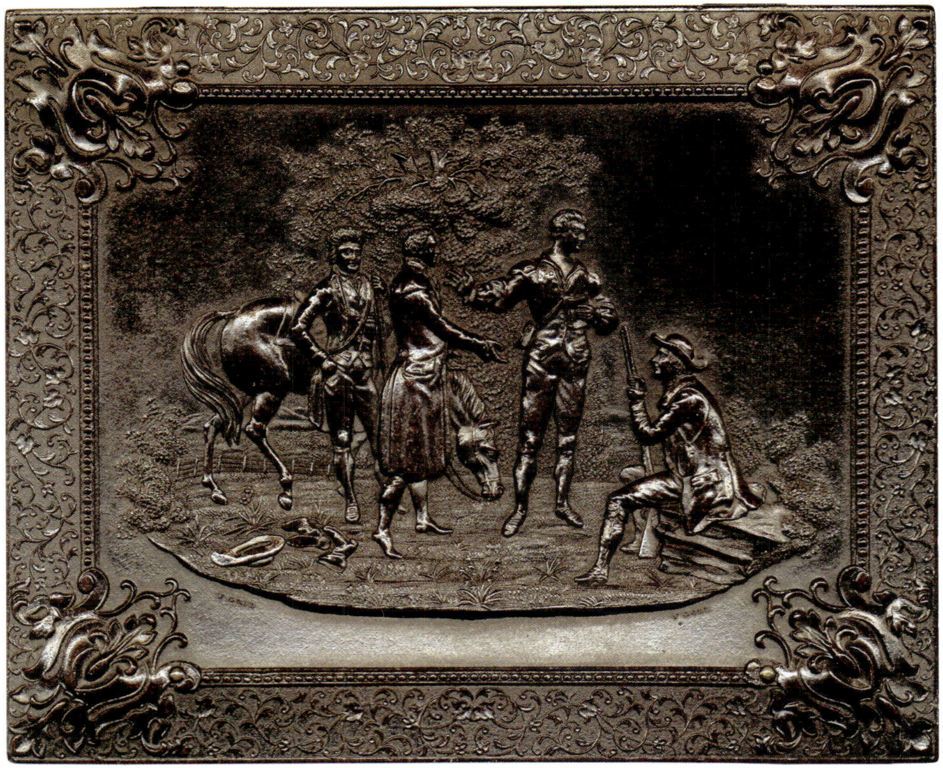

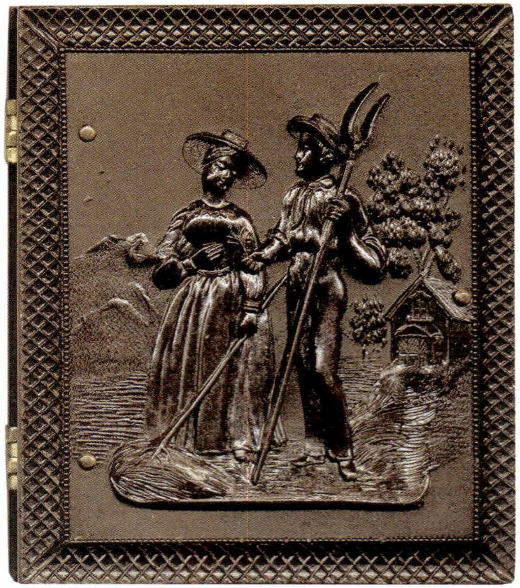

Above: 'The Capture of Major André' a quarter plate case engraved by Frederick Goll and produced by Peck and Halvorson, recalls an incident in the American War of Independence. André, an officer in the British Army, and operating behind the lines as a spy, was eventually captured and hanged in 1780. Case shown actual size

Top right: 'American Gothic' showing a farmer and his wife, complete with hayfork, has an unusual cushion border used in several other case designs from Littlefield, Parsons & Co. Shown actual size.

Bottom right: Ninth plate case with cutout centre, backed with blue velvet, shown actual size. A number of examples of this style of case produced by Littlefield, Parsons & Co., have been found in quarter, sixth and ninth plate sizes.

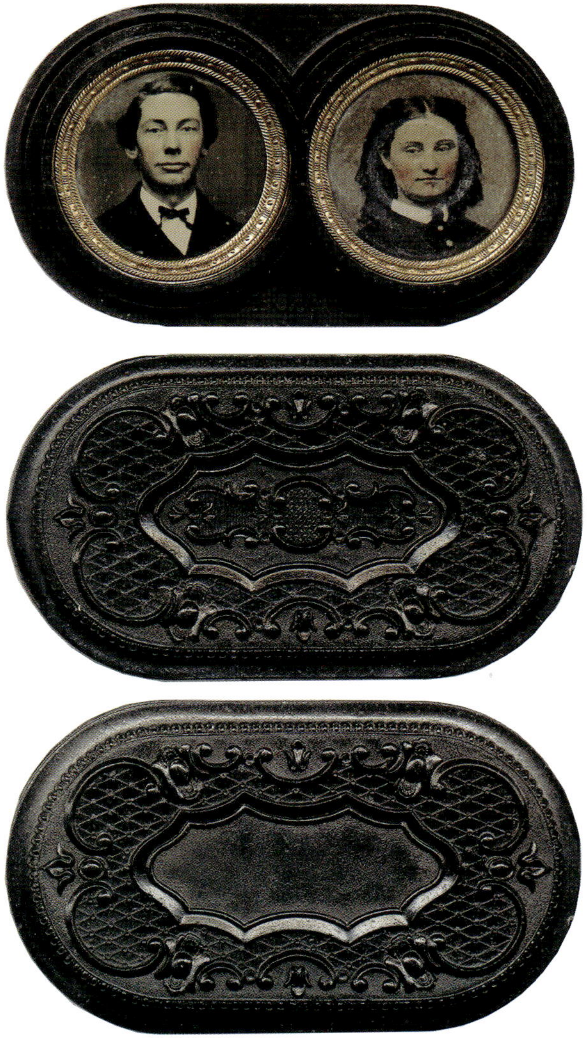

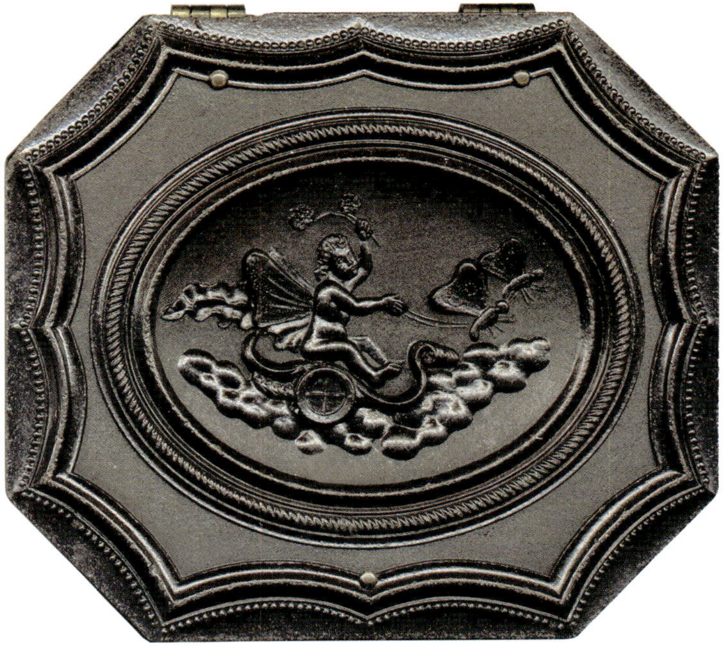

Left: This extremely rare 'double sweetheart' size of case contains two circular sixteenth plate size tintypes. The two halves of the case simply press together, and are not hinged. This style of closure is the norm for the many circular sweetheart 'oreo' or 'cookie' cases which are very rare outside America. Only two double sweetheart case designs have so far been identified. The casemaker for neither is known. Shown actual size.

Above: 'The Butterfly Chariot' a sixth plate design from Littlefield, Parsons & Co., a fanciful design showing an angel on a chariot being pulled across clouds by two butterflies. The origin of this symbolic image is unknown. The case contains the tinted ambrotype illustrated on page 79. Shown actual size.

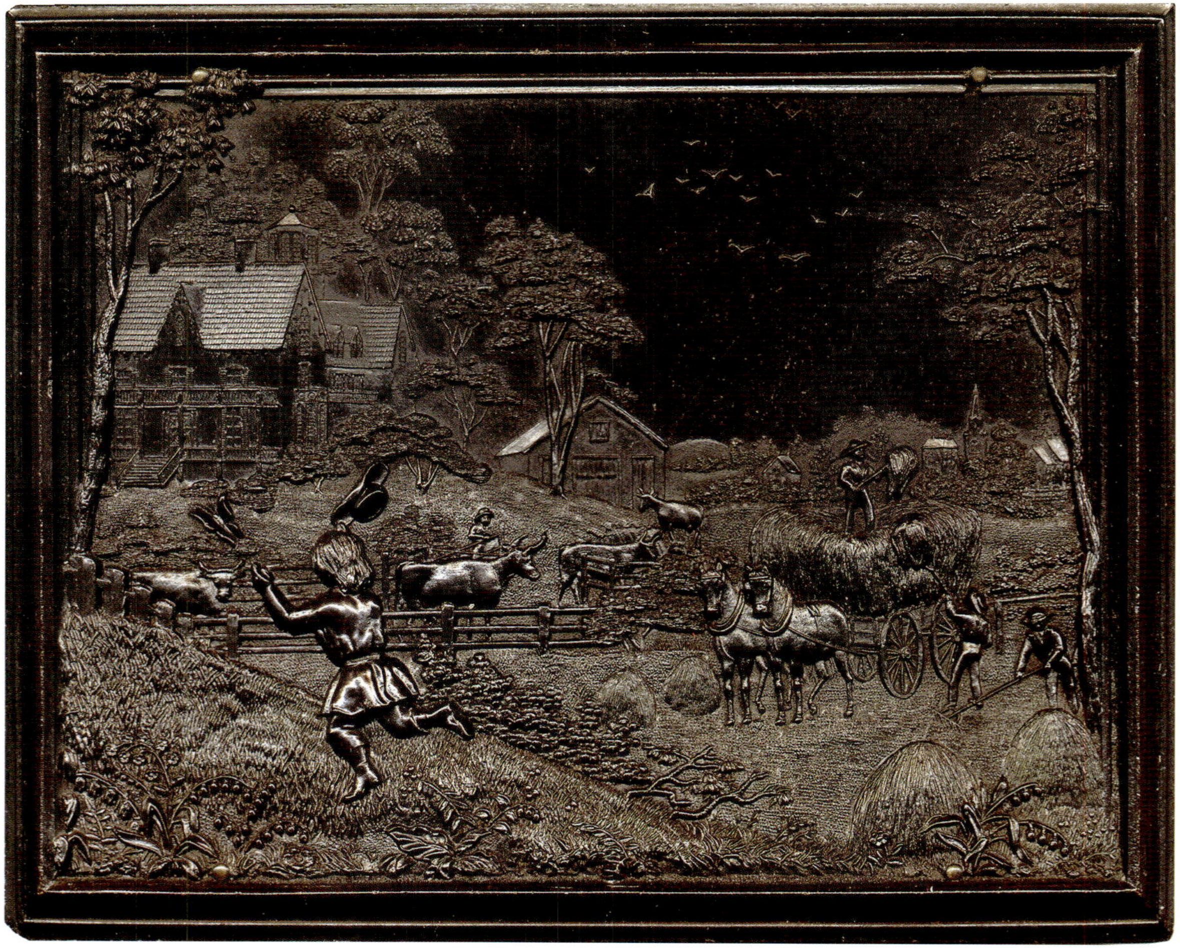

Above: There is no record of the die-engraver for Littlefield, Parsons & Company's beautiful half plate case design 'A Summer's Evening'. The design of the case is based on a section of a lithographic print published in 1855 by Nathaniel Currier. The case probably appeared no more than three or four years later. Three variants of this design have been identified in America. Shown actual size.

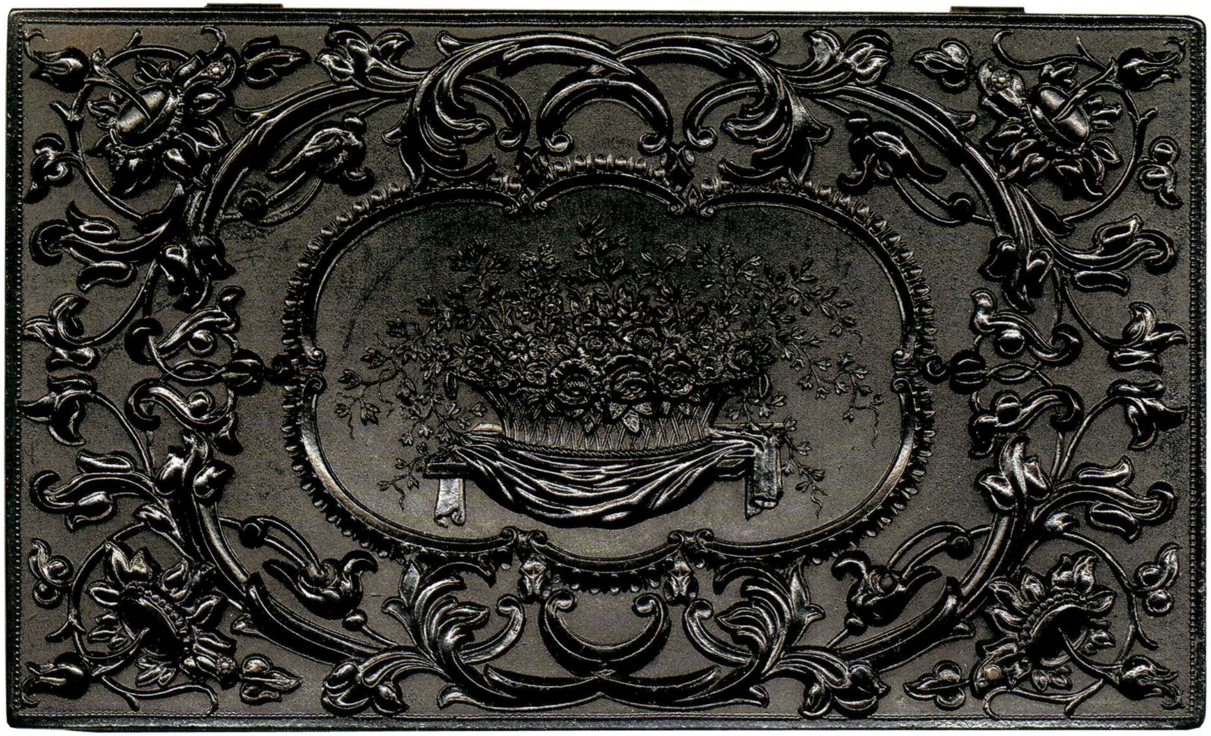

Basket of Flowers, double sixth plate union case by Littlefield, Parsons & Co., c.1860. The woven basket is a recurring theme in many union cases by both Littlefield, Parsons & Co and Holmes Booth & Hayden, sometimes filled with flowers, but more usually filled with fruit. Only nine cases this size have yet been identified. Case shown here actual size.

Footnotes

1. Gutta Percha was manufactured from the latex sap of certain Malayan or Brazilian trees. While not produced in as large quantities as from rubber trees, the material was found to be available in commercial quantities from the *palaquium oblongifolia* tree and was first introduced to Europe as early as the middle of the 17th century. It became plastic at temperatures above 65°C, and as it became rigid when moulded, and yet not brittle, it was ideal for a wide variety of moulded products, such as dishes and utensils for the processing of photographic plates. In the USA today, the thermoplastic used for union cases is often mistakenly referred to as gutta percha. It is, however, shellac rather than latex based.
2. Bois Durci, literally 'hard wood' was produced in France from the early 1860s, and used for a wide variety of moulded products, and for several carte-de-visite album covers. An example is illustrated in the next chapter.
3. 'Parkesine' was evolved into 'Xylonite' by Parkes' successor, Daniel Spill and the business became known as the British Xylonite Company.
4. Peck's first US Patent, No. 11,758, and variously titled *Manufacture of Daguerreotype Cases,* and *Making Photographic Picture Cases* was granted on October 3rd 1854, a fact Peck printed on the label of every union case he produced. It was the first of nine patents relating to union cases, seven in the United States and two in Britain.
5. US Patent No. 20,436, Edward G Kinsley & S. A. W. Parker, *Hinges for Daguerreotype and Other Cases*, 1st June 1858.
6. The Thorvaldsen bas reliefs 'Day' and 'Night' would already have been well known to the buyers of union cases. Thorvaldsen himself had died in 1844, but the popularity of his work remained long after his death. The original marble medallions are in the Thorvaldsen Museum in Copenhagen.
7. British Patent No.1503, *Improvement in the Manufacture of Composition Jewellery and Ornaments, and in Cases for Jewellery, Photographs, and for Other Similar Purposes*, 21st June 1859
8. US Patent No.21,285, Improvement in Composition for miniature cases, &c., August 24th 1858

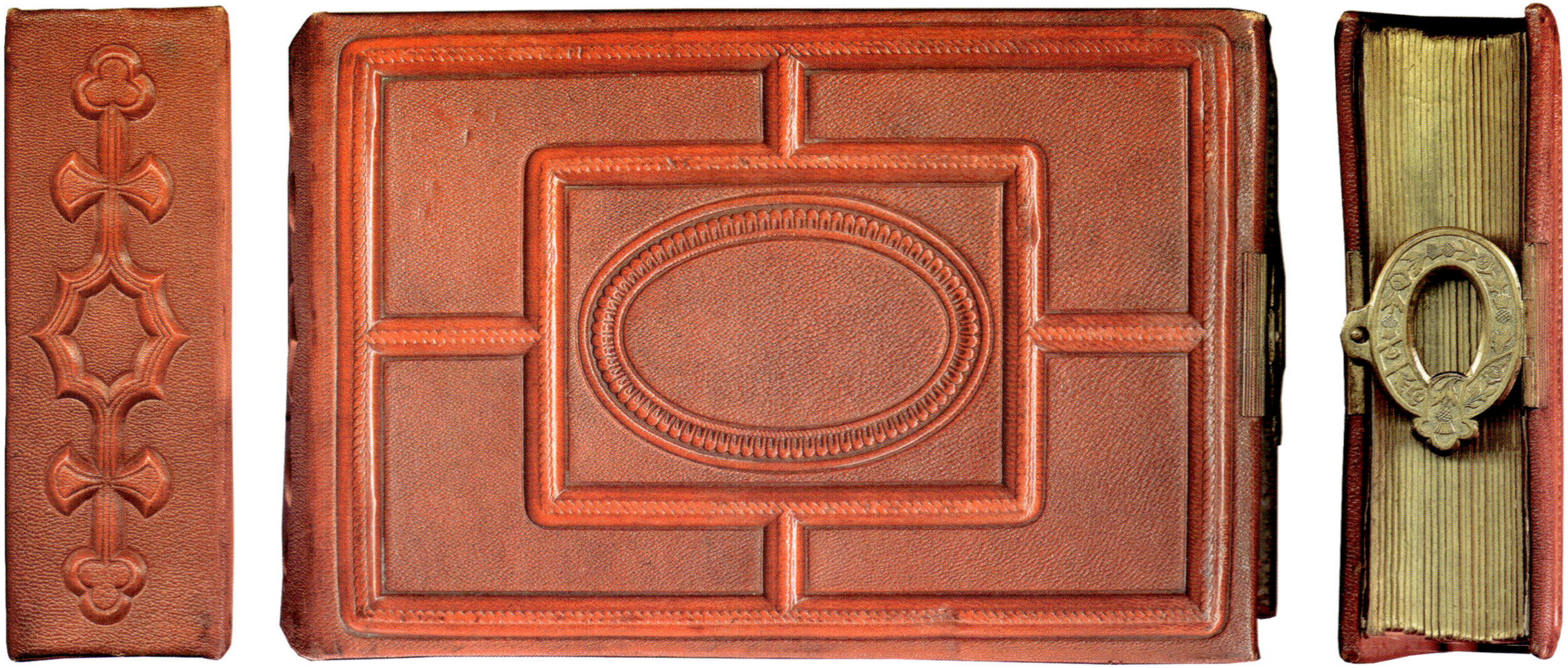

Red leather carte-de-visite album, designed to take two portraits per page, with a capacity of one hundred cartes. Carte apertures have gilded edges and rounded corners. The album dates from the mid 1860s and is fitted with an elaborate English and Scottish motif clasp of intertwined roses and thistles. The album has silk-effect end-papers and gilded edges to the pages. There is no identification of the manufacture. Early carte-de-visite albums suffered from an inability to be opened completely flat. In the early 1860s, however, a series of patents in Britain and Europe introduced albums which could be laid flat open, thanks to ingeniously designed spines, and ingenious methods for holding the pages together.

Albums of this period cost from as little as a shilling for one designed to take twelve cartes, to upwards of six guineas for the really lavish variety. Albums such as the one illustrated here probably cost in the region of £1.50–£2. Actual album size 230mm x 115mm.

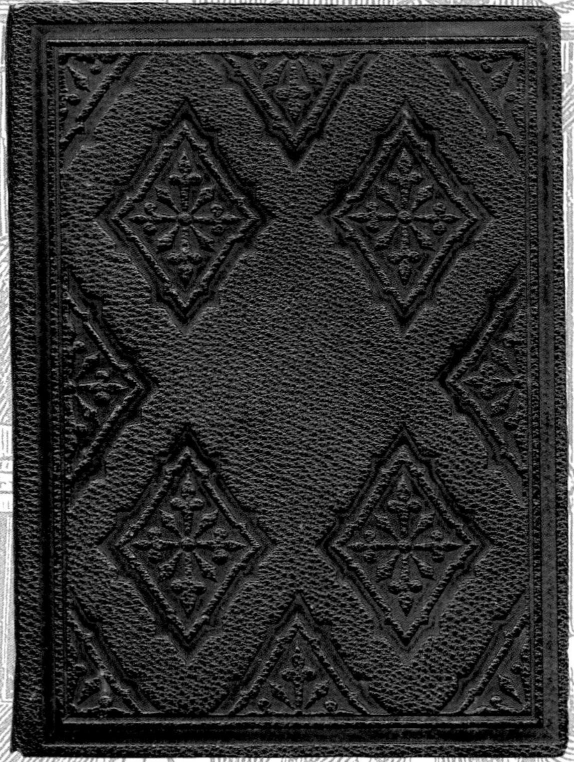

Chapter Seven

The Family Album, the Framed Portrait and changing attitudes to photography

Sixth plate tinted and gilded ambrotype of a young child in an early Victorian style gilded frame more usually used to house a miniature painting. The portrait was taken by an unknown Glasgow photographer in the late 1850s, and was framed by James McClure & Sons, Carvers, Gilders and Printsellers to the Queen, at 83 Renfield Street Glasgow.

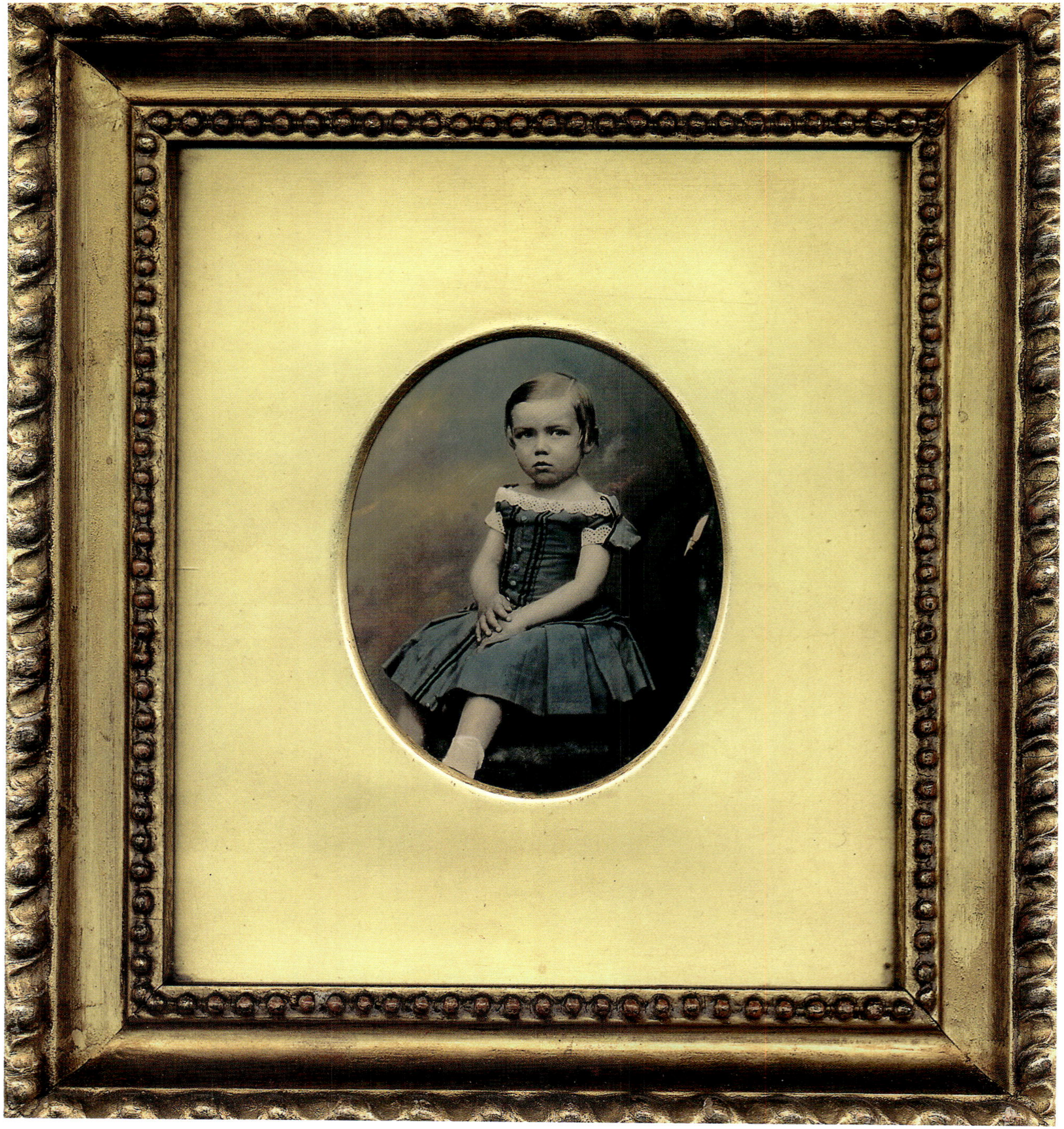

Chapter Seven:

The Family Album and the Framed Portrait

The carte-de-visite, introduced by André Adolphe Eugène Disderi of Paris, reduced the price of the photographic portrait overnight from pounds to pennies, and the expensive case's days were numbered.

The ambrotype survived for a few more years but, along with the tintype, it was eventually relegated to the itinerant photographer, and in particular in Britain, the beach photographer, whose business depended on the production of a 'finished' picture in a few minutes. As the carte-de-visite used a glass negative from which any number of prints could be made, it was by necessity a more time consuming process for a single image.

Ambrotype and tintype photographers, producing unique positives in the camera, could satisfy their customers in a matter of minutes, albeit with a product which was sometimes less durable, if less care was taken over its production.

There did remain, however, a significant market for larger framed ambrotypes throughout the 1860s, and a wide variety of elaborate wooden, plaster, metal and plastic frames were manufactured to meet that demand.

Despite the undoubted quality of these large and unique portraits, both in their execution and their subsequent colouring, very few photographers identified their work. Framed ambrotypes in both half plate and full plate sizes became the top end of the market for many of those portraitists whose prices were being forced down by the competitive nature of the carte-de-visite market. And as the wet collodion negative used for the carte was effectively the same process as employed for the ambrotype, the two coexisted easily.

At the smaller end of the scale, quarter and sixth plate portraits could also be purchased in wood and plaster frames, while pressed metal frames, many made in France, were available for ninth plate and sixth plate images.

Within a few years of the introduction of the carte-de-visite in 1857, it was the family album rather than the cased or framed portrait which was in the ascendancy.

Legend has it that Napoleon III, while leading his army out of Paris, stopped at the studio of his court photographer, A. A. E. Disderi[1], and had portraits of himself produced and distributed to his generals and troops – supposedly so that they would know who not to shoot! Like many legends, while very attractive, it is without substance. The original cartes appear to have been produced for Count Parma who had the idea of sticking small albumen paper prints of himself on to his visiting cards.

It was Disderi, however, who first marketed the format and the idea of ready card-mounted portraits. The change was to replace the owner's name and address on the card with that of the photographer, and to offer the small prints for a price which considerably opened up the photographic market.

While the ambrotype remained relatively expensive – somewhere between ten shillings and a guinea for a cased portrait in sixth or quarter plate – the carte was, from the outset, offered for a fraction of that cost.

Between four and ten shillings – 20-50p – for a sitting and a dozen card-mounted prints, brought photography within the reach of the masses and very quickly expanded the total market several-fold.

The logical successors to the photographic case were the desk-frame (see page 91) and the family album.

The family album, at first a simple affair, evolved into a Victorian treasure with the pages richly decorated by the daughter of the house. Later albums were published pre-printed – many by Marion & Co. of Paris[2] – and they survive to this day in their thousands. They were filled with cartes-de-visite at usually two or four to a page, and cabinet prints one to a page.

While there was no way that the delicate glass ambrotype could be incorporated into the family album, the tintype, once considered the poor relation of photography, and usually in Britain used only by itinerant and beach photographers, did find a place in the new order. The ninth plate tintype – once sold in a cheap pressed metal matte and paper frame – was given a new lease of life by

A Page from a 'Jewel' carte-de-visite album made by Marion & Co. of Paris and given as an engagement present to a Lancashire Sunday School teacher in 1888. The album contained cartes-de-visite and cabinet prints of all her friends at the local Sunday School. While early albums were often decorated by the daughter of the house, by the 1880s lavishly printed examples like this were widely available.

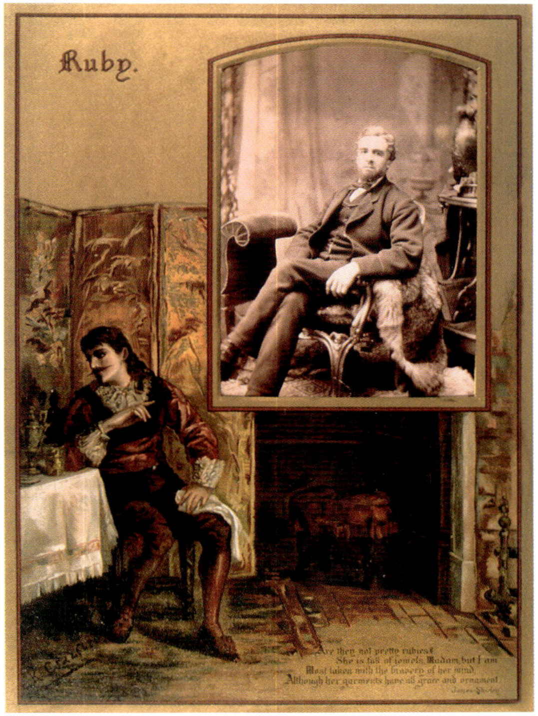

Half plate gilded ambrotype of a recently married couple in a painted wood and plaster frame, 1860s. The portrait, like many ambrotypes, is laterally reversed. Thus the new bride is showing her wedding ring on her right hand. Her husband wears a flower in his lapel. Photographer unknown. The unusual brown matte has a gilded edge. Frame size 235mm x 264mm.

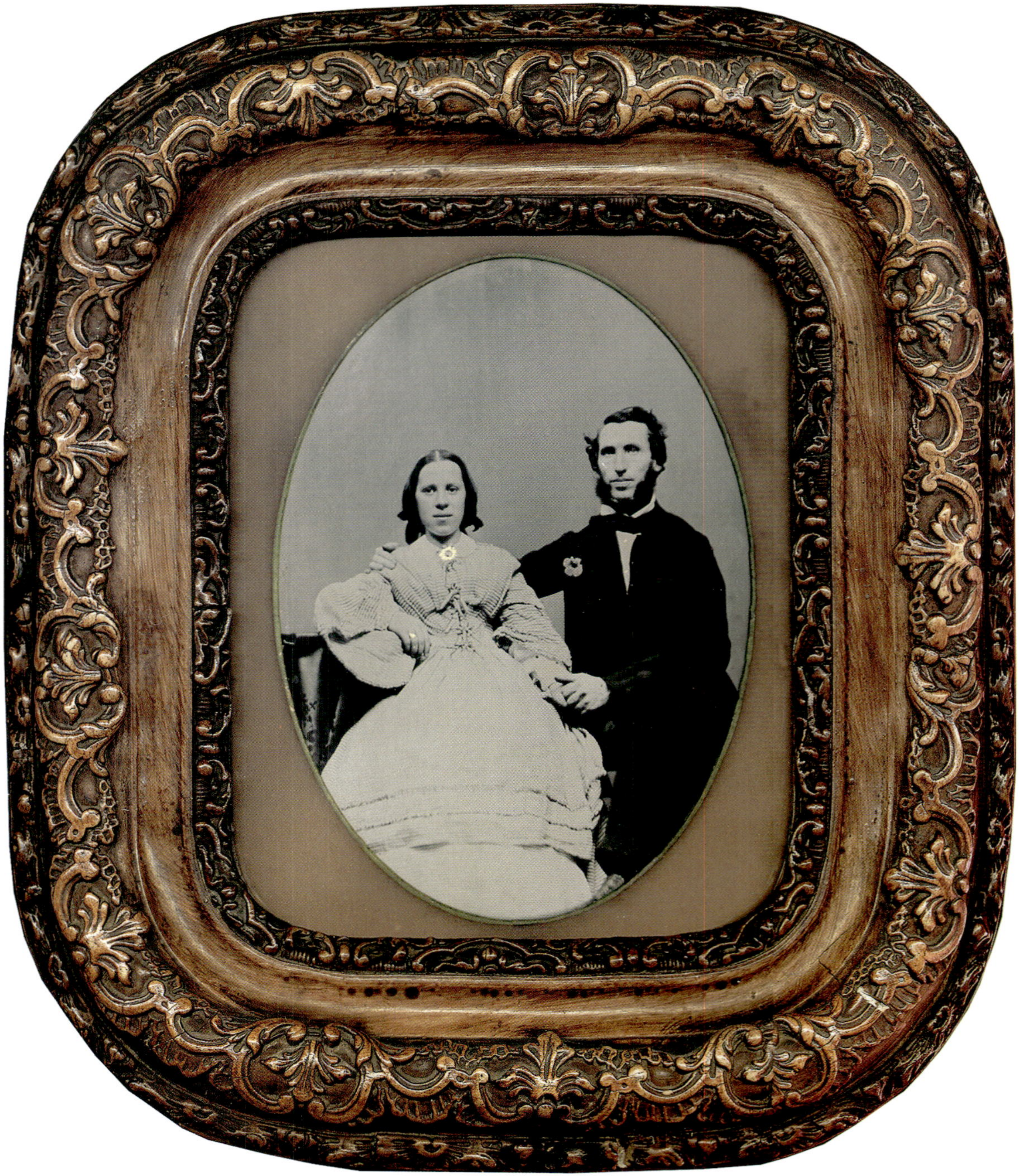

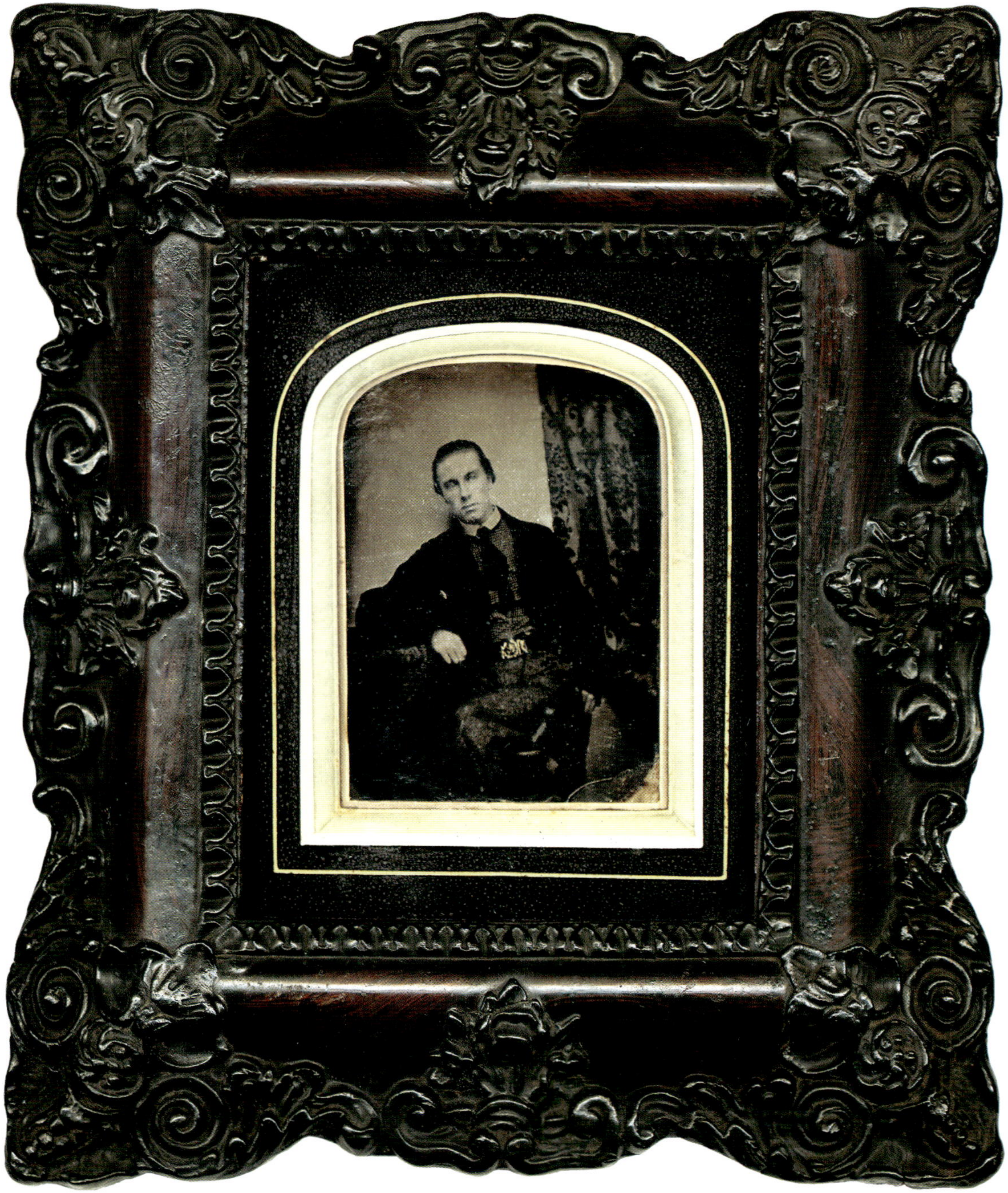

Sixth plate ambrotype in wood and plaster frame. Frames like this became quite common in the late 1850s and the 1860s. Crudely made, and produced in large numbers in a variety of sizes, they offered a more lavish alternative to the simple wood and paper frame, adding scale and value to the small ambrotype image. Examples for sixth plate, quarter plate and half plate ambrotypes have been identified. Given the appearance of the subjects usually found in these frames, they were at the lower price end of the market. Typically measuring 180mm x 205mm, the frames were available in a variety of wood effects.

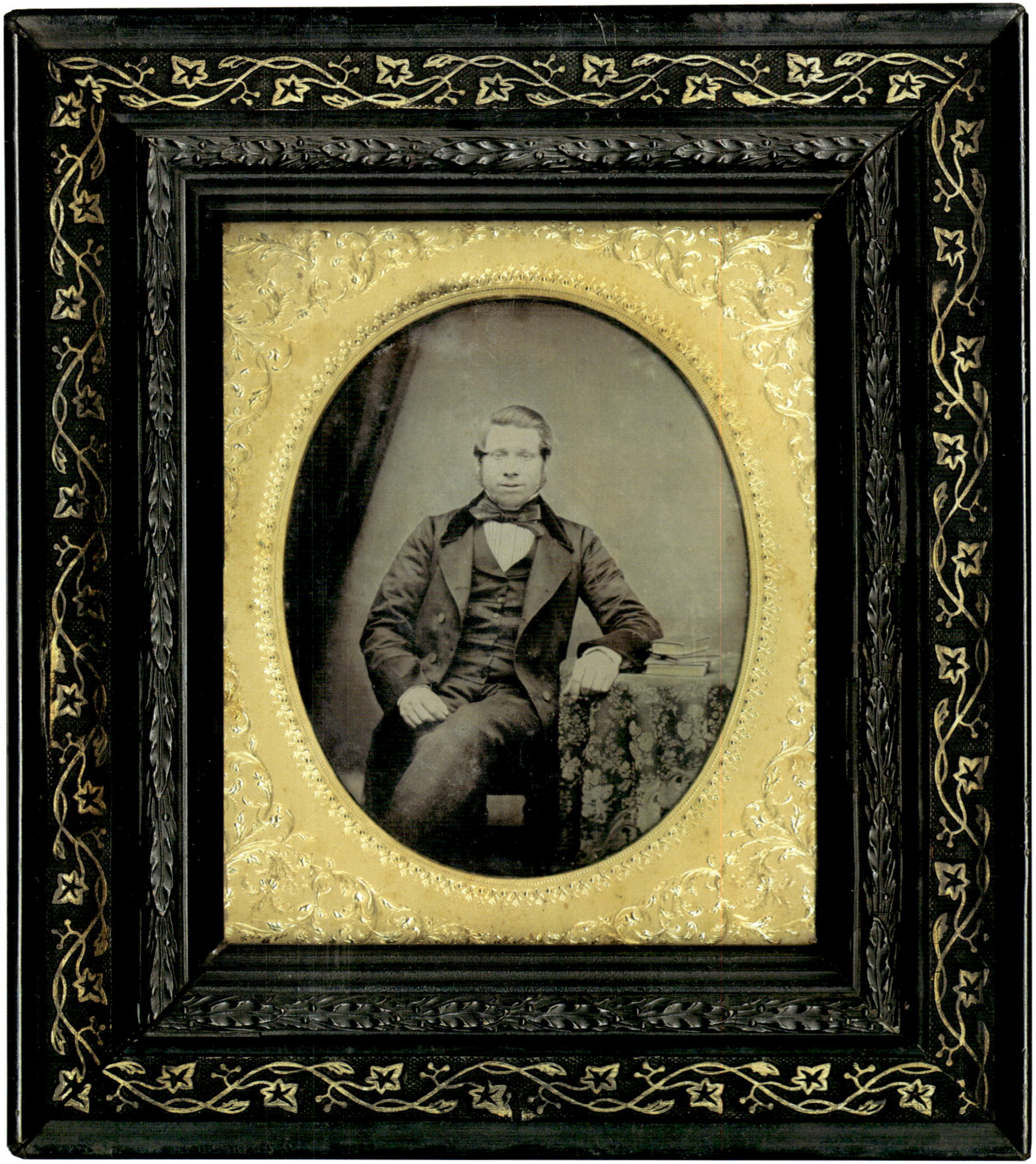

Half plate tinted ambrotype in wood and plaster frame with ornate chased matte, 1860s. This ambrotype is mounted behind one of the most elaborate mattes yet identified, and in such a finely decorated and gilded frame, presentations like this were a long way in price and availability from the small wooden or pressed metal frames illustrated opposite.

mounting it on a carte-de-visite card with an oval hole punched out.

The 'gem' tintype[3] – one twenty-fourth plate size – and hitherto a beach or fairground novelty, also found its place in the album.

At first restricted to photographs of the immediate family, the album later contained a much wider variety of imagery. Local photographers bought and sold images of the famous, the infamous and the downright weird, offering them to their customers at 6d to 1/- (2.5p-5p) each. Thus albums could contain photographs of royalty – many by Mayall, the royal photographer – of clergy, of stars of the music hall and theatre, and of freaks, a particular fascination of the Victorians.

While many photographers are reported as having refused to entertain the idea of producing ambrotypes – considering them distinctly inferior to daguerreotypes – few seem to have been slow to see the potential of the carte-de-visite market. So cartes can be found in humble family albums bearing the imprint of such well known photographers as Nadar, Claudet, Matthew Brady, Mayall, and others.

A single negative could be produced in a relatively short time – and the sales potential of a new portrait of a member of the royal family was considerable, running to many thousands of prints. In many ways, the carte-de-visite assumed the role of informer – letting the population at large see what the monarch, the prime minister and other dignitaries looked like. In that respect it served the same need that had once prompted Roman Emperors to put their heads on their coinage, and is today served by the media.

Just as the ambrotype and daguerreotype had spawned a large packaging industry, and a small novelty packaging industry, so did the carte-de-visite.

In addition to the conventional albums and small slot-in frames, carved wooden frames and multi-print frames were soon available.

Cartes-de-visite were incorporated into fans, wallets, decorative fire screens and a host of other novelties.

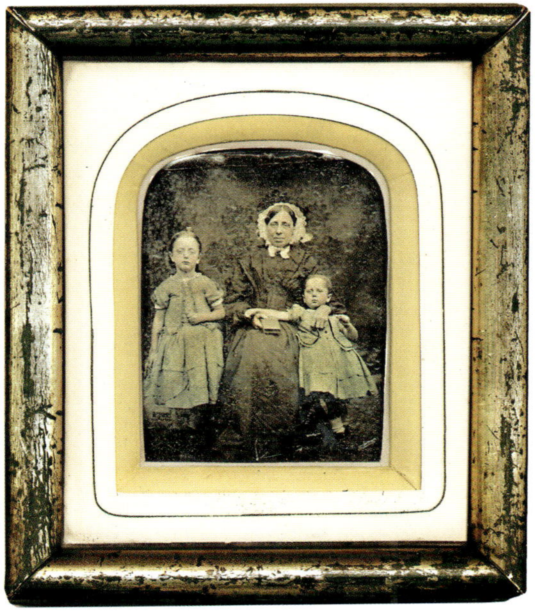

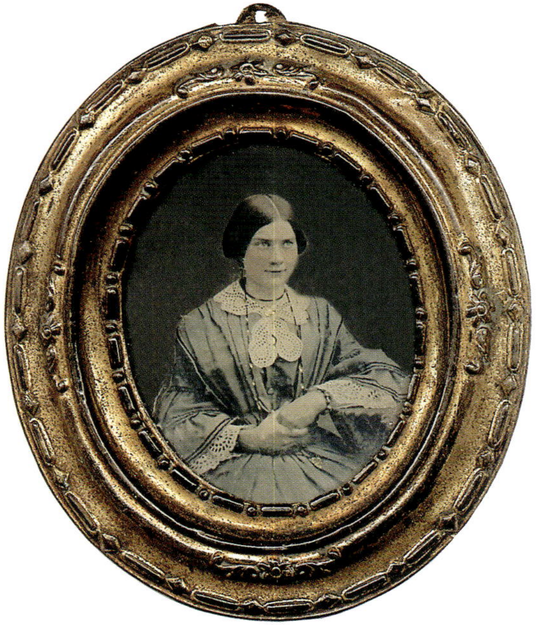

Above left: Mother and daughters, sixth plate tinted ambrotype in simple gilded wooden frame, early 1860s, actual size 127mm x 145mm. Photographer unknown.

Above: This French pressed-metal crimped frame houses a ninth plate ambrotype, and has a recessed rear pan to hold the ambrotype plate in place – a rectangular plate held in an oval frame. The metal hanger at the top is part of the pressed metal frame front. Frame size 77mm x 91mm. Photographer unknown.

Album covers – at first plain leather – evolved into ornamental tooled affairs. A few were even made out of thermoplastic. Others, inlaid with cameos, mother of pearl or even jewels were produced, while the really ostentatious could have carved walnut covers, or velvet, metal, or highly decorated and painted affairs.

The moulded plastic cover – developing into the album format technology previously restricted to the union case – was available in a variety of styles by the 1870s. The plastic album cover, however, could not have survived had it been made of the brittle shellac based thermoplastic used for union cases. An altogether more robust material was needed – and just such a material was found in a patent proposal published in London and Paris as early as 1855.

Bois durci – literally hard wood – offered greater strength and greater resistance to chipping and abrasion than the plastics favoured by the American casemakers – so much so that one is left wondering why cases were not made of it also. There appears to be only marginal differences

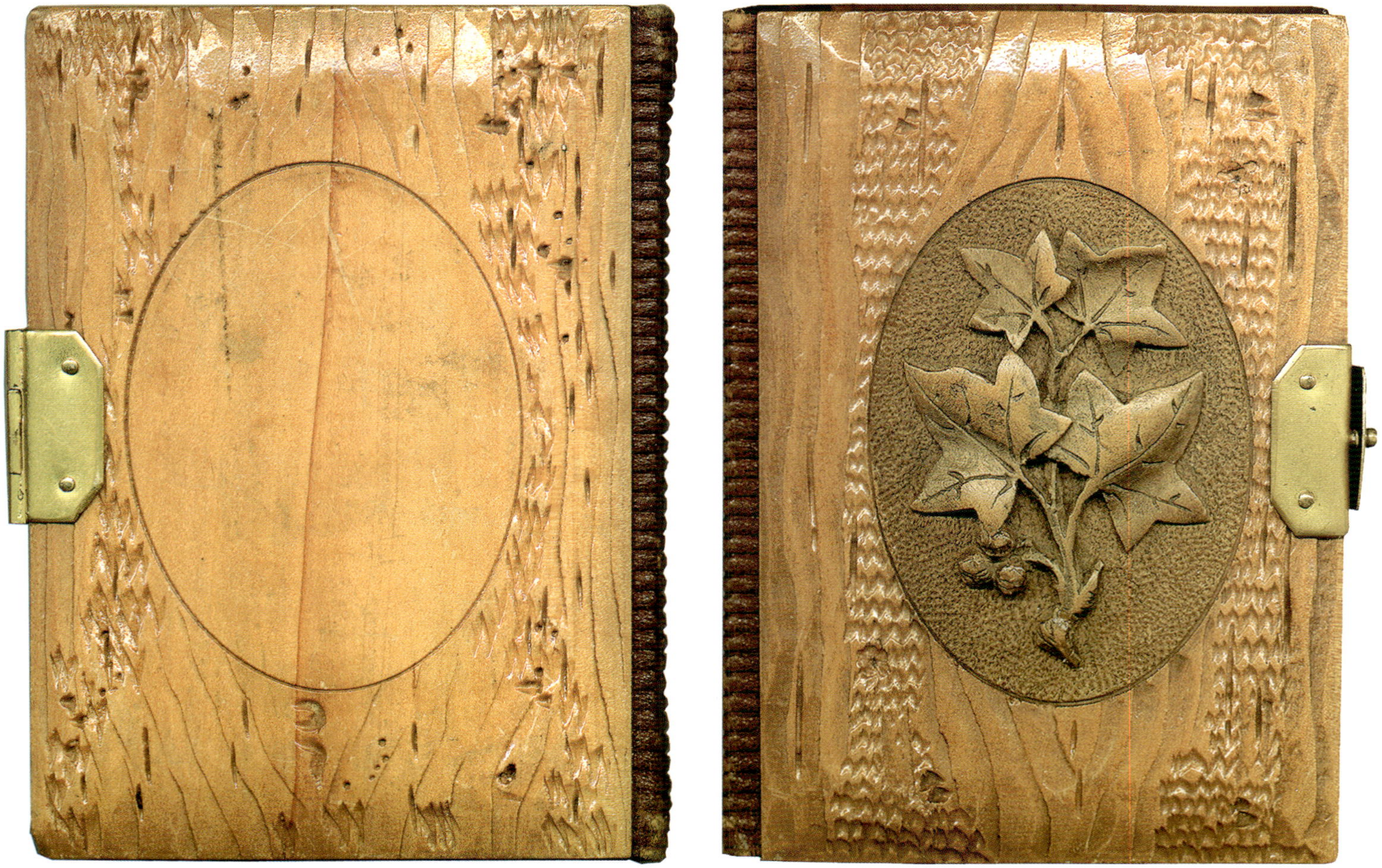

Small photograph album designed to take one carte-de-visite per page, this example has moulded 'bois durci' covers designed to look like inlaid carved wood and probably dates from the 1860s. It holds twenty-four portraits in pages with an embossed motif surrounding the aperture. The back cover is much simpler than the front, without the inlaid 'carved leaf' motif, and the two faces are held together by a strong banded leather spine. A very simple undecorated brass clasp holds the album closed. Album is shown here actual size.

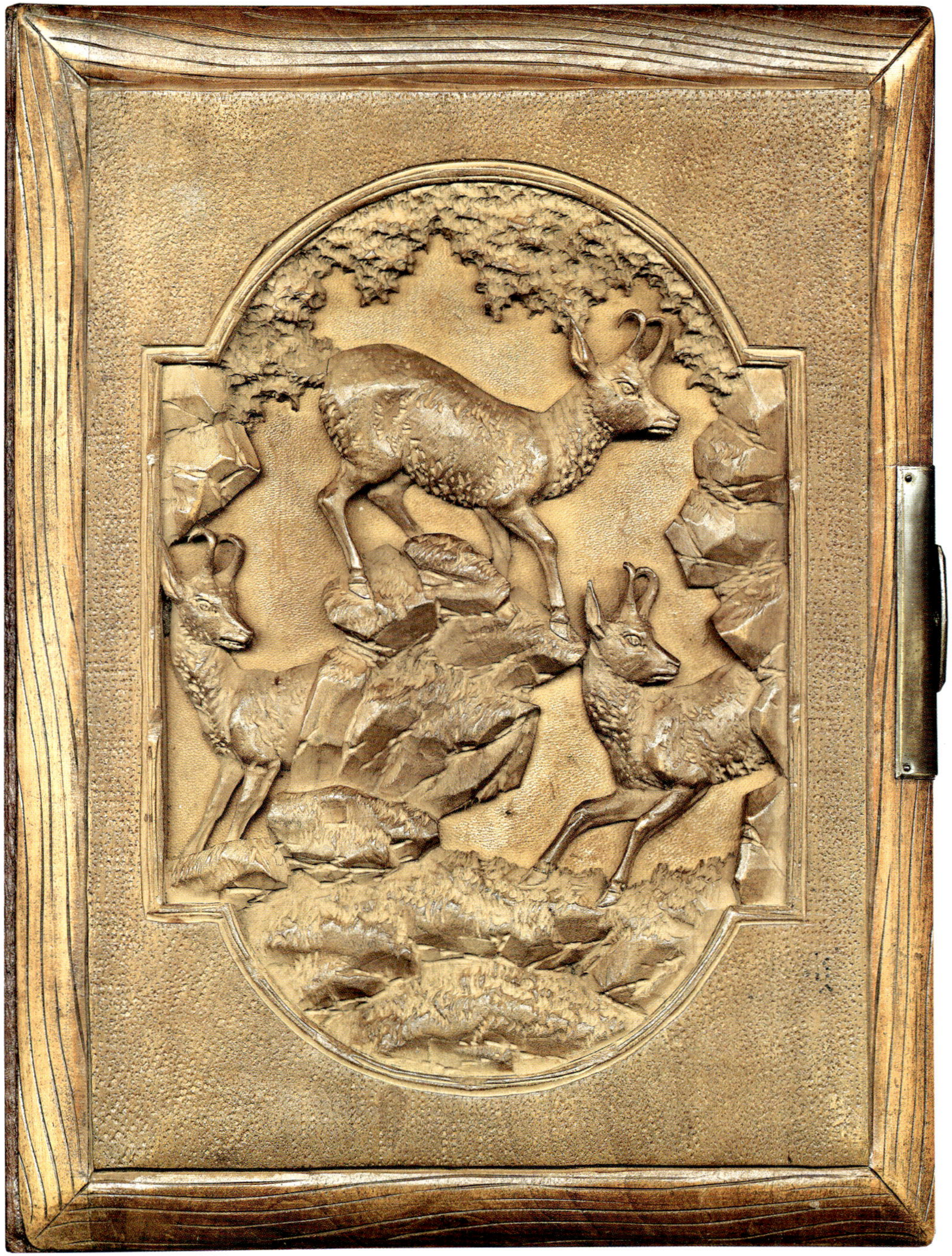

This magnificent album from the late 1870s has an elaborate moulded cover of bois durci or similar material. The ornate cut-out motif is backed with beige leather to give a heightened relief effect. It is remarkable that a product of this quality, and exhibiting this level of technological achievement bears no maker's identification whatsoever. Album size 230mm wide x 292mm tall. The back cover, also thermoplastic, is flat and bears a moulded carved wood effect. A strong leather spine, and a large but plain and simple metal closure complete the piece. The case was designed to hold twenty four cabinet prints and one hundred and four cartes-de-visite.

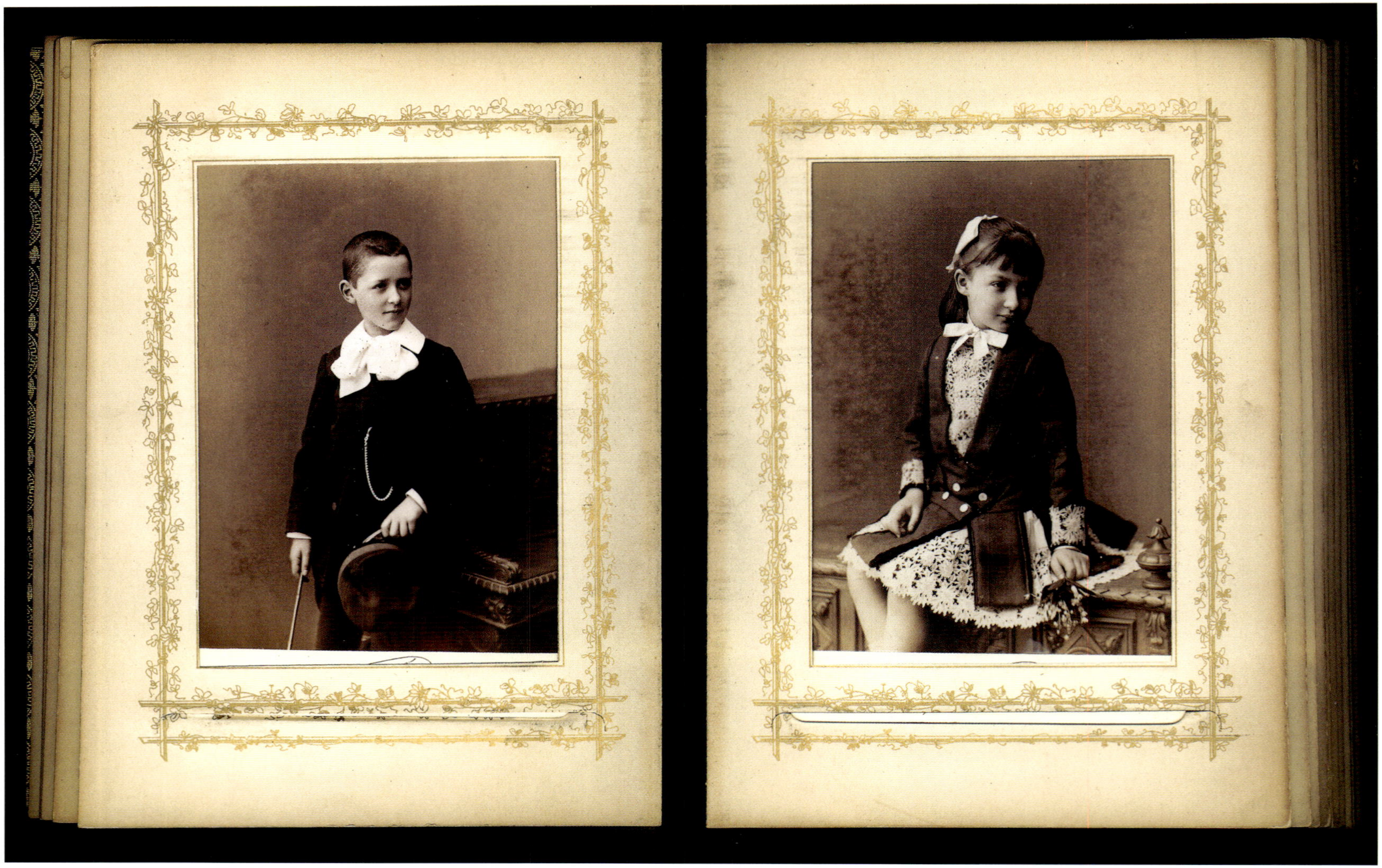

The interior of the black thermoplastic album illustrated opposite contains a collection of French family portraits. These two cabinet portraits of children were photographed c.*1880 at the Maison L Bacard, successor to A. Courrier of 59 Rue de Rivoli, Paris.*

between the clarity of image and fineness of moulding possible with bois durci and that obtained in union cases. And given the greater inherent strength of the material, much of the chipping and cracking to which so many union cases have succumbed might have been avoided.

The material was patented in 1855 simultaneously in Paris by a Monsieur Latry and in London by Francois Charles Lepage[4] and had much in common with the thermoplastic favoured by Samuel Peck in that both depended on finely ground wood fibre for their bulk.

While the union case depended on shellac for the binding material, bois durci used a mixture of albuminoid and other glutinous materials heated and moulded under pressure[5]. Colouring was achieved using anything from lamp black to vegetable dyes, for the undyed material itself was relatively colourless. This meant that bois durci was capable of being offered in a wide range of colours and, indeed, in the many examples of it which survive, that range of colours is clearly apparent.

Chessmen, jewel boxes, umbrella handles, ornaments and a host of other applications were found for the new material before covers for family albums were ever considered. Indeed, portrait medallions were probably the most common – notable examples being Napoleon III, Empress Eugénie, Molière, Wellington and the Algerian patriot Abd-el-Kader.

So robust was bois durci, that it could be engraved – offering the potential for personalised album covers. The example illustrated here has

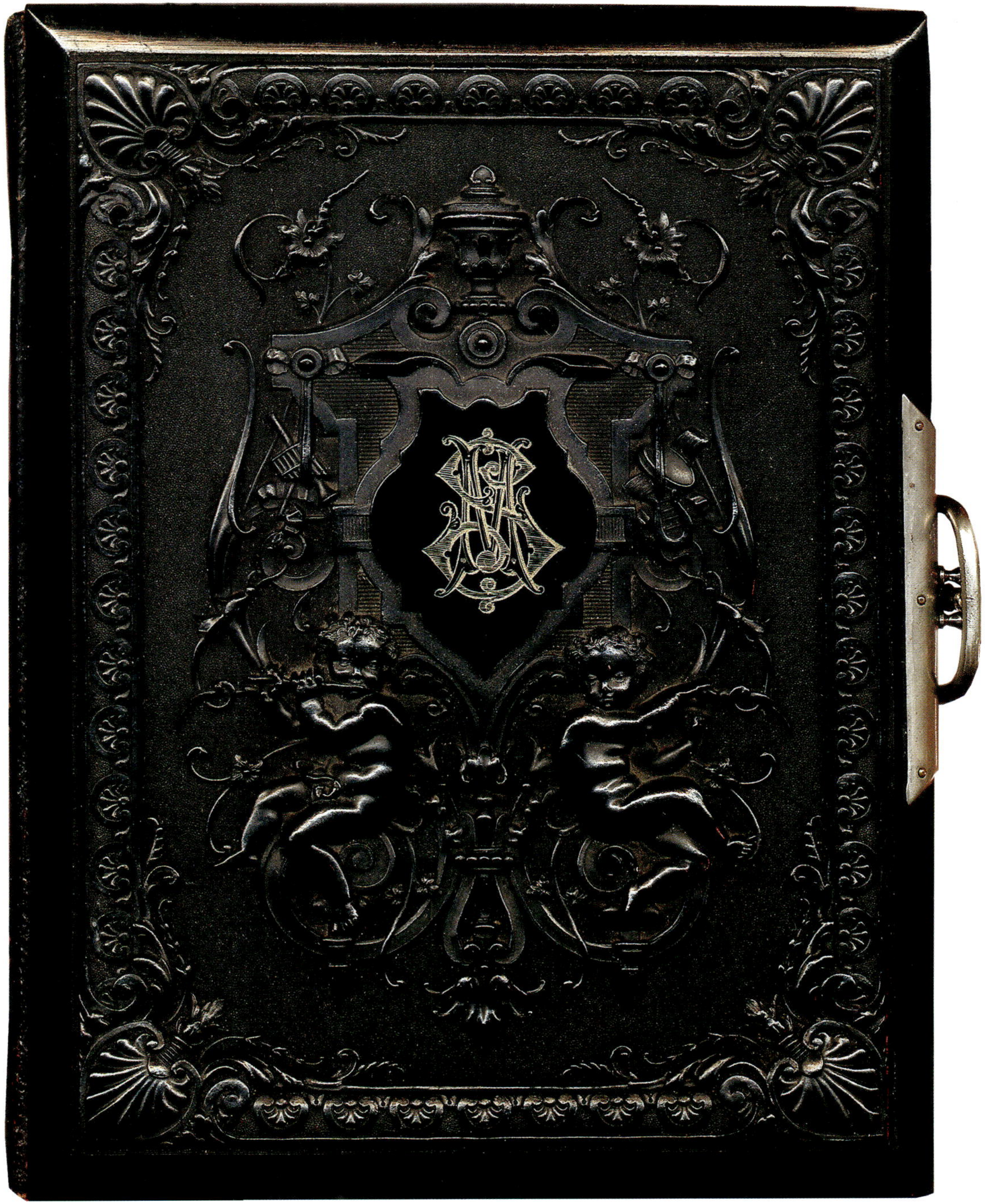

Right: Black thermoplastic album manufactured in France in the 1880s. The back cover has the same border, but a plain ground. The album has slots for twenty-two cabinet prints and sixteen cartes-de-visite. By this time, the cabinet print was in the ascendancy, the larger format being the preferred size for the well-to-do. The clasp carries two patent dates – June 22nd 1875, and December 5th 1881. It contains portraits by the Reutlinger studio, and the Langlois studio, both of Paris. Actual album size 177mm x 223mm.

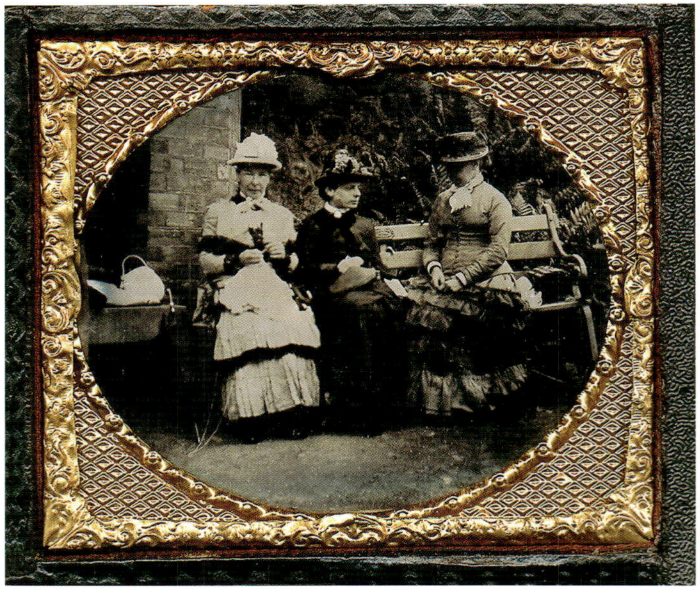

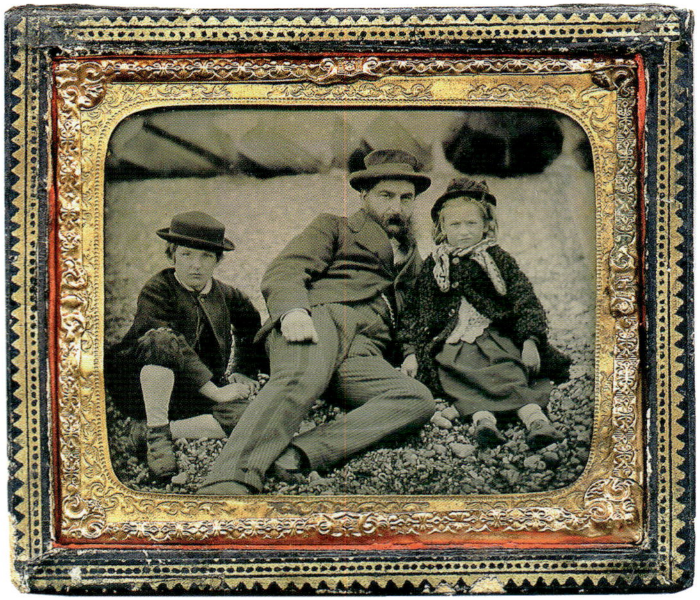

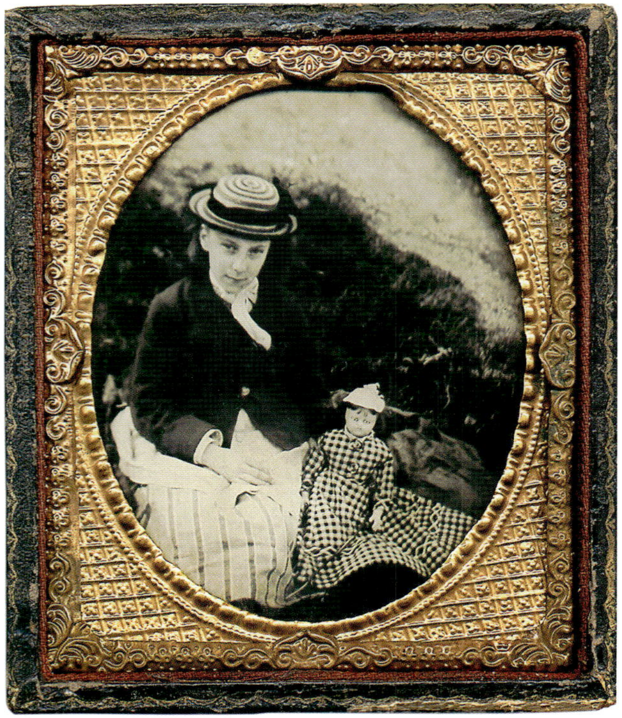

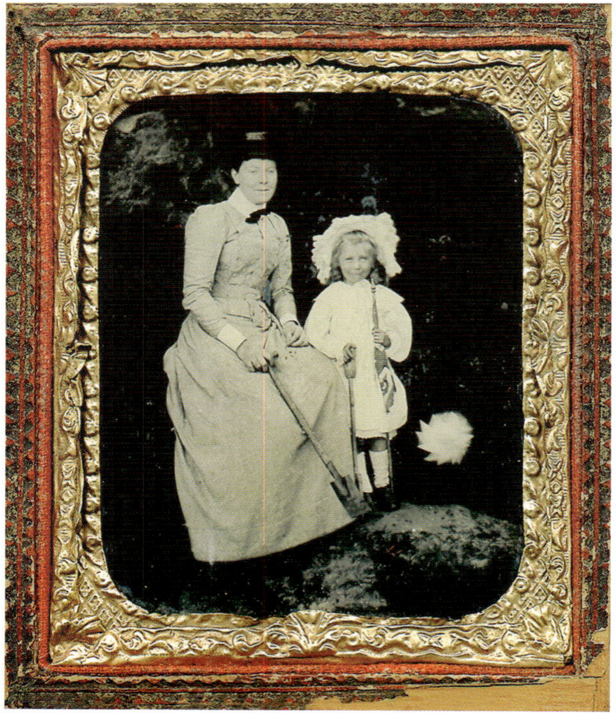

Four typical examples of the output of itinerant photographers using the ambrotype in cameras with internal processing. All are sixth plate size. Such photographer worked beaches, fairgrounds and the parks and public spaces of holiday towns in the 1870s. Their images were processed on the spot, and sold in cheap wood and paper frames for a few pennies each. Each frame has a simple wire ring for hanging on a wall. Actual image sizes are: Ladies knitting – 95mm x 80mm, Father and children on shingle beach – 99mm x 86mm, Girl with doll – 81mm x 94mm, and Mother, child and windmill – 82mm x 95mm.

been engraved with the initials 'SM' or 'MS' in a panel clearly intended for just that purpose. At least fifteen different designs of 'Couvertures de Livres et Albums' were available from the company by 1865. This example is later, as the clasp has a patent date of 1881 stamped into the metal.

The range and quality of carte albums quickly expanded to cover all tastes at a wide range of prices. Today, albums with fine covers are collected just as avidly as cases.

Within a few years of the introduction of the carte-de-visite, its dominance over the photographic portrait market was almost total. And it was not just in portraiture that the format was a success.

Many photographers who had earned their reputations producing large format architectural and landscape prints to be pasted into the family scrapbook, and who had later taken up the small stereoscopic camera to produce image pairs to meet the demand established by that craze, also produced view cartes.

These were often created by cropping one of the two images which made up a stereo pair and mounting that on a visiting card as well. It was not just images of family and friends which the family album preserved and celebrated, but the places they visited as well. While scenic, architectural and landscape daguerreotypes and ambrotypes were relatively rare, this was definitely not the case with cartes-de-visite.

Photographers such as Francis Bedford – official photographer to the Prince of Wales – even pioneered the idea of multi-image cartes-de-visite. In the 1870s he produced large 12" square albumen prints from large glass negatives, and prepared a large montage of images and typography which was then photographed again using a carte-de-visite camera. The resulting copy prints were the predecessor of the multi-view postcards of today.

Few daguerreotypes were produced after about 1860, and few ambrotypes after 1870, although the ambrotype enjoyed a brief revival in popularity

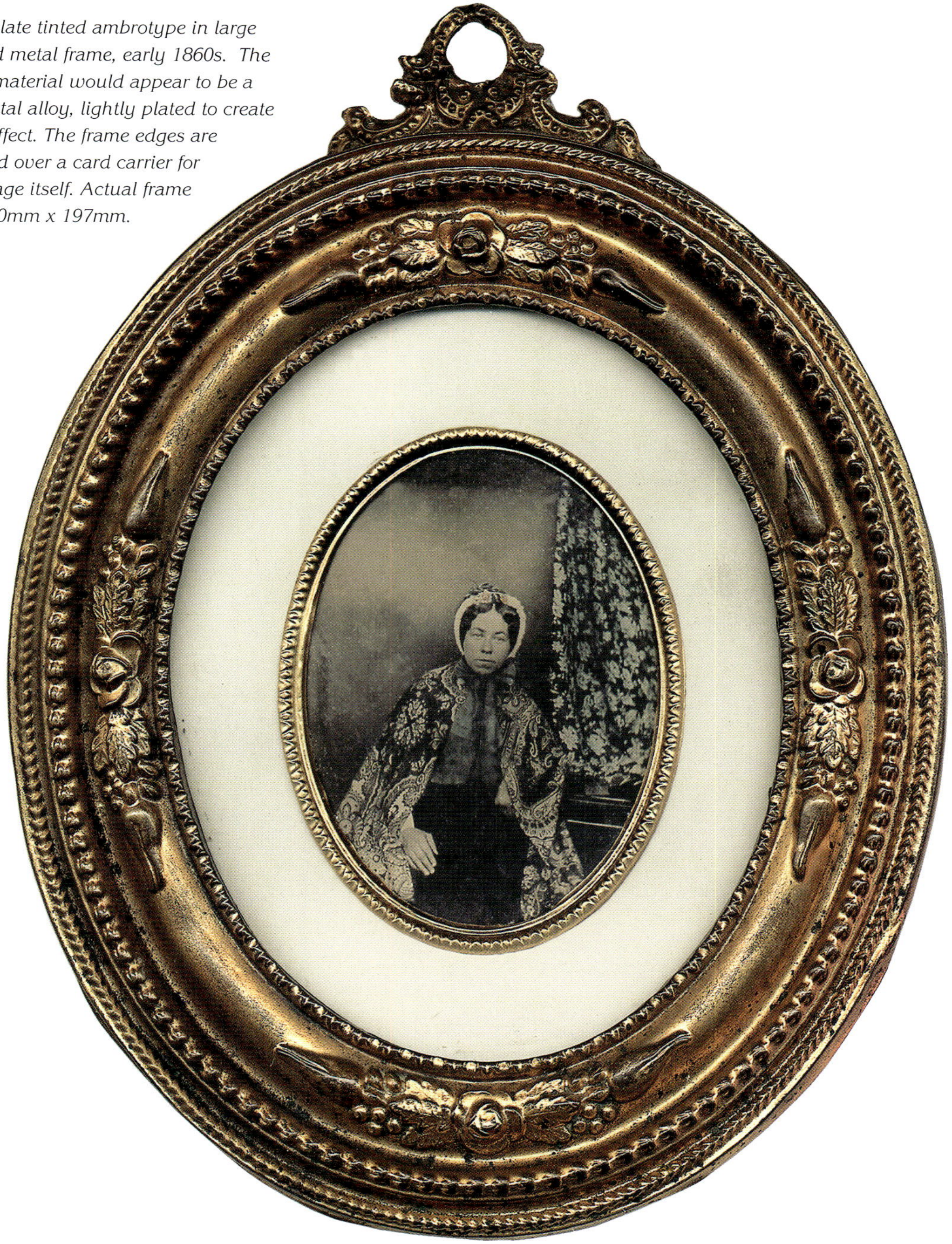

Sixth plate tinted ambrotype in large pressed metal frame, early 1860s. The frame material would appear to be a soft metal alloy, lightly plated to create a gilt effect. The frame edges are crimped over a card carrier for the image itself. Actual frame size 150mm x 197mm.

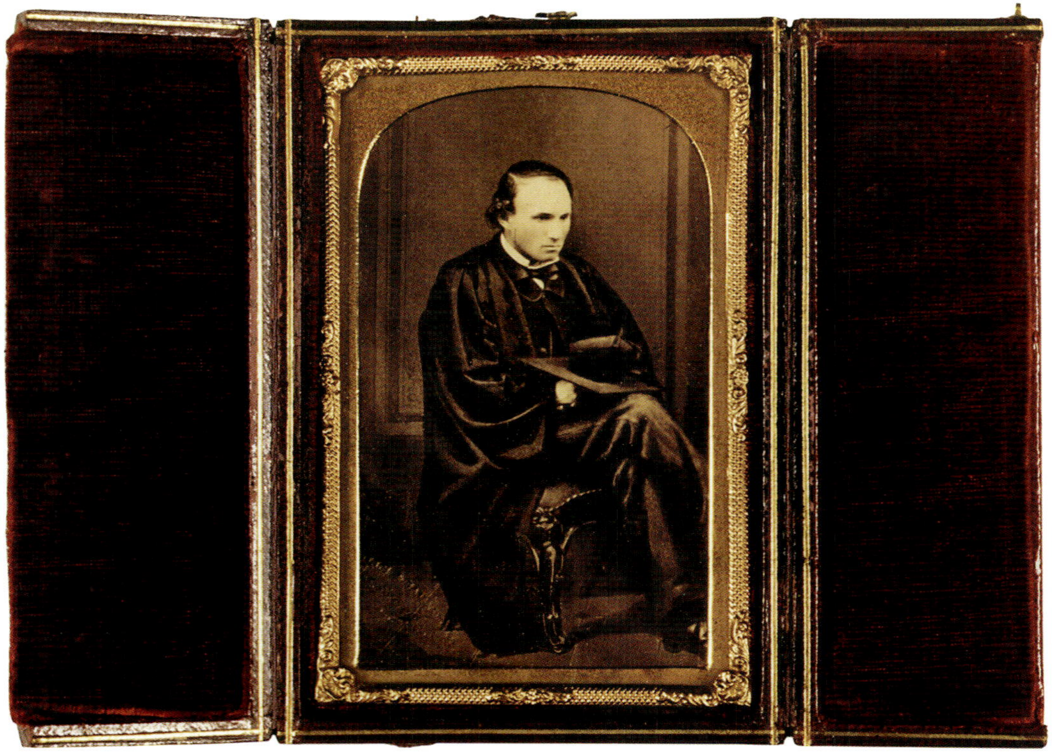

Carte-de-visite of academic with cap and gown, by Hill & Saunders 'Photographers to the Prince of Wales', taken at their studio in Oxford, 1860s. The case in which this carte-de-visite is packaged recalls the double-fronted cases often used for miniature paintings in the years before photography. Actual case size 75mm x 110mm closed, 155mm x 110mm open. A fold out stand in the back of the case enabled it to be displayed open.

as the century came to a close. The negative reigned supreme and the unique photographic portrait disappeared almost totally from view until it enjoyed a resurgence of interest this century with the emergence of Polaroid and other instant picture materials.

It was inevitable that as the professional portrait photograph reduced in importance and novelty, and as amateur photography took over from the professional in the production of the majority of photographic keepsakes, the lavish range of presentation styles and materials would disappear.

Albums continued to enjoy some popularity until the outbreak of the First World War, but with less individuality, and in a much more limited range of materials than in the early days.

As enlargers[6] became more commonplace, and the enlarged portrait became the norm rather than the exception, the framed portrait on the drawing room wall took over from the smaller portrait.

It was, however, the concealed nature of the early photograph, preserved in a cases or in the pages of albums, and thus shielded from damaging light, which has ensured the survival of the huge legacy of Victorian photography which we enjoy today.

Footnotes

1. As a declared means of reducing the unit price of a photograph, André Adolphe Eugène Disderi patented the carte-de-visite under French patent No.21502, November 27th 1854, and with it the idea of exposing up to ten pictures either in series or simultaneously (with a multiple lens camera) and therefore being able to print them together, thus considerably reducing the time taken per sitting.
2. Marion & Co dominated the market for both the pre-printed photographers' cards used to hold the carte-de-visite print, and the albums in which they were housed. As an early example of the importing of photographic goods from mainland Europe, many British photographic studios, large and small, had their cards produced by the French firm, and Marion's imprint can be found on cartes from both small studios in provincial towns, and major London studios.
3. The tintype, ferrotype of melainotype first appeared in 1856 as a cheaper alternative to the ambrotype. It was still enjoying considerable popularity in fairgrounds and holiday resorts at the outbreak of the First World War. The tintype was originally available in all the standard sizes down to 1/16th plate size, but the gem format was only introduced in the 1860s.
4. Francois Charles Lepage, British Patent No.2232, 5th October 1855.
5. With albumen derived from egg white, a colourless material was produced to which a range of pigmented materials could be added. With albumin from blood, only browns and blacks were possible.
6. Although solar enlargers had been used since the 1850s, modern darkroom enlarging became commonplace only in the 1880s.

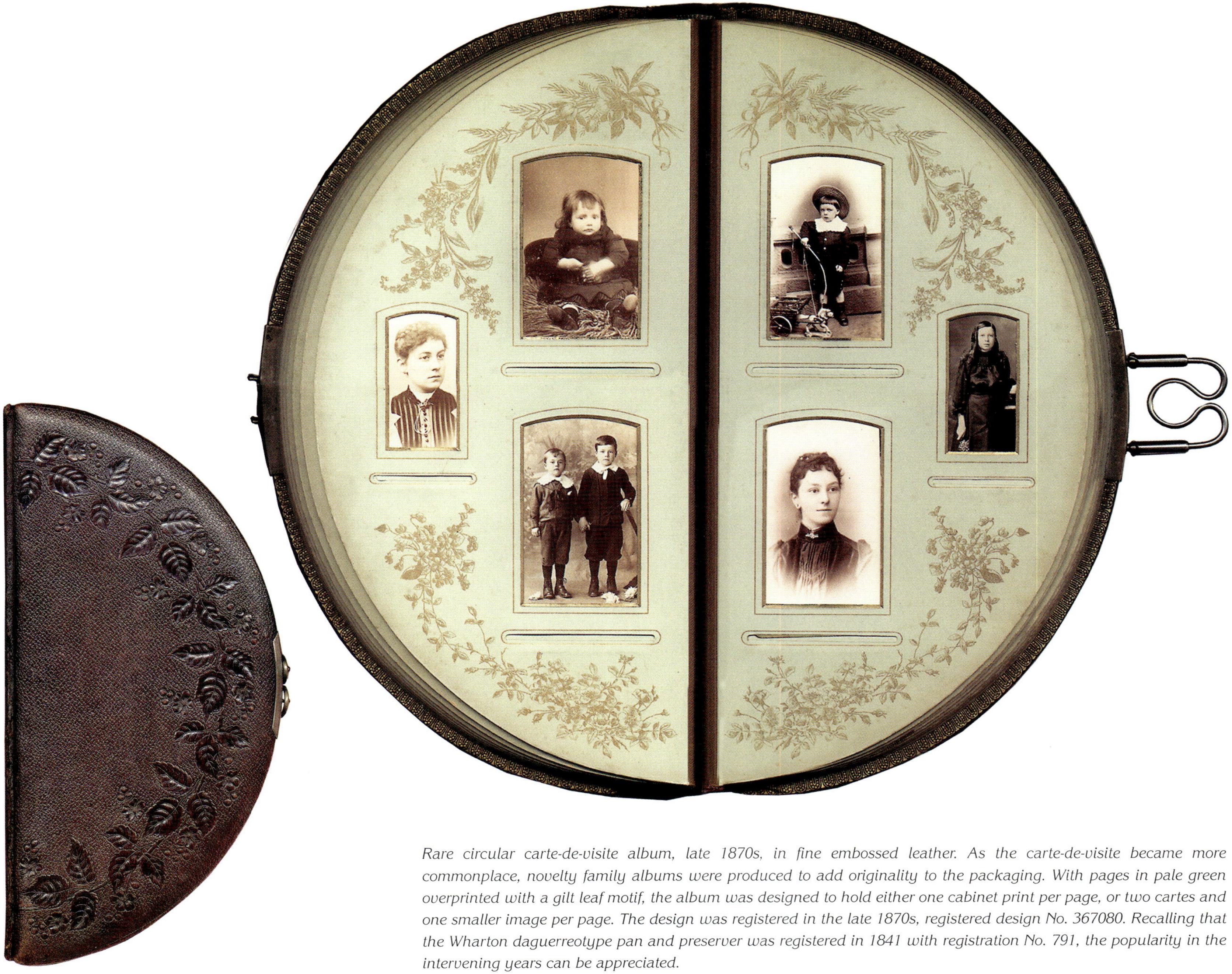

Rare circular carte-de-visite album, late 1870s, in fine embossed leather. As the carte-de-visite became more commonplace, novelty family albums were produced to add originality to the packaging. With pages in pale green overprinted with a gilt leaf motif, the album was designed to hold either one cabinet print per page, or two cartes and one smaller image per page. The design was registered in the late 1870s, registered design No. 367080. Recalling that the Wharton daguerreotype pan and preserver was registered in 1841 with registration No. 791, the popularity in the intervening years can be appreciated.

At the top end of the ambrotype market, simplicity was often the order of the day – a high quality image framed immaculately. This whole plate ambrotype from the later 1850s is framed in a high quality gilded wooden frame with applied plaster decorative border, and is set behind a thin wooden oval matte. Frame size 285mm x 345mm. The jointing of the framing bars, and the overall quality of the craftsmanship is exemplary.

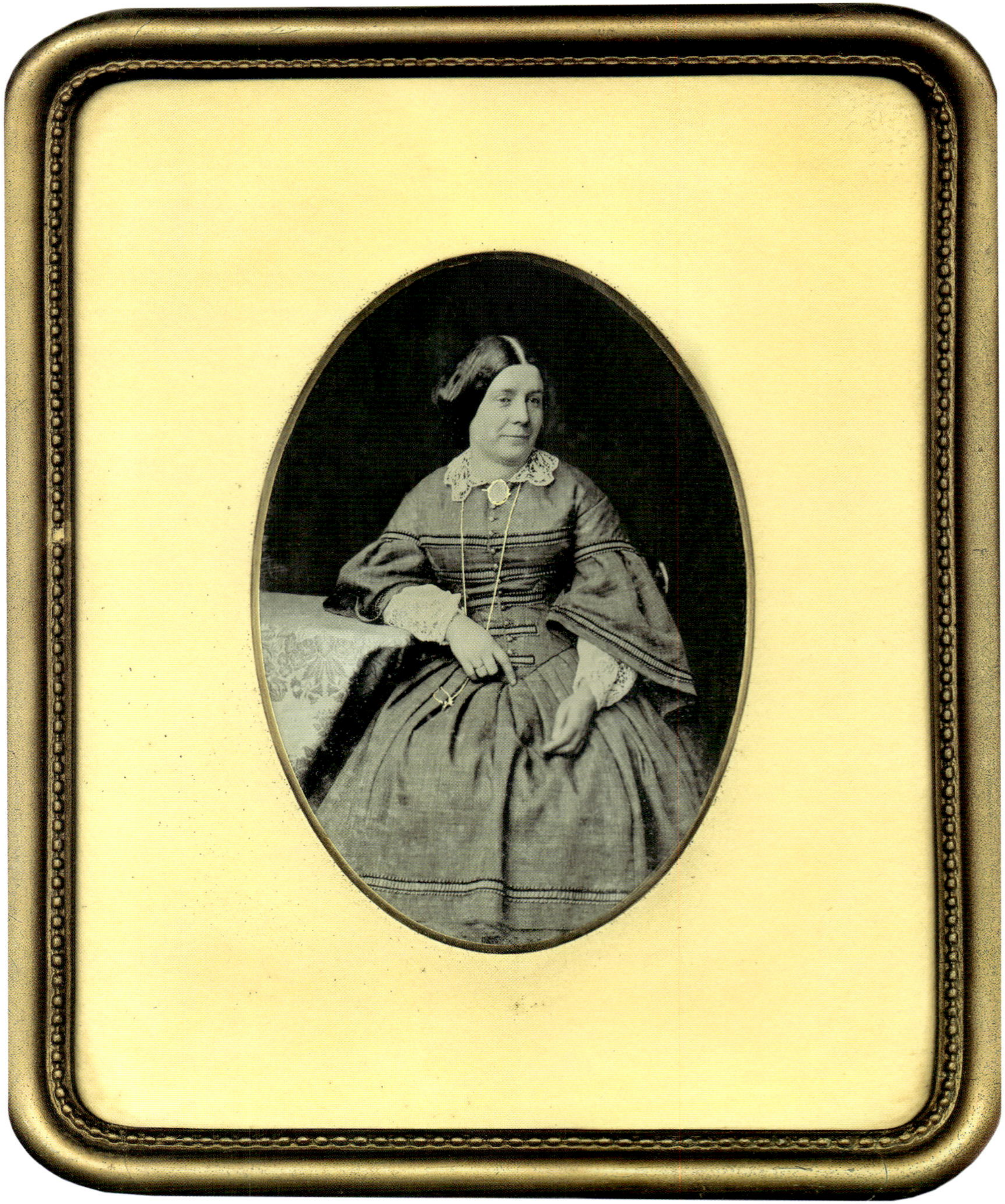

Glossary:
People & Processes

Ambrotype
The name 'ambrotype' was originally coined in the US, while the British preferred the 'collodion positive' title. Eventually, 'ambrotype' became the most widely used term. Invented by Frederick Scott Archer (qv) in 1852, the ambrotype portrait became widely popular from the mid 1850s until *c.*1875. Although Archer invented the process, he never patented it in Britain, although American patents were taken out claiming the invention with several slight modifications. The process enjoyed a slight resurgence of interest in the 1890s.

Anthony, Edward T.
From his New York manufactory and shop, Anthony supplied photographic materials, equipment and cases worldwide, including a direct-mailing service to British customers, advertised widely in the late 1850s.

Archer, Frederick Scott
(1813-1857) Inventor of both the wet collodion process and the collodion positive, Archer never patented his ideas, and as a result did not profit from their phenomenal success, living out his last few years in poverty at the height of his process's universal success.

Bois Durci
Invented by Francois Charles Lepage and patented by him in 1855, bois durci was a more robust material than shellac-based thermoplastics, but could not be moulded in quite such intricate detail.

Brookes & Adams
Die engravers based in Birmingham, England, Brookes and Adams made the dies for the British union case maker John Smith. The company is still operating today.

Cabinet Print
The cabinet portrait format was introduced in 1866 by a British photographer, F. R. Window, and achieved extensive popularity. It continued to be popular long after the smaller carte-de-visite (qv) went out of fashion. Cabinet albums were marketed up until the outbreak of the Great War. The image format was 140mm x 120mm, mounted on a card measuring 165mm x 127mm.

Carte-de-Visite
Introduced by Disdéri in Paris, the carte-de-visite became the ubiquitous format for the portrait photograph from the later 1850s. It transcended class, being available both from society photographers and the more humble local studio. The 90mm x 57mm albumen paper print was mounted on a 140mm x 102mm card, the traditional size of the Victorian visiting card.

Collodion Positive
The British name for the ambrotype (qv), collodion positives greatly reduced the cost of the portrait photograph in the 1850s and 1860s.

Critchlow, Alfred P. & Company
Despite being known for his union case manufacturing in the United States, Critchlow was born in Nottingham, England, where he learned die engraving, and worked as a horn button maker. In the US, he developed Florence Compound, his shellac based thermoplastic material from which he manufactured union cases. He patented his embracing riveted hinge, US Patent No.15,915, October 14th 1856.

Daguerre, Louis Jacques Mandé
(1787-1851) Former theatrical designer and painter, Daguerre collaborated with J. N. Niepce before developing his own eponymous process. He died in the year of the Great Exhibition, the year which saw the introduction of the wet collodion process which eventually displaced his silvered copper plate.

Eichmeyer, Harold A.
Originally a daguerreian artist in his own right, Eichmeyer is better known for the unique design of leather case which he pioneered in 1855, with rounded edges, raised relief leather banding, and ornate clasps.

Edward Anthony's New York shop as featured in his 1854 catalogue. That catalogue listed thousands of items of photographic paraphernalia, including several hundred variants on the simple case.

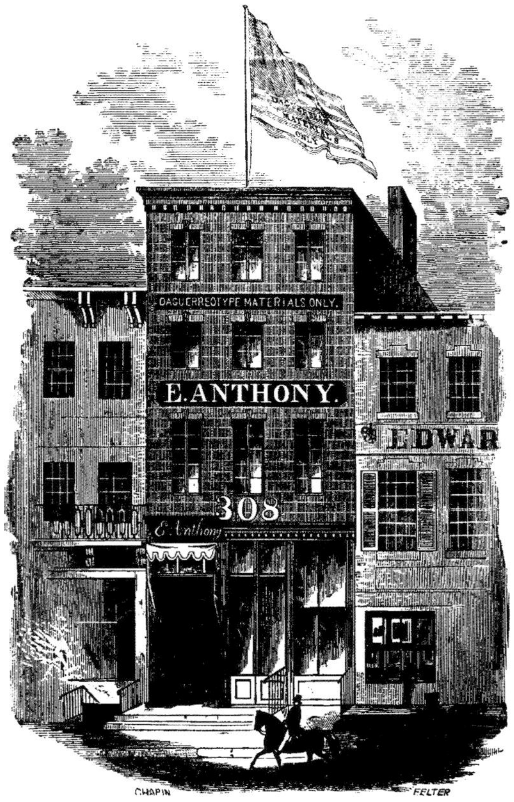

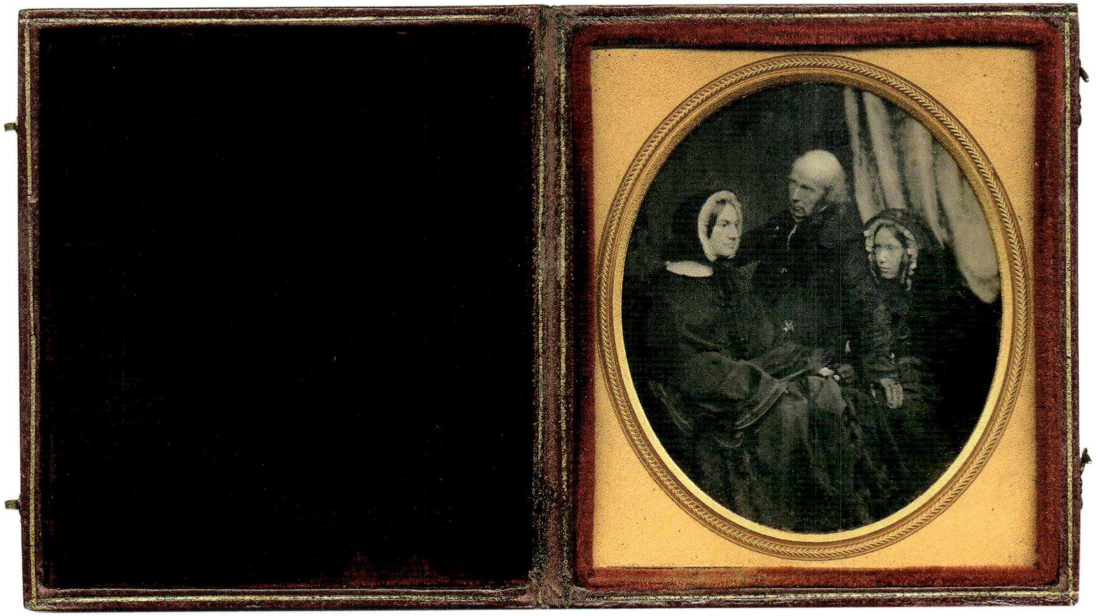

Beautifully posed sixth plate ambrotype of a family by W. W. Law who operated a studio at 49 Gold Street, Northampton in the early 1860s.

Ferrotype
Also known as the tintype and the melainotype (qv), the ferrotype used a blackened tin plate as a replacement for the glass of the collodion positive. It achieved considerable popularity from 1855 (when it was patented in the US by Hamilton Smith of Gambier, Ohio) thanks to its durability and its popularisation by itinerant photographers in the UK and the US. The name 'Ferrotype' was adopted by Victor Griswold when he acquired Smith's patent rights in 1856. British patents followed in the same year. The process remained in use by fairground and beach photographers well after the Great War.

Florence Manufacturing Company
Successor to Littlefield, Parsons & Co., the company took the name of Alfred Critchlow's original Florence Compound as their name, and traded thus from 1866. A few late union cases bear this name. The company went on to manufacture a range of plastic products.

Goll, Frederick P.
Die engraver who produced some of the finest designs for both Samuel Peck, and Littlefield, Parsons & Co.

Gutta Percha
Latex-based material used to mould a wide range of utensils and objects from the 1850s.

Gyde, James & Edwin
Successors to British union casemaker, John Smith, the Gydes marketed cases under the Improved Patent Union Case label.

Halvorson, Halvor
Married to Samuel Peck's sister, Halvorson was closely involved in the development of Peck's union cases, and was responsible for developing a process for gilding union case faces, under US Patent No.13,410, August 7th 1855.

Henning & Eymann
Die engravers responsible for some of the finest Holmes Booth & Hayden (qv) union cases including *The Vision of Ezekiel* and *The Holy Family* illustrated in this book.

Holmes, Booth & Haydn
Israel Holmes, John Booth, and Hiram, James and Henry Haydn went into union case production around 1857. Originally brass founders, their factory was in Waterbury, Connecticut.

Key, Frederick, & Co.
Engraved several dies for Samuel Peck, as well as manufacturing cases under his own name in the early 1860s.

Kinsley & Parker
Edward Kinsley and Samuel Parker entered the union case making business in the late 1850s, with their unusual design for the external hinge used exclusively on Wadhams' union cases. They were based in Stoughton, Massachusetts. Three cases have been identified which bear the Kinsey &

Parker label as makers rather than just suppliers of hinges.

Littlefield, Parsons & Co.
Isaac Parsons, long time collaborator with Alfred Critchlow (qv) eventually bought the Critchlow business in late 1857, and traded as LP&Co. from 1858.

Marion & Co.
Originally of French origin, Marion & Co. established a London office in Soho Square early in the carte-de-visite era. Operating subsequently as A. Marion & Co. and A. Marion, Son & Co., they grew to be the largest supplier of mounts in Europe, and dominated the photographic card and album publishing market for decades, developing a huge US clientele as well. At the height of their success, they acted as distributors for many of the royalty and celebrity cartes which found their way into family albums.

Melainotype
Introduced by Adolphe Mestin in France in 1853, it produced a low quality image on blackened tin, lacking in highlights, and was rejected by the French buyers of photography. It was patented three years later as the Ferrotype (qv) or Tintype and enjoyed considerable success. The 'Melaintype' name was reintroduced in America by Neff after 1856.

Patent American Union Case
A marketing 'brand name' for a range of union cases imported into the UK. The examples with this brand label so far identified have been re-labelled Littlefield, Parson's & Co. patterns.

Peck, Samuel
Onetime grocer, as well as a photographer, Peck made his name as a manufacturer of photographic accessories and cases. His leather and paper case designs were sidelined with his introduction of the union case in 1853 developed with Halvor Halvorson (qv). Patents in 1854, 1855 and 1856 detailed his methods and his compound, and his cases were manufactured at the Scovill Company in New Haven, Connecticut.

Plate Sizes
Most cased images were supplied in approximate fractions of the 'whole plate' size of 165mm x 216mm. Half plate was the one size which was not widely agreed, and half plate images can measure anything from 115mm x 140mm up to 115mm x 165mm. quarter plate usually measured 83mm x 108mm, sixth plate 71mm x 83mm, ninth plate 51mm x 64mm, and sixteenth plate 35mm x 41mm.

Smith, Frederick, and Hartmann, Hermann
Die engravers responsible for the creation of the two magnificent pictorial whole plate cases, *The Landing of Columbus*, and *Washington Crossing the Delaware.*

Smith, John (UK)
Former horn button maker, John Smith and his successors are the only British Union case makers so far identified.

Smith, John (US)
The American John Smith was a die engraver based in new York, responsbile for several Peck union case designs.

Tintype
See under 'melainotype' and 'ferrotype'.

Union Case
Despite present day claims to the contrary by several American dealers and writers, the union case was made exclusively of shellac-based thermoplastic materials, and not gutta percha (qv).

Wadhams Manufacturing Company
A late entrant into the union case market, Wadhams made fewer than twenty different case designs, all using the Kinsey & Parker external hinge (qv).

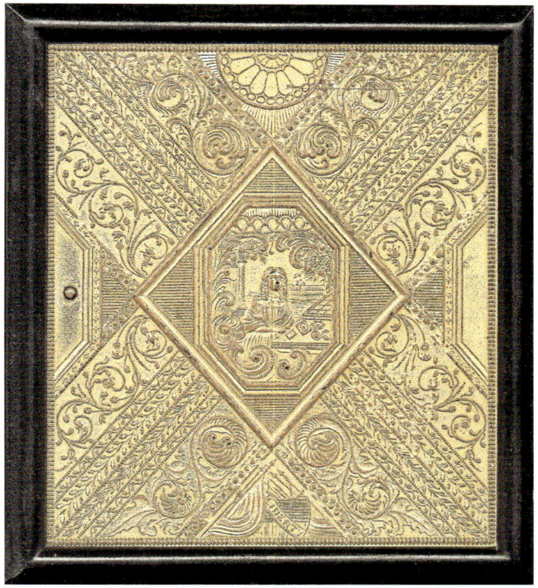

The sixth plate union case 'The Daguerreian Gallery', by Samuel Peck & Co. is available in plain brown or black thermoplastic, and also covered in gold leaf. It is the most completely gilded of all the union cases, and the gilding was applied at the moulding stage, a thin sheet of gilded paper being placed in the bottom of the mould. The gilding process was described in detail in Peck's 1854 US Patent No.11758. Such cases are rare. 86mm x 96mm.

Index

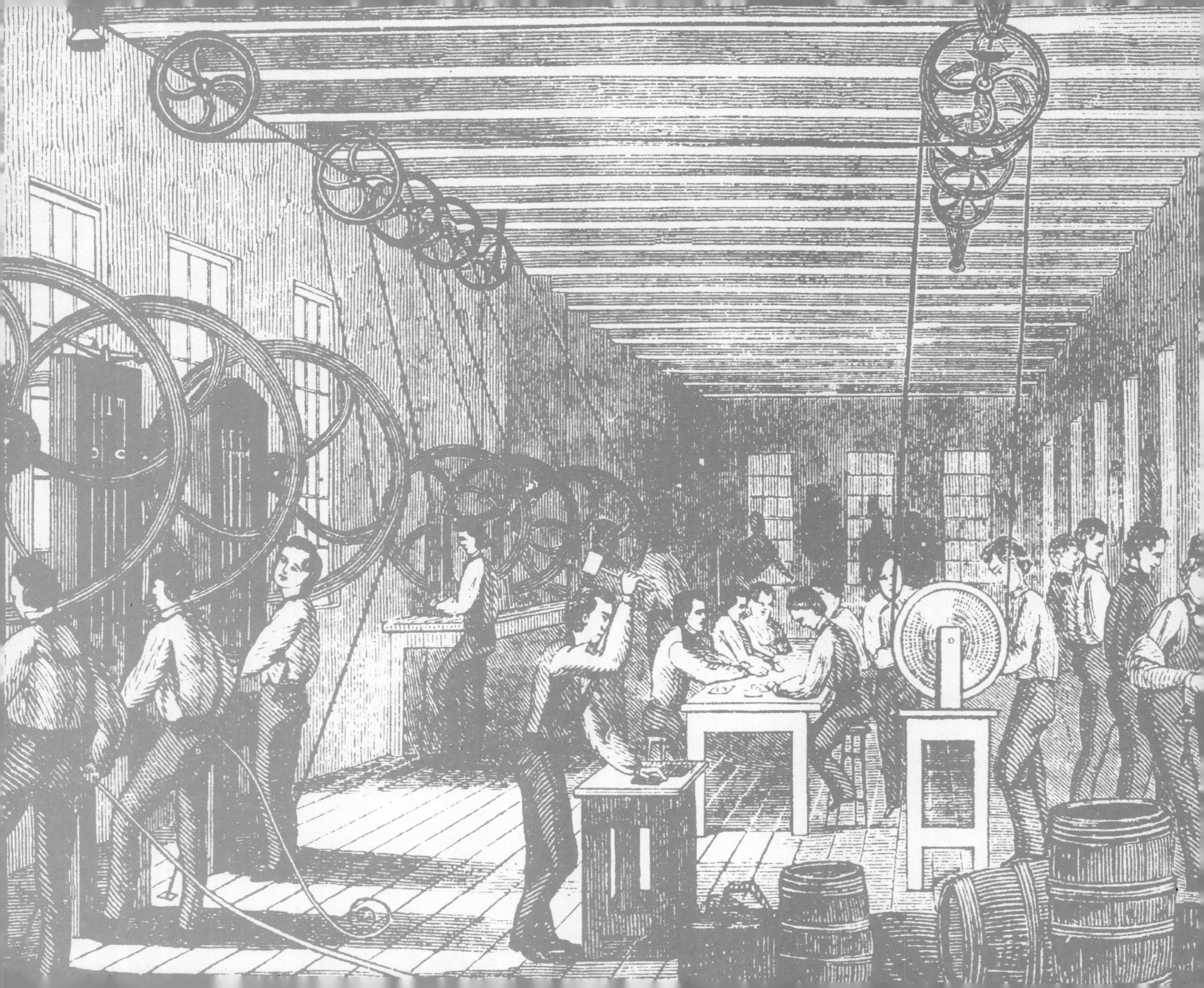